The CD-ROM Book

Steve Bosak

Jeffrey Sloman

que

The CD-ROM Book

Library of Congress Catalog No.: 93-85045

ISBN: 1-56529-292-8

95   94   4   3   2

Interpretation of the printing code: the rightmost double-digit number is the year of the book's printing; the rightmost single-digit number, the number of the book's printing. For example, a printing code of 93-1 shows that the first printing of the book occurred in 1993.

Publisher: David P. Ewing

Director of Publishing: Mike Miller

Managing Editor: Corinne Walls

Marketing Manager: Ray Robinson

About the Authors

Jeffrey Sloman is a freelance writer and consultant based in Franklin, Indiana. He is a contributing editor to *Windows* magazine, where he writes the monthly Windows Networking column. His consulting practice includes all aspects of Microsoft Windows as well as marketing and strategic-direction support for high-tech companies. In a previous life, he worked at the Museum of Science in Boston, Massachusetts, where he designed and built electronic and electromechanical components for exhibits.

Steve Bosak has been writing about high technology and computers since the late 70s for a variety of publications, including *PCWorld*, *Byte*, and *Microsystems Journal*. He is director of the Professional Writing Program at Columbia College in Chicago. Interested readers can contact him on MCI Mail at **IDsbosak**.

Credits

Publishing Manager
Don Roche, Jr.

Acquisitions Editor
Sherri Morningstar

Product Directors
Timothy S. Stanley
Brian Underdahl

Production Editor
Alice Martina Smith

Copy Editors
Barbara Koenig
Cindy Morrow
Heather Northrup

Technical Editor
Baird Peterson

Book Designer
Amy Peppler-Adams

Cover Designer
Tim Amrhein

Production Team
Jeff Baker
Angela D. Bannan
Danielle Bird
Katy Bodenmiller
Laurie Casey
Charlotte Clapp
Scott Cook
Brook Farling
Teresa Forrester
Heather Kaufman
Tim Montgomery
Shelley Palma
Ryan Rader
Dennis Sheehan
Sue VandeWalle
Mary Beth Wakefield
Lillian Yates

Indexer
Joy Dean Lee

Composed in *ITC Century Light* and *MCPdigital* by Que Corporation

Acknowledgments

Steve and Jeff would like to thank...

Alice Martina Smith for her good humor, sharp editing skills, and superhuman efforts in pulling together disparate elements in a timely fashion (we won't comment on her typing skills).

Don Roche for backing this project 100 percent.

Amy Peppler-Adams for helping to make this book noticeably different.

Linda Baliman and **Lou Mier** at Takin' Care of Business for their outstanding negotiations with software vendors.

Kim Sudhalter and **Audrey Mann** at Technology Solutions, Inc., for technical information.

Richard Bowers at Optical Publishers Association for encouragement, support, and direction.

Renée and Jonathon Sloman for putting up with Jeff while this book was being written.

All the vendors, too numerous to name, who supplied products for evaluation in this book.

And thanks to Que in general for allowing us to make this book just what we wanted it to be.

Trademark Acknowledgments

Dedications

To Renée, Jonathon, Arnold, and Barbara.

—js

To Maureen and Ian for understanding where I disappear to for hours on end every night, and to Scott and Stephanie for their consummate game-playing skills and honest consumer opinions.

—sb

Contents at a Glance

Table of Contents

9 CD-ROM for After Hours

225

10 Copyright Laws   251

11 Beyond the Basics   257

Introduction

Thank you for buying *The CD-ROM Book*. This book is designed to help you learn about CD-ROM and the sort of technology available. It is written to answer three questions:

➤ What is CD-ROM?

➤ How do I use CD-ROM?

➤ What products are available in the CD-ROM arena?

We—the authors, editors, and designers of this book—have worked very hard to make this book especially helpful and easy to use. You will notice right away that this book looks different than other computer books. This difference in appearance is a product of the special features built into the book.

First is the easy-to-read double-column style, reminiscent of a magazine. We chose this layout because it is easier to read and nicer to look at. Second are the numerous side bars (set off from the text) and margin notes (in a special place at the edge of the page). These devices help maintain a smooth flow of thought in the body of the book, while still providing related information, clarifications, and definitions where they can be useful. In the text, references to margin notes appear in a **special typeface** to alert you that a margin note can be found for that topic. This is a printed version of the hypertext found in electronic publications.

Another special feature of the book is the use of tables and icons that provide information at a glance. In places where products are discussed, specifications and classifications are right up front so that you can easily scan for items of interest. Where there are tables, features are marked with checkboxes; an X in the box means that the feature is part of that product; an empty box means that the feature is not available. This approach is familiar to users of graphical user interfaces like Windows; it lets you see what is not there as well as what is—so that you don't have to try to remember what *could be* there.

The book is designed to be used like a database, in a random-access fashion. Although you could read it from cover to cover, we don't expect you to. Instead, it is designed so that you can use it as a reference; each paragraph and chapter is substantially independent, with references to other information as needed. This means that if you are interested in some aspect of CD-ROM technology, you can look at just what you are curious about without jumping around or reading more than you want.

In a way, this book is an experiment. It represents a rethinking of books in the light of how we use information today. The book is designed to be as "interactive" as a printed book allows. We expect that the times you cannot find the information you need (to learn about what CD-ROM is, how it works, and what you can do with it) will be few.

A Guide to Special Features

The margin notes in this book include icons that depict the nature of their contents. There are six types of margin notes:

What Is a Note?

A note is a piece of related information that would have been out of place in the text. Notes are designed to point out important ideas and concepts that might not otherwise be obvious.

What Is a Caution?

A caution is just what it says; it warns you about some aspect of the information provided in the text. Cautions help you avoid damage to equipment, data, or yourself.

What Is an Explanation?

An explanation is either a definition or a glossary-type entry. It is connected with some particular word or concept in the text.

RULE OF THUMB

What Is a Rule of Thumb?

The rule of thumb margin note includes a general rule about some piece of technology. It is used to help you make a decision when the rules are fuzzy and clear-cut recommendations are impossible.

TIP

What Is a Tip?

A tip is designed to make some processes easier. Tips are usually related to some particular action being described in the text.

AWARD OF EXCELLENCE

What Is an Award of Excellence?

In writing *The CD-ROM Book*, we came across products in all categories that stood out from the rest. We felt the need to recognize these special products beyond giving them our recommendation; these are the recipients of the Award of Excellence. There were no fixed criteria used to determine award winners; each was distinguished by some special characteristic that made the product an example to be followed. In each case, the logic for our decision is spelled out so that you can understand why the choice was made.

We feel the winners of *The CD-ROM Book* Award of Excellence are all examples of products that offer something exceptional. These products get our recommendation—as well as our admiration for what they do well.

Icons without Text

A few icons used in the book are not accompanied by text. These icons indicate a fixed idea about a product, making the information easy to absorb without having to search the text.

 Products that bear the Recommended icon have our approval. These are products we recommend as among the best in their class. Products without the Recommended icon are not without merit, however; if the product is in the book, we thought it was worth considering and purchasing. We avoided products we thought were a waste of time. On the other hand, please note that the absence of a product from this book does not condemn it—some product information was not available in time to make the printing deadline.

 The Highly Recommended icon indicates that we thought the product exceeded the expectations for a Recommended rating. The Highly Recommended icon distinguishes products than stand out as particularly useful, fun, or interesting. The Highly Recommended rating can be assumed for any product that has an Award of Excellence.

  Hardware products are rated graphically with a set of CD icons. These ratings reflect a relatively complex formula based on fact and opinion. The fact portion involves the tallying of points for various features and specifications. The opinion portion is an additional set of points we added, based on the drive's qualities relative to the rest of the field. The opinion portion of the score is worth about 1/3 of the total; although we could not overly influence the results, we could break ties.

 These icons are used with educational software and are intended to help you determine—at a glance—which applications may be of interest to you or your children. More than one icon may be "active" at the same time to indicate a range of ages.

What's in This Book

As innovative as this book may be, it *is* a book and books have chapters. Here's a run-down on what you will find in each chapter:

> **The CD-ROM Book on Disc**
>
> Did you know that this book is available in a disc-based version? The disc packaged with this book contains the entire text of this book. You can pop the disc into your drive and click on the blue words in the text to jump around from chapter to chapter instead of flipping through paper pages.

Chapter 1, "What Is CD-ROM?," introduces you to the fascinating world of compact disc read-only memory. What is it? Why do you need it? What do you need to know about the technology to keep up with the fast-changing world?

Chapter 2, "CD-ROM Specifications Explained," clarifies some of the most confusing aspects of CD-ROM technology. If you've ever wondered what "Yellow Book Specifications" have to do with CDs—or are looking for some comprehensible details about more complex issues—look no further.

Chapter 3, "How To Select CD-ROM Drives," describes more than 40 products. The specifications you need for each drive are presented consistently, making it easier for you to make an informed decision about the drive you need. We rate each drive to further assist your purchasing decision.

Chapter 4, "How To Install Your CD-ROM Drive," takes you through the doesn't-have-to-be-so-messy chore of introducing your computer to your new CD-ROM drive. You learn how to set jumpers on an adapter card, install the card, connect the drive, install the software drivers, and—finally—access data on a disc.

Chapter 5, "How To Network Your CD-ROM Drive," explains how to make your state-of-the-art CD-ROM drive available to everyone on the network. Perhaps more importantly, the chapter explains why you'd want to. Setting up your drive for use with Windows for Workgroups and Lantastic—and an easy alternative to the horrors of configuring NetWare—are some of the topics covered.

Chapter 6, "What Is Multimedia?," introduces you to multimedia—a world made practical by the storage capacities of CD-ROM. Because a major element in multimedia presentations is sound, this chapter describes some of the best sound boards and speakers available.

Chapter 7, "CD-ROM in Business," groups application titles commonly found in business environments. General business, marketing, sales, law, accounting, finance, education, library-science, and medical application titles are described.

Chapter 8, "CD-ROM for Reference and Education," gives you an idea of the plethora of CD titles available in the reference and education realms. Imagine an entire shelf of encyclopedia volumes reduced to a single shiny disc, or a dictionary that pronounces *onomatopoeia* for you. Now imagine every document of importance to the history of the United States, all Shakespeare's works (in the Queen's English), and a French lesson that talks taking

up no more than a few inches of shelf space.

Chapter 9, "CD-ROM for After Hours," was the most fun for us to research. We're confident our information is good, thanks to the help of our expert consultants Scott and Stephanie. In this chapter, we talk about some of the best games on CD-ROM.

Chapter 10, "Copyright Laws," presents specific information about copyright laws—and copyright infringement—in clear language. Before you use parts of a CD-ROM in your next multimedia presentation, read this.

Chapter 11, "Beyond the Basics," will be helpful when your thirst for data outgrows the capabilities of a single CD-ROM drive. And in case you fancy creating your own CDs, this chapter includes a primer about developing an application and mastering a disc that you can then mass produce (as well as a look at several software and hardware options that can make it all possible).

Chapter 12, "CD-ROM on the Road: Going Portable," reassures those whose offices are the front seats of their cars that you really can take it with you. CD-ROM drives come in several packages that make transporting reams of data to remote locations as easy as taking the disc—and the drive—with you.

Chapter 13, "CD-ROM in the Family Room," draws the line between the CD-ROM drive used with your computer and the CD-ROM drive that may be hooked up to your television-based Sega home-game system. Although these two systems—and the discs they use—are not fully compatible, you will want to know more about their differences.

Chapter 14, "Video on Disc: CD-ROM and Full-Motion Video," explains what full-motion video is and why CD-ROM makes the propagation of it possible. For real propeller heads, this chapter describes some of the video standards and code boards required for developing applications that make use of full-motion video.

Chapter 15, "The Future of CD-ROM," is more than an editorial. It provides some facts about the future of the CD-ROM industry, some tidbits about what's up-and-coming, as well as our opinions about the whole scenario.

The appendixes in this book contain lots of information tangential to the main flow of the text in the chapters. In these sections, you will find names and addresses of CD-ROM drive manufacturers, software developers and publishers, and hardware and software vendors. Some instructions for taking care of your precious data discs, a list of hundreds of software titles and their publishers, and some suggestions about where you can turn for additional information about CD-ROM round out the appendixes.

How To Use the Disc

Handsomely framed by the front cover of this book is a disc. A real CD. Encoded in its plastic and metal layers are the entire contents of this book as well as some software demos you might like to experience (we would have said "look at," but the CD-ROM necessitates the use of a stronger word). To use the disc in your CD-ROM drive, first remove it from this book. Then place it in the drive (don't forget the caddy if your drive needs one), open your Windows Program Manager, and select Run from the File menu. Assuming that your CD-ROM drive is configured to be drive D, type **D:\INSTALL.EXE** and click on OK.

Enjoy.

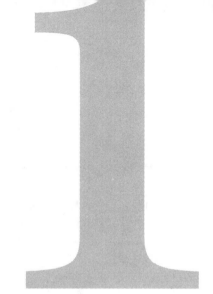

Chapter 1

What is CD-ROM?

Before you begin a serious investigation into any new field, some familiarity with the terms used by people in that field is essential. Beginning your CD-ROM education is no exception. This chapter introduces you to CD-ROM terminology, briefly explains the evolution of the CD-ROM, and provides some reasons why you need to know more about this cutting-edge technology.

CD-ROM: A Brief History

In 1978, two companies—Philips and Sony— joined forces to produce the audio compact disc (CD). Philips had already developed commercial laser-disc players, and Sony had a decade of digital recording research under its belt. The two companies were poised for a battle—the introduction of potentially incompatible audio laser disc formats—but they came to terms on an agreement to formulate a single audio technology.

Sony pushed for a 12-inch disc. Philips wanted to investigate smaller sizes, especially when it became clear that they could pack an astonishing 12 hours of music on 12-inch discs.

By 1982, the companies announced their standard, which included the specifications for recording, sampling, and above all, the 5-inch format we live with today. To be specific, the discs are 12 centimeters in diameter. As legend has it, this size was chosen because it could contain Beethoven's Ninth Symphony.

With the continued cooperation of Sony and Philips through the 1980s, additional specifications were announced concerning the use of CD technology for computer data. These recommendations have evolved into the computer CD-ROM drives we use today. Where engineers once struggled to find the perfect fit between disc form-factor and the greatest symphony ever recorded, software developers and publishers are cramming these little discs with the world's information.

Understanding and using this CD-based cornucopia of knowledge can enrich your business, your career, and your leisure. The technology is affordable and easy to add to an existing PC.

A Library on Your Desk

Within minutes of inserting a compact disc into your computer, you have access to information that may have taken you days, or even weeks, to find a few years ago. Science, medicine, law, business profiles, and educational materials—every conceivable form of human endeavor or pursuit of knowledge—are making their ways to aluminum-coated, 5-inch plastic discs called **CD-ROMs**, or compact disc-read only memory.

Although only dozens of CD-ROM discs, or titles, were published for personal computer users in all of 1988, the Software Publishers Association predicts that in 1993, publishers will offer over 3,000 individual titles, containing data and programs ranging from worldwide agricultural statistics to preschool learning games. Individual businesses, local and federal government offices, and small businesses also will publish thousands of their own, limited-use titles.

The Infinite Index

Aside from the sheer avalanche of data available on CD-ROM, this medium of delivering information has unique properties. Imagine, for example, a 300-volume library of classic literature with an *infinite index*—the ability to search and perform a cross-reference on every work in a text. By entering the word **Dickens**, for example, you can be presented with a list of all the Dickens titles on the CD—

no more remarkable than the traditional card catalog found in your neighborhood library. But if you then narrow your search by typing **work house**, you are presented with an index listing of every passage in every Dickens work that mentions the words *work house*. Finding the Shakespeare play that contains the quotation, "Alas, poor Yorick!" is as simple as typing it in. Within seconds, the software whisks you to that famous graveside passage in Hamlet.

Because every word, number, or symbol on a disc can be located in seconds, information that might take hours to retrieve in printed form is merely a few keystrokes away on a PC equipped with a CD-ROM. Suppose, for example, that you need to find the address and phone number of Que Corporation, the publisher of this book, with nothing more to go on than the company's name. To complicate matters, you have no idea what city or state the corporation is in, which means that the phone company and a phone directory is of no use—even if your local library stocks every phone book in the country! By using a single business-directory CD, you can type **Que Corp** and instantly see the company's address (see fig. 1.1).

As you can see, the nearly limitless way in which you can use CD-ROMs to search for data makes them even more approachable and useful, in many cases, than their printed counterparts.

The Talking Papyrus

When the Egyptians began using papyrus—man's first paper—to record information, it was a technological innovation. It sounds funny now, but it's true. Where previous cultures had

EXPLANATION

CD-ROM

The CD-ROM (compact disc-read only memory) is a read-only optical storage medium capable of holding 660 megabytes of data (approximately 500,000 pages of text), about 70 minutes of high-fidelity audio, or some combination of the two. The CD-ROM is very similar to the familiar audio compact disc and will, in fact, play in a normal audio player. The result, however, is noise, unless there is audio along with the data on the CD-ROM. When accessing data, a CD-ROM is somewhat faster than a floppy disk, but considerably slower than a modern hard drive. The term *CD-ROM* refers to both the discs themselves and the drive that reads them.

used rocks, wood, tree bark, and cave walls to inscribe information, the papyrus allowed the Egyptian culture to leapfrog its predecessors in information technology. The papyrus was easier to store, easier to read, and certainly more portable than the stone tablets being lugged around.

But the most useful feature of papyrus was its ability to store a virtually unlimited amount of information; a collection of scrolls could contain a lengthy piece of work, not possible with other "technologies" from the past. Scrolls eventually evolved into the handwritten, then printed, books of today.

But CD-ROMs have upped the ante. Although the book you're holding right now contains over 100,000 words, the enclosed CD can hold millions of words, with room to spare for audio and video.

Even if CD-ROMs were strictly limited to publishing text, you have already seen how powerful the medium is in locating the tiniest bits of information. Although this electronic papyrus has nearly unlimited potential for text indexing and retrieval, its capabilities do not end with the printed word.

The same CD-ROM technology that offers the full text of Shakespeare, business databases, and an entire dictionary all on one CD is capable of *speaking* to you as well. Publishers of CD-ROMs have begun to take advantage of the audio capabilities of the data CD technologies in inventive ways. The same CD that holds text can also simultaneously incorporate audio—speech, music, or sound effects—to enhance its text presentations.

Perhaps you've always been a bit reluctant to use the word *forte* because you are not sure how it's properly pronounced. If you look up *forte* in Microsoft's Bookshelf for Windows CD-ROM, you are presented with the screen shown in figure 1.2.

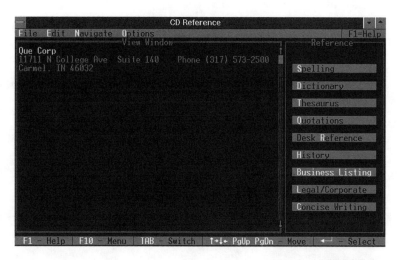

Art, Photos, and Video

CD-ROM can also provide visual information: a full-color image of *Guernica* as you read a short biography of Picasso; photos of Saturn taken by the Voyager spacecraft when you reference an article on unmanned space exploration; or a clip of film—complete with sound—of President Nixon's resignation speech when you read about Watergate.

Complex theories and mechanisms can be explained and demonstrated through animation and narration. Databases of visual information can be searched as effortlessly and endlessly as their written counterparts by using index information provided on the disc.

This combination of text, sound, graphics, and animation on CD-ROM is called **multimedia. Multimedia is explained in greater detail in Chapter 6, "What Is Multimedia?"**

The use of multimedia CD-ROMs for PCs is just beginning to be explored by innovative publishers. The years ahead will see a tremendous growth in both the number and variety of titles.

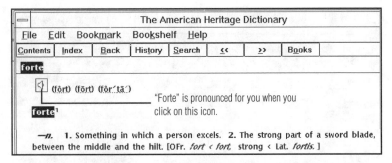

The American Heritage Dictionary

File   Edit   Bookmark   Bookshelf   Help

| Contents | Index | Back | History | Search | << | >> | Books |

forte

(fôrt) (fôrt) (fôr´tā´)

"Forte" is pronounced for you when you click on this icon.

forte[1]

—*n.* **1.** Something in which a person excels. **2.** The strong part of a sword blade, between the middle and the hilt. [OFr. *fort* < *fort,* strong < Lat. *fortis.*]

FIGURE 1.2

Clicking on the speaker icon next to the definition provides you with a spoken pronunciation of that bothersome word, recorded by a professional elocutionist. Public speaking can now be your forte.

Handling CD-ROMs

CD-ROM media should be handled with the same care afforded a photographic negative. The CD-ROM is an optical device and degrades as its optical surface becomes dirty or scratched. If your drive uses a *caddy*—a container for the disc that rules out the need to handle the disc itself—you should purchase a sufficient supply of these to reduce disc handling. Should your CD-ROM become scratched or dirty, however, it is possible to recover the CD-ROM to usable condition.

For more information on maintenance, see Appendix F, "Care and Feeding of CD-ROMs."

What's Playing on CD-ROM?

Each CD-ROM has a capacity of over 600 megabytes of storage. In terms of data, that capacity is roughly the equivalent of 500,000 pages of text. With all this available storage, single CD-ROMs can pack an enormous amount of data. The variety is staggering, as the following list shows:

➤ The entire listings from all Yellow Pages throughout the United States

➤ Full-color maps containing every street in the country

➤ Facsimile numbers for all publicly held businesses and all government institutions

➤ A visual tour of the Smithsonian Institute

➤ A 21-volume encyclopedia, complete with full-color pictures, illustrations, sound annotations, and full-motion video clips

With all this cheap, efficient storage power, virtually every facet of life is already being transformed by this technology:

➤ Businesses are using CD-ROM technology for marketing and marketing research, business reference, and lead generation.

➤ Schools have adopted CD-ROM for referencing and as an exciting new tool for interactive education.

➤ Scholars use CD-ROM technology to cut research time and to publish data for a fraction of the cost of paper-bound materials and publications.

➤ The government is in the process of converting massive amounts of paper documents to CD-ROM in an effort to conserve space and preserve its archives.

➤ At home, CD-ROMs can replace shelves of reference materials, add a new dimension to a child's learning, and transform your PC into a multimedia playground with the most visually stunning games and entertainment software yet developed.

Now that you have an idea of what CD-ROM technology can do on your PC, you should understand how it works.

Compact-Disc Technology

Although identical in appearance to audio CDs, computer CDs store both data *and* audio. The CD drives that read the discs when attached to PCs also bear a strong resemblance to an audio CD. The methods of handling discs, inserting them into the CD drive, and ejecting them when finished are all familiar to anyone who has used an audio CD. Both forms of CD operate on the same general mechanical principles.

The disc itself, nearly 5 inches in diameter, is made of a polycarbonate wafer. The wafer's base is coated with a metallic film, usually an aluminum alloy. The aluminum film is the portion of the disc that the CD-ROM drive reads for information. The aluminum film, or strata, is then covered by a **plastic coating** that protects the underlying data.

Mass-Producing CD-ROMs

Although a laser is used to etch data onto a master disc, this technique is impractical for the reproduction of hundreds or thousands of copies of the disc. Each production of a master disc can take more than 30 minutes to encode. In addition, master discs are made of materials that aren't durable enough for continued or prolonged use. In fact, unless you are using a CD-R (CD-Recordable) or CD-WO (CD-Write Once) for mastering discs or storing data, the material used for master CDs is made of glass. Only the CD-R and CD-WO drives use metal-coated discs for making masters or writing data.

For limited-run productions of CDs, an original master is coated with metal in a process similar to electroplating; once the metal is formed and separated from the master, the metal imprint of the original is used to stamp copies, not unlike the reproduction of vinyl records. This process works effectively for small quantities, but eventually the stamp wears out.

To produce a large volume of discs, a three-step process is employed:

1. The master is, once again, plated and a stamp is produced.

2. This stamp is used to create a duplicate master, made of a more resilient metal.

3. The duplicate master is used to produced numerous stamps.

This technique allows a great many production stamps to be made from the duplicate master, preserving the integrity of the original encoding. It also allows the mass-production discs to be made from inexpensive materials. The CDs you buy are coated with aluminum after they are stamped into polycarbonate; then they are protected with a thin layer of plastic. The thin, aluminum layer that coats both the etched pits and smooth surfaces enables the reading laser to determine the presence or absence of strongly reflected light.

This mass-manufacturing process is identical for both data and audio CDs.

CDs, in some respects, are similar to an older technology, the phonograph record (which the CD has made nearly obsolete). On a CD, microscopic pits stamped into a polycarbonate layer and coated with aluminum replace the vinyl record's grooves. These pits are called **data bits**.

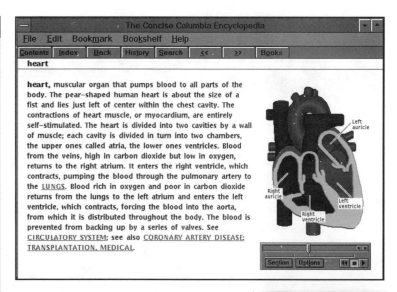

heart, muscular organ that pumps blood to all parts of the body. The pear-shaped human heart is about the size of a fist and lies just left of center within the chest cavity. The contractions of heart muscle, or myocardium, are entirely self-stimulated. The heart is divided into two cavities by a wall of muscle; each cavity is divided in turn into two chambers, the upper ones called atria, the lower ones ventricles. Blood from the veins, high in carbon dioxide but low in oxygen, returns to the right atrium. It enters the right ventricle, which contracts, pumping the blood through the pulmonary artery to the LUNGS. Blood rich in oxygen and poor in carbon dioxide returns from the lungs to the left atrium and enters the left ventricle, which contracts, forcing the blood into the aorta, from which it is distributed throughout the body. The blood is prevented from backing up by a series of valves. See CIRCULATORY SYSTEM; see also CORONARY ARTERY DISEASE; TRANSPLANTATION, MEDICAL.

Reading back the information is a matter of reflecting a lower-powered laser off the aluminum strata. A receiver or light receptor notes where light is strongly reflected and where it is absent or diffused. Diffused or absent light is caused by the recorded pits in the CD. Strong reflection of light indicates no pit—an area called a *land*. The light receptors within the player collect the reflected and diffused light as it is refracted from the surface. As the light sources are collected from the refraction, they are passed along to microprocessors that translate the light patterns back into data or sound.

Compact discs resemble their old vinyl predecessors in yet another way: CD tracks are not concentric circles across the surface, but one long spiral of pits and lands leading into the disc's center, just as a phonograph record's long groove leads toward the label of the record. This spiral of CD data is nearly three miles long.

When a CD—audio or data—seeks a bit of data from the disc, it looks up the address of the data from a table of contents and positions itself near the beginning of this data across the

FIGURE 1.3

The text article on the human heart is accompanied by an animation of a heart in action. A voice-over explains the action as it proceeds.

EXPLANATION

Data Elements: Bits, Nybbles, and Bytes

The term *bit* is a contraction of BInary digiT. A bit is the atomic—smallest, indivisible—element used to represent data in a computer's memory. A bit is binary, that is, it can have only one of two values: 1 or 0. Bits are grouped together to represent symbols and for easier manipulation. The most common grouping is eight bits, called a *byte*. One byte can represent 255 different values. In the case of text, these are the 255 characters in the American Standard Code for Information Interchange (ASCII). A *nybble* is four bits—or one-half byte. The nybble is useful in some obscure cases, but certainly shows that at least some computer scientists have a sense of humor.

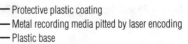

— Protective plastic coating
— Metal recording media pitted by laser encoding
— Plastic base

A CD-ROM is composed of layers of plastic, polycarbonate, and aluminum.

EXPLANATION
Error Correction

To prevent a single scratch or flaw in a CD-ROM from destroying the disc's value, an error-correction scheme is used. The CD-ROM uses a scheme called *Reed-Solomon ECC* (Error Correcting Code). This code works by storing the data on the disc more than once, allowing the recovery of a missing bit (or bits) by using the surrounding data. A key element to error correction is error detection. An error-detection algorithm (a mathematical "mechanism") allows the drive to identify damaged data and employ the error-correcting code.

spiral, waiting for the right string of bits to flow past the laser beam.

Inside Data CD-ROM Drives

The microprocessor that decodes the electrical impulses—or pits and lands of the disc's reflected light—is the key difference between music and data compact players. This decoder must pass along digital information to a digital target—a PC. The audio CD player, on the other hand, must pass along digital information to an analog processor—a stereo amplifier.

A CD-ROM drive has internal components that operate in the following manner:

1. The *laser diode* emits a low-energy beam toward a reflecting mirror.

2. The *servo motor*, on command from the microprocessor, positions the beam onto the correct track on the CD-ROM by moving the reflecting mirror.

3. Once the beam hits the disc, its refracted light is gathered and focused through the first lens beneath the disc, bounced off the mirror, and sent toward the beam splitter.

4. The *beam splitter* directs the returning laser light toward another focusing lens.

5. The last lens directs the light beam to a *photo detector*, which converts the light into electrical impulses.

6. The incoming impulses are decoded by the microprocessor and sent along to the host computer as data.

Although the simplicity of data or binary language seems to imply that a data CD optical reader would need to be less sensitive to incoming signals than an audio CD reader, that is not the case. Because the encoding pits on a

data CD are uniform in size, the presence or absence of the pitting must be measured precisely, thereby signaling the 1 or 0 of binary code. Even one **misreading** of the space or pit can cause the entire data file to lose integrity, or become useless. Therefore, the tracking mechanism—the motor that moves the laser beam across the surface—and the receptors of the refracted light must be more tightly integrated with each other and more accurate in reading the recording surface than those in an audio CD reader.

In the case of an audio CD, missing data can be "interpolated." That is, the information follows a predictable pattern that allows you to guess the missing value. For example, suppose that a series of three values—10, 13, and 20—are stored on an audio disc. If the middle value is missing because of damage or dirt on the CD's surface, you can interpolate a middle value of 15, which is midway between the values 10 and 20. Although this guess is not exactly correct, in the case of an audio recording, it is not noticeable to the listener. If those same three values appear on a CD-ROM in an executable program, there is no way to guess the correct value for the middle sample. Interpolation cannot work because executable program data follows no natural law for the data in a series of values. To guess that the missing value is 15 is not just slightly off, it is completely wrong.

Because of the need for such precision, CD-ROM drives for PCs were later to market than their audio counterparts. When first introduced, CD-ROM drives were too expensive for widespread incorporation. In addition, drive manufacturers were slow to adopt standards, causing lag time in the production of CD-ROM titles. Without a wide base of software to drive the industry, acceptance was slow.

As this book will show, the game has changed considerably. Software titles are pouring out from major commercial, academic, and government publishers, and small and large businesses are adding this powerful technology to their competitive arsenals. Drive manufacturers have improved their products, moved to more standard interfaces, and dropped their prices. When data CD-ROM drives were first introduced, only three or four manufacturers made all the available drives, but now there are dozens of suppliers.

With greater competition, better mass-manufacturing techniques, and increased demand, drives can be purchased today for as little as $250. Many drive systems include a bundle of CD-ROM software discs, making the purchase even more attractive.

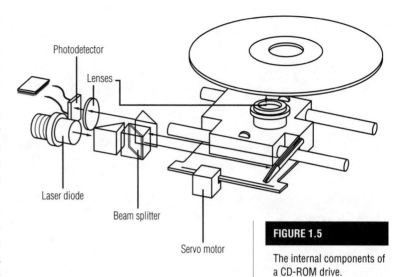

Photodetector

Lenses

Laser diode

Beam splitter

Servo motor

FIGURE 1.5

The internal components of a CD-ROM drive.

Chapter 2

CD-ROM Specifications Explained

If you are considering the purchase of a CD-ROM drive, you have undoubtedly been bombarded with advertising lingo and the conflicting advice of competing advertisements. What do you look for in a CD-ROM drive? How do you know exactly what a CD-ROM drive can do? How do you know whether drive X is better than drive Y? Unlike searching the Personal section of the local paper for the perfect mate, there are some standards used in advertisements for CD-ROM drives. This chapter helps you determine what all the hype means.

Drive Attributes

When purchasing a CD-ROM drive for your PC, you should consider three distinct sets of attributes of CD-ROM drives:

➤ The drive's specifications

➤ The format or formats it is capable of reading

➤ The interface it requires for connection to your PC

The variance in any of these categories is enormous; in fact, single vendors offer entire lines of drives that vary in performance specifications, format-reading capabilities, and the type of adapters they can use to connect to your PC. For these reasons, drive prices vary widely. First-generation CD-DA drives, for example, are available for as little as $190. You'll probably be disappointed in the drive's performance and capabilities, however, and may be better off looking elsewhere. Before you buy, know the drive's characteristics.

This chapter discusses all three drive characteristics, giving you a better understanding of what type of drive you need to buy.

CD-ROM Drive Specifications

Drive specifications tell you the drive's performance capabilities. If you're shopping for a sports car, for example, and the dealer tells you the car can accelerate from a standing stop to 60 miles per hour in 6 seconds, you know you've got a hot car. The car's horsepower, displacement in liters, and number of cylinders and valves are also specifications you use to determine how fast the car can run.

CD-ROM drive specifications tell the shopper much the same thing. Typical performance figures published by manufacturers are the data transfer rate, access time, internal buffers (if any), and the interface used.

Data Transfer Rate

The **data transfer rate** tells you how much data the drive can read from a data CD and transfer to the host computer when reading one large, sequential chunk of data. The standard measurement in the industry is kilobytes per second, usually abbreviated as KB/s. If a manufacturer claims a drive can transfer data at 120 KB/s, it means that a drive reading a sequential stream of data from the CD can achieve 120 kilobytes per second after it has come up to speed.

Note that this is a sustained and sequential read—not access across the data disc from different portions of the platter. In other words, the read is taking place as one long gulp of data from a single continuous track, rather than random accesses from various parts of the disc. Obviously, the data transfer specification is meant to convey the drive's peak data-reading capabilities. A higher rate of transfer might be better, but a number of other factors come into play.

A higher transfer rate might not be useful if the software accessing the data or the PC using the data does not need the information in such high volume.

If you expect to run a variety of CD-based software on your system, you need a drive with a high data transfer rate. Applications that employ full-motion video, animation, and sound require high transfer rates; you'll be disappointed in the results of a slower drive.

Access Time

A CD-ROM drive's access time is measured the same as it is for PC hard drives. In other words, the **access time** is the delay between the drive receiving the command to read and its actual first reading of a bit of data. The time is recorded in milliseconds (ms); a typical manufacturer's rating may be listed 350 ms.

The amount of time it takes to perform a series of random reads from a number of different positions on the disc is called the *average access rate*; the true access time depends entirely on where the data is located on the disc. Positioning the read mechanism to a portion of the disc near the narrower center of the disc gives you a faster access rate than positioning it at the wider outer perimeter. Access rates quoted by many manufacturers are an average taken by calculating a series of random reads from a disc.

Obviously, a faster average access rate is desirable, especially when you are relying on the drive to locate and pull up data quickly. Access times for CD-ROM drives are steadily improving; these advancements are discussed later in this chapter.

Note that these average times are significantly slower than those for PC hard drives, ranging from 500 to 200 ms (compared to 20 ms on a typical hard disk). Most of the speed difference lies in the construction of the drive itself; hard drives have multiple read heads and range over a smaller surface area of media. CD-ROM drives have only one laser read beam that must be positioned over the entire range of the disc. In addition, the data on a CD is organized in a long spiral from the outer edge inward. When the drive positions its head to read a "track," it must estimate the distance into the disc and skip forward or backward to the appropriate point in the spiral. Reading off the outer edge requires a longer access time than the reading off the inner segments.

EXPLANATION

Data Transfer Rate

Data transfer rate is the rate at which data moves from its resting place on storage media (like the CD-ROM) to a place where it can be used by your application. It is a *rate* because it is measured as a quantity over time. The higher the data transfer rate, the better.

RULE OF THUMB

Recommended Transfer Rate Minimum: 150 KB/s.

EXPLANATION

Access Time

Access time is the measure of how long it takes the CD-ROM drive to find a particular spot on the disc. Because the current position of the laser pickup influences how long it takes for the drive to locate an area, access time is expressed as an average. CD-ROM drives have access times far greater (in other words, worse) than typical hard drives because of the large size of the laser unit. The smaller the access time, the better.

One way to visualize a CD-ROM data disc is to think of a phonograph record; the record, like the CD, holds data in a spiral down the platter. New tracks, or songs, are merely different segments along the spiral. CDs and records differ in one significant way, however; the CD's spiral of data moves from the inside toward the outer edge as it fills with data (the analog spiral of the phonograph record moves from the outer edge inward).

Buffer

Some drives are shipped with internal buffers or caches of memory installed on-board. These buffers are actual memory chips installed on the drive's board that allow data to be staged or stored in larger segments *before* being sent to the PC. A typical buffer for a CD-ROM drive is 64 kilobytes (KB). There are several advantages to having buffer memory on the CD-ROM drive. Buffers can ensure that the PC receives data at a constant rate; when an application requests data from the CD-ROM disc, the data is probably scattered across different segments of the disc. Because we know that the drive has a relatively slow access time, the pauses between data reads may cause a drive to send data to the PC sporadically. You may not notice this problem in typical text applications, but a slower access-rate drive coupled with no data buffering is very noticeable—even irritating—in the display of video or some audio segments. In addition, a drive's buffer, when under the control of sophisticated software, can read and have ready the disc's table of contents, making the first request for data faster to find on the disc platter.

Interface

A CD-ROM's **interface** is the physical connection of the drive to the PC's expansion bus. The interface is an important element—the pipeline of data between the drive and the computer.

SCSI Standard Interfaces

SCSI, or the *Small Computer System Interface*, refers to a group of adapter cards that conforms to a set of common commands. These adapter cards also allow computer users to string a group of devices along a chain from a single adapter, avoiding the complication of inserting new adapter cards into the PC bus slots every time a new hardware device, such as a tape unit or additional CD-ROM drive, is added to the system. These traits make SCSI interfaces preferable for connecting peripherals such as a CD-ROM drive to your PC.

All SCSI adapters are not created equal. Although they may share a common command set, they can implement these commands differently—or not at all—depending on how the adapter's manufacturer designed the hardware. Furthermore, although the adapter may use **SCSI commands** to operate the CD-ROM drive, it may not allow the chaining of devices, defeating one of the chief purposes of implementing a SCSI interface.

SCSI-2 and ASPI

As is usual with standards, the original SCSI specification did not take into account the rapid enhancements to the technology involved. Changes to the amount of data that

RULE OF THUMB

Recommended Access Time: 350 ms or better.

RULE OF THUMB

Recommended Buffer: 64KB or better.

EXPLANATION

Interfaces

In the world of computers, interfaces are everywhere. An *interface* is simply a place where information moves from one system to another—for example from a CD-ROM drive to the computer's memory for use by an application, or from the computer to a printer for hard copy. The "user" interface—where you type and use your mouse—is where the data is moved between the computer and you.

EXPLANATION

SCSI Commands

SCSI commands are low-level requests, acknowledgments, and signals passed from the PC to the peripheral device with which it is communicating. SCSI commands may be as simple as finding all connected devices or asking whether a device is busy or idle. If devices, host adapters, and software drivers all use the same commands that are implemented the same way across all hardware, you've avoided another standards war and entered nirvana.

SCSI devices are expected to move, and the sophistication of the devices themselves, required enhancements to the original specification.

The SCSI-2 standard incorporates several enhancements, including the following:

➤ SCSI Fast, a special high-speed mode that greatly increases *throughput* (the amount of data moved on the SCSI bus).

➤ SCSI Wide, an enhancement that adds a second cable. This cable is used to widen the data bus to 32 bits, which also enhances throughput.

➤ Scatter/Gather, intelligent data reads and writes that minimize seek times by scheduling activity based on the data's physical location under the control of the SCSI host adapter.

The Advanced SCSI Programming Interface (ASPI) standard was designed by Adaptec—a manufacturer of SCSI host adapters—to ease the development of SCSI hardware device drivers. ASPI provides a standard software interface to the host adapter hardware. A SCSI device manufacturer can write a single, ASPI-compatible device driver that works with any ASPI-compatible host adapter or interface card made by Adaptec or another manufacturer.

The ASPI standard interface is made possible by the **ASPI driver** for a particular host adapter. The ASPI driver is a small device driver that translates the peculiarities of a particular manufacturers hardware into the standard ASPI interface.

Nonstandard SCSI

Some drive manufacturers ship their own controller cards with their drives. These controllers may be called SCSI, but may not be compatible with the ASPI or SCSI-2 specifications. When a manufacturer claims a drive has a SCSI interface, you may be getting far less than you need.

If you don't intend to install multiple SCSI devices, however, a proprietary controller or adapter is acceptable. Just beware of the limitations on expansion and compatibility.

CD-ROM Disc and Drive Formats

As was explained in Chapter 1, compact discs are pitted to encode the binary bits 0 and 1. Without a logical organization to this disc full of digits, however, the CD-ROM drive and PC would be at a loss to find any discernible data in all those numbers. To this end, the data is encoded to conform to particular standards. When a drive encounters particular patterns, it—and the PC—"recognize" the organization of the disc and find their way around the platter. Without standard data formats, the CD-ROM industry would be dead in the water; vendors of particular discs and disc drives would be producing incompatible discs and drives, thereby limiting the number of units that could be sold.

Formats are also needed to advance the technology. For example, hard rubber wheels and no suspension were fine for the first automobiles that cruised along at the breakneck speed of 30 miles per hour. But hitting a pothole at 60 miles per hour in such a vehicle could cause serious damage to the vehicle—and the riders. Consequently, inflatable tires and shock absorbers became a necessary component of the modern car.

Similarly, the standards for disc formats have evolved. The first compact data discs stored only text information that was relatively easy to encode. Graphics produced a greater challenge, and the standards evolved to incorporate them. The use of animation with synchronized sound, and then live-motion video, called for other expansions to the standards in which CDs store data.

TIP

CorelSCSI!

Corel Corporation, the same people who bring you CorelDRAW!, has done more than any single company to help standardize SCSI on the PC. By taking Adaptec's ASPI interface and creating a standard set of requirements for it, Corel certifies hardware for compatibility. Corel's own product, CorelSCSI!, provides drivers for a wide array of SCSI devices at a single low cost. If you want or need to use SCSI, check out CorelSCSI!.

For manufacturer information on CorelSCSI!, see Appendix D, "Where To Buy: Hardware and Software Vendors."

RULE OF THUMB

Recommended Interface: SCSI-2 or ASPI compatible.

Advanced CD-ROM standards are still evolving. Multiple vendors are deploying a number of different techniques for expanding the capabilities of CD-ROM technology. These techniques can be incompatible with each other or immature in their development. Consequently, acceptance of some of these newer standards by software vendors is essential to the widespread use of these newer standards. You need to be familiar with these issues before you purchase a drive; consider the formats that the drive is capable of reading—both now and in the future.

The majority of drives available today, however, do comply with earlier CD-ROM formats, ensuring that the vast library of CD-ROM applications available can be used on these drives.

First Data Standard: ISO 9660

Manufacturers of the first CD-ROM data discs produced their discs for one particular drive. In other words, a data disc produced for company A's drive could not be read by anyone who had purchased company B's drive; the disc was formatted for each manufacturer's drive. Obviously, this incompatibility stalled the industry's development. Philips and Sony—the original collaborators for the standards incorporated in audio CDs—developed the "Yellow Book" specifications for data CD-ROMs.

An extension of the way in which audio data was stored on disc, the Yellow Book specification details how data can be organized on a disc for later retrieval. The International Standards Organization (**ISO**) refined this specification in such a way that every vendor's drive and disc would expect to find a table of contents for a data disc. This is known as a *Volume Table of Contents*, and in theory is similar to a standard book's table of contents. ISO 9660 did not completely solve compatibility problems, however. The incor-

poration of additional data to aid and refine the search for data on a disc, as well as to format the data blocks, was still left to each separate vendor's design.

> ### Books, Books, Everywhere...
>
> Colors of books are used to define CD-ROM specifications because of the binders in which the specifications were originally held. The Yellow Book specification, for example, gets its name because the specifications were originally contained in a yellow binder. Following is a list of the book colors and a brief description of the CD-ROM format specifications they contain.
>
> | Color | Description |
> | --- | --- |
> | Red | Audio |
> | Yellow | Data (CD-DA) |
> | Green | CD-I (Philips), CD-ROM-XA |
> | Orange | Recordable (CD-WO, CD-R) |

High Sierra Format

It was in the interest of all manufacturers to resolve the compatibility issue. In a meeting in 1985 at the High Sierra Hotel and Casino in Lake Tahoe, California, leading manufacturers of CD-ROM drives and CD-ROM discs came together to resolve the differences in their implementation of the ISO 9660 format.

The agreement became known as the *High Sierra format*, and is now a part of the ISO 9660 specification document. This expansion enabled all drives to read all ISO 9660-compliant discs, opening the way for the mass-production of CD-ROM software publishing. Adoption of this standard also enabled disc publishers to provide cross-platform support for their software, easily manufacturing discs for DOS, UNIX, and other operating system formats. Without this agreement, the maturation of the CD-ROM marketplace would have taken years longer and stifled the production of available ROM-based information.

The exact and entire specifications for how to format the CD media is complex, strewn

EXPLANATION

ISO

The International Standards Organization is a committee responsible for developing standards that allow international trade by ensuring compatibility among manufacturers.

with jargon you may never need, and superfluous to your understanding of drive capabilities. You should know the basics, however, because they give you a glimpse at the inner workings of retrieving data so quickly from such an enormous well of data.

To put basic High Sierra format in perspective, the disc layout is roughly analogous to a floppy disk. A floppy has a system track that not only identifies itself as a floppy and its density and operating system, but also tells the computer how it's organized—into directories, and within the directories, into files.

Basic CD-ROM formats are much the same. The initial **track** of a data CD identifies itself as a CD and begins synchronization between the drive and the disc. Beyond the synchronization lies a system area that details how the entire disc is structured; as a part of the system area, the disc identifies the location of the volume area—where the actual data is held. The system area also contains the directories of this volume, with pointers or addresses to various named areas. A significant difference between CD directory structures and DOS directory structures is that the CD's system area also contains direct addresses of files within their subdirectories, allowing the CD to seek to a specific location on the spiral data track.

CD-DA (Digital Audio)

Data drives that can read data *and* audio are called CD-DA. Virtually any data drive now being sold can read both types of discs. When you insert a disc, the drive reads the first track of the disc to determine what type is loaded. Most drives ship with **audio CD** software that allows you to play audio CDs from your PC. You can use headphones, or if you have installed a sound card, you can connect speakers to the system. Some external drives ship with

standard Left/Right audio plugs; just plug them into any external amplifier.

PhotoCD

Kodak first announced the PhotoCD in 1990, but it was not available until 1992. Kodak is now shipping in quantity the home CD drives that display your own photographs on your television. You merely drop off a roll of film at a participating Kodak developer and later take home a PhotoCD and drop it into your Kodak PhotoCD-compatible disc player. But what's a PhotoCD-compatible player?

The home unit is designed to play your PhotoCDs as well as your audio CDs. Because virtually all data-ready CD drives can also interpret audio, it's no surprise that the Kodak PhotoCD players play audio discs. The player merely reads the first track and determines what type of disc you've fed it. The real breakthrough is in the drive's capability to determine whether the data disc contains one, two, or dozens of individual photo "sessions."

CD Sessions

Remember from the discussion of the High Sierra format that each data disc holds a Volume Table of Contents (VTOC) that tells the CD reader where—and how—the data is laid out on the disc. CD data has, until this point, been single-session in its encoding. In other words, when a CD master disc was created, all the data that would ever reside on the disc was recorded in a single session. Neither the format nor the media contained any provision for returning later to append more information. The PhotoCD format—along with the XA and CD-I formats covered in the section, "CD-ROM-XA Extended Architecture," later in this chapter—not only allows for multiple sessions, but allows multiple sessions to be read back on a fully PhotoCD-capable CD-ROM drive. The drive must be capable of finding the multiple VTOCs associated with the appended sessions, however.

This is where some confusion arises. When Kodak first released the PhotoCD, the company maintained that a drive must be CD-ROM-XA-compliant to use PhotoCD. As of January 1992, however, Kodak tested non-XA drives with new software drivers and okayed them as single-session PhotoCD-compatible. In other words, many of the drives shipping right now—in fact a majority of the drives—may be perfectly suited to reading PhotoCD discs that contain a single session of photos. The drive can recognize only the first session and ignores any data or subsequent volume entries made after the initial session.

PC-based CD-ROM drives, if supplied with the proper device driver and Kodak-based software, can read single-session **PhotoCD** images. Kodak is licensing the "viewer" portion of its software so that it can be incorporated into existing software packages. Special filters—or decoders—will be added to desktop publishing, word processing, and PC-paint software to enable you to import PhotoCD images into documents created using these packages.

Kodak has plans to incorporate synchronized audio and text into its existing photo format. To take advantage of these capabilities, the drive that reads these advanced discs must be XA-compatible. In addition, drives must be XA-compatible to read any disc that contains multiple recordings.

Volume Table of Contents

Disc ID	Data Block 1 Address	Data Block 2 Address	Data Block 3 Address	etc...

How Do They Do It?: PhotoCD Production

When you drop off your roll of film, the Kodak developers produce prints, just as they do normally. After the prints are made, however, the process goes high-tech. Using high-speed UNIX operating system-based SUN SparcStations, the prints are scanned into the SparcStation using ultra-high resolution scanners. To give you an idea of the amount of information each scan carries, one color photograph can require 15 to 20 megabytes of storage space. After the image is stored on disk, it is compressed using Kodak's own custom software. The compressed, stored images are then encoded onto special writeable CDs. The finished product is packaged in a familiar CD case and shipped back to your local developer for pickup.

Even though these scanned images occupy an enormous amount of media space, the capacity of CD technology can easily carry 100 photos—at the highest possible resolution. Because existing television, and even most home computers, cannot use these ultra-high-resolution photos, the typical home or PC-based PhotoCD can hold hundreds of images. (See table 2.1 for more details.) Because most of us rarely have this many photos developed at the same time, Kodak developed the system in conjunction with Philips so that multiple sessions can be recorded on one disc. You can have your Thanksgiving photos developed and recorded to disc in November, for example, and bring the same disc back in late December to have other holiday photos added. You can continue to bring in the same disc until it is full.

FIGURE 2.1

The basic organizational format of a CD-ROM.

 TIP

Using PhotoCD

Although PhotoCD can be used as the modern equivalent of the slide show when the discs contain photos of your vacation, this technology is also a wonderful opportunity for DTP (desktop publishing) enthusiasts and other desktop document creators. Even if you have a scanner and can create your own images, you probably can't duplicate the quality and convenience of the PhotoCD. For the pros and semipros, Kodak's offering may be a liberating technology.

For a lot more information about PhotoCD, see Chapter 13, "CD-ROM in the Family Room."

Table 2.1 Photo CD Resolutions

Resolution (in Lines)	Uses
256 by 384	Fine for most conventional TVs and low-resolution VGA adapters.
512 by 768	Good for S-VHS TVs and VGA adapters with 1 MB or more of memory.
1024 by 1536	Beyond current TV technology but ready for high-definition TV; even Super VGA can't use all the data.
2048 by 3072	Beyond TV or current PC capacities.

EXPLANATION

Backwards Compatibility

Backwards compatibility means that a new or improved system or technology can work with its predecessors. Backwards compatibility is very important to vendors as they design new products. Consumers do not want their supply of data, media, equipment, or the like to become suddenly obsolete. Backwards compatibility, however, is a double-edged sword. In order to ensure this compatibility, trade-offs are always made, and these trade-offs generally mean that the new technology does not achieve its full potential.

EXPLANATION

Forms and Modes

The terms *Form 1* and *Form 2* refer to two separate audio and video tracks that can be interleaved in Mode 2. Because Mode 1 doesn't expect interleaved data, Form 1 and Form 2 have no effect on it.

As of this writing, many current CD-ROM drives can read Kodak PhotoCD discs in single-session mode. Philips CD-I home entertainment systems and the Kodak systems can use multi-session discs. To take advantage of multi-session capabilities and to use audio and text on a PhotoCD for the PC, you must have an XA-compatible CD-ROM drive.

CD-ROM-XA Extended Architecture

CD-ROM-XA, or eXtended Architecture, is **backwards-compatible** with the earlier High Sierra or ISO 9660 CD-ROMs. It adds another dimension and added capabilities to the world of CD-ROM technology.

Interleaving

CD-ROM-XA drives employ a technique known as *interleaving*. The XA specification calls for the ability to encode on disc whether the data directly following an identification mark is graphics, sound, or text. Graphics may include standard graphic pictures, animation, or full-motion video. In addition, these blocks can be *interleaved*, or *interspersed*, with each other. For example, a frame of video may start a track followed by a segment of audio that accompanies the video, followed by yet another frame of video. The drive picks up the audio and video sequentially, buffers the information in memory, and then sends it to the PC for synchronization.

In short, the data is read off the disc in alternating pieces, and then synchronized at playback so that the result is a simultaneous presentation of the various kinds of data.

Mode 1 and Mode 2, Form 1 and Form 2

To achieve this level of sophistication, the CD format is broken up so that the data types are layered. Mode 1 is CD data *with* error correction. Mode 2 is CD data *without* error correction. The Mode 2 track, however, also allows what are called **Form 1 and Form 2** tracks to exist—one after the other—to allow for interleaving. These interleaved tracks may include their own error correction and may be any type of data.

For a drive to be truly XA-compatible, the Form 2 data encoded on the disc as audio must be ADPCM audio. Therefore, the drive or the SCSI controller must have a signal processor chip that can decompress the audio during the synchronization process.

What all this translates into is that drives currently available may be *partially* XA-compliant. They may be capable of interleaving data and reading multi-session discs, but may not have the ADPCM audio component on the disc or its controller.

Currently, the only fully XA-compliant drives are produced by Sony and IBM. The Sony drive incorporates the ADPCM chip. The IBM XA drive is for IBM's proprietary Micro Channel Architecture bus and is designed for the high-end PS/2 computers.

Manufacturers may claim that their drives are "XA-ready," which means they are capable of multi-sessions and Mode 1 and Mode 2, Form 1 and 2 reading, but they do *not* incorporate the ADPCM chip. Software developers, including Kodak, have yet to produce many XA software titles. IBM has a few under its Ultimedia program, but others have not yet hit the market.

If you purchase a drive that is fully mode-compatible, form-compatible, and capable of reading multiple sessions, you may have the best available at this time. The XA specification is currently waiting for acceptance. Audio and video interleaving *is* possible without full XA compliance, as MPC applications under Microsoft Windows demonstrate.

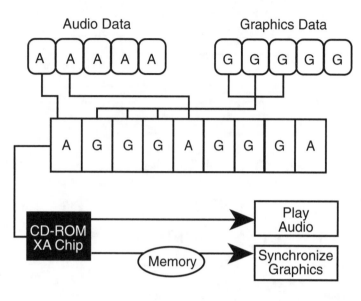

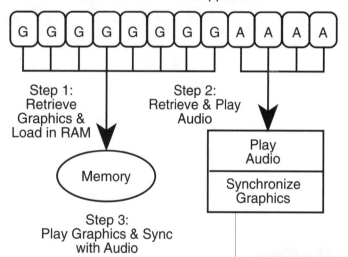

FIGURE 2.2

CD-ROM-XA architecture adds the ability to "interleave" different types of data.

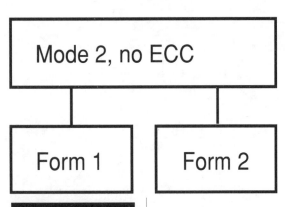

Mode 1, ECC

Mode 2, no ECC

Form 1	Form 2

FIGURE 2.3

A simple schematic of the use of modes and forms in a CD-ROM-XA format. Both modes can be used on one disc.

TIP

Using CD-R

Although writeable CD-ROM may not be ready for consumer prime time, it is a great business tool. CD-R has two important applications. First is desktop database publishing, in which the high capacity and low cost of CD-ROM media make small production runs of large databases possible. The second is internal or external distribution of large amounts of data. This application is useful to organizations that must distribute a great deal of data to only a few locations—not enough to justify the production of a normal CD-ROM. This data could be a catalog, an inventory, or even executable programs.

CD-R

Sometimes known as CD-WORM and CD-WO, the **CD-R** format allows you to write your own CDs.

As with mastering any CD, data must be laid out or formatted before it is recorded to the CD-R unit. Often, this layout is performed on a PC with large hard disks or other magnetic and removable media.

The CD-R is not quite the CD you might expect, however. Instead of the recording beam burning pits into a metallic or glass strata, the CD-R media is coated with a dye that has the same reflective properties as a "virgin" CD disc—in other words, a CD reader sees an unrecorded CD-R disc as one long land without any pits. When the recording laser begins to burn data into the CD-R media, it heats the gold layer and the dye layer beneath. The result of heating these areas causes the dye and gold areas to diffuse light in exactly the same way that a pit does on a glass master disc

or a mass-produced CD. The reader is fooled into thinking a pit exists; there is no actual pit, however—just a spot of less-reflective disc caused by the chemical reaction of heating the dye and gold.

Golden Memories: Gold Metal in CD-ROMs

The Kodak PhotoCD discs you receive from a developer look like bright gold. This regal color is not a marketing gimmick; the discs actually contain a film of gold. The Kodak PhotoCD system is a variant of the CD-R recorder. Your memorable photos are, in fact, etched in gold.

Many of the newer-model CD-R units support all the formats covered in this chapter: from ISO 9660 through CD-ROM-XA. In addition, these drives also read the formats, serving as a ROM reader. Prices have fallen, but they're still around $5,000. A number of models are discussed in Chapter 11, "Beyond the Basics," which covers capabilities, price, and the cost of recordable CD-R media.

Other Standards and Designations

When discussing CD-ROM drives, applications, and software, a number of additional standards and terms may be used. The following sections are a round-up discussion of these standards and designations.

Multimedia CD-ROM

Multimedia is not a specific standard but a descriptive term. Any CD that incorporates text with graphics or sound or video is, by definition, multimedia. **Multimedia CDs** exist for DOS, Macintosh System 7, MegaDOS, Windows, and UNIX operating systems and may be available in many different formats.

MPC CD-ROMs

A consortium of hardware and software manufacturers led by Microsoft Corporation announced the formation of the Multimedia PC Marketing Council at Fall COMDEX in 1991. This council described the recommended platform for implementing multimedia on PC systems; as more manufacturers joined the council, applications and hardware conformed to the proscribed specifications.

The MPC Council recommends the following minimum performance requirements for MPC-compatible CD-ROM drives:

➤ CD-DA drive with external audio output. ("External audio output" can be as simple as a headphone jack. Most drives have headphone jacks and a 4-pin audio edge connector or standard RCA audio plugs.)

➤ 150 KB/s transfer rate, required for animation or video.

➤ 500 ms access speed. This rate is unrealistically low, however. Most drives have much better access rates; if you use a lot of graphics and video, you'll want a drive with better performance than 500 ms.

Far from being an exact specification or format for data, MPC CD-ROM is a convention for storing audio, animation, video, and text for synchronization under Microsoft Windows using data received from an MPC-compliant CD-ROM. Microsoft has developed Windows Application Programmer's Interface software, which allows CD-ROM software manufacturers to organize data on their CDs so that information can be passed to Windows for processing.

Note that discs labeled *MPC* only run under Microsoft Windows 3.0 or higher with the Microsoft Multimedia Extensions. If a drive meets the minimum MPC Council recommendation for performance, it can run MPC CD-ROMs under Windows.

MultiSpin and High-Speed Drives

Audio drives deliver sound at a preset transfer rate to the Digital to Analog Converters (DACs).

MultiSpin drives, a term coined and trademarked by NEC, Inc., allow the drive to **spin faster** and deliver data at rates far higher than the audio equivalent. There is no reason why the computer must restrict itself to receiving data at the slower audio rate if the CPU, memory, and application software are capable of handling faster data rates.

NEC's line of high-speed drives were the first on the market in 1992, and these drives deliver data to the PC at roughly twice the speed of earlier CD-ROMs. Particular applications, such as live-motion video, especially benefit from this technology—data is delivered in a constant stream, allowing the PC to process the video frames at a smoother rate. Some drives without high-speed technology, especially those that have no buffering capabilities, deliver video in a jerky and uneven manner.

A number of vendors, including NEC, Texel, Toshiba, and Chinon, are now supplying high-speed versions of their drives. The Pioneer minichanger offers what the company calls *QuadSpin*—speeds up to four times the base delivery rate for data.

Other Drive Features

Given all the technical specifications such as transfer rates, buffers, and interfaces, you must also evaluate other aspects of a drive's construction, design, and manufacture when choosing a CD-ROM.

EXPLANATION
Spinning Speeds

The CD format was originally designed to store audio, not data. For audio reproduction, the speed at which the disc spins must send the data to the DACs—Digital to Analog Converters, which turn the digital information stored on the disc into the sound you hear—at a rate that provides the data when it is needed for the sound. This data rate is fixed, even though the disc spins more slowly at its center—where the data starts—than at its outside edge. The laser speed varies to compensate for the higher angular velocity that the larger diameter at the edge causes. This speed is perfect for audio; for data, however, the faster, the better. New drives can adjust themselves to higher spinning speed for data or the standard speed for audio.

Using Terms Correctly

As a rule of thumb, *multimedia CD-ROM* is a term used to describe any disc that uses multiple media. Other specifications and terms are more specific to operating systems or CD-ROM disc formats.

For a lot more information on multimedia, see Chapter 6, "What Is Multimedia?"

To find out about multimedia at home, see Chapter 13, "CD-ROM in the Family Room."

Drive Seals

Dirt is your CD-ROM's biggest enemy. Dust or dirt, when it collects on the lens portion of the mechanism, can cause read errors or severe performance loss. Many manufacturers seal the lens and internal components in airtight enclosures from the drive bay. Other drives, while not sealed, have double dust doors—one external and one internal—to keep dust from the inside of the drive. These features help prolong the life of your drive.

Caddies

Most CD-ROM drives require that you first insert the CD into a caddie and then insert the caddie into the drive. Some drive manufacturers, however, have built-in caddies—drawers that slide out when you push the Eject button. The disc is merely inserted into the drawer. Both methods have pros and cons.

Caddieless Drives

CD-ROMs without caddies require you to spend less time fumbling around with your CDs. This method has two slight hitches, however. First, you must make certain that the CD drawer is kept very clean; the easiest way to foul the reading of disc, and potentially damage a drive, is to introduce dirt into the mechanism. Second, if the drawer hinge fails, you must send the entire drive in for repair.

Drives with Caddies

You need a phone number for a business in Los Angeles, so you open the CD case for your American Business Phone Book CD. You eject the CD already in the drive, remove it, and replace it in its case. You take out the Phone Book CD and insert it into the caddie. Then....

You get the picture. Using caddies is a time-consuming bother if you deal with a number of different CDs. This inconvenience is the only drawback to caddies. The individual caddies are easy to clean; when they show signs of wear, you simply throw them away. You can pick up caddies for about five or six dollars each; it's worth the small investment to buy each of your most-used CDs their own caddies.

Self-Cleaning Lenses

If the laser lens gets dirty, so does your data. The drive spends a lot of time seeking and reseeking—or finally giving up. **Lens-cleaning discs** are available, but built-in cleaning mechanisms are now included on some model drives. You may want to consider this feature, particularly if you work in a less-than-pristine work environment or, like us, you have trouble keeping your desk clean—let alone your CD-ROM drive lens.

TIP

Cleaning Your Drive's Lens

The collimating lens on the laser pickup assembly tends to get covered with dust, which can cause errors. If your drive is not self-cleaning, special CDs are available that, when inserted into a CD drive, use a soft brush to dust the drives lens. These CDs are available at audio and discount stores.

For more information about caring for your discs and drives, see Appendix F, "Care and Feeding of CD-ROMs."

Internal versus External: Some Considerations

You need to consider whether you want an internal or external drive. Think about where and how you intend to use your CD-ROM drive. What about the future expansion of your system? There are pluses and minuses to both drive types. Take a look at some of the issues.

External Enclosures

Drives with external enclosures tend to be rugged, portable, and large—in comparison to their internal versions. Buy an external drive if you have the space and are considering or already own other external SCSI peripherals you can chain to the same adapter. You may also consider an external drive if you want to move the drive easily from one PC to another. If each PC has its own SCSI adapter, you simply unplug the drive from one adapter and plug it in to the other.

Internal Enclosures

Internal drives clear off a portion of your desk. Buy an internal drive if you already have internal SCSI devices you can chain to your adapter, have ample drive bay space, or intend to keep the CD-ROM drive exclusively on one machine.

Chapter 3

How To Select CD-ROM Drives

You now have a good idea what a CD-ROM drive can do for your personal and business computing. There's one problem: where once there were only a handful of CD-ROM drives to choose from, now there are dozens, with new models and manufacturers releasing new products virtually every month. These drives can vary widely in performance, design, and construction. This chapter compares many of the currently available CD-ROM drives.

How To Use This Chapter

In this chapter, you find descriptions of many kinds of CD-ROM drives. Because there are so many different brands available, this chapter narrows the search down to some of the best. Each drive is rated with a number of compact-disc icons. The maximum rating is five icons (rounded to the nearest half icon). The rating system considers the performance and specifications of the drive; a subjective "value" score was added to the overall total. This value score factors in our opinion of the drive based on price, quality, features, and how it compares with the available field. This rating is designed to help you narrow the choices available; it is not foolproof or scientific.

Because advertisements aren't always consistent in what they tell you about the product, this chapter incorporates specification charts into the descriptions of the various products. The charts provide the same information about each product so that you can compare all the important aspects of the drives before you make a purchasing decision.

A special icon, called the Award of Excellence, is used to mark superlative products (we explain why these products are cream of the crop in the margin-note text accompanying the award icon).

CD Technology

Based in Sunnyvale, California, CD Technology's primary product is their CD Porta-Drive, a lightweight, portable Mac-compatible and PC-compatible CD drive (see fig. 3.1). CD Technology claims that, unlike other portable or lightweight CD-ROM drives, theirs is free from possible contamination because of a "quadruple seal" approach: the outside power supply is sealed, the drive mechanism is sealed, an additional barrier is provided with the popular "garage door-style" disc opening, and a self-cleaning lens mechanism adds another level of contamination protection. The drive is based on the Toshiba XM-3401 mechanism, one of the fastest on the market. The unit is light—a mere three pounds—and has a standard SCSI connection.

The suggested price includes drive, caddy, power supply, enclosure, and instructions. SCSI cards are sold separately by CD Technology, but Adaptec, Future Domain, and Procom SCSI adapters should be fine, with appropriate drivers for the Toshiba.

The internal Porta-Drive model comes with a caddy and a standard SCSI flat ribbon cable with connectors for three SCSI devices (with three connectors, you can "daisy chain" devices on the cable). Although the company offers standard 8-bit and 16-bit SCSI adapters, virtually any SCSI card supported by CorelSCSI! should work. Because this drive is essentially a Toshiba drive, the SCSI kit supports it.

SCSI Adapters without SCSI Cards

CD Technology sells a parallel-to-SCSI adapter—a SCSI-on-the-printer-port solution for the external drive—making it possible to easily attach the drive to a notebook computer that has no slot available for a SCSI card, or for users and system administrators who are squeamish about opening up PCs and messing with SCSI interface cards.

The CD Porta-Drive T3401 from CD Technology.

CD Porta-Drive Model T3401

External (Portable)	
[x] PC compatible	
[x] Macintosh compatible	
[x] MPC compliant	
[x] PhotoCD, single session	
[x] PhotoCD, multi-session	
Interface:	
[x] SCSI	
[x] SCSI-2	
[ ] Proprietary	
Average access time	200 ms
Transfer rate	330 KB/s
Memory buffer	256KB
Audio:	
[x] Standard RCA jacks	
[x] Headphones	
[ ] 4-pin CD audio out	0
Suggested list price:	$850

CD Porta-Drive Model T3402-INT

Internal	
[x] PC compatible	
[x] Macintosh compatible	
[x] MPC compliant	
[x] PhotoCD, single session	
[x] PhotoCD, multi-session	
Interface:	
[x] SCSI	
[x] SCSI-2	
[x] Proprietary	
Average access time	200 ms
Transfer rate	330 KB/s
Buffer	256KB
Audio:	
[ ] Standard RCA jacks	
[ ] Headphones	
[x] 4-pin CD audio out	
Suggested list price	$700

Chinon

Chinon America, Inc., carries a full line of CD-ROM drives, multimedia upgrade kits, and 3.5-inch Magneto Optical drives. Although primarily known in this country as a manufacturer and supplier of printers, the Chinon CD-ROM drive line covers PC and Macintosh platforms, with both internal and external versions (see fig. 3.2).

The CDX-535 comes with a power supply, one CD caddy, and documentation. An optional PC Interface Package bundles an 8-bit SCSI card, SCSI cable, Microsoft MSCDEX extensions, and documentation.

The drive comes with a power supply, one CD caddy, and documentation. The Macintosh Interface Package, an added option, includes Mac drivers, a connector cable to the Mac SCSI bus, and CD Play Software.

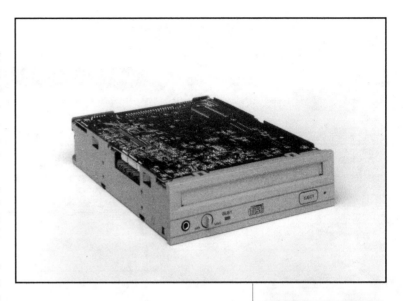

FIGURE 3.2

The Chinon CDS-535 double-speed cached drive.

Chinon CDS-535

Internal	
[x] PC compatible	
[x] Macintosh compatible	
[x] MPC compliant	
[x] PhotoCD, single session	
[x] PhotoCD, multi-session	
Interface:	
[x] SCSI	
[x] SCSI-2	
[ ] Proprietary	
Average access time	280 ms
Transfer rate	300 KB/s
Buffer	256KB
Audio:	
[ ] Standard RCA jacks	
[x] Headphones	
[x] 4-pin CD audio out	
Suggested list price	$645

Chinon CDX-535, PC

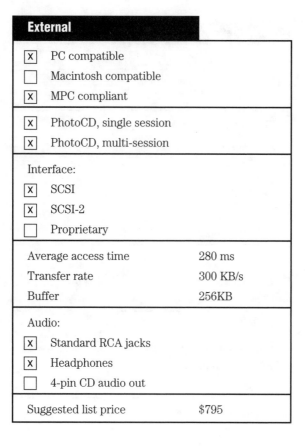

External

☒	PC compatible
☐	Macintosh compatible
☒	MPC compliant

☒	PhotoCD, single session
☒	PhotoCD, multi-session

Interface:

☒	SCSI
☒	SCSI-2
☐	Proprietary

Average access time	280 ms
Transfer rate	300 KB/s
Buffer	256KB

Audio:

☒	Standard RCA jacks
☒	Headphones
☐	4-pin CD audio out

Suggested list price	$795

Chinon CDA-535, Mac

External	
☐ PC compatible	
☒ Macintosh compatible	
☐ MPC compliant	
☒ PhotoCD, single session	
☒ PhotoCD, multi-session	
Interface:	
☒ SCSI	
☒ SCSI-2	
☐ Proprietary	
Average access time	280 ms
Transfer rate	300 KB/s
Buffer	256KB
Audio:	
☒ Standard RCA jacks	
☒ Headphones	
☐ 4-pin CD audio out	
Suggested list price	$795

Hitachi

The Hitachi company has been in the CD-ROM drive business since the beginning, producing some of the first and fastest drives in the early market. They have a wide range of drives; in fact, no other vendor offers such a wide product line. The Hitachi drives are high quality, easy to install and configure, and have very competitive prices (see fig. 3.3).

In their extensive line of internal and external drives, Hitachi has a model and price range for virtually any user or organization.

With a larger buffer than the 1700S and a SCSI interface, the Hitachi 1750S D-ROM drive can be a good choice for multimedia systems with standard SCSI. The drive meets MPC specifications, and the buffer should ensure smooth video playback.

This model is a solid, basic, MPC-compliant or Macintosh CD-ROM drive.

Installation kits are available for Mac, PC, and PS/2 MCA bus machines.

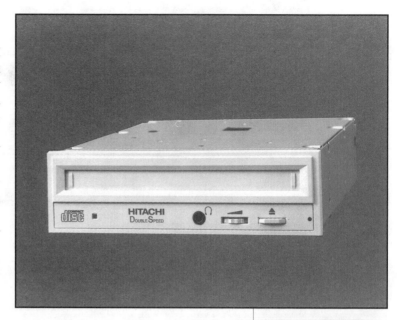

FIGURE 3.3

A Hitachi CD-ROM drive.

Hitachi CDR-1700S

External	
[x] PC compatible	
[ ] Macintosh compatible	
[x] MPC compliant	
[x] PhotoCD, single session	
[ ] PhotoCD, multi-session	
Interface:	
[ ] SCSI	
[ ] SCSI-2	
[x] Proprietary	Hitachi Bus
Average access time	320 ms
Transfer rate	153.6 KB/s
Buffer	32KB
Audio:	
[x] Standard RCA jacks	
[x] Headphones	
[ ] 4-pin CD audio out	
Suggested list price	$815

Hitachi 1750S

External	
☒ PC compatible	
☒ Macintosh compatible	
☒ MPC compliant	
☒ PhotoCD, single session	
☐ PhotoCD, multi-session	
Interface:	
☒ SCSI	
☐ SCSI-2	
☐ Proprietary	
Average access time	320 ms
Transfer rate	153.6 KB/s
Buffer	64KB
Audio:	
☒ Standard RCA jacks	
☒ Headphones	
☐ 4-pin CD audio out	
Suggested list price	$915

Hitachi 3700

Internal	
[x] PC compatible	
[x] Macintosh compatible	
[x] MPC compliant	
[x] PhotoCD, single session	
[ ] PhotoCD, multi-session	
Interface:	
[ ] SCSI	
[ ] SCSI-2	
[x] Proprietary	Hitachi Bus
Average access time	370 ms
Transfer rate	153.6 KB/s
Buffer	64KB
Audio:	
[ ] Standard RCA jacks	
[x] Headphones	
[x] 4-pin CD audio out	
Suggested list price	$745

Hitachi CDR-3750

Internal	
☒ PC compatible	
☐ Macintosh compatible	
☒ MPC compliant	
☒ PhotoCD, single session	
☐ PhotoCD, multi-session	
Interface:	
☒ SCSI	
☐ SCSI-2	
☐ Proprietary	
Average access time	370 ms
Transfer rate	153.6 KB/s
Buffer	64KB
Audio:	
☐ Standard RCA jacks	
☒ Headphones	
☒ 4-pin CD audio out	
Suggested list price	$865

Hitachi CDR-6700

Internal	
[x] PC compatible	
[x] Macintosh compatible	
[x] MPC compliant	
[x] PhotoCD, single session	
[x] PhotoCD, multi-session	
Interface:	
[ ] SCSI	
[ ] SCSI-2	
[x] Proprietary	Hitachi Bus
Average access time	260 ms
Transfer rate	300 KB/s
Buffer	128KB
Audio:	
[ ] Standard RCA jacks	
[x] Headphones	
[x] 4-pin CD audio out	
Suggested list price	$995

Laser Magnetic Storage

The Colorado-based Laser Magnetic Storage (LMS) company is a subsidiary of Philips. Not surprisingly, LMS drives are Philips mechanisms with LMS cases (see fig. 3.4). And these are not trivial enhancements. On some models, for example, a motorized caddy smoothly ejects the disc. When you're playing audio CDs, the front-panel display allows easy track-skipping with the simple push of a button. Other features include a good-sized volume control and easy-to-read LEDs. Another salient feature of the LMS line is of great importance—price. The LMS line is very reasonably priced.

All LMS retail drive packages come with an adapter card, cables, and all necessary installation software.

According to a company spokesperson, LMS is the only U.S.-based manufacturer of CD-ROM drives. The company sells drives through distributors and OEM relationships with other vendors.

The list price is astoundingly low for an internal double-speed drive, especially considering that the mechanism is a Philips—

one of the pioneers in CD-ROM technology. The drive has loads of important user features. These are "must see" units when you're considering purchasing any new CD-ROM drive.

External models of the LMS drive will be available shortly.

FIGURE 3.4

The LMS CM206 double-speed drive has a motorized disc tray for loading CDs and a very attractive $499 suggested list price.

LMS CM206

Internal	
X PC compatible	
☐ Macintosh compatible	
X MPC compliant	
X PhotoCD, single session	
X PhotoCD, multi-session	
Interface:	
X SCSI	
X SCSI-2	
☐ Proprietary	
Average access time	350 ms
Transfer rate	300 KB/s
Buffer	64KB
Audio:	
☐ Standard RCA jacks	
X Headphones	
X 4-pin CD audio out	
Suggested list price	$499

LMS CM215

Internal	
[x] PC compatible	
[ ] Macintosh compatible	
[x] MPC compliant	
[x] PhotoCD, single session	
[x] PhotoCD, multi-session	
Interface:	
[x] SCSI	
[x] SCSI-2	
[ ] Proprietary	
Average access time	360 ms
Transfer rate	153.6 KB/s
Buffer	64KB
Audio:	
[ ] Standard RCA jacks	
[x] Headphones	
[x] 4-pin CD audio out	
Suggested list price	$499

Liberty Systems

Liberty is best known for bundling a variety of mass-storage devices with SCSI and parallel-to-SCSI interfaces. Liberty specializes in removable media drives such as Syquest systems and high-end optical products. Their portable CD-ROM reader is a Toshiba drive in a Liberty enclosure with parallel-to-SCSI, Mac, and standard PC SCSI connection options. It prices out much lower than CD Technology's portable, based on the same Toshiba XM-301 drive mechanism, so if you want a solid portable at an attractive price, take a look at the Liberty drive.

The 115CD-P has a parallel-port SCSI and a price of $799. All systems—Mac, PC, or parallel—ship with cable, power cord, and software for drive installation. An optional padded carrying case is $29.

Liberty 115 Series

External (Portable)	
[x] PC compatible	
[x] Macintosh compatible	
[x] MPC compliant	
[x] PhotoCD, single session	
[x] PhotoCD, multi-session	
Interface:	
[x] SCSI	
[x] SCSI-2	
[ ] Proprietary	
Average access time	200 ms
Transfer rate	300 KB/s
Buffer	256KB
Audio:	
[x] Standard RCA jacks	
[x] Headphones	
[ ] 4-pin CD audio out	
Suggested list price	$699

NEC

NEC was a pioneer in bringing CD-ROM to the desktop. Their CD art-gallery disc was one of the first commercially available and useful applications, which clearly demonstrated to most users the capabilities of CD technology for computing. NEC was also first in providing double-speed drives, a technology that NEC refers to as *MultiSpin* (see fig. 3.5). As you know, double-speed drives give PCs more muscle when processing multimedia video and animations, making PC video a smooth, more life-like representation than the jerky, out-of-sync playback you experience on drives with 150 KB/s transfer rates.

Macintosh Drivers with NEC

If you're a Mac user, make certain that you have the latest drivers for the NEC when using System 7. Some users have experienced problems with their PostScript interpreters when using older NEC drivers, and the problem is particularly difficult to track down unless you know what to suspect.

The portable MultiSpin-38 drive has a higher access time and less of a buffer than the Multi-Spin-74 or the MultiSpin-84. Still, the MultiSpin-38 has an amazing price for a portable using double-speed technology. The MultiSpin-38 drive is more than adequate for multimedia tasks, including full-motion video in QuickTime for the Mac or Video for Windows.

FIGURE 3.5

The NEC family of MultiSpin CD-ROM drives.

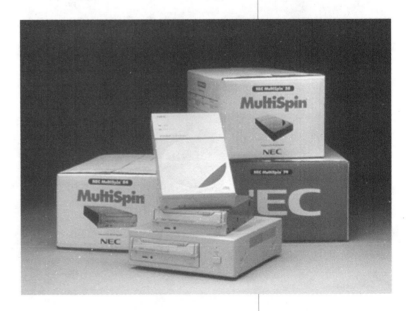

NEC MultiSpin-74

External	
☒ PC compatible	
☒ Macintosh compatible	
☒ MPC compliant	
☒ PhotoCD, single session	
☒ PhotoCD, multi-session	
Interface:	
☒ SCSI	
☒ SCSI-2	
☐ Proprietary	
Average access time	280 ms
Transfer rate	300 KB/s
Buffer	256KB
Audio:	
☒ Standard RCA jacks	
☒ Headphones	
☐ 4-pin CD audio out	
Suggested list price	$615

NEC MultiSpin-84

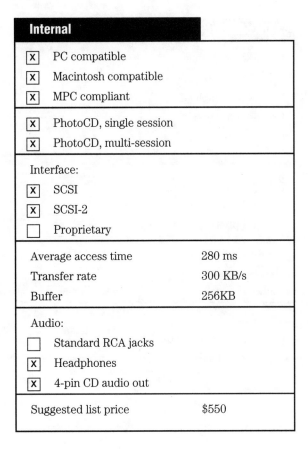

Internal	
☒	PC compatible
☒	Macintosh compatible
☒	MPC compliant
☒	PhotoCD, single session
☒	PhotoCD, multi-session
Interface:	
☒	SCSI
☒	SCSI-2
☐	Proprietary
Average access time	280 ms
Transfer rate	300 KB/s
Buffer	256KB
Audio:	
☐	Standard RCA jacks
☒	Headphones
☒	4-pin CD audio out
Suggested list price	$550

NEC MultiSpin-38

External (Portable)	
☒ PC compatible	
☒ Macintosh compatible	
☒ MPC compliant	
☒ PhotoCD, single session	
☒ PhotoCD, multi-session	
Interface:	
☒ SCSI	
☒ SCSI-2	
☐ Proprietary	
Average access time	400 ms
Transfer rate	300 KB/s
Buffer	64KB
Audio:	
☒ Standard RCA jacks	
☒ Headphones	
☐ 4-pin CD audio out	
Suggested list price	$465

Philips Consumer Electronics

Philips invented CD-ROM. The company does well in recordable, CD-I, and portable optical technologies. It's no surprise that their CD-ROM drives are some of the best in the business, nor that many manufacturers are repackaging the Philips mechanism in multimedia PCs and in their own enclosures.

Philips recently announced a new series of CD-ROM drives.

The Philips CDD462BK drive is an excellent choice for the multimedia user. It comes with a host adapter, cable, MSCDEX drivers, and documentation.

The Philips CDD462RS system comes with all cables, the Philips adapter card, software extensions for DOS, a bundled set of speakers, and a selection of popular CD titles. All you need for a multimedia upgrade, therefore, is a sound card.

Double-speed and a very respectable access time make the Philips RapidReader CM405ABK a good multimedia drive. The standard SCSI interface is also a big plus, making Mac or daisy-chained PC installations possible.

The RapidReader CM425ABK is the external version of Philips' double-speed contender. It is Mac, PC, and PS/2 compatible, with a standard SCSI interface. The 265-ms access rate makes it perfect for multimedia applications that use Video for Windows or QuickTime.

The Philips CM205XBK drive alone is $499, but it requires the Philips adapter, which boosts the price to $599. This model is a good, basic MPC-compliant drive.

Philips RapidReader CM405ABK

Internal	
☒ PC compatible	
☒ Macintosh compatible	
☒ MPC compliant	
☒ PhotoCD, single session	
☒ PhotoCD, multi-session	
Interface:	
☒ SCSI	
☒ SCSI-2	
☐ Proprietary	
Average access time	265 ms
Transfer rate	300 KB/s
Buffer	64KB
Audio:	
☐ Standard RCA jacks	
☒ Headphones	
☒ 4-pin CD audio out	
Suggested list price	$599

Philips CDD462RS

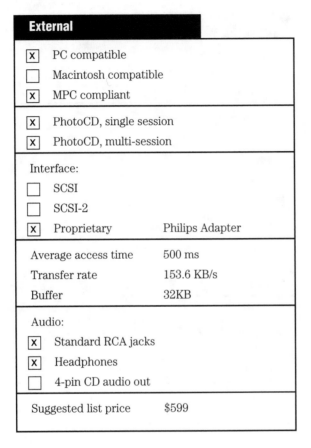

External

☒	PC compatible
☐	Macintosh compatible
☒	MPC compliant

☒	PhotoCD, single session
☒	PhotoCD, multi-session

Interface:

☐	SCSI	
☐	SCSI-2	
☒	Proprietary	Philips Adapter

Average access time	500 ms
Transfer rate	153.6 KB/s
Buffer	32KB

Audio:

☒	Standard RCA jacks
☒	Headphones
☐	4-pin CD audio out

Suggested list price	$599

Philips RapidReader CM425ABK

External	
[X]	PC compatible
[X]	Macintosh compatible
[X]	MPC compliant
[X]	PhotoCD, single session
[X]	PhotoCD, multi-session
Interface:	
[X]	SCSI
[X]	SCSI-2
[ ]	Proprietary
Average access time	265 ms
Transfer rate	300 KB/s
Buffer	64KB
Audio:	
[X]	Standard RCA jacks
[X]	Headphones
[ ]	4-pin CD audio out
Suggested list price	$699

Philips CDD462BK

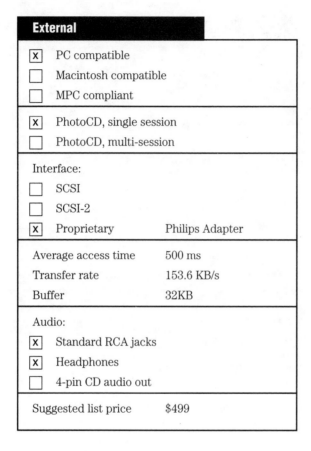

External

- [x] PC compatible
- [ ] Macintosh compatible
- [ ] MPC compliant

- [x] PhotoCD, single session
- [ ] PhotoCD, multi-session

Interface:
- [ ] SCSI
- [ ] SCSI-2
- [x] Proprietary   Philips Adapter

Average access time	500 ms
Transfer rate	153.6 KB/s
Buffer	32KB

Audio:
- [x] Standard RCA jacks
- [x] Headphones
- [ ] 4-pin CD audio out

Suggested list price	$499

Philips CM205XBK

External	
[X] PC compatible	
[ ] Macintosh compatible	
[X] MPC compliant	
[X] PhotoCD, single session	
[ ] PhotoCD, multi-session	
Interface:	
[ ] SCSI	
[ ] SCSI-2	
[X] Proprietary	Philips Adapter
Average access time	375 ms
Transfer rate	153.6 KB/s
Buffer	32KB
Audio:	
[X] Standard RCA jacks	
[X] Headphones	
[ ] 4-pin CD audio out	
Suggested list price	$599

Procom Technology

Procom is perhaps best known for their SCSI Xelerator adapters, which they put to good use in these CD-ROM packages. The drives are based on Toshiba's latest mechanisms, and the performance of the Procom kits are comparable. The drives and drive/adapter bundles sold by Procom are a great value (see fig. 3.6).

All Procom systems have electronic caddy ejection—vastly preferable over the mechanical ejection mechanisms, which jam and often malfunction. The caddy can be ejected by software command as well.

The Procom SiCDS is a blazing internal drive, especially when used with a Procom adapter and CorelSCSI!. A fabulous access rate, a high transfer rate (the highest now available), and a hefty 256KB buffer make this drive a real multimedia racehorse.

The price is right. The fastest-shipping CD-ROM at the time this book was printed, the Procom MCD-DS external drive, is a great value.

The Procom PxCDS is a very affordable, multi-session, and MPC-compliant drive with a standard SCSI interface.

If you want multi-session and MPC capabilities in an extremely affordable internal CD-ROM drive, consider the Procom PiCDS.

If you don't mind forgoing multi-session PhotoCD capabilities but want a good multimedia drive, the Procom PiCDL internal drive is priced right. Its price includes the drive, adapter, cables, and installation.

This external drive comes with an adapter, cables, and documentation.

The Procom MacCD/LX is a good QuickTime-ready drive.

The Procom MacCD/MX is fast and PhotoCD multi-session compatible, making it a good high-end drive for Mac users.

FIGURE 3.6

The double-speed drives from Procom are a great value for such high-end performance.

Procom SiCDS

Internal	
☒ PC compatible	
☐ Macintosh compatible	
☒ MPC compliant	
☒ PhotoCD, single session	
☒ PhotoCD, multi-session	
Interface:	
☒ SCSI	
☒ SCSI-2	
☐ Proprietary	
Average access time	200 ms
Transfer rate	330 KB/s
Buffer	256KB
Audio:	
☐ Standard RCA jacks	
☒ Headphones	
☒ 4-pin CD audio out	
Suggested list price	$645

Procom MCD-DS

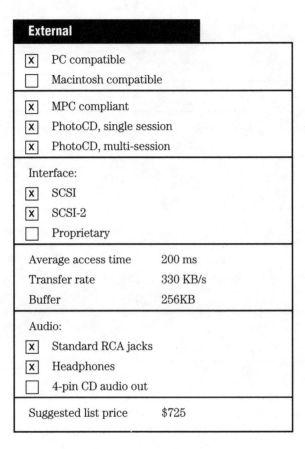

External

- [x] PC compatible
- [ ] Macintosh compatible

- [x] MPC compliant
- [x] PhotoCD, single session
- [x] PhotoCD, multi-session

Interface:
- [x] SCSI
- [x] SCSI-2
- [ ] Proprietary

Average access time	200 ms
Transfer rate	330 KB/s
Buffer	256KB

Audio:
- [x] Standard RCA jacks
- [x] Headphones
- [ ] 4-pin CD audio out

Suggested list price	$725

Procom PxCDS

External	
[x]	PC compatible
[ ]	Macintosh compatible
[x]	MPC compliant
[x]	PhotoCD, single session
[x]	PhotoCD, multi-session

Interface:

[x]	SCSI
[x]	SCSI-2
[ ]	Proprietary

Average access time	490 ms
Transfer rate	150 KB/s
Buffer	64KB

Audio:

[x]	Standard RCA jacks
[x]	Headphones
[ ]	4-pin CD audio out

Suggested list price	$425

Procom PiCDS

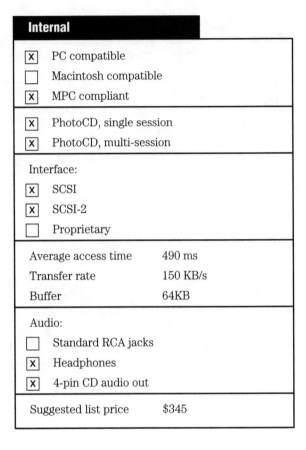

Internal	
[X]	PC compatible
[ ]	Macintosh compatible
[X]	MPC compliant
[X]	PhotoCD, single session
[X]	PhotoCD, multi-session

Interface:

[X]	SCSI
[X]	SCSI-2
[ ]	Proprietary

Average access time	490 ms
Transfer rate	150 KB/s
Buffer	64KB

Audio:

[ ]	Standard RCA jacks
[X]	Headphones
[X]	4-pin CD audio out

Suggested list price	$345

Procom PiCDL

Internal		
[X]	PC compatible	
[ ]	Macintosh compatible	
[X]	MPC compliant	
[X]	PhotoCD, single session	
[ ]	PhotoCD, multi-session	
Interface:		
[ ]	SCSI	
[ ]	SCSI-2	
[X]	Proprietary	LMSI Adapter
Average access time		375 ms
Transfer rate		153 KB/s
Buffer		32KB
Audio:		
[X]	Standard RCA jacks	
[X]	Headphones	
[ ]	4-pin CD audio out	
Suggested list price		$325

Procom PxCDL

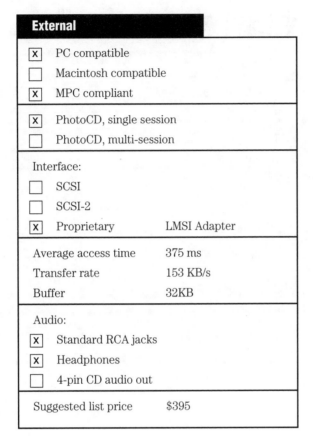

External

- [x] PC compatible
- [ ] Macintosh compatible
- [x] MPC compliant

- [x] PhotoCD, single session
- [ ] PhotoCD, multi-session

Interface:
- [ ] SCSI
- [ ] SCSI-2
- [x] Proprietary   LMSI Adapter

Average access time	375 ms
Transfer rate	153 KB/s
Buffer	32KB

Audio:
- [x] Standard RCA jacks
- [x] Headphones
- [ ] 4-pin CD audio out

Suggested list price	$395

Procom MacCD/LX

External		
☐	PC compatible	
☒	Macintosh compatible	
☐	MPC compliant	
☒	PhotoCD, single session	
☐	PhotoCD, multi-session	
Interface:		
☒	SCSI	
☒	SCSI-2	
☐	Proprietary	
Average access time		380 ms
Transfer rate		150 KB/s
Buffer		64KB
Audio:		
☒	Standard RCA jacks	
☒	Headphones	
☐	4-pin CD audio out	
Suggested list price		$595

Procom MacCD/MX

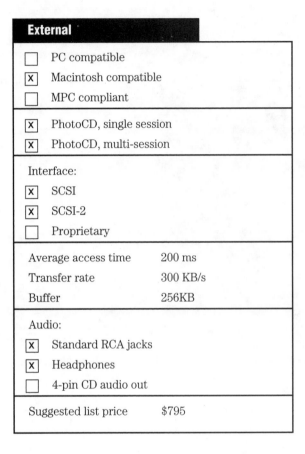

External

- [ ] PC compatible
- [x] Macintosh compatible
- [ ] MPC compliant

- [x] PhotoCD, single session
- [x] PhotoCD, multi-session

Interface:
- [x] SCSI
- [x] SCSI-2
- [ ] Proprietary

Average access time	200 ms
Transfer rate	300 KB/s
Buffer	256KB

Audio:
- [x] Standard RCA jacks
- [x] Headphones
- [ ] 4-pin CD audio out

Suggested list price	$795

Sony Corporation

Sony recently announced double-speed drives for multimedia applications (see fig. 3.7). The drives—internal and external—shipped in the summer of 1993.

The Sony CDU-561 double-speed CD-ROM drive is designed for high-performance workstations and multimedia applications.

Sony CDU-561

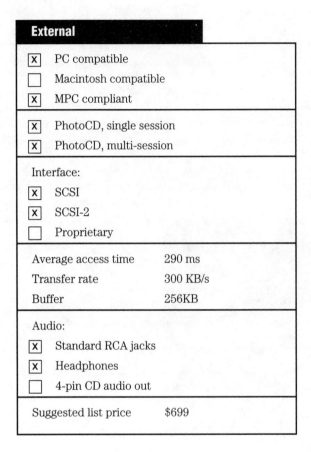

External	
☒	PC compatible
☐	Macintosh compatible
☒	MPC compliant
☒	PhotoCD, single session
☒	PhotoCD, multi-session

Interface:
- ☒ SCSI
- ☒ SCSI-2
- ☐ Proprietary

Average access time	290 ms
Transfer rate	300 KB/s
Buffer	256KB

Audio:
- ☒ Standard RCA jacks
- ☒ Headphones
- ☐ 4-pin CD audio out

Suggested list price	$699

Texel Drives Models DM-3024 and DM-5024

Texel provides high performance, rugged, well-engineered drives at a modest price. There may be drives of comparable speed on the market today, but Texel leads the way in construction and pricing. Some Texel drives can be found on the street for as little as $400, making them an excellent buy.

Texel

There's a lot to like about the Texel line. Although it's limited to two drives, those drives are the best two on the market (see fig. 3.8). Texel is the U.S. subsidiary of the Shinano Kenshi electronics firm, where high-speed motor and ruggedized components for CD-ROM drives are developed. The drives are rugged, fast, easy to install, and give excellent performance for the money. All models—including the multimedia kits—are an exceptional value for such quality products. The

Texel drives support all the CD-ROM formats you can use on a PC or Mac at the time of this writing, and further improvements and enhancements are scheduled in the near future for this drive line. Although the name *Texel* may not be a PC-household word yet, that may change soon. For the money, these drives are the best. Period. If you're in the market for PhotoCD, MPC, and a standard SCSI interface drive, you won't go wrong purchasing these drives.

For the price, the Texel DM-3024 drive can't be beat. If you're considering an internal drive, you can't find a better value.

With a rugged case, great performance, and an incredible price when compared to the competition, the Texel DM-5024 is your best bet for an external CD-ROM drive.

FIGURE 3.8

The Texel series of high-performance drives.

Texel DM-3024

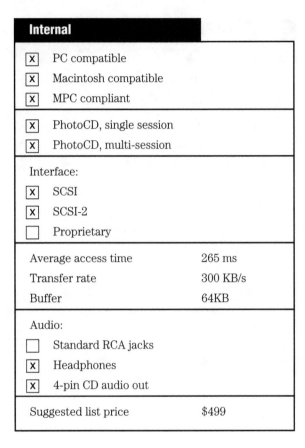

Internal

[X]	PC compatible
[X]	Macintosh compatible
[X]	MPC compliant

[X]	PhotoCD, single session
[X]	PhotoCD, multi-session

Interface:

[X]	SCSI
[X]	SCSI-2
[ ]	Proprietary

Average access time	265 ms
Transfer rate	300 KB/s
Buffer	64KB

Audio:

[ ]	Standard RCA jacks
[X]	Headphones
[X]	4-pin CD audio out

Suggested list price	$499

Texel DM-5024

External	
☒	PC compatible
☒	Macintosh compatible
☒	MPC compliant
☒	PhotoCD, single session
☒	PhotoCD, multi-session

Interface:	
☒	SCSI
☒	SCSI-2
☐	Proprietary

Average access time	265 ms
Transfer rate	300 KB/s
Buffer	64KB

Audio:	
☒	Standard RCA jacks
☒	Headphones
☐	4-pin CD audio out

Suggested list price	$599

Toshiba

When this book went to press, Toshiba boasted the fastest drives on the market, and their drive line focuses exclusively on double-speed models. The Toshiba drive—like Sony, Philips, and Hitachi—are sold under other brand names, with only some modifications to the cabinet.

The Toshiba XM-3401B is an internal speed demon that is perfect for multimedia applications, PhotoCD, and full-motion video. The price is reasonable when you consider its features and performance.

The Toshiba TXM-3401E is a great drive for any application dealing with full-motion video (look at its transfer rate and 256K buffer); but this external version of the Toshiba is a high-end drive, with a higher-than-average price.

The TXM-3401P is Toshiba's portable version of the double-speed drive, with specifications identical to the internal and external models.

Toshiba XM-3401B

Internal	
☒ PC compatible	
☒ Macintosh compatible	
☒ MPC compliant	
☒ PhotoCD, single session	
☒ PhotoCD, multi-session	
Interface:	
☒ SCSI	
☒ SCSI-2	
☐ Proprietary	
Average access time	200 ms
Transfer rate	330 KB/s
Buffer	256KB
Audio:	
☐ Standard RCA jacks	
☒ Headphones	
☒ 4-pin CD audio out	
Suggested list price	$695

Toshiba TXM-3401E

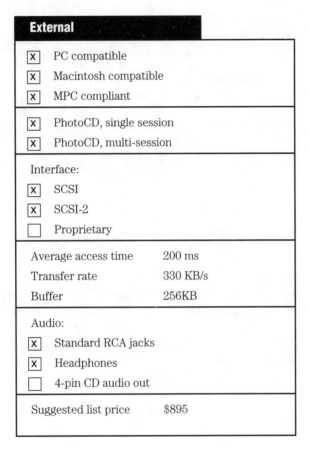

External

- [x] PC compatible
- [x] Macintosh compatible
- [x] MPC compliant

- [x] PhotoCD, single session
- [x] PhotoCD, multi-session

Interface:
- [x] SCSI
- [x] SCSI-2
- [ ] Proprietary

Average access time	200 ms
Transfer rate	330 KB/s
Buffer	256KB

Audio:
- [x] Standard RCA jacks
- [x] Headphones
- [ ] 4-pin CD audio out

Suggested list price	$895

Toshiba TXM-3401P

External (Portable)		
[X]	PC compatible	
[X]	Macintosh compatible	
[X]	MPC compliant	
[X]	PhotoCD, single session	
[X]	PhotoCD, multi-session	
Interface:		
[X]	SCSI	
[X]	SCSI-2	
[ ]	Proprietary	
Average access time		200 ms
Transfer rate		330 KB/s
Buffer		256KB
Audio:		
[X]	Standard RCA jacks	
[X]	Headphones	
[ ]	4-pin CD audio out	
Suggested list price		$925

Multimedia Upgrade Kits

This section gives you a sample of the more popular multimedia upgrade kits now available for the Mac and PC. Most bundles include a sound card, CD-ROM drive, and at least a few CD titles to get you started. Some systems also include speakers, although they don't come close to the fidelity of full-blown multimedia amplifiers and speakers such as the Altec Lansing ASC series. Although the prices may be attractive, be careful: some bundles are proprietary—the drive and the interfaces used are not compatible with other host adapters or sound boards. This section presents only a representative sample of what's out there; it gives you a good idea of what questions to ask and what features to expect when you buy an upgrade system.

What To Look For

Although price may be an issue, consider paying a bit more for a system that gives you a good drive and good sound; anything else may be obsolete soon or give you less-than-satis-factory results when you use applications with full-motion video.

Price Isn't Everything

Even though price is almost always a mitigating factor, look over the upgrade kits you are considering and compare both their drive and sound-card specifications.

For a lot more information about sound cards, see Chapter 6, "What Is Multimedia?"

Bundled Software

All things being equal—sound-card performance, CD-ROM drive specifications, and interface type (proprietary or standard)—the deciding factor in which upgrade kit you buy may be the CD titles the manufacturer decides to throw into the pot to sweeten the deal. If you don't want or need a Carmen San Diego disc, for example, consider a drive package in the same price range but that ships with titles you think you'll really use. Bundled titles change regularly, too, so check with the retailer or distributor to ensure that you're getting the titles you're expecting. Titles listed in this section with the multimedia bundles are those shipped at the time of this book's printing.

No ratings?

Note that we did not provide iconic ratings for the multimedia upgrade kits.

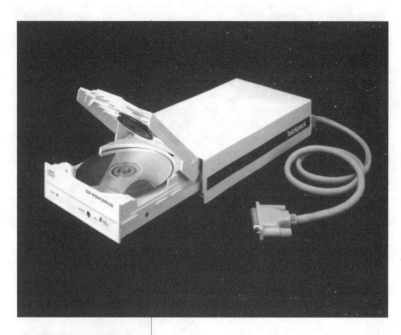

FIGURE 3.9

The CD Edutainment 16 Upgrade Kit includes Sound Blaster 16, a CD-ROM drive, speakers, and several software titles from Creative Labs.

Creative Labs

Creative Labs has a number of bundles—the drive, the sound card, and accessories are all the same—but the types of software in each bundle are different.

As the following chart indicates, the drive and CD-ROM drive are proprietary. If you're not happy with the CD-ROM performance specifications on this system, we recommend passing it up. Pricing and bundled titles are the only things going for this system.

Variations of this Creative Labs system offer fewer and different titles at different prices.

CD Edutainment 16 Upgrade Kit

Internal or External

[X]	PC compatible
[ ]	Macintosh compatible
[X]	PhotoCD, single session
[ ]	PhotoCD, multi-session

Interface:

[X]	SCSI	
[ ]	SCSI-2	
[ ]	Proprietary	Panasonic/ Matsushita

Average access time	400 ms
Transfer rate	153.6 KB/s
Buffer	32KB

Sound:

[X]	8-bit
[X]	16-bit
[X]	MIDI
[ ]	Sampled

Bundled software:

Multimedia Animals!

Monkey Island

Secrets of the Luftwaffe

Sherlock Holmes

Just Grandma and Me

Loom

Speakers included	Hi-Tex CP-10
Suggested list price	$799 (internal)
	$899 (external)

Media Vision

The Media Vision multimedia upgrade kits come in a number of flavors—from a single-unit CD-ROM, sound card, and speaker system that sits under your monitor to an internal CD-ROM, sound card, and desktop speaker system.

Media Vision products are affordable and provide good sound. The Pro 16 kit has a respectable CD drive and should do well with multimedia animation and video.

Media Vision Fusion CD 16

Internal or External	
[X] PC compatible	
[ ] Macintosh compatible	
[X] PhotoCD, single session	
[ ] PhotoCD, multi-session	
Interface:	
[X] SCSI	
[ ] SCSI-2	
[ ] Proprietary	
Average access time	380 ms
Transfer rate	153.6 KB/s
Buffer	32KB
Sound:	
[X] 8-bit	
[X] 16-bit	
[X] MIDI	
[ ] Sampled	
Bundled software:	
Where in the World Is Carmen San Diego?	
Compton's Family Encyclopedia	
Ultima Underworld	
Wing Commander II	
Speakers included	Labtec
Suggested list price	$799

Media Vision Pro 16 Multimedia System

Internal

[x]	PC compatible
[ ]	Macintosh compatible
[x]	PhotoCD, single session
[ ]	PhotoCD, multi-session

Interface:

[x]	SCSI
[ ]	SCSI-2
[ ]	Proprietary

Average access time	280 ms
Transfer rate	300 KB/s
Buffer	64KB

Sound:

[x]	8-bit
[x]	16-bit
[x]	MIDI
[ ]	Sampled

Bundled software:

Where in the World Is Carmen San Diego?

Lotus 1-2-3 for Windows

Compton's Encyclopedia

King's Quest V

MacroMind Action! on CD

Nautilus Multimedia CD

Music and Sound Effects Library

Speakers included	0
Suggested list price	$1,099

Procom

Procom has both Macintosh and PC upgrade kits—on both ends of the price and performance spectrum. The Mac kit is bundled with seven CD titles and a pair of amplified speakers. PC kits have sound boards, speakers, and either an MPC-compliant Sony drive or a double-speed Toshiba drive. Contact Procom or your local distributor for pricing and CD bundling for the PC kits.

For $995, you can get the MacCD/MX—the same as the MacCD Station package but with a faster, 200-ms drive.

MacCD Station

External	
☐ PC compatible	
☒ Macintosh compatible	
☒ PhotoCD, single session	
☒ PhotoCD, multi-session	

Interface:	
☒ SCSI	
☒ SCSI-2	
☐ Proprietary	

Average access time	380 ms
Transfer rate	150 KB/s
Buffer	64KB

Sound:	
☐ 8-bit	N/A
☐ 16-bit	N/A
☐ MIDI	N/A
☐ Sampled	N/A

Bundled software:

Mozart Dissonant CD Companion

Sherlock Holmes

Procom's Music Sampler

Illustrated Encyclopedia

World Atlas

Quantum Leap MegaROM Shareware CD

Nautilus CD

Speakers included	Yes
Suggested list price	$845

Sony

Sony has two multimedia upgrade kits available now. The more recently introduced package, described here, has a more capable drive, is multi-session compatible, and packs a more varied bundle of CDs than the original upgrade kit.

The CDU7305 is the external version of this system and lists for $1,069.

Desktop Library CDU31A-LL

Internal	
[X] PC compatible	
[ ] Macintosh compatible	
[X] PhotoCD, single session	
[X] PhotoCD, multi-session	
Interface:	
[X] SCSI	
[ ] SCSI-2	
[ ] Proprietary	
Average access time	550 ms
Transfer rate	150 KB/s
Buffer	64KB
Sound:	
[X] 8-bit	
[X] 16-bit	
[X] MIDI	
[ ] Sampled	
Bundled software:	
Grolier Multimedia Encyclopedia	
Where in the World Is Carmen San Diego?	
The Presidents	
Time Magazine Almanac	
Tempra ACCESS for Photo CD	
Great Wonders of the World I	
Speakers included	Sony
Suggested list price	$849

Turtle Beach

The Turtle Beach sound card—called MultiSound—on which this system is based, is the finest-quality audio card on the market. To make matters even better, Turtle Beach chose a Texel drive to bundle with the system—the best with the best. Although it's pricey, the system is not short on quality, and the titles bundled with it are high quality as well. The only disappointment here is the hefty price tag. If you add the list price of the MultiSound sound card ($599) to the list price of the Texel drive ($599), the combined bundle is still more than buying them separately. Granted, there are CD titles bundled with the system, but the price still seems high by at least $200.

IThe Turtle Beach System is a one-stop multimedia presentation package. With the included software, businesspeople can produce very acceptable multimedia presentations.

Desktop Library CDU31A-LL

External
[x] PC compatible
[ ] Macintosh compatible
[x] PhotoCD, single session
[x] PhotoCD, multi-session

Interface:	
[x] SCSI	
[x] SCSI-2	
[ ] Proprietary	

Average access time	550 ms
Transfer rate	150 KB/s
Buffer	64KB

Sound:	
[x] 8-bit	
[x] 16-bit	
[x] MIDIX	
[x] Sampled	(on-board ROM w/samples)

Bundled software:
WAVE for Windows
MediaBlitz
Band in a Box
Make Your Point
Sound Effects CD
Compton's Encyclopedia
Kings Quest V

Speakers included	0
Suggested list price	$1,499

Texel

Texel offers a wide range of CD-ROM multimedia bundles for the home, for the office, and for multimedia presentation development. Each bundle includes either an internal or external Texel CD-ROM drive, a 16-bit sound card, speakers, headphones, and an assortment of titles (depending on the emphasis of the package: business, home reference, or entertainment). The following list shows some of the bundles currently available:

➤ *Home:* Eight CDs of entertainment and reference, including over 5,000 shareware programs.

➤ *Education:* Nine CDs ranging from reference and educational games to a multimedia encyclopedia.

➤ *Multimedia:* Twelve CDs that include top-rated games, a multimedia encyclopedia, and animation and presentation packages.

➤ *Business:* Ten CDs, including a national telephone directory, reference CDs, and desktop publishing and database software.

Texel

External	
[x] PC compatible	
[ ] Macintosh compatible	
[x] PhotoCD, single session	
[x] PhotoCD, multi-session	
Interface:	
[x] SCSI	
[x] SCSI-2	
[ ] Proprietary	
Average access time	265 ms
Transfer rate	300 KB/s
Buffer	64KB
Sound:	
[x] 8-bit	
[x] 16-bit	
[x] MIDI	
[ ] Sampled	
Bundled software:	(see preceding lists)
Speakers included	Yes
Suggested list price	(varies with bundle)

Chapter 4

How To Install Your CD-ROM Drive

You've read Chapter 3 and decided on the drive you want. You ordered it. It's arrived at your doorstep. What next?

Installation of a CD-ROM drive is as difficult—or as easy—as you make it. If you know a little about SCSI interface devices such as your CD-ROM drive, and plan ahead, the installation should go smoothly.

This chapter walks you through the installation of typical internal and external CD-ROM drives. It also includes tips and pointers that often aren't included in the manufacturer's installation manuals. Even after you've installed the hardware, however, you need to do more than turn on the drive and toss in a CD. You first must load special software onto your PC. Relax; this chapter also walks you through the software installation.

Preparing the Adapter Card

Regardless of the type of installation—internal or external drive—you need to check your CD-ROM drive's SCSI host adapter before installation.

Carefully remove the adapter card from its protective, antistatic bag.

Static Protection

Static electricity is the enemy of your electronic equipment. Sensitive CMOS (Complimentary Metallic Oxide Semiconductor) components are easily damaged by static discharge—a static "shock" can have as many as 250,000 volts! This problem is particularly severe when humidity is low—like in the winter. You can avoid damage by taking some simple precautions:

➤ Leave your PC plugged into (but turned off!) a *grounded* outlet and touch the exposed metal case of the power supply to discharge any static charge built up in your body.

➤ Better yet, buy a static discharge wrist strap (inexpensive versions are available from Radio Shack and other electronics suppliers. *Do not attempt to make your own; wrist straps require special safety features to prevent potentially fatal shocks.* By wearing the wrist strap, you will continuously drain your static charge.

➤ Try to work in an uncarpeted room, if possible.

➤ Remember that static discharge damage is not always *immediately* fatal to your equipment. Without some precaution, you can do damage that may show up only after some use of the device.

Lay out the card on the antistatic bag; the IC chips, transistors, and processors should be face up; the external connector should be to your right. Virtually all documentation for adapter cards assumes that the cards are oriented this way when you configure them.

The single most important step in installing any SCSI device, including a new CD-ROM, is properly configuring, or making the correct settings, for the adapter card in front of you. If you pay special attention to this part of the installation, you'll avoid 90 percent of the problems with installing SCSI devices.

Check the adapter's documentation for the default settings of the card. These specifications are generally indicated in a list near the beginning of the documentation or by notation throughout the manual. *Don't* worry about pin settings, jumpers, or anything else other than copying the default settings to a piece of paper. Look for the following default settings:

➤ IRQ

➤ DMA channel

➤ I/O address or memory address

➤ Adapter SCSI ID

Don't panic! You don't need to know exactly what each of these settings means. In any event, we'll provide explanations along the way....

The following is a typical list of default settings for a SCSI adapter:

> IRQ: 11
> DMA channel: 5
> I/O address: 330
> SCSI ID: 7

Don't worry if your **settings** are different; we discuss each of the settings in this chapter.

If you want to avoid hair pulling, teeth gnashing, and general frustration, you must now check the SCSI card default settings for possible conflicts with other cards already installed in your PC. You *cannot* have two cards with the same settings for IRQ, DMA, or

I/O address or the drive—and possibly your PC—will lock up or operate erratically.

Here are some cards you should check to make sure that your CD-ROM settings do not duplicate the IRQ, DMA, and I/O port address settings for these cards:

➤ Network interface cards (Ethernet, ARCNet, and so on)

➤ Sound cards

➤ Scanner interfaces

➤ Internal modems and fax modems

➤ Other SCSI cards for hard drives, Bernoulli drives, or other added peripherals such as tape-backup units

If you value your time and your sanity, keep a record handy of these important settings for all your adapter cards. Write down the current settings on a piece of paper, for example, and tape that paper into the PC's owner manual or inside your PC's case. This way, any time you add a new adapter card or must reconfigure one already installed, you'll have a reference. Otherwise, you may find yourself pulling out every peripheral adapter in your machine to check its settings. Obviously, any time you add a new card or change the settings of one installed, change your note card. (For more information about upgrading your computer, and how to maintain a list of settings for your computer, see *Easy Upgrading and Troubleshooting*, published by Que Corporation.)

If you did not keep records for previously installed devices and need to check for existing settings, refer to each card's documenta-

Getting All or Most of the Settings

Some proprietary SCSI host adapters may have some, all, or just a few of these settings available. In any case, jot down whatever defaults are listed in the manual.

tion. You may also purchase a PC diagnostic software program—many are currently available. These programs scan installed adapter cards for occupied interrupts and DMA channels. QA/Plus, WIN Sleuth, and Quarterdeck's Manifest are some popular choices.

Make a note of any conflicts. It will probably be easier to reset the defaults on the CD-ROM SCSI card, which is already out of the PC and sitting in front of you. But don't make changes yet. Just take notes.

The next step is to make sure that the defaults listed in the manual are, in fact, the defaults actually set on the board. Everyone makes mistakes, including your manufacturer. Although this type of error is relatively uncommon, it's best to double-check the manual's default listings against the physical defaults set on the card before you've gone too far into the installation process.

Jumpers and Switches

Adapter-card configurations are set with *jumpers*—tiny plastic-covered shunts that fit over pin-pairs on the adapter card. These rows of jumper pins may run left to right or up and down across the card. Configuring the board is a matter of having the jumpers on or off a pair of pins.

These rows of jumper pins are labeled with a letter and a number, such as J5 or W1. Your adapter-card manual or pamphlet has a diagram of these jumper rows, or *banks*, as they're called (see fig. 4.1). Carefully check the pin settings against your manual. Make sure that pins are jumpered where they should be. Just as important, make sure that there are no extra jumpers on any of the pins.

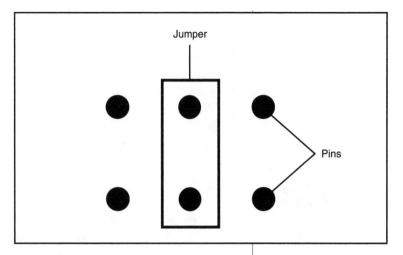

DIP Switches

Some SCSI adapters, such as the Trantor 130, configure the cards using rocker switches—called *DIP switches*—instead of jumpers (see fig. 4.2). DIP is an acronym for *Dual Inline Package*, which refers to the configurations of the pins on the switch's "package." This configuration places the electrical connections in an industry-standard layout. The pins are lined up on the top and bottom of the switches in two rows (dual, inline).

FIGURE 4.1

A SCSI card with jumper banks.

As you're checking the **jumper blocks**, make sure that you are checking the correct bank of jumpers; there may be a number of banks of blocks on the card. After you verify that the pins are set to the correct defaults, you're ready to resolve any possible interrupt conflicts.

Adapter Cards without Jumpers

Newer adapter cards from Proc Technology, Adaptec, and Future Domain are virtually jumperless. Your particular adapter card may not have jumpers; it may have rocker-switch (DIP-switch) settings or software-selectable interrupts. With the latter cards, you use software to set open DMA and interrupt channels; you make settings on the card entirely from the keyboard. If we're all very lucky, most hardware manufacturers will soon be shipping software-configurable adapter cards.

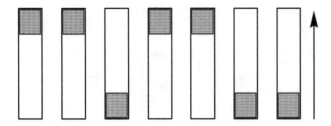

FIGURE 4.2

Some adapters use DIP
switches rather than
jumpers to set configuration
options.

Irksome IRQs

The most common cause of a system lock-up after an installation is an IRQ conflict. Avoid problems up front by making sure that you have no conflicts now. Table 4.1 lists common IRQ numbers and which ones are typically open. Remember that you may already have an installed card occupying one of the interrupt request lines. In addition, if you have an 8-bit SCSI card, you are further restricted in the number of available IRQs: from 0 to 7 only.

If you find a conflict, consult your adapter-card manual for help selecting a different IRQ. To set up the adapter card to use a particular IRQ, remove or move a jumper from one pin-pair to another. Although you can remove jumpers with your fingers, you risk handling chips that may be near the jumpers. It's better to use a pair of tweezers (especially those included in a computer tool kit) to carefully remove the jumper. Reset the jumpers according to the manual's diagrams for the new IRQ.

IRQs

The letters IRQ are shorthand for *Interrupt ReQuest*. An IRQ is part of the hardware architecture of the IBM PC, which is an "interrupt-driven design." IRQs are used by hardware to notify the microprocessor—your PC's CPU (Central Processing Unit)—that some service is needed. If IRQs were not used, the CPU would have to wait for the completion of the current hardware activity before it could move on to another task. To make this clearer, let's look at how this works in the case of a CD-ROM drive connected with a SCSI adapter.

When an application needs some data from the CD-ROM drive, it requests the information from the operating system (OS). The OS, in turn, makes the request to the CD-ROM drive through the SCSI host adapter. The CD-ROM drive receives the request through the host adapter and goes off to find the requested data. This operation is not instantaneous; it takes some time for the drive to do its job. To us, it is almost no time, but to the CPU it is a long time indeed. The CPU could keep asking the adapter if the data was available, a technique called *polling*, but this would be a waste of time that could be used to service other requests from programs and hardware. Instead of polling the drive, the CPU does some real work, like handling the movement of the mouse pointer, accepting keystrokes, and the like.

When the data is finally ready for the CPU, the SCSI host adapter gets the attention of the CPU by "pulling on" an IRQ—the one to which it is connected. The CPU knows, by referring to the SCSI device driver, that the particular IRQ it just detected is associated with the host adapter. The CPU then completes the request the application made for data by receiving the data that is now waiting at the host adapter. Although this explanation is simplified, it should give you some idea what is going on in your machine.

You may also hear IRQs referred to as "interrupt levels." This is because, in IBM-PC compatible machines, IRQs have priority levels: 0 is the highest priority and 15 is the lowest. The IRQs are serviced in the order of their priority. When PCs were equipped with relatively low-powered microprocessors, this priority system was critical, and you had to choose an IRQ that provided a high-enough priority for your purpose. Today, machines are much more powerful, so prioritization is no longer a concern.

Table 4.1 Common IRQ Assignments

IRQ	Use
IRQ 0	Timer Interrupt
IRQ 1	Keyboard Interrupt
IRQ 2	Cascade to IRQ 9
IRQ 3	COM 2 and COM 4
IRQ 4	COM 1 and COM 3
IRQ 5	LPT 2 (parallel printer port)
IRQ 6	Floppy Disk
IRQ 7	LPT 1 (parallel printer port)
IRQ 8	Real Time Clock
IRQ 9	Cascade to IRQ 2
IRQ 10	Available to user
IRQ 11	Available to user
IRQ 12	Mouse Port on PS/2
IRQ 13	80x87 Math Coprocessor
IRQ 14	Hard Disk
IRQ 15	Available to user

EXPLANATION

DMA

Direct Memory Access (DMA) is a technique that speeds up access to memory for expansion cards. Because it avoids the intervention of the CPU, this technique is "direct." There are seven DMA channels in an IBM-AT compatible machine.

DMA Conflicts

DMA, or Direct Memory Access, settings have less serious consequences than IRQ settings when they are in conflict. A typical symptom of a DMA conflict is no response from one of the cards in conflict. For example, if you have a sound card and a CD-ROM SCSI card set for the same DMA channels, one—or both—of the cards may not function. Check DMA settings on the cards, but be aware that getting the proper DMA channel may require more than one jumper setting (you may have to change two or three jumpers to change the DMA channel). The Adaptec 1540 SCSI card, for example, has a default DMA of 5, but jumpers pertaining to the DMA selection are on jumper block 5 *and* on jumper block 9. To set all DMA

jumpers to the same DMA channel on the Adaptec card, you must set DMA Channel Select, DMA Request, DMA ACKnowledge, and DMA INTerrupt Request on these two separate blocks.

Most SCSI cards come set with a default of DMA channel 5. This should be fine for most PCs because few other adapter cards occupy these channels. Some of the newer, 16-bit sound cards have DMA channel 5 set as the default, however, making them likely culprits in any conflict with your SCSI cards.

I/O Port Addresses

No two cards can live at the same **I/O port** address. More importantly, I/O port addresses are really base addresses—they describe the

EXPLANATION

I/O Ports

An I/O (Input/Output) port is just what its name says: a port for the movement of data. I/O ports allow the operating system to communicate with adapter cards in the computer's bus. The addresses used by these ports are arbitrary memory locations to which the adapter's hardware is mapped. In other words, the adapter gives the appearance that its hardware resides at the selected address. The "memory space" used by the PC for I/O ports is completely separate from that used by RAM (Random Access Memory), where programs are stored, and ROM (Read Only Memory), where system software is stored.

starting address the card occupies. The full range of the memory address must be taken into consideration when resolving conflict with other cards. For example, if a sound card occupies memory address 220, you may assume that a SCSI card can exist at address 230. Not necessarily so. If the sound card's memory range is 220 to 235, you've just introduced a conflict.

We've noticed some typical conflicts of late in the way types of adapter cards are shipped in their default state. Most SCSI cards ship with base I/O port addresses of 220, 300, or 330. Many sound boards and internal fax modem cards may also occupy these addresses in their default configurations. Network interface cards are often set in the 300 to 360 range by default, too. If you need to change your I/O port address to resolve a conflict, make certain that you know the *range* of the possible conflict.

Typical symptoms of I/O conflict are similar to those that occur with DMA conflicts: one or both of the cards in conflict does not respond. Another symptom of memory conflict is disconcerting, but harmless: your machine may go through the boot process of checking memory, loading drivers, and so on, get to the end of the boot, and then reboot all over again. If this happens, you can be certain you have an I/O port conflict.

Installing the Card and Attaching the Drive

After you configure the card correctly, resolve all potential conflicts, and are thoroughly tired of looking at the manual's hazy diagrams for jumper blocks, you're ready to insert the SCSI card into the PC.

Selecting a Slot

To begin, turn off the power to the computer. Unscrew the case cover and remove it. Look at the available or unoccupied slots in your PC bus. These card slots may come in 8-bit, 16-bit, or 32-bit lengths (8-bit slots are the shortest and 32-bit slots are the longest and usually the last slots in the case). If your CD SCSI adapter is an 8-bit adapter, it has one set of gold edge-connectors; the 16-bit cards have two sets—one short and one long. Make the most of the real estate inside your PC case. Don't put an 8-bit card in a 16-bit slot unless you have no other choice—you may want that 16-bit slot later on for a true 16-bit card. Unscrew from the back of the PC the slot cover for the bus slot you've selected. Hang onto this screw.

Hold the card by its top edges and slide it firmly into the expansion bus; the connector edge should be facing through the open slot in the back of the PC chassis. Press down firmly. You'll feel the card seat itself—pop into the connector. Be careful not to press down too hard—you might damage the motherboard under the connector. Make sure that the card is evenly seated, front to back. Most SCSI cards have cable hooks on either side of the outside connector that can get in the way when you put the card into the bus (see fig. 4.3). If one of these hooks gets caught between the chassis and the card, you'll have a difficult time seating the card properly. Move the hooks straight up, parallel with the connector, so that they slide easily through the slot in the back of the PC.

Gently move the adapter flange with its slotted top away from the screw hole in the PC chassis. Put the screw from the slot plate (the one you saved when you removed the slot cover) into the hole and give it a few turns—enough to start it solidly. Slide the card flange under the screw and secure it firmly. By starting the screw into the chassis first and then sliding the card into place beneath it, you avoid the problem of trying—often without luck—to align the adapter bracket flange and PC chassis hole for the screw. A common hassle here is dropping the screw into the PC case while trying to secure the card. Keep a flashlight handy to peer between the cards and locate dropped screws; those tweezers you used for changing jumpers can come in handy to carefully remove misplaced screws. If you've grounded yourself, you won't do any damage if you're careful in removing a dropped screw.

The worst part is over.

Do not replace the cover of the PC yet. If some lingering conflicts exist or the card is not fully seated in the slot, you may need to do more inside work. You can replace the PC case after you've installed the drive, rebooted the system, installed the driver software, and (whew!) tested the drive...not before.

Attaching the CD-ROM Drive

Once the card is in and properly seated, you can hook the card to the drive. Depending on your configuration—external or internal—read the appropriate section that follows.

External CD-ROM Drives

Unpack the CD-ROM drive carefully. When you purchase an external drive, you should receive the following items:
- ➤ External drive
- ➤ Power cord
- ➤ SCSI cable (if the SCSI card came bundled with the drive)

This is the bare minimum to get the drive up and running. You may also find a CD caddy, a manual or pamphlet for the adapter card, and, possibly, a sampling of CDs to get you started.

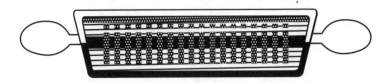

Configure and check the adapter card as described in "Preparing the Adapter Card," earlier in this chapter.

Take a look at your work area and the SCSI cable that came with the drive. Where will the drive find a new home? You're limited by the length of the cable. Find a spot for the drive and insert the power cable into the back of the unit. Make sure that you have an outlet, or preferably a free socket in a surge-suppressing power strip into which you can plug the new drive.

Plug one end of the supplied cable into the connector socket of the drive, and one onto the SCSI connector on the adapter card. Most external drives have two connectors on the back—either connector can be hooked to the PC (see fig. 4.4); we'll discuss the extra connector later in this chapter. Use the guide hooks, if they're provided, to secure the cable to both the drive and adapter connector. Some SCSI cables supplied with Future Domain 16-bit controllers have a micro-connector for the adapter end that simply clips into place.

The external CD-ROM drive should have a SCSI ID select switch on the back. This switch sets the identification number for the drive when it is hooked to the host adapter. The adapter, by most manufacturer's defaults, should be set for SCSI ID 7. Make sure that you set the SCSI ID for the CD-ROM drive to any other number—6, 5, or 4, for example. The only rule is to make certain you do not set the CD-ROM drive to an ID that is already occupied—either by the card or by any other SCSI

FIGURE 4.3

A SCSI connector, showing hooks that can get in the way of installation.

Loose Screws

Never, under any circumstances, leave loose or dropped screws in the computer case. They inevitably short something out, doing severe damage to your main PC board and any cards in the expansion bus.

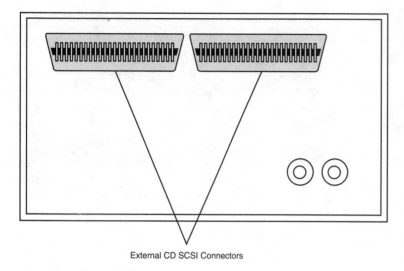

External CD SCSI Connectors

FIGURE 4.4

External CD-ROM drive
SCSI connectors.

peripheral on the chain. Most SCSI hard drives, as a rule, occupy SCSI IDs 0 and 1; if you have SCSI hard drives, be certain that you do not set the CD-ROM drive to occupy a hard drive SCSI ID number.

Finally, you must terminate the drive by placing the terminating resistor cap on the second SCSI connector on the back panel of the drive. This resistor cap may already be in place. For a detailed description of how to set SCSI IDs and properly terminate a drive, see "Identifying and Terminating with Care," later in this chapter. If you are dealing with multiple SCSI devices and your new CD-ROM drive is one in a chain, read this termination section carefully.

Turn on the power for the drive and the PC and install the SCSI software according to your SCSI adapter manual.

Internal CD-ROM Drives

Unpack the internal drive kit. You should have the following pieces:

➤ Internal drive
➤ Power cord
➤ SCSI interface board

➤ Internal SCSI ribbon cable
➤ Floppy disks with device driver software and manual
➤ Drive rails or mounting screws

Your manufacturer also may have provided a power-cable splitter—a bundle of wires with plastic connectors on each of three ends. A disc caddy and owner's manual may also be included.

Configure and check your card according to the instructions in "Preparing the Adapter Card," earlier in this chapter. Make sure that the PC is turned off and that the cover is off. Before installing the card into the PC bus, however, you should connect the SCSI ribbon cable to the adapter card.

The ribbon cable should be identical on both ends. You'll find a red stripe or dotted line down one side of the outer edge of the cable. This stripe is the pin-1 designation and ensures that the SCSI cable is connected properly into the card and into the drive. If you're lucky, the manufacturer supplied a cable with notches or keys along one edge of the connector. With such a key, there is only one way to insert the cable into the card and drive. You must hook up an unkeyed cable according to the pin-1 designation.

Along one edge of the SCSI adapter card is a double row of 50 brass-colored pins. This is the 50-pin connector. In small print along the base of this row of pins are at least two numbers: 1 and 50. Aligning the ribbon cable's marked edge over pin 1, carefully—and evenly—insert the ribbon cable connector.

Now insert the adapter card into an open expansion slot in the PC, leaving the drive end of the cable loose. Choose one of the drive bays the front of the machine for the internal drive. Make sure that the bay is easily accessible and not blocked by other items on your desk—you'll be inserting the CDs here, and you'll need the elbow room.

Remove the drive bay cover. Inside the drive bay is a metal enclosure with screw holes for mounting the drive. If the drive has mounting holes along its side and fits snugly into the enclosure, you won't need mounting rails. If it's a loose fit, however, mount the rails along the sides of the drive with the rail screws, and then slide the drive into the bay. Secure the drive into the bay with four screws—two on each side. If the rails or drive don't line up evenly with the four mounting holes, make sure that you use at least two screws—one mounting screw on each side. Because you will insert and eject a lot of CDs over the years, making sure that the drive is mounted securely is a must.

Find the striped side of the ribbon cable and align it with pin 1 on the drive's edge connector. To determine which is pin 1, refer to either the diagram in your owner's manual or to the designation on the connector itself.

The back of the CD drive has a power connector outlet. Inside the case of your PC, at the back of the floppy or hard disk, are power cords in a bundle—two black, one red, and one yellow—attached with plastic connectors to the floppy and hard drives. You may already have a free power connector laying open in the case. Plug the open connector into the back of the power socket on the CD-ROM drive (these connectors go in only one way). If you do not have an open connector, use the power-cable splitter provided by the manufacturer (see fig. 4.6): Disconnect a floppy drive power cord, attach the splitter to the detached power cord, and plug one of the free ends of the splitter into the floppy drive and the other end of the splitter into the CD-ROM drive. Read the following section, "Identifying and Terminating with Care," for final installation information.

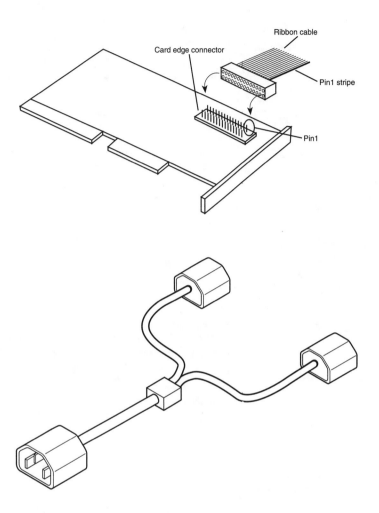

Do not replace the PC cover yet—you need to make certain that everything is running perfectly before you seal the case. You're now ready to turn on the computer. For the drive to work, however, you need to install the software drivers.

FIGURE 4.5, top

Ribbon cable connection to SCSI adapter.

FIGURE 4.6, bottom

Power cord splitter and connector.

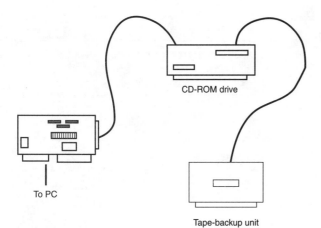

CD-ROM drive

To PC

Tape-backup unit

A SCSI chain of devices on an adapter card.

TIP

Internal Termination

Some external drives have *internal termination*. In other words, the manufacturer installed terminating resistors—much like the ones installed on the adapter card—onto the drive's IC board inside the drive case. If your drive has internal termination, you **must not** put a terminator cap on the external connector. Check the manual that came with your drive to ensure that the drive has no internal termination. Thankfully, few external drives are internally terminated.

NOTE:

Terminating Resistors

Most internal SCSI devices ship with terminating resistors on board. Check the user manuals for the locations of these resistors. There may be one, two, or even three resistors on any given device.

SCSI Chains: Internal, External, and a Little of Both

Remember that one of the primary reasons for using a SCSI controller for your CD-ROM drive is that you can chain several peripherals to one adapter card—preserving card slots inside the PC and limiting the nightmare of tracking IRQs, DMAs, and memory addresses.

You can add scanners, tape-backup units, and other SCSI peripherals to this chain (see fig. 4.7). There are only a few things to keep in mind: chief among them is SCSI termination.

Identifying and Terminating with Care

The first rule of SCSI device chaining is simple: each end of the SCSI chain must be terminated: the first device must contain a termination resistor and the last must also have a terminator attached. All devices between the first and last should be free of any terminator.

The second SCSI rule is that all SCSI devices must be set to a unique ID number. For the external drive installed in an example earlier in this chapter, the SCSI adapter was set for ID 7 and the CD-ROM drive was set for ID 6. Any additional SCSI devices added must take the IDs 1, 2, 3, 4, or 5. Remember that the SCSI adapter takes an ID, and its default is usually ID 7.

Example One: All External SCSI Devices

Suppose that you've installed a CD-ROM drive and added a tape device to the chain with the extra connector on the back of the CD-ROM drive. The first device in this SCSI chain is the adapter card itself. All SCSI cards have a series of long, ceramic-tipped components plugged into the board in a group of two or three components. These are the **terminating resistors** for the card (see fig. 4.8). From the card, you've run an external cable to the CD-ROM drive, and from the CD-ROM drive, you've added another cable to the back of the tape unit. The tape unit must be terminated as well, because it's the last device in the chain. Only the first and last devices—the SCSI card and the tape drive, in this example—must be terminated. Most external units are terminated with a *SCSI cap*—a small connector that plugs into the unused external SCSI connector.

These external drive connectors come in two varieties: a SCSI cap and a pass-through **terminator**. The cap plugs over the open connector and covers it. The pass-through terminator, however, plugs onto the connector and has an open end into which you can plug a SCSI cable. This type of connector is essential if your external drive has only one SCSI connector—you can plug in the drive *and* make sure that it's terminated by using only one connector.

Example Two: Internal Chain and Termination

The same SCSI termination and ID rules apply to internal chains as they do to external chains: all the internal devices must have unique SCSI ID numbers and the first and last devices must be terminated. In the case of internal devices, however, you must check for termination. Internal devices have *terminating resistors* or packs similar to the ones installed on the adapter card. If you install a tape unit as the last device on the chain, for example, it must have resistors on its circuit board. If you place a CD-ROM drive in the middle of this chain, its resistors must be removed. The adapter card, at the front end of the chain, should keep its resistors: *do not* remove them.

Example Three: Internal and External SCSI Devices

If you mix and match external and internal devices, follow the rules for assigning SCSI ID and termination outlined in "Identifying and Terminating with Care," earlier in this chapter. In the third example shown in figure 4.9, an internal CD-ROM drive is terminated and set for SCSI ID 6; the external tape unit is also terminated and assigned SCSI ID 5. The SCSI adapter itself is set for ID 7, and—the most important point—its terminating resistors have been **removed**.

Installing Driver Software

After you configure the adapter card correctly, insert it into the PC, and ensure that the drives

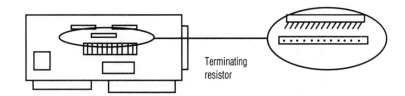

Terminating resistor

are connected and terminated properly, you're ready for the last step: installing the CD-ROM software.

Putting CD-ROM Software on the PC

If you purchased your drive as a drive/adapter-card bundle, the manufacturer has included the appropriate software disk and documentation for installing the SCSI software. If you purchased your drive and card separately, the software components you need may have come with the adapter card. In any case, the CD-ROM drive needs three software components to operate on a PC:

➤ A SCSI adapter driver
➤ A SCSI driver for the specific CD-ROM drive you've installed
➤ MSCDEX—Microsoft CD Extensions for DOS

The first two drivers—the SCSI adapter driver and the CD-ROM driver—are loaded into your system at start-up by placing command lines in the CONFIG.SYS file. The MSCDEX, or DOS extension, is an executable file added to the system through the AUTOEXEC.BAT file.

Installing the SCSI Adapter Driver

Each SCSI adapter model has a specific driver that allows communications between the PC

FIGURE 4.8

SCSI adapter-card terminating resistors.

EXPLANATION
SCSI Termination

Signals on the SCSI bus have a high enough frequency to act as radio waves. When a radio signal travels down a wire, it reflects from the end unless it finds an "impedance match." The terminators on the SCSI bus are used to absorb these reflections, which would otherwise interfere with legitimate SCSI signals and cause errors.

Removing Resistors

Be careful when handling the adapter card—static discharge can damage the IC chips contained on the card. Make sure that you ground yourself before you start and never hold the card by its edge connectors. Chip pullers—specially made tweezers found in most computer tool kits—are especially useful in removing resistor packs from adapter cards and from internal peripherals such as CD-ROM drives. The resistor packs have very thin teeth that bend easily; once bent, they're really tough to straighten out and reinsert.

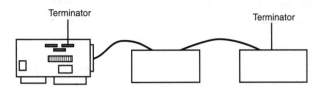

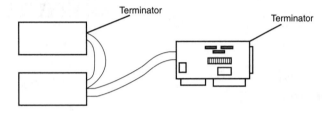

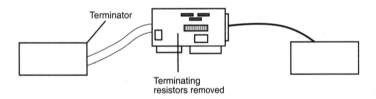

FIGURE 4.9

Examples of SCSI termination.

and the SCSI interface. This driver should have been provided with your SCSI drive and adapter kit. Documentation should also have been included, which walks you through the installation of the software. You can manually add the SCSI device driver to your CONFIG.SYS file.

To add the SCSI device driver to your CONFIG.SYS file, go to the top of the CONFIG.SYS file. Use the DEVICE= statement to add the name and path of the driver:

DEVICE=C:\DRIVERS\MYSCSI.SYS

In this sample statement, C:\DRIVERS is the subdirectory to which the SCSI device

driver, MYSCSI.SYS, has been copied. Some drivers have option switches or added commands that, for example, allow you to view the progress of the driver being loaded. Option switches are usually added to the end of the DEVICE= statement.

Installing the CD-ROM Device Driver

The CD-ROM device driver, as well the SCSI adapter driver, should be a part of your basic installation kit. If not, contact the drive's manufacturer for the proper CD-ROM device driver for your SCSI card.

The device driver should come with an installation program that prompts you for the memory I/O address for the SCSI adapter on which you installed the CD-ROM drive. The device driver allows communication with the drive through the SCSI bus to your PC. Installation programs add a line similar to the following to the CONFIG.SYS file:

DEVICE=C:\DRIVERS\MYCDROM.SYS
/D:mscd001

In this sample statement, C:\DRIVERS is the subdirectory that contains the driver MYCDROM.SYS, the CD-ROM driver for your specific CD-ROM drive. The /D:mscd001 option after the statement designates this CD-ROM driver as controlling the first (001)— and only—CD-ROM drive on the system. This portion of the device-driver statement identifies the drive as a Microsoft DOS Extensions CD-ROM (MSCDEX designates CD-ROM drives in this fashion: mcs001, mcs002, and so on).

Installing the Microsoft CD Extensions File

The Microsoft CD Extensions file allows DOS to identify and use data from CD-ROMs attached to the system. Because the original DOS had no provisions for this technology, "hooks" for handling this unique media are not a part of the basic operating environment. Using Microsoft CD Extensions is convenient for all the software components involved, however. As CD-ROM technology changes, the MSCDEX file also can be changed, independent of the DOS system. For example, most PhotoCD, multiple-session CD-ROM drives require MSCDEX.EXE Version 2.21, which has been modified from earlier versions to accommodate the newer CD format. MS-DOS 6 includes Version 2.22.

MSCDEX.EXE should be in the software kit that came with your drive. If not, obtain the latest copy directly from Microsoft. The latest version of CD Extensions is also available on CompuServe in the Microsoft forum. If you are a registered user of the DOS operating system, MSCDEX is free. Read the licensing agreement that appears on the disk or in your manual for the proper licensing of MSCDEX files.

Your installation software should add to your AUTOEXEC.BAT file a line similar to the following:

C:\WINDOWS\MSCDEX.EXE /d:mscd001

In this sample statement, C:\WINDOWS is the directory to which the MSCDEX.EXE file has been copied. MSCDEX assigns a DOS name or drive letter to the CD-ROM drive when it is installed. The /d:mscd001 portion of the statement tells MSCDEX the DOS name or drive of the device defined by the **CD-ROM device driver** in the CONFIG.SYS file. In this example, the DOS name is d: (the D drive).

Sound complicated? Don't worry. As long as these three drivers are loaded properly in the system, the CD-ROM drive will operate as transparently as any other drive in the system.

MSCDEX.EXE has a variety of options or switches you can add to its command line in the AUTOEXEC.BAT file. (See the table on the following page.)

Getting Ready for Lift-Off

Your drive should come with installation software that copies the device-driver files to the hard drive and adds the necessary command lines to the CONFIG.SYS and AUTOEXEC.BAT files. After the drivers are loaded and the files are modified, you can reboot the machine and look for signs that all went smoothly in the software installation.

The SCSI driver is the first to load. You see an on-screen message from the driver that includes the software version number and the model of the SCSI adapter card it found.

Then the CD-ROM adapter driver loads, showing its software version and the drive it supports.

Finally, MSCDEX loads, telling you the buffer size, the memory allocated to the drive, and what DOS drive letter has been assigned to the CD-ROM drive.

Once you're sure that the software is loaded correctly, test the drive by inserting a CD into the disc caddy and loading it into the CD-ROM drive. Type **DIR/W G:** at the DOS prompt to see a directory of the CD you just inserted (see fig. 4.10). (If your CD has been assigned a drive letter other than G, use that drive letter instead.)

You can log onto the CD-ROM drive just as you can onto any DOS drive. CD-ROM drives look like network drives to the operating system; they support any DOS commands that work on a network drive and that do not write the drive. CDs, remember, cannot be overwritten, erased, or formatted.

If you have logged onto the CD-ROM drive and can receive a directory of a sample CD, you're all set. The drive is correctly installed.

Now you can power down the PC and replace the cover.

Driver Names

The MSCDEX and CD-ROM device driver names must match (for example, they both must be msc000 or msc001—the defaults provided by most installations are used in this example). As long as the two names are the same, the drivers can "find" one another.

Switch	Function
/V	This option is called Verbose; causes the screen to display at start-up information about memory allocation, buffers, drive-letter assignments, and device-driver names.
/L: <letter>	Designates which DOS drive letter is assigned to the drive. For example, /L:G assigns the drive letter G to the CD-ROM drive. Two conditions apply: You must not have another drive assigned to that letter and the LASTDRIVE= statement in the CONFIG.SYS file must be equal to or greater than the drive letter assigned here. For example, LASTDRIVE=G is fine, but LASTDRIVE=F causes an error if you attempt to assign the letter G to the CD-ROM drive with the /L: switch.
/M: <buffers>	Allows you to buffer data from the CD-ROM drive. This switch is useful if you want faster initial access to the drive's directory. Buffers values of 10 to 15 are more than enough for most uses—any more is overkill. Because each buffer is equal to 2KB of memory, a /M:10 buffer argument, for example, takes 20KB of memory. Note that the buffer allocation does not significantly increase the overall performance of the drive—just DOS's initial access to the drive and the access of large data blocks when the drive is gulping down live-motion video, for example. You can't turn a 400 millisecond drive into a speed demon by adding a 200KB buffer. With no /M: argument added, MSCDEX uses a default of six buffers, which is fine for most PCs and CD-ROM drives.
/E	Loads the buffers into DOS expanded memory, freeing space in the conventional 640KB. Early versions of MSCDEX—anything below Version 2.1—do not load into expanded memory. You must have DOS 5.0 or higher for this option to load into high memory.
/S	Enables you to share your CD-ROM drive on a peer-to-peer network, like Windows for Workgroups.
/K	Kanji support.

Using a CD-ROM in Microsoft Windows

Once you add a CD-ROM drive to your system, Windows knows about it through DOS. You'll suddenly find a few changes in your Windows environment. Open up the File Manager by double-clicking on its file-cabinet icon. You see the new CD-ROM drive among the old, familiar drive icons across the top of the window (see fig. 4.11). Notice that the CD-ROM drive icon is highlighted with a miniature CD disc and that the drive carries the title *CD-ROM*. The DOS Extensions mentioned earlier tell Windows the media type (removable, read-only) of your new drive.

Using Media Player

You can set your CD-ROM player to play audio CDs as you work in Windows. You first must hook your drive to a sound card and speakers or connect the CD's audio ports to a stereo. Go to the Windows Control Panel by selecting the Control Panel icon from the Main group; select the Drivers icon from the Windows Control Panel. If you do not see [MCI]/CDAUDIO among the files in the drivers list, insert the Windows Installation disk that contains the CDAUDIO driver, choose Add, and double-click on Un-listed or Updated Driver from the menu at the top of the screen. At the prompt, type the drive letter of the Windows Installation disk. After the driver appears in the Control Panel list, double-click on it to add it to the Windows configuration, and then exit the Drivers and Control Panel windows.

Double-click on the Media Player icon; from the Devices area of the screen, select CD. A list of the track numbers on the audio CD installed in the CD-ROM drive appears along the bottom edge of the Media Player window. The controls in Media Player are similar to those on an audio CD player, including track select, continuous play, and pause (see fig. 4.12). You can configure Media Player to display the CD audio line in either tracks or time duration by choosing the Scale option from the menu at the top of the screen.

Many drive manufacturers supply DOS-based CD audio players with their systems. Check your installation manual and software disks for these utilities.

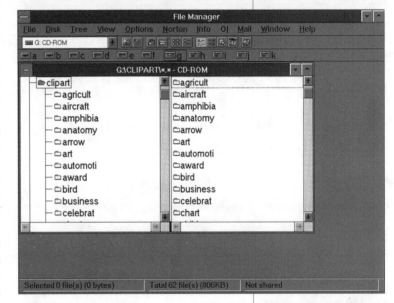

Moving Onward

Your hardware is all set. You're ready to explore the thousands of CD-ROM titles available. Look through the coming chapters for our selections of a few of the best titles released to date.

FIGURE 4.10, top

The directory of a CD after installing the drive.

FIGURE 4.11, bottom

The CD-ROM icon is automatically added to the Windows File Manager window.

Other chapters in this book show you how to share your CD-ROM drive across various networks and how to add multimedia capabilities to your system. The addition of a CD-ROM drive is the cornerstone for many new additions to your system.

Congratulations! You've entered the information age of CD-ROM!

FIGURE 4.12

The Media Player with an audio CD loaded.

Chapter 5

How To Network Your CD-ROM Drive

Computer networks are no longer just for large companies and educational institutions. Peer-to-peer networks like Lantastic and Windows for Workgroups make networking a real possibility for the ever more common multicomputer household.

In this chapter, you learn how to make CD-ROM drives available across a small network so that all users can access CD-ROM data. Take careful note of CD-ROM software licensing agreements before networking any CD-ROM-based application: the very act of providing shared access to the CD over a network may violate the terms of the software license.

There are two basic reasons to provide networked access to a CD-ROM drive:

1. The cost of a CD-ROM drive prevents the purchase of enough drives for all users.

2. Many or all of the users on the network must share a database stored on CD-ROM.

The two peer networks covered in this chapter are appropriate for home and small-business networks. If you are a Windows user, Windows for Workgroups probably makes the most sense for you. If you stay in DOS most of the time, look at Lantastic.

Using Windows for Workgroups

For Windows users, Windows for Workgroups (WFW) is a great way to get connected. WFW is actually a version of Windows with built-in peer networking capabilities. This program lets a Windows workstation share its disk drives, including CD-ROM, and printers. It's a snap to install, and it can run alongside **Novell NetWare**.

One of the best things about WFW is its ease of installation. Its installation program is very good at determining your hardware setup and configuring itself appropriately. If you are installing Windows for Workgroups for the first time, as a pilot, or just between two workstations, the best choice is to buy the WFW Starter Pack (available from your Microsoft dealer). The Starter Pack includes software for two stations, two NICs (Network Interface Cards), two BNC T connectors and terminators (required for the connection), and a 25-foot cable.

EXPLANATION
Peer-to-Peer

A *peer-to-peer* (or just *peer*) *network* is a network of computers that all have equal status. Theoretically, all computers can be both clients and servers on a peer network. Practical management considerations, however, usually dictate the dedication of a particular machine to do the bulk of the server work. Peer networks contrast with *client/server networks*, in which a dedicated file server provides file and print services to clients called workstations.

A *file server* is a computer whose disk drives are used by workstations on the network for common and private storage of files. A *client* is a computer that uses the services of a file server. Print services include giving clients access to print *queues* that allow clients to send print jobs to a printer.

Novell NetWare

Although Windows for Workgroups is a fine way to provide some level of CD-ROM sharing over a NetWare network, there is more than one native solution you can use to connect the CD-ROM drive to a NetWare file server or to provide CD-ROM services through specialized hardware. One very good solution (which brings other benefits as well) comes from Corel Corporation in the form of CorelSCSI! Pro. CorelSCSI! is an amazing product that provides ASPI-compatible device drivers for just about any optical-drive device, including CD-ROM, R/W optical disk drives, and WORMs.

The Pro version of the product also comes with many NetWare drivers and utilities, including software to share CD-ROM drives from the file server.

For more information about how to contact Corel, see Appendix D, "Where To Buy: Hardware and Software Vendors."

Bytes or Bits?

LAN speeds are generally measured in mega*bits* per second; data transfer rates from disk drives and the like are generally measured in mega*bytes* per second.

The included NICs use Ethernet, a networking standard that allows the stations to communicate at a very high data rate: 10 Mb/s (**megabits** per second). This rate is probably faster than the disk drive of an ISA (Industry Standard Architecture, or AT-style) machine can move data.

Ethernet can run over a variety of cable types. The simplest to implement is 10Base2, which uses a coaxial cable. 10Base2 gets its name because its two conductors share an axis, one running through the center of the other. This cable is very similar to the cable used for your cable-TV connection, with slightly different electrical properties.

The 10Base2 standard is the most economical way to network for smaller groups because the addition of a station requires only a T connector and a segment of cable. The cable terminates in BNC connectors. These connectors are industry-standard bayonet locking connectors. Setting up the physical cabling requires only a little understanding and no special technical skills.

You are also very likely to hear about the 10BaseT standard. This cabling scheme uses UTP (Unshielded Twisted Pair), which is very similar to the wiring used in telephone systems. This system has advantages for larger systems but requires extra hardware in the form of *hubs* or *concentrators*.

As far as WFW is concerned, once the CD-ROM drive is correctly installed, it is just like any other disk drive. Sharing a CD-ROM drive with WFW is almost completely transparent to the user. Even installation is essentially transparent.

Installing a CD-ROM Drive with WFW

The first step in the installation of the CD-ROM drive is to install the drive so that it

works with DOS. You must be sure that you have the appropriate driver software installed:

➤ The driver for the CD-ROM adapter

➤ If you are using SCSI/ASPI, the ASPI driver for the SCSI adapter

➤ The ASPI driver for the CD-ROM drive

➤ MSCDEX (Microsoft CD-ROM Extensions)

The next step is to install Windows for Workgroups or, if you are already using Windows, perform an upgrade. During this process, WFW notices that you have a CD-ROM installed and does a couple of things for you automatically. It updates the MSCDEX file to version 2.21 (required if you want to share the CD-ROM drive) and it adds the /S (share) switch to the MSCDEX command line.

WFW, NetWare, and CD-ROM Drives

WFW is a great way to share a CD-ROM drive on a NetWare network, but one very common problem can drive you crazy if you don't catch it. So that you can access your NetWare file server, Microsoft provides a special, WFW-compatible driver called MSIPX.

If other stations are to share your drive, you must place MSCDEX after Net Start, but before MSIPX in the AUTOEXEC.BAT file. If you don't, workstations attempting to share the CD-ROM drive get an error message instead of a file list when they try to look at the drive in File Manager.

Amazingly enough, that's all it takes. If you already have Windows for Workgroups installed, just install the CD-ROM drive for DOS and make these changes yourself:

1. If your MSCDEX version is not 2.21 or higher (or the replacement for MSCDEX provided by Corel), update it. You can find the 2.21 version on the WFW distribution disks.

2. Add the /S switch to the MSCDEX command line in AUTOEXEC.BAT.

Sharing the Drive with WFW

Making your CD-ROM drive available to other users on the network is simple once you install the drive. Using File Manager, follow these steps:

1. In the toolbar at the top of the screen, click on the icon for your CD-ROM drive (or the one you want to share, if you have more than one). It has a picture of a CD on it. A file list from the CD-ROM in that drive appears (see fig. 5.1).

2. Click on the Share button in the toolbar if you want to generally share the drive so that, for example, others can place disks in the drive and use them. The Share button shows a little hand and a file folder. After you click on the Share button, the Share Directory dialog box appears (see fig. 5.2).

If you intend to share only a specific directory on a specific disc, make that directory the current directory by clicking on it in the right pane of the display, and then click on the Share button.

3. In the Share Directory dialog box, tell WFW just what to do by filling in the form provided:

The **S**hare Name is the name that others on the network see when they browse for the drive. You can call the drive anything you like, but make the name something clear like *Joe's CD-ROM Drive*.

The **P**ath line is filled in for you, so leave it alone.

Use the **C**omment line to specify a comment for others to see.

The Re-share at Start**u**p check box determines whether this share is a persistent share. A *persistent share* is automatically remade the next time you start WFW. You probably want this to happen (which is why this is the

default). If you don't want this share to be made the next time you start WFW, click on the box to turn off the option. Some drives generate an error message if there is no disc in them at startup when this option is selected. This is nothing more than an annoyance and doesn't hurt anything.

The Access Type set of radio buttons determines what sort of access users have to the drive. For normal drives, this feature is important, but because users cannot write to the CD-ROM drive, you can ignore this option.

The Passwords options let you set a password that users who want to share your drive have to type. The password is the same for everyone who uses the drive and should not be considered particularly secure.

4. After you fill in the Share Directory dialog box, click on the OK button to complete the operation. Your drive is now available to others in the workgroup.

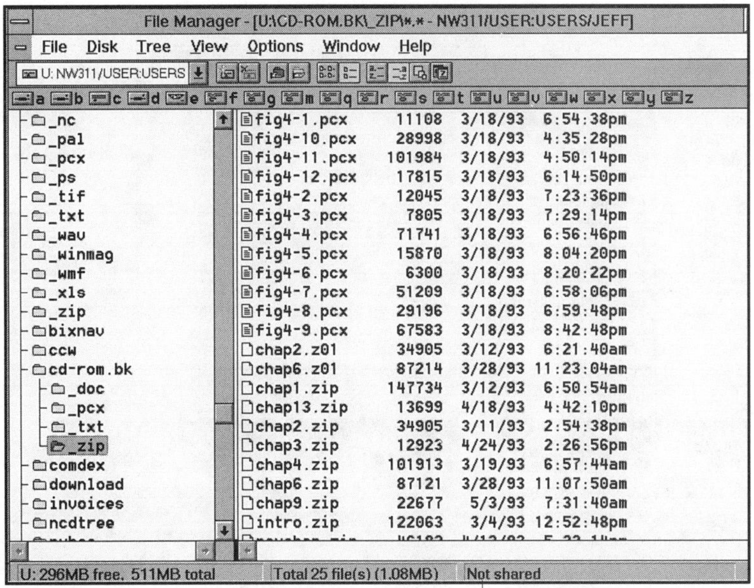

FIGURE 5.1

WFW's File Manager is the control center for sharing and connecting drives.

EXPLANATION

Ethernet

Ethernet is one of many standards used in computer networking. It is essentially a description of how the signal should look on the wire. Nearly every NOS (Network Operating System, the software that provides network services) out there, from the simplest to the most complex, can use Ethernet.

Ethernet was developed by Xerox Corporation at their Palo Alto Research Center (known as PARC). It has been adopted as the most prevalent standard for networking, and is used by the largest computer network in the world, the Internet, which connects literally millions of computers worldwide.

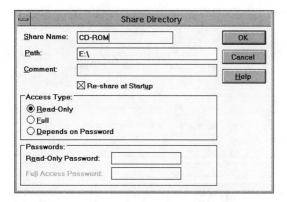

FIGURE 5.2

The Share Directory dialog box.

What's a Share?

A share is a path that is shared by the machine's user. It can be all or just part of the drive.

Licensing

Just because you *can* share a CD-ROM disc does not mean you are allowed to. Please carefully read the license agreement that came with the disc to make sure that you comply with its terms before allowing multiple users to access the CD-ROM at the same time. Some applications can detect when they are running across the network and refuse to work.

Connecting to Another Drive with WFW

It is just as easy to access someone else's drive with WFW as it is to make your drive available to others in the workgroup. It also involves File Manager and a few simple operations:

1. Click on the Connect button (the first button) on the toolbar in the WFW File Manager window. The Connect Network Drive dialog box appears (see fig. 5.3).

2. Fill in the appropriate options in the Connect Network Drive dialog box:

Use the **D**rive combo box to choose the drive letter assigned to the shared CD-ROM

drive. The combo box defaults to the next available drive, but you can choose another. Your choice must be no higher in the alphabet than the LASTDRIVE= statement in your CONFIG.SYS file.

The **P**ath combo box is filled in automatically as you browse for the CD-ROM drive. You can ignore it for now.

The Reconnec**t** at Startup check box serves the same purpose as its partner in the Share Directory dialog box: it decides whether the connection is persistent (automatically remade next time you start Windows). A noncritical error occurs if there is no disc in the drive when you start Windows; a dialog box appears to allow you to continue.

3. In the **S**howed Shared Directories On list box, locate the machine on which the drive you want to access is located and click on its icon. This list box allows you to browse for **shares** on other machines in your workgroup and is where you find the CD-ROM drive you want to share. Each machine on the network is listed in this box with both an icon and a name.

4. After you select a machine, the pane in the bottom half of the dialog box displays any directories available on that machine. Click on the CD-ROM drive's share. With any luck, it has been given an obvious name. This action fills in the **P**ath combo box you ignored earlier. If you know exactly what you want and where it is (if you're a propeller head), you can skip the browsing and type the path in the **P**ath box directly.

5. Click on the OK button and supply the password, if one is requested. Now you can access information on the CD-ROM you chose.

Understanding Performance Issues

Windows for Workgroups makes sharing CD-ROM drives easy and relatively inexpensive. It also brings the added benefits of sharing other drives and printers. The downside, however, is that you may suffer performance degradations on both the CD-ROM-based application and on the machine sharing it.

Become familiar with the problem signs so that you can decide whether you need to purchase another CD-ROM drive and use it directly. The first sign is **poor performance** of CD-ROM applications that move lots of data from the CD. Applications that use complex graphical images, sound, or other multimedia-style elements may show problems. You may also see some slowing of applications on the host machine during access.

Of more concern is the fact that some applications with timing-critical sections geared around audio or animation sequences may lock up if you attempt to run them across the network. This problem is less common now than it was when multimedia applications were first created, but watch for it so that you don't mistake it for another problem.

Using Lantastic

Lantastic is another peer-to-peer networking product that comes in two flavors: DOS and Windows. Actually, the Windows version of Lantastic is simply a Windows interface to the network. If you want to enable networking under Windows, you must load the basic Lantastic network before loading Windows (after Windows loads, Lantastic for Windows loads).

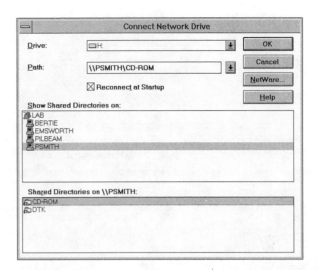

Sharing the Drive with Lantastic

Sharing a CD-ROM drive with other members of your workgroup under Lantastic is a fairly straightforward procedure. Carry out the following steps on the machine to which the CD-ROM drive is physically connected. Regardless of the installation—DOS or Windows Lantastic—you must take the following preliminary steps:

1. Make sure that all SCSI, CD-ROM, and DOS drivers for the CD-ROM drive are installed and functioning properly. To make sure that the CD-ROM drive is properly installed, use the DOS prompt to switch to that drive and get a directory of files on a disc in that drive.

2. Install Lantastic. Make sure that all members of the workgroup can access and share selected drives.

3. Remove the MSCDEX command from your AUTOEXEC.BAT file.

4. In the STARTNET.BAT file (which contains commands to start Lantastic), make sure that the MSCDEX command originally found

---

FIGURE 5.3

The Connect Network Drive dialog box lets you browse through and connect to drives owned by other users.

TIP

How To Correct Some Performance Problems

You may be able to correct the slow-down problem somewhat by using the Performance Tuning adjustment available in the Control Panel. This slider control lets the machine's owner select the priority of foreground over background operations.

in the AUTOEXEC.BAT file falls between the Lantastic REDIR and SERVER command lines. For example, position the MSCDEX statement as follows:

```
REDIR SERVER1
MSCDEX.EXE /D:MSCD0001 /L:D
SERVER
```

5. Save the STARTNET.BAT file.

6. Type **NET_MGR** at the DOS command line and press Enter to access Lantastic's Network Resource Manager.

7. Select Shared Resources Management from the menu. A list of resources pops up on the screen.

8. Press the Insert key, type an identifying name for the CD-ROM drive—up to eight characters long (for example, **MY_CDROM**)—and press Enter.

9. When NET_MGR asks you for the true link, or true name for the CD-ROM drive, type the DOS drive name (for example, type **D:** or **E:**).

10. That's it! Press the Escape key to exit the menus and NET_MGR. Each workstation on the peer network can now access the shared CD-ROM drive.

Connecting to Another Drive with Lantastic

Once you set up the CD-ROM drive to be shared across the Lantastic network (as described in the preceding section), you must connect each workstation that is to share the CD-ROM drive to the drive over the network. To connect a workstation to the shared drive, follow these steps on the machine that is to access the drive:

1. Type **NET** at the DOS prompt and press Enter to access Lantastic's Peer NET program.

2. Select Network Disk Drives and Printers

from the Main Functions menu.

3. Select the drive designation you want the CD-ROM to use under that machine's Lantastic sessions. Suppose that the workstation has two floppies and one hard drive (that is, it has drives A through C); you may want to make the CD-ROM drive D. Specify the DOS drive name you want the CD-ROM drive to become for this workstation and press Enter.

4. The next list displays available servers. Select the server that contains the CD-ROM drive you want to access. For example, if the machine to which the CD-ROM drive is physically connected is called EMSWORTH, select EMSWORTH as the server to which you want to connect.

5. Select the CD-ROM drive from the list of available drives on the selected server and press Enter. The name you select here is the same name you gave to the drive when you accessed Lantastic's Network Resource Manager, selected Shared Resources Management, and pressed Insert (refer to the preceding section for more information about setting up a drive to be shared on Lantastic).

6. Press the Escape key to back out of all menus and return to the DOS prompt.

Once you install Lantastic for Windows, you'll find that all Lantastic's Network Manager tools now show the shared CD-ROM drive. No additional work need be done under the Windows version of the interface.

Using CD-ROMs with NetWare

NetWare LAN administrators and users have a number of ways to attach CD-ROM drives and applications to their networks in order to share network-licensed CD-ROM applications. The majority of these solutions involve attaching the CD-ROM drives directly to a NetWare server, running special NetWare Loadable Modules (NLMs) to access the drives through the SCSI interface, and then allowing network access to the drives for groups of users. This sounds like a relatively painless process, but in real life it isn't. SCSI conflicts, NLM incompatibilities, and myriad other complications often arise.

Thankfully, someone has done something to ease the pain of networking CD-ROMs under NetWare.

discport

Microtest has come up with an ingenious hardware and software package that makes the installation and networking of CD-ROM drives under NetWare 3.11 as easy as installing a drive in a single PC. The product is called discport and retails for about $695—and is worth every penny.

The package consists of a discport "black box" that houses an Ethernet port, a SCSI port, a CD-ROM SCSI cable, a power supply, and software. Installation is this simple:

1. Plug the Ethernet port on the discport box into the network on any available Ethernet socket.

2. Plug your standard (SCSI 2) CD-ROM drive into the SCSI port on the discport box.

3. Plug the discport into a power outlet.

4. Install the software.

That's it!

Drives can be chained—up to seven CD-ROMs on each discport box. And to make management easy, you don't have to attach the discport box to the server; you can put it anywhere out on the LAN where authorized users can change discs.

It's the software that makes this package really hum, however. One of the most confusing issues for NetWare LAN users is how to find the CD-ROM applications out on the network. The masterful discport Windows and DOS end-user software displays in a list all CD-ROMs available to users—with familiar application names rather than cryptic volume labels.

Network administrators can control who has access to CD-ROMs and can assign members of a workgroup as CD-ROM managers, allowing them to change CDs and publish the applications to others within their group.

This is a fabulous product at a great price. Don't network without it.

AWARD OF EXCELLENCE

discport

Don't even think about networking CD-ROMs under NetWare without Microtest's discport. It's *the* easiest way to add CD-ROM to NetWare, period. Now if every SCSI device were this easy to configure....

Chapter 6

What Is Multimedia?

Although the title and focus of this book is CD-ROM technology, this chapter examines one of the most exciting developments in personal computing in the last five years: multimedia. CD-ROM is not a requirement for multimedia on a PC, but its impressive capacity makes data-intensive multimedia applications practical. Nothing short of a CD-ROM can deliver the raw storage capacity required for these ambitious, exciting software packages.

Most multimedia applications, however, require more than just a CD-ROM drive to be effective. The addition of a sound card, for example, is essential for most multimedia applications.

In this chapter, we explain the basic components of multimedia and examine specific models of multimedia hardware you can add to your system—in addition to a CD-ROM drive. In particular, we focus on sound cards that contain CD-ROM-drive hardware interfaces; these boards may prove the most economical for multimedia upgrades to your current PC.

Understanding Multimedia

Multimedia on a computer is any application that employs more than one medium to convey information. The following list runs through the possible combinations for multimedia presentations from the least to the most complex:

Text with graphics
Text with photos
Text with sound
Text with animation
Text with video
Graphics with sound
Photos with sound
Animation with sound
Video with sound

Enhancing Multimedia

Most multimedia applications on PCs are still primarily text-based with multimedia aspects added to them. For example, figure 6.1 is from

The Term Multimedia

The term *multimedia* can be construed to mean something as simple as a word processing document. Because of this ambiguity, the term itself is subject to abuse. Don't count on the word multimedia to mean anything in particular when it appears on a software package or elsewhere. Look for terms that are specific and unambiguous, such as MPC (discussed later), when shopping for software.

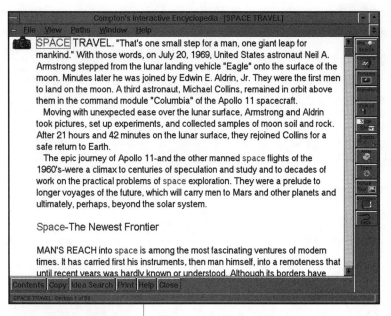

Many multimedia applications are not text-based, however. They use graphics, sound, animation, and/or video. CD-ROM based games and education applications may consist entirely of animation and sound.

Understanding Storage Requirements

In terms of complexity and required storage, the **media** used in multimedia applications have a broad range.

Text files with graphics images are the base level of multimedia. Text and graphics in one file or presentation on a PC require relatively little storage space. For example, a five-page report about the increased sales of baseball bats to the Pacific Islands that includes three-color bar charts consumes no more than 100 kilobytes of disk space.

If you present the same information in a five-minute graphic slide-show format with a dubbed stereo soundtrack of music to accompany the graphics, however, the presentation blossoms into a sound-with-graphics multimedia presentation that requires nearly 40 megabytes of drive storage space.

The table at the bottom of this page gives some rough estimates of how storage hungry various multimedia elements are.

FIGURE 6.1

Compton's Multimedia Encyclopedia, showing an article with graphics enhancement.

EXPLANATION

Media

The term *media* (plural) or *medium* (singular) is used in two ways that can be easily confused. One sense is the *storage medium*, such as the CD-ROM itself. The other sense is the *presentation medium*, such as the graphics, text, and sound. You may see both senses in the same paragraph, so pay careful attention to context to avoid confusion.

Compton's Multimedia Encyclopedia. Next to the great article on space exploration that occupies most of the right portion of the screen, notice the icon that represents a multimedia enhancement to the article. Clicking on this camera icon displays a picture of an Apollo moon landing.

Sound enhancements to articles are handled similarly. Figure 6.2 is an example from Quanta's Consumer Information CD. By clicking on the headphone icon next to the backache article, you can hear a brief spoken introduction to the text. Other text-based multimedia applications incorporate animation, video, and video with sound.

Multimedia Element	Amount of Storage Space Required
One minute of audio, mono	700K
One minute of audio, stereo	1.5M
One minute of animation	2.5 to 5.5M
One minute of video	20 to 30M, compressed

It's easy to see from these kinds of numbers that the use of multimedia in mass-produced applications requires the storage capacity of CD-ROM.

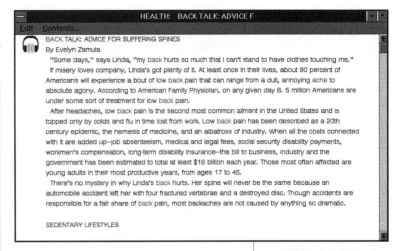

Enabling Technology

In the world of technology, an innovation in one area sometimes leads to radical changes in other technologies. These new technologies are called *enabling technologies*. CD-ROM is an enabling technology. The compact-disc media can record any form of digital information—and any sort of information can be encoded digitally. As long as standards are in place for the orderly recording and playback of the information, CD-ROM technology can deliver all forms of information. For these reasons, CD-ROM enables multimedia to be widely distributed and exploited in a variety of applications. In the case of multimedia, the CD-ROM allows the digital storage of sound and images. This technique is replacing the traditional method of analog recordings and 35mm transparencies or overhead foils.

➤ 101-key keyboard
➤ Mouse (with a minimum of two buttons)
➤ Joystick (not all applications use this)
➤ Serial, parallel, and MIDI (Musical Instrument Device Interface) ports

FIGURE 6.2

Quanta's Consumer Information CD, showing an article with audio enhancement.

Looking at the MPC Standard

MPC (Multimedia PC) is a standard created by a consortium of companies including Microsoft Corporation. This group met and developed a list of requirements for hardware designed to be used in multimedia presentations. This list is a great advantage to you as a multimedia consumer. It guarantees that if you own an MPC, you can successfully run any application labeled with the MPC logo. The basic requirements for an MPC are as follows:

➤ CPU: 386SX (or better)
➤ RAM: 2M (more is *definitely* better)
➤ Disk drives: **Floppy disk**: 3.5" high-density; **Hard disk**: 30M (or larger)
➤ CD-ROM with CD-DA output
➤ MPC-compliant sound card
➤ VGA display adapter (or better)

Understanding Sound Cards

All CD-ROM drives for PCs are capable of playing standard CD audio, so why the need for yet another piece of hardware? The trouble with sound is that there are many techniques for providing digital audio for applications; CD audio (CD Digital Audio, or CD-DA) is just one of them. For one thing, CD-DA eats up enormous disc space. In a multimedia application that requires sound, video, text, and graphics, even the CD-ROM's enormous storage capacity can be stretched to the max. Also, the synchronization of audio with video or animation is technically more difficult with CD audio. To get around some of these drawbacks, software developers use a variety of audio recording techniques to provide voice, sound effects, and music. Sound cards offer an effective means of taking CD-ROM-based audio and synchronizing it for multimedia applications.

The following sections provide some basic information about sound-card technology and describe some popular sound cards (at least, those that include interfaces for attaching CD-ROM drives) currently shipping. One section describes speaker systems especially designed for the multimedia CD-ROM market.

Digital Audio and What Is Covered Here

The field of digital audio and the creation of multimedia presentations is vast—too big to cover thoroughly in this book. This book assumes that you want information to help you purchase an appropriate audio card to play back multimedia applications. Therefore, it covers only audio that pertains directly to your purchase of a sound board as a compliment to your CD-ROM drive.

If you're going to delve heavily into the creation of your own multimedia presentations, this section of the book provides basic background on audio, but doesn't give you all the information you need to create applications.

Sound Sources

Unfortunately, not all sound is created—or reproduced—equally on a PC. The recording, creation, and reproduction of sound can be handled in a variety of ways with a number of different technologies. The following sections explain the differences between these technologies and their relative merits

Sampled Sound

Analog sounds—sounds that exist in the physical, real world—are vibrations of air. In effect, these sounds are waves of differing heights and widths. Additionally, analog sound is continuous, so that the wave's modulations blend from beginning to end, without interruption, throughout the sound event. When you drop a pot lid on the floor, the analog sound of the crash goes through many peaks, valleys, and gradually diminishing spikes until the sound disappears altogether.

Digital recording onto CDs is *sampled audio*. Instantaneous snapshots of the original sound are taken at regular intervals, encoded to digits, and captured to the recording media. The greater the rate at which the sound is sampled, the more closely the digital recording resembles the original.

Figure 6.3 represents, in a graphic wave format, a single analog cough. If the cough is sampled at a low rate, the resulting wave might look the wave shown in figure 6.4. Notice that many of the peaks and valleys have not been captured. The second sample may not even be discernible as a cough when played back because so much information is missing.

Taking many more samples of the sound gets us closer and closer to the original analog sound. There is a diminishing point of returns, however, because each sample needs storage space. Theoretically, you can sample an analog sound into infinity—but you also need infinite storage space. Luckily, the human ear is not infinitely capable of discerning sound quality.

The more complex a sound is, the greater the sample rate that must be used to reproduce it accurately. Human speech, for example, is capable of a fairly limited range of sounds and can be reproduced with a relatively low sample rate. Music, on the other hand, is complex and requires a higher sample rate if it is to be reproduced without noticeable loss of sound quality.

By understanding these inherent characteristics of different types of sounds, software developers can utilize the most appropriate sample rates to capture multimedia audio, reducing significantly the CD-ROM space needed to record voice overs, music, and sound effects.

Sample rates are expressed in **kilohertz**, which is the number, in thousands, of samples per second. Some typical sample rates are 11, 22, and 44 KHz. The highest, 44 KHz, is the rate of CD audio recordings. This rate was established as a result of an idea called the *Nyquist limit*, which says that the highest frequency that can be reproduced is one half the sample rate. Therefore, the theoretical high-frequency limit of a CD recording is 22 KHz (22,000 Hz). This frequency is just about the upper limit of human hearing and is considered high fidelity.

8-Bit and 16-Bit Sound

In addition to sample rate, the data bits available for capturing sound also come into play. 8-bit samples are capable of representing a wave in one of 256 possible states. 16-bit samples, on the other hand, can express over 65,000 possible states, dramatically expanding the recording's **dynamic range**.

Obviously, 16-bit cards are superior in dealing with sound samples. Only 16-bit cards can deliver 44 KHz, CD-audio-quality sound through the PC. In addition, some hardware manufactures are currently shipping cards that support 12-bit sound. All cards do not record and play back at the same resolution; for example, some cards can record only at 8-bit resolution but can play back 16-bit sound files.

Sound Encoding

In addition to employing sampled sounds to create audio in digital format, software and hardware can compress or encode that digital data even more, enabling better use of the CD storage space. One standard for encoding these sound bits is called PCM (Pulse Code Modula-

tion). The sound board uses a DAC (Digital to Analog Convertor) to take the digital information representing the sound and convert it to analog signals for speakers and, ultimately, your ears.

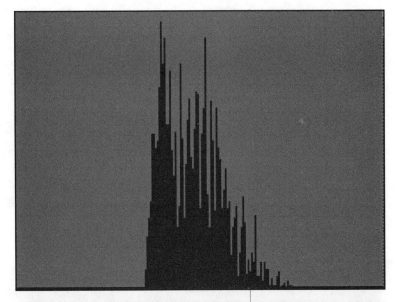

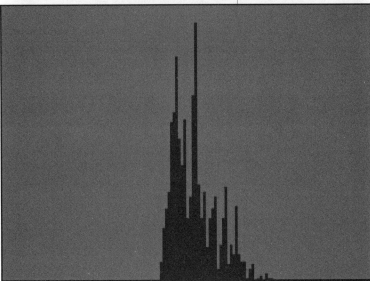

FIGURE 6.3, top

An analog representation of a cough.

FIGURE 6.4, bottom

A sample of a cough, with few samples recorded.

Hertz and CPS

The technical term for CPS (Cycles Per Second) is Hertz. It is named after Hienrich Hertz, a German physicist. The prefix *kilo* multiplies it by 1000; the prefix *mega* increases it to one million.

EXPLANATION

Dynamic Range

Although sample rate (*time-domain resolution*) determines the *frequency response* of a digital recording, the number of bits in each sample (*amplitude-domain resolution*) determines the *dynamic range*. The dynamic range is simply the difference between the quietest and loudest reproducible sounds. A 16-bit recording, when compared to an 8-bit recording, has a superior dynamic range.

ADPCM (Applied Differential Pulse Code Modulation) is a refinement of PCM that provides more efficient encoding than PCM and is a part of the CD-ROM-XA (Extended Architecture) specification. To date, however, few applications use ADPCM digital encoding, and not many sound boards have ADPCM chipsets on them. ADPCM may become the standard for multimedia sound encoding in the future, however, for a number of reasons. First, ADPCM requires much less storage space compared to conventional PCM encoding. ADPCM-enabled multimedia applications can store up to 16 times more audio information than is possible with the PCM method, leaving more space for text, graphics, and video. Perhaps the most important reason behind the use of ADPCM, however, is that the sound can be effectively interleaved with other data types under the XA format. Present multimedia applications must use PCM or CD audio; these formats must be clearly defined on the disc as a separate audio track or stored in a sound file.

Different Sound Formats

All sounds are not created equal. The actual sounds themselves are represented in different formats in multimedia applications. Just as sample rates affect the quality of a recording, so does the manner in which the sound is generated. The following sections describe the available formats and point out the drawbacks and merits of each in representing sound in multimedia applications.

FM Synthesis

FM, or *frequency modulation*, synthesis is used in the development of sound effects and synthesized music. Synthesized music is the music most people commonly refer to as *computer music* because it generally lacks the richness expected from natural sounds

(although it does use a technique very similar to the way real sounds are produced). All the tones and effects are produced by mixing and modulating simple tones in different patterns with specialized hardware. One pattern may provide a cymbal-like crash, for example, and another pattern may produce a musical tone.

Because the variety and complexity of tones is limited by the synthesizer's capabilities, nuances or shadings of sound are generally beyond the capabilities of the relatively simple synthesizers supplied on sound boards. As a consequence, these sounds have limited appeal, but are perfectly suited to certain background and sound-effect functions in multimedia presentations. Earlier FM synthesis cards provided only 10 or 11 simultaneous sounds or voices, but most cards now use 20-voice stereo chipsets (the minimum you settle for in a synthesis-based sound card).

MIDI

MIDI is short for Musical Instrument Digital Interface and really is not a method for recording music as much as it is a way for recording commands to be sent to a musical instrument (like a keyboard). A MIDI file—often designated with the extension MID—contains references to notes, not an actual recording of the music itself. When MIDI-compatible sound cards read the MIDI files, the cards take the references and look them up in a MIDI table. The table indicates which sound should be played for each reference. For example, the MIDI table may define a cymbal crash as number 55. When the sound card reads a MIDI file and sees the reference to 55, it provides the cymbal sound. You can play MIDI files through the FM synthesis (described in the preceding section) or you can tie MIDI files to a ROM-based sample of real sounds with the ROM chips residing on the sound board.

ROM-Based Sound Samples

Some sound cards have on-board ROM-based memory chips that carry actual recordings of instruments. These recordings are stored according to the MIDI standard table and can be referenced in that way. ROM-based samples sound more real than their mechanically synthesized counterparts and include all the nuances of live musical instruments.

Providing ROM-based memory chips capable of holding the range of musical instruments and sounds in the MIDI standard, however, requires expensive chips and technology. Sample-based sound cards are more expensive than their synthesized cousins, but you may find the difference worth the added expense. Also, as mass manufacturing and competition heats up even more in the sound-card market, prices will fall to reasonable levels.

WAVE

PCM and ADPCM (described in "Sound Encoding," earlier in this chapter) are techniques for digitally *encoding* sounds; WAVE is a *file format*, that is, a standard way to store encoded data. WAVE files are digital recordings, just like CD audio, but they are saved in file form rather than recorded on a CD track. WAVE files usually have the extension WAV, but this extension is not required. WAVE files can be stored in 8-bit or 16-bit format and can be recorded at 11, 22, or 44 KHz. Many current multimedia titles rely on applications reading a WAV file and playing it at the same time that a graphics or photo file is displayed.

Storing a sound in WAVE format on CD is not the most productive use of the CD space, but it provides independence for the audio element. The WAVE file can be assigned or used by any application at any time and need not be a synchronized, interleaved part of the multimedia application. The key asset of WAVE files is their versatility; they can reside on the hard drive, floppy drive, or CD-ROM.

WAVE files created by different applications may be in different file formats, much as graphics formats may differ. Files created with Sound Blaster software, for example, have a VOC extension and must be converted to WAV format for use with Microsoft Windows WAVE applications.

A Sound Summary

Now that you know where all the sound is coming from on PCs these days, keep a few things in mind when purchasing a sound board with a CD-ROM interface:

➤ Music scores stored in MIDI files only sound as good as the on-board capabilities of the card you buy. Some cards use FM synthesis and others use real samples of instruments. Sampled sound is superior in quality to synthesized sound, but you pay for the improvement. Even those cards that use instrument samples have differing qualities: some use samples at the 44-KHz range and others use 22-KHz samples.

➤ Only 16-bit sound boards are capable of playing or recording full CD-audio quality 44 KHz WAVE files and CD audio tracks.

➤ Cards that offer compression techniques (such as ADPCM) may be positioned for use in multimedia applications that use the CD-ROM-XA specification. On-board compression of audio is also a plus if you plan to record your own sound: you can conserve hard disk storage space with such features.

PC Sound Boards with CD-ROM Interfaces

Because sound boards are a must for multimedia applications (most worthwhile multimedia applications are published on CD-ROM), it makes sense for users to buy a sound board that incorporates a CD-ROM interface (a built-in connector for your CD-ROM drive), so that you can eliminate the need for yet another board in your PC. In most cases, this solution makes for a cleaner installation: you set only one set of interface-card jumpers, take up only one slot, and so on.

Most cards come with SCSI-2 connectors, allowing you to choose exactly which drive you'd like to pair up with the audio card. Because some of the CD-ROM interfaces may not be standard, you may be limited to a choice of only a few CD-ROM drives. Although such non-standard CD-ROM interfaces may be cheaper, you have to settle for their CD-ROM drive options, not yours.

The following sections detail the sound cards with CD-ROM interfaces that are currently available. Keep in mind, however, that you do not need any of these combination sound/CD-ROM cards to get full multimedia performance (these sound cards may have a proprietary CD-ROM interface—buy your own CD-ROM-drive and SCSI cards and plug them into the sound card). Many sound cards that do not provide CD-ROM interfaces can be perfectly suitable for use in your PC. In this case, a separate sound card hooked to your CD-ROM drive audio port gives you full multimedia.

Sound Blaster Pro

Suggested list price: $199

Sound Blaster has been around a long time. Creative Labs pioneered the acceptance of audio on the PC with this affordable, easy-to-install card. Most software programs list *Sound Blaster or fully compatible* in their installation requirements when describing the equipment needed to play the audio portions of their programs.

The Sound Blaster Pro uses a Yahmaha FM synthesizer chipset to provide MIDI services and uses 8-bit AD-DAC chips for the conversion of analog sound to digital and digital to analog. The board's top sample rate is 22 KHz in stereo and 44 KHz in mono. For most purposes, this rate is perfectly adequate. Spoken multimedia applications, for example, won't suffer much under the 8-bit constraint. CD audio will suffer, however.

The board has a 4-watt on-board amplifier to drive external speakers and an external volume dial to control the output level. This amplifier has more than enough power to drive the speaker systems designed for use with PCs.

You'll notice some distortion and interference if you hook the board up to most stereo systems, however. Even with the volume output turned all the way down, there is noticeable buzzing. Don't use Sound Blaster Pro with an external amplified source without using a pad or attenuating adapter, available from places like Radio Shack.

The Sound Blaster Pro card offers a full range of inputs and outputs, including those listed in the table at thop of the next page.

The bad news is that Sound Blaster Pro uses a proprietary SCSI interface that limits you to the proprietary version of a Panasonic CD-ROM (either internal or external). No other drives will work with this sound card.

The Panasonic/Mashushita drive is serviceable enough, conforming to MPC specifications and allowing single-session PhotoCD. But the drive's low speed isn't well suited to full-motion video and causes jerky, staccato playback of video clips.

Input/Output	Purpose
Line in	For external audio sources
Line out	For connection to amplified speakers or a stereo receiver
Microphone in	A standard microphone jack for recording
MIDI in/out	For use with MIDI-equipped keyboards and mixers
Joystick port	Standard PC joystick port

For the money, Sound Blaster Pro is a good entry-level sound card. You may want to use this card for sound only, and ignore the proprietary SCSI port that limits you to the lackluster Panasonic/Mashushita CD-ROM.

Sound Blaster 16 ASP

Suggested list price: $349

The Sound Blaster 16 ASP card is Sound Blaster Pro's big brother (see fig. 6.5). Recently released, it is Creative Labs' answer to 16-bit sound, and the improvement over the 8-bit Sound Blaster Pro is notable. The Sound Blaster 16 ASP handles audio CDs remarkably well and is very capable in recording 44 KHz stereo sound with playback through both external stereo amplifiers and external speakers. One big plus is the new board's ability to turn off the on-board amplifier if you intend to hook up the card to a stereo system. This feature virtually eliminates any transient noise or distortion, giving you clean sound through the amplifier. Sample rates go from 5 to 45 KHz.

The sound generation is still limited to FM synthesis, however. Any MIDI-based music produced by the Sound Blaster 16 ASP sounds identical to that produced by the Sound Blaster Pro. Creative Labs has announced a WAVE daughterboard (a module that plugs onto the main board) that provides ROM-based samples as a $249 option.

The card also incorporates a set of ADPCM signal processors, so it has the equipment necessary for compression and decompression of ADPCM-encoded CD-ROM material for XA-format applications. Sony's first CD-ROM-XA discs, however, developed for their portable CD player, do not work with the ASP's ADPCM processors. Perhaps CD-ROM-XA applications will work on ADPCM-based sound boards in the future.

The Sound Blaster 16 ASP card incorporates all the standard inputs and outputs (see the table top of the next page).

HIGHLY RECOMMENDED
Sound Blaster 16 ASP

FIGURE 6.5

Creative Labs'
Sound Blaster 16 ASP.

Input/Output	Purpose
Line in	For external audio sources
Line out	For connection to amplified speakers or a stereo receiver
Microphone in	A standard microphone jack for recording
MIDI in/out	For use with MIDI-equipped keyboards and mixers
Joystick port	Standard PC joystick port

AWARD OF EXCELLENCE

NOTE:

Sound Blaster as the Universal Solvent of Audio Cards

Most sound cards are Sound Blaster compatible because most multimedia software developers write the audio portion of their software to the Sound Blaster specifications.

Creative Labs uses the same proprietary CD-ROM interface on the Sound Blaster 16 ASP card as it does on the Sound Blaster Pro, severely limiting your drive choices. This board isn't good for hooking up to a CD-ROM because there are too many good drives you can't use with it.

The Sound Blaster 16 ASP is a solid 16-bit board; it's a shame it is crippled with a proprietary CD-ROM interface. The performance is good, the sound quality is excellent, and the circuitry, particularly the ADPCM compression, ensures that this board won't become obsolete anytime soon. The WAVE daughterboard may be a good additional investment. Don't buy this card for the CD-ROM interface, however, unless you're comfortable using the two models of Panasonic/Mashushita drives it supports.

Media Vision's Pro Audio Spectrum 16

Suggested list price: $349

Much like the Sound Blaster 16 ASP, the Pro Audio Spectrum 16 is a 16-bit card that delivers a full 44 KHz stereo sampling range. Audio quality is good, and MIDI sounds are represented through standard FM synthesis.

DMA, IRQ, and memory I/O for the Pro Audio Spectrum 16 and its **Sound Blaster emulation** are set with board jumpers or through software configuration and setup.

The Pro Audio Spectrum 16 card has 16-bit AD-DAC chips throughout, and the inputs and outputs listed in the following table.

Input/Output	Purpose
Line in	For external audio sources
Line out	For connection to amplified speakers or a stereo receiver
Microphone in	A standard microphone jack for recording
MIDI in/out	For use with MIDI-equipped keyboards and mixers
Joystick port	Standard PC joystick port

Unlike the interface on the Creative Labs sound cards, the Pro Audio Spectrum 16 card's SCSI interface is a standard ASPI-compatible connector. You can choose from any of dozens of compatible CD-ROM drives to add to the Pro Audio Spectrum 16 card. If you want choice, this sound card makes a price-compatible alternative to the Sound Blaster 16.

Priced lower than most 16-bit cards, with a standard SCSI connector, this card is an excellent choice if you want a reasonably priced card that allows you to select your own CD-ROM drive.

Turtle Beach MultiSound

Suggested list price: $599

Turtle Beach was the first company to introduce memory-chip-based instrument samples on-board the sound card (see fig. 6.6). Their MultiSound board holds 4 megabytes of 126 sound samples in standard MIDI table format, sampled at a rate of 44 KHz in stereo. All MIDI files are played back through the sampled sound base, so music sounds like real music.

Although the Turtle Beach MultiSound **does not** contain a built-in SCSI interface for CD-ROM, this high-quality board deserves mention here.

Continuing its commitment to clear sound reproduction, the specification for the Turtle Beach MultiSound card's distortion is incredibly low— less than 0.01 percent. Frequency response and signal-to-noise ratio also come in at remarkable rates, making this card one of the cleanest on the market today.

Turtle Beach also claims superior performance for their product. The board has an on-board, 24-bit Motorola DSP-56001 digital-signal processor, which provides extra horsepower in processing sound, leaving the PC's CPU to perform other chores. Lesser digital-

signal processors rely on CPU usage through the DMA channels for some processing, resulting in possible system degradation in the process.

The company also claims that the card is software upgradeable, allowing the customer to make upgrades from a floppy disk. It's unclear whether you can make upgrades for newer forms of compression, such as ADPCM, in such a fashion. Because the Motorola chip is programmable, such upgrades are a possibility.

The MultiSound board has the inputs and outputs listed in the table at the top of the next page.

Turtle Beach MultiSound

Clean sound, superior circuitry, and easy installation make this the best multimedia sound card available for the PC today.

FIGURE 6.6

The Turtle Beach MultiSound card.

Input/Output	Purpose
Digital audio line in	For external audio sources
Auxiliary line in	For external CD-ROM
Line out	For connection to amplified speakers or a stereo receiver
MIDI in/out	For use with MIDI-equipped keyboards and mixers
Joystick port	Standard PC joystick port

Sampling versus Synthesis

There are two basic ways to produce musical sounds on demand. The least expensive way is through synthesis. This method involves using various signal generators and filters to approximate the natural sound of a musical instrument by imitating its acoustical characteristics. Practical synthesis usually falls short of ideal sound because of the complexity of most natural sounds.

Sampling, the other approach, actually records examples of the instruments playing various notes and then plays the notes back to create the music. Although this idea is simpler than a synthesizer in some ways, the technology involved is more complex. What makes this method practical is that MIDI is used to instruct the sound board as to what it should play; although MIDI does provide for arbitrary sounds, it also has standard musical-instrument sounds. This feature means that when a program needs a piano sound, it can ask for the sound, and the board can provide the appropriate piano sample.

The MultiSound board is top of the line in both quality and price. The addition of a CD-ROM drive requires a separate SCSI interface, however. The Turtle Beach folks claim that removing extraneous electronics from the board cuts down on electronic interference and distortion. They may be right. The 16-bit samples and clean-sound reproduction make this board the premiere sound board—but at a premium price.

The Cyber Audio Card by Alpha Systems Labs

Suggested list price: $349

The new Cyber Audio card by Alpha Systems Labs strikes a balance somewhere between the Sound Blaster 16 ASP and the MultiSound card. Although the sound isn't 16-bit sampled, it's a vast improvement over the FM synthesis provided by other sound cards.

ASL went to great lengths to ensure that the system was Sound Blaster-compatible, reserving a Sound Blaster hardware jumper on the card for compatibility configuration. The card handled all software we had previously installed and configured for Sound Blaster, and replaced FM synthesis with WAVE-sampled sound in a noteworthy fashion.

Sound is reproduced using the on-board WAVE samples through the Sierra Semiconductor Aria chipset—and the result is quite good. The card supports full 16-bit sound playback, all the way to 45 KHz in stereo, and the results are as good as—if not better than other cards described in this chapter. Sample rates for recording, however, are limited to 12-bit samples. The board has an ADPCM chipset, making it CD-ROM-XA-ready.

A nifty bonus to this card is its Aria Listener software. The card ships with a microphone headset that allows you to program the card—

Input/Output	Purpose
Line in	For external audio sources and microphone
Line out receiver	For connection to amplified speakers or a stereo
MIDI in/out	For use with MIDI-equipped keyboards and mixers
Joystick port	Standard PC joystick port

and Windows—for voice recognition. For example, you can train Windows to open Word for Windows when you say "Open Word" by passing the appropriate voice-recognition software command to a macro in Windows. Although the Microsoft Sound card also has this capability, it lacks all the sound features of the Cyber Audio card. The Aria Listener software worked well in our tests.

The Cyber Audio card has the following inputs and outputs listed in the table at the top of this page.

The SCSI interface is a standard, fully ASPI-compatible SCSI interface. You can hook any high-performance drive to this interface. The SCSI interface, coupled with a good driver package, makes your choices for a CD-ROM drive pretty extensive with this card.

ASL has done a good job making sure that this card delivers high quality at a reasonable cost. The standard SCSI interface, sampled sound, and true 16-bit operation make it a good choice. The included voice-recognition module and competitive price make the Cyber Audio card one of the most desirable on the market.

Cardinal Technologies: Cardinal SoundVision

Suggested list price: $399

If you're really on the lookout to save slots in your PC and are not worried about CD-quality recording, consider buying the Cardinal SoundVision card.

Cardinal has been a player in the video-adapter market a long time; they've bundled their basic SVGA card with a sound card and SCSI interface—all on one board.

With all those chips on one board, something has to give. SoundVision only plays back and records in 8-bit and 12-bit modes, making sound less than superior, but more than adequate for most uses, including business presentations.

Input/Output	Purpose
Line in	For external audio sources and microphone
Line out receiver	For connection to amplified speakers or a stereo
MIDI in/out	For use with MIDI-equipped keyboards and mixers
Joystick port	Standard PC joystick port

FIGURE 6.7

The ATI Stereo F/X CD card.

ATI Stereo F/X CD

Suggested list price: $199

ATI, long known for their video accelerator cards, has entered the multimedia sound and CD-ROM arena with the Stereo F/X CD card (see fig. 6.7).

The Stereo F/X CD card uses standard FM synthesis for MIDI services. The major drawback to the card is that it's only 8 bits, which means that the largest stereo sample rate you can produce from the Stereo F/X CD is 22 KHz (the mono rate is 44 KHz). The 8-bit design causes the playback of audio CDs to degrade noticeably. ATI claims that they chose an 8-bit design to hold down prices; it's true that the card is priced below many of its competitors.

The Stereo F/X CD card also has an 8-watt amplifier with bass-boost capabilities. ATI claims that its simulated stereo effect is equal to 16-bit boards on the market today.

The ATI Stereo F/X CD card has the inputs and outputs at the bottom of this page.

A MIDI I/O—for controlling instruments like keyboards—is optional.

ATI implemented a proprietary SCSI interface so that it could connect to CD-ROM drives, and it is unclear what drives are currently supported. ATI will sell drive upgrade kits, but there is no information about the upgrade kits at this time. Drive selection will probably be very limited. ATI claims they've developed "Quiet CD" circuitry for this board that cuts

The SoundVision card has the following inputs and outputs:

The Cardinal SoundVision card carries a standard SCSI interface that is compatible with standard SCSI drives such as the NEC and Toshiba. Some other cards have pseudo-SCSI interfaces capable of supporting only their proprietary drives.

The video portion of the Cardinal SoundVision card offers resolutions all the way up to 1048-by-768 in 256 colors. This card is not one of Cardinal's Windows accelerator cards, however, so performance on the video side is average. The sound card, standard SCSI interface, and video package are a good combination if you're looking for all three at the same time and budget is an issue.

Input/Output	Purpose
Line in	For external audio sources
Line out	For connection to amplified speakers or a stereo receiver
Microphone in	A standard microphone jack for recording
Joystick port	Standard PC joystick port

down on signal interference from the CD-ROM attached to the card.

Price is the prime factor when talking about the ATI Stereo F/X CD card; serious CD-ROM drive users will no doubt be limited in drive selections because of the proprietary interface. The 8-bit design also limits sound capabilities. The card, even at suggested retail, is a true bargain, however. Its sound quality is excellent for its limited 8-bit range.

Logitech SoundMan 16

Suggested list price: $299

The SoundMan 16 by Logitech is similar to both the Sound Blaster 16 ASP and the Pro Audio Spectrum. It uses 16-bit ADC (Analog-to-Digital Convertor) and DAC (Digital-to-Analog Convertor) chips for true 44-KHz sound in and out and standard FM synthesis for sound production.

The SoundMan 16 is fully configurable through software—virtually all other cards require the user to change jumpers on the board for the IRQ, DMA, and memory I/O settings.

A standard 8-bit SCSI connector for the SoundMan 16 is available as an option. Check with the manufacturer for drive compatibility and availability of CD-ROM drivers for the SCSI connector.

It's too early to tell how CD-ROM friendly the SoundMan 16 will be, but the sound capabilities are priced very attractively.

Gravis UltraSound

Suggested list price: $199

The Gravis UltraSound card provides 16-bit, 32-voice sound capabilities in a very affordable package (see fig. 6.8). The card is based on wave-table synthesis rather than FM synthesis, making the quality far superior to some other cards on the market.

In addition, you can upgrade the wave tables to a full 6.5 megabytes of 16-bit sampled sound. The Gravis UltraSound card uses disk-based samples, rather than on-board ROM, to store the wave tables. Upgrades to the UltraSound tables are only a few floppy disks away (with ROM-based cards, you have to physically remove the ROM modules and replace them with the upgrades).

Sampling runs to full stereo 44 KHz, and the UltraSound card includes 256KB of memory for improved throughput of sound recording or WAVE file playback. This memory is expandable on-board to a full megabyte to cache the disk-based samples.

The Gravis UltraSound card has the inputs and outputs listed in the table at the top of the following page.

RECOMMENDED
Gravis UltraSound

FIGURE 6.8

The Gravis UltraSound card.

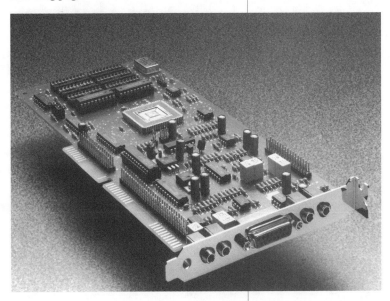

Input/Output	Purpose
Line in	For external audio sources
Line out receiver	For connection to amplified speakers or a stereo
Microphone in	A standard microphone jack for recording
Joystick port	Standard PC joystick port

An optional add-on daughterboard that plugs into the basic card adds a standard SCSI-2 CD-ROM interface, making your choice for CD-ROM drives more extensive than that available on other cards.

The Gravis UltraSound card offers great value; you can add modules as you need them for upgrades such as the full 6-or-more mega-byte MIDI sound samples.

Speakers

The most practical way to get sound to your ears from a PC sound card is by using specially designed external speakers. These small, self-powered units come with special magnetic shielding; this shield prevents the speaker's magnets from distorting a monitor display or interfering with the viability of your hard drive. An unshielded speaker can corrupt data on a floppy disk, so the shielding is essential.

PC speakers don't have to be expensive to be effective. Unless you want chest-thumping volume as you sit at your PC, most of the speaker systems described in the following sections should be adequate for your needs. If you have to crank your multimedia to the max, you may be better off simply hooking the sound card to a full-blown stereo.

If you invest in a 16-bit sound card, you won't notice a drastic difference between it and your old 8-bit card until you plug the 16-bit card into a great stereo or buy a good pair of speakers.

The speaker systems in the following sections are just a sampling; many other brands and styles, including those that use subwoofer systems, are hitting the market. You can spend up to $600 on PC speakers alone—if you're so inclined. Look at your desktop real estate and your sound requirements. Few people require the monster speaker systems that are available, but if you intend to produce your own multimedia presentations, the investment may be worthwhile.

Labtec 88-700

Suggested list price: $99

Probably the most popular speakers on the market for PCs, the Labtec 88-700 are small, moderately priced speakers that deliver clean sound at a good price. Labtec's speakers are powered by batteries or through a DC power adapter you can plug into the wall. A nice feature is the bass, treble, and mid-range equalizers on each speaker that enable you to fine-tune the response. Each speaker has a separate volume control as well.

Sony

Suggested list price: $129 to $199, depending on model

You can find Sony speaker pairs everywhere, and the prices are right. They provide basic stereo in battery-powered enclosures that fit easily on any desk. Don't look for real high-end sound in the Sony line, however; just solid performance at reasonable prices.

Hi Tex CP-18

Suggested list price: $69

The Hi Tex CP-18 are the speakers of choice for manufacturers bundling speakers with their systems. They're a bit taller than the Sony or Labtec systems, and their sound quality is about the same. The Hi Tex speakers have volume controls for each speaker. These speakers don't give you concert-hall sound, but they're an excellent value.

Roland Monitors

Suggested list price: $170 to $320, depending on model

Roland, the MIDI pioneers, make a number of speaker systems. The Monitor series includes speaker pairs with separate bass, treble, and volume controls for each speaker. These speakers are larger than most PC speakers. They're also rugged, high fidelity, and provide higher output than the average PC speaker.

Altec Lansing ACS300

Suggested list price: $400

The Altec Lansing ACS300 speakers are favorites in the industry. At a recent trade show, virtually every multimedia system vendor showed off their wares with the Altec Lansings—and for good reason. The fidelity is great, the construction is sturdy, and they require the minimum in desktop real estate. These speakers deliver real 25-watt stereo in a surprisingly small package. The price is right, too, considering the amazing quality.

Altec Lansing ACS300 speakers contain a subwoofer that delivers the cleanest bass riffs

imaginable; the left and right speaker shells contain controls for bass, treble, presence, balance, and other spatial and special effects.

Altec Lansing ACS300 speakers are, for the price, the best speakers you can buy for your PC. They are highly recommended.

Altec Lansing ACS100 models are a great bargain at only $180, if you can forgo the woofer and some of the special controls and mixing capabilities. A woofer can be added later for an additional $150.

How To Install Sound Boards with CD-ROM Interfaces

Sound boards interact with your computer's hardware on a low level, meaning that they need to access the computer through hardware interrupts, DMA channels, and memory input/output addresses. **For a lot more information on IRQ, DMA, and many memory addressing, see Chapter 2, "CD-ROM Specifications Explained."**

Most sound cards require you to change jumper pins on the board if you need to change the default settings. Before attempting an installation, check the card's defaults against any previously installed adapter cards to make sure that there are no conflicts. Cards that may already be installed in your system and might cause conflicts include the following:

➤ SCSI adapters
➤ Bus mouse
➤ Scanner cards
➤ Network interface cards
➤ Modem or fax cards

After you reconfigure the card or decide that the defaults will work, write down all the card's settings. You'll need this information during software setup and to resolve any possible conflicts when you add other adapter cards in the future.

Altec Lansing ACS300

Floor-thumping subwoofer and stereo-satellite speakers with a plethora of useful controls make this speaker system the ultimate in its price range.

Hardware Conflicts

Most hardware conflicts that cause system freeze-ups, erratic performance, or video problems can be traced to conflicts with improperly installed sound cards.

After you set the DMA, memory, and IRQ settings properly, insert the card into an open slot in your PC. Make certain that you handle the card properly: **do not** handle the card by the gold edge connectors and ensure that you're static-free by discharging yourself (touch the grounded computer case). Remove the slot-cover screw and plate; keep the screw. Make certain that you insert the card straight in the slot and make sure that it is well seated in the full expansion bus slot. Secure the card with the slot-cover screw.

Install your CD-ROM drive according to the instructions in Chapter 2: make sure that you've chosen an appropriate and **readily accessible** drive bay, secured the drive into the bay, and plugged in the power by using a power splitter.

After the drive and card are mounted, you can attach the SCSI ribbon cable from the drive to the sound card's edge connector. Make sure that the cable is oriented correctly. Pin 1 of the cable is indicated by a stripe; pin 1 on the drive and card are marked.

Your CD-ROM drive should also have a small, four-pin plug near the ribbon cable. This plug is the CD audio output. The sound card has a similar plug. The sound card or the CD-ROM drive should include a cable with four-pin connectors for attaching the CD-ROM audio to the card. This cable is keyed on each end to ensure that you connect the cable in only one direction.

After you hook up the SCSI cable and CD-audio feed to the sound card, you're ready to attach speakers or hook up the system to a stereo with the output jack. Check your sound-card manual for the exact location of this output jack. With so many ports on the back of the adapter card, you can easily get them confused.

After you connect the speakers, turn on the PC and install the sound-system software that came with the card. The software setup installs drivers for the sound card and sets the PC's environment to look for the sound card at specific IRQ, DMA, and memory locations each time the machine starts up. This setup probably includes a short test program that checks all the hardware settings and plays a test music file. Check your sound card's manual for information on these test programs.

After you test the card and install the drivers so that DOS can recognize and locate the sound card, you can install the Windows drivers. But before you close up your machine and restart the PC, make sure that you know your card's IRQ, DMA, and memory settings and check for any hardware conflicts.

Troubleshooting

If you have difficulty with the installation of your sound cards or sound-card/CD-ROM-drive combinations, check the following areas for potential problems:

➤ Make sure that there are no IRQ, DMA, or memory conflicts with existing cards in your system.

➤ Make sure that all CD-ROM software drivers are loaded properly.

➤ Check that both data and power cables are properly connected.

For detailed troubleshooting information and explanations of drive and IRQ conflicts, see Chapter 4, "How To Install Your CD-ROM Drive."

Installing Windows MPC Drivers

After you jumper the sound card, plug it in, and give it a quick sound check with the manufacturer's audio test program, you're ready to install the card for use under Microsoft Windows 3.1. The card manufacturer should provide you with Windows MPC drivers on disk. Check the sound-card manual to determine which disk these drivers are on, because Windows will ask for them.

Crowded Cases

If your drive bay and case are crowded, connect the ribbon cable to the drive and feed it through the case when you slide the CD-ROM drive into the bay. You may attach the cable to the sound card as well, and slide the card in after you attach the SCSI cable.

Click on the Control Panel icon in Windows. All the available Control Panel icons appear. Click on the Drivers icon; the dialog box in figure 6.9 appears.

Click on the Add button and follow the instructions for adding the drivers from a floppy disk. The appropriate drivers are copied into the Windows System subdirectory. Now you must tell Windows how these drivers can find your sound-card hardware. The driver-configuration process should have added the files listed in the table at the bottom of this page.

The driver file names given in this table are examples. The disk that came with the sound card contains the appropriate drivers for your card. Use those drivers—they are probably the most current available.

Highlight each of the first three drivers and configure them one at a time. If you have auxiliary audio and MIDI synthesizer drivers, you must configure only their memory address ports. The standard default for this address is 220 hex. Refer to your own card installation to make sure that you provide Windows with the proper setting. If you provide the wrong memory address, when you restart Windows, Windows tells you that the card's configuration and the setting you chose for the Windows drivers do not match.

The WAVE and MIDI driver requires a bit more setup. Highlight this driver and click on Setup. The window shown in figure 6.10 appears.

Notice that you need to set the memory address, the IRQ channel, and both high and low DMA channels for the 16-bit sound card.

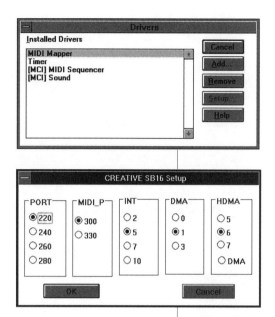

8-bit cards do not require setups for high and low DMA. If you didn't keep records of these settings when you installed the card, you'll be kicking yourself now. (If your card was installed with the defaults, you can look them up in the sound card's user manual and enter them here.) When you're finished, click on Close. Windows tells you that the changes will not take effect until you restart Windows and gives you the option to do so. Restart Windows.

Your Windows environment is now sound-enabled, allowing you full access to Windows multimedia applications.

FIGURE 6.9, top

The Windows 3.1 Driver-configuration dialog box.

FIGURE 6.10, bottom

The WAVE and MIDI Driver Setup window.

Windows File Name	Purpose
Auxiliary Audio	Handles CD and Line in audio through Windows
MIDI Synthesizer	The basic MIDI driver
WAVE and MIDI	Driver for handling WAVE files and MIDI files

Chapter 7

CD-ROM in Business

Information is money. CDs are the most cost-effective way to disseminate information. If your business is not using CD-ROM technology—especially if you are in a professional field such as marketing, law, or medicine—you can be assured that your competition is. CD-ROMs save you the paper chases and high costs of searching for information through expensive online databases. In fact, much of the database and research information discussed in this chapter was only available through online electronic databases until the enormous storage capacity of CD-ROM technology made wider distribution possible. CD-ROM research is convenient and cost-effective; rather than contracting specialized research firms or devoting key employees to full-time research, you can train an unlimited number of employees to take advantage of CD-ROM resources on-site. By using network versions of business CDs, any number of people can access the information they need to develop sales leads, track the competition, and make informed, strategic decisions.

About This Chapter

This chapter explains CD-ROM business software, providing an overview of the capabilities of this kind of software. The chapter also covers possible application to everyday business needs and explains the flexibility and capability of the user interface and search-and-retrieval engine.

Note that many business applications are expensive. The time and resources required for publishers to gather, verify, and master information for these applications is not insignificant. In many cases, the cost of securing rights for the data is an enormous financial risk the publishers must take. For these reasons, many discs are not even sold outright; you rent or purchase a subscription to the data, much as you purchase a subscription to a newsletter or journal. For this reason, we've stated whether applications are available through a subscription, an outright purchase, or both.

And because CD-ROM information for the business sector is particularly time sensitive, we've indicated whether updates to the discs are available—where applicable—and the frequency of the updates.

The variety and magnitude of information available for businesses is staggering. This chapter provides an in-depth tour of some of the more common, less specialized, applications available. But don't let your curiosity end here; there are literally thousands of specialized databases and applications on CD-ROM; they cover virtually every conceivable business research requirement. You can expand your search for CD-ROM information in two places beyond this chapter. First, Appendix C, "Additional CD-ROM Software Titles," lists hundreds of business, professional, and research-oriented CD-ROMs. Second, the best place to look for CD-ROMs is on CD-ROM, as described in the following section.

Discs of Discs

The first category of CD-ROMs described in this chapter contains a single entry: a disc about discs. That is, the CD-ROM described in the following section contains all the information you can possibly want about CD-ROMs currently available for purchase or rental.

The CD-ROM Directory on Disc

**HIGHLY
RECOMMENDED**

TFPL Publishing/Pemberton Press	
Operating System:	DOS 3.3 or above
Class:	CD-ROM database
Search and Retrieval:	DataWare
Updates:	Every six months
Subscription:	Quarterly
Purchase:	Yes
Licensing:	Quarterly

The CD-ROM Directory on Disc from Pemberton Press and TFPL Publishing is the most exhaustive compendium of CD-ROMs in print. This CD-ROM lists over 3,500 current CD-ROM applications in every imaginable category. And it does more than merely list titles: the listings include brief descriptions of many titles and full information regarding the developer—not just name, address, and phone, but what related products and services they provide as well as the number of employees and years in business. The directory is international in scope; it represents CD-ROMs in print from all over the world.

In addition to application information, The CD-ROM Directory on Disc also includes extensive listings for hardware manufacturers and distributors, detailing the products offered. Additional material includes retrieval and authoring software supplies and books, journals, conferences, and exhibitions for the CD-ROM industry.

The directory is updated every six months and is also available in book form.

This disc is a must for companies investing in CD-ROM technology, for researching available titles, or for library and research institutions that need the latest information concerning available CD-ROM titles.

The CD-ROM Directory on Disc is, in effect, a one-stop resource guide to the CD-ROM industry. Using DataWare's search-and-retrieval software—a vast improvement over the previous search engine used for this data—you can search the following separate databases on The CD-ROM Directory on Disc:

➤ **Titles:** Names of CD-ROM applications and databases

➤ **Companies:** Company names

➤ **Hardware:** Hardware product name or category

➤ **Software:** Software name or category

➤ **Conferences:** International conference schedules and details

➤ **Journals:** A comprehensive listing of journals, journal articles, and similar materials related to CD-ROMs

➤ **Books:** An exhaustive bibliography of CD-ROM technology and resources books currently in print, with full bibliographic information

The DataWare search-and-retrieval information is highly flexible as well. You can combine searches in one session, complete with multiple Boolean operations across various search fields—all of which provide you with a *customized* list of results. For example,

you can search the software titles with the category **Education** and enter **<500** under the Price field to obtain all educational software titles at 500 dollars or less.

The distributors, Pemberton Press, sell The CD-ROM Directory on Disc mainly by subscription, and you can purchase a multiple-year subscription. Single editions of the CD-ROM are available, but if you anticipate ongoing research into CD-ROM applications, the subscription is the better value.

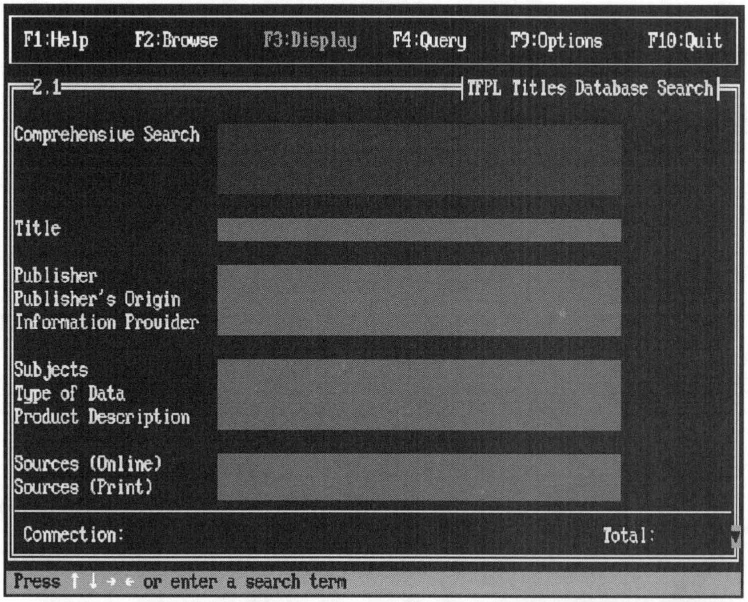

General Business Discs

Many applications—not just reference, bibliographies, and databases—are moving to the roomy environs of CD-ROM. You expect to purchase spreadsheet, word processor, and database applications on traditional floppy disks. But if you purchase all these packages at once, installing them from one CD-ROM is a significant advantage.

FIGURE 7.1

The CD-ROM Directory on Disc is the "mother of all discs"—you can find up-to-date information on everything currently published on CD-ROM.

Because some traditional applications are becoming so complex and offer so many features, they may strain your installation patience by forcing you to use 10, 15, or even 20 floppy disks just to get the program running. Some applications—especially those that include significant clip art, graphics samplers, and graphics templates—are impractical to ship on floppies; in some cases, installing these applications would require nearly 100 disks! By using CD-ROMS, developers can deliver more program for far less money. Distribution on CD-ROM for these applications is a time-saver for you—and a money-saver for application developers. One CD-ROM costs significantly less in initial production, packaging, and shipping than the horde of floppies often needed.

In addition, some CD-ROM applications can be run directly from the CD-ROM, freeing your PC hard drive for more data, applications, and utilities.

Microsoft Works

RECOMMENDED

Microsoft Corporation	
Operating System:	DOS 3.3 or above
Class:	Integrated office-automation software
Search and Retrieval:	N/A
Updates:	N/A
Subscription:	N/A
Purchase:	Yes
Licensing:	Single user

One of the chief challenges of running a small office or workgroup is selecting a suite of applications that are easy for every employee to use and that work well with each other. The Microsoft Works package fits this bill nicely (see fig. 7.2). The sum here is greater than the parts because all the applications share similar interfaces, the applications can easily share information with one another, and the fact that you can install the programs from one CD makes this a veritable office in a box.

In the learning department, Microsoft has included a fabulous multimedia tour and tutorial of the Works suite of products. The animation, sound, and interactive lessons make learning the program entertaining as well as informative; even the most computer-reluctant person in your office can learn quickly and effectively by using Works' online education.

Because the tutorial doesn't cover every feature of Works, the Works CD also includes full documentation for all the components. In addition, a coupon in the CD package entitles registered users to a full printed version of the documentation. When you combine the tutorial, the online manual, and the program's easy, intuitive interface, however, the paper manual is probably not necessary.

This disc of products is the perfect personal productivity set for users in a small business or workgroup. The following list details the various Microsoft Works modules:

➤ **Word Processor.** Although this isn't an industrial-strength Word for Windows word processor, the Works word processor is no lightweight. It easily imports data from the spreadsheet, database, and drawing components of the package. In addition, it does all the things good word processors must do: paragraph and page formatting, font selection, spelling checking, and so on.

➤ **Spreadsheet.** The Works spreadsheet includes basic spreadsheet functions for managing and crunching numbers. In addition, the package includes a handy graphing component with 31 templates for displaying your work in a variety of graphs and charts.

➤ **Database.** The Works database is very easy to use and customize. Although you won't want to keep highly complex datasets in the database, it's perfect for other tasks such as business addresses, contact data, and small inventories. The customizable report output is great for creating printed phone and contact lists. You can access all the print functions with a few mouse clicks, and predefined forms make organization and presentation easier than with most databases. The database module is perfect for tracking individual sets of informa-

tion, and you can create any number of separate databases.

➤ **Drawing.** Simple drawing tools in the Works drawing module enable you to draw freehand or with the aid of geometric tools. You can dress up charts or tables by using the import and export features. And because you can easily add the finished drawings to documents in other Works modules, this module is preferable to a high-end drawing package when you need only a quick graphic and not an elaborate presentation.

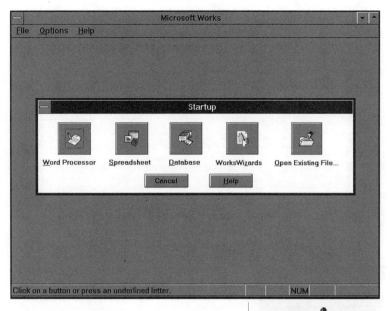

FIGURE 7.2

Microsoft Works packs a word processor, spreadsheet, database, and drawing program onto one CD-ROM.

HIGHLY RECOMMENDED

Microsoft Office

Microsoft Corporation	
Operating System:	Windows 3.1
Class:	Office-automation suite
Search and Retrieval:	N/A
Updates:	N/A
Subscription:	N/A
Purchase:	Yes
Licensing:	Single user

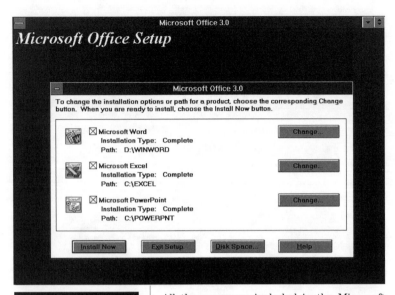

Microsoft Office is all you need to run your office on one CD-ROM.

Word Processing: Word for Windows

Word for Windows has garnered numerous awards and countless user testimonials. When Microsoft was developing the version 2 package, they went through an extensive usability study: they used actual workers in a controlled laboratory, engineers examined people using the software and scientifically measured how easy or difficult certain word processing chores were to accomplish. After these studies, the interface and other design elements of the word processor were further refined. The efforts show. Many confirmed users of other word processors have switched, mainly because of the ease with which complicated tasks such as reformatting, indexing, bulleting, and moving text can be accomplished in the Word for Windows environment.

This book is not the place for a full review or checklist of features, but let us say this: Word for Windows has everything you need in word processing. From simple one-page memos to book-length projects incorporating graphics, indexes, and footnotes, Word for Windows is a superior word processor. When used with the other programs in Office, Word for Windows is a key component in a smooth-running operation.

Presentations: PowerPoint

Making presentations for use on the computer screen or making full-color slides is easy with PowerPoint, a full-featured presentation package. The program includes a number of predefined presentation backgrounds and templates, making your presentations as easy as plugging your text and charts into existing slides.

PowerPoint's extensive importing capabilities—from the other components in Microsoft Office or from other Windows-based applications—allow you to produce highly sophisticated presentations with the tools you're most

All the programs included in the Microsoft Office CD-ROM are best sellers: Word for Windows, PowerPoint, Excel, and Mail (see fig. 7.3). You get a workstation's worth of productivity software on a single disc (the floppy-based version must require at least 20 or 30 disks). When you add the fact that all the documentation, tutorials, and templates for the applications are also on the disc, you save your desktop literally pounds of printed manuals, disks, disk cases, and an assortment of slipcases. In addition, Microsoft Office is priced well below what you'd spend if you bought the programs separately. Saving money and space at the same time—a great use of technology!

Saving Time

Network administrators can save a lot of time by picking up multiple packs of Microsoft Office to install on individual desktops. One disc per desktop does it; and a reduction in boxes, manuals, and assorted paper is part of the bargain.

The following sections describe each of these powerful applications in more detail.

comfortable with. You can create presentation slides with text from a word processor, graphics from a drawing package, and charts and numbers from a spreadsheet.

PowerPoint supports a number of file formats including the SCODL file format (used by most 35mm slide-production facilities) for turning computer presentations into slide shows. Overhead transparencies, speaker's crib-notes, and printouts of slides for handouts are other features. The automated computer-screen slide-presentation module lets you show your presentation on computer.

Spreadsheet: Excel for Windows

Excel for Windows is the Windows-based spreadsheet that has been giving Lotus 1-2-3 a run for its money. In fact, Excel for Windows lets you import Lotus files and has a cross-referenced online help facility and a macro program that converts Lotus command keystrokes to Excel keystrokes on the fly; Lotus users, in effect, don't even have to learn new keyboard commands.

Extensive use of templates, macros, and Windows toolbars makes former multikey and multilevel menu tasks a matter of single-clicking the mouse. Because Excel is a full-blown Windows product, it supports the drag-and-drop interface and connections to other Windows applications as well.

Mediasource

Microsoft Mail

E-mail is here to stay—and electronic mail in Windows with Microsoft Mail is the easy way to manage it. You can E-mail virtually anything you create in a Windows application with this program, and you can E-mail to virtually any computer's E-mail system: it doesn't have to be a Microsoft Mail platform.

One of the best features of Mail is its ability to send mail from any Windows application; no need to disturb your work or shut down an application just to use the mail.

If you've wondered how to paste together the right set of programs to make your desktop work, look no farther than Microsoft Office.

Marketing and Sales Discs

Presentation charts, research, lead development, phone numbers, and contacts; it seems marketing and sales is *all* data. What better place to find data than on CD-ROMs? The titles in the following sections are a few of the latest general-purpose marketing and sales tools on CD-ROM. They have many uses, are very flexible, and—of late—have become very affordable.

Applied Optical Media Corporation	
Operating System:	Windows 3.1
Class:	Multimedia clip-art database
Search and Retrieval:	N/A
Updates:	Various volumes
Subscription:	N/A
Purchase:	Yes
Licensing:	Single user

Mediasource is a new twist on a traditional CD-ROM application. There are many CD-ROM discs of clip art—from color illustrations to photographs—but few have done what Applied Optical Media Corporation has: Mediasource combines audio, photography, and illustrated images onto one disc. Discs—or volumes—are grouped according to themes: business, places, sports, and so on.

You can choose from a variety of clip media discs, too. General topics, sports, and business-theme discs are available. You are free to include the images in any multimedia presentation as long as the images are not a part of a commercial product.

HIGHLY RECOMMENDED

PhoneDisc USA: Business

Digital Directory Assistance, Inc.	
Operating System:	DOS 3.3 or above
Class:	Business database, telephone listing
Search and Retrieval:	Proprietary
Updates:	N/A
Subscription:	No
Purchase:	Yes
Licensing:	Single user

Phone books are a perfect example of the utility of CD-ROM. Type a name, a partial name or number, press a key, and presto!—up pops the number and address you're looking for. One of the best products in this category of business software is PhoneDisc USA: Business (see fig. 7.4).

Individual businessmen will want a copy of the business disc for their own desktops. If you forget the phone number for that contact and can't find his or her business card, PhoneDisc USA is there.

PhoneDisc USA has an easy-to-use interface: no searching through submenus or search-result lists to scan for the number you're after. Just type the name, and a list of numbers comes up. Most entries include full addresses and phone numbers.

You can search by business type or search by name and by limiting words. For example, you can conduct a search by typing **Que** in the name field and **Indianapolis** in the city field; you get one result, of course: Que Corporation in Indianapolis, Indiana.

You can print the results of a search, but the program does not support tagging multiple entries or tagging entries for export to disk files. Digital Directory Assistance offers database-mailing-list services if you have to compile mailing lists for marketing campaigns.

Digital Directory Assistance also sells the following CD-ROM directories:

➤ **PhoneDisc USA: Residential:** A database of over 75 million US residents, mostly from the east and west coasts. You can search by name and narrow your search with limiting words as with the business directory. This directory comes on two CD-ROMs.

➤ **PhoneDisc Reverse:** Do you have a number you've forgotten the name for? Have client numbers wound up in the wrong data file? Input the number in this reverse directory and it'll give you the name and address of its owner. Five regional discs are included.

➤ **PhoneDisc QuickRef+:** This one CD is a compilation of 100,000 most frequently called businesses, government offices, institutions, and schools. This directory comes on one disc.

➤ **PhoneDisc New York and New England:** This regional directory is comprehensive—all residential and business numbers have been licensed from the regional phone companies. This set is updated monthly.

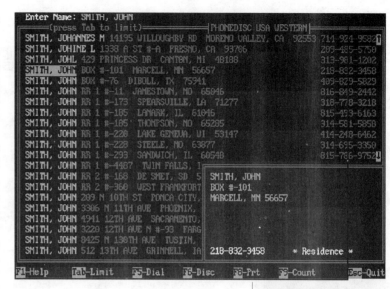

American Business Phone Book

American Business Information	
Operating System:	DOS 3.3 or above
Class:	Business database, telephone listing
Search and Retrieval:	Proprietary
Updates:	Yearly
Subscription:	No
Purchase:	Yes
Licensing:	Single user

When you use the American Business Phone Book, you can search for businesses across the name by name and then narrow the search with city, state, ZIP code, and business type (see fig. 7.5). The software is easy to use and can print individual records, although you can't print a compilation of them. You can also do a reverse search (enter the number and find the business assigned to it).

The American Business Phone Book is updated yearly. One drawback is the use of a meter; you can do 5,000 searches per disc; once the limit is reached, the software ceases to function. Still, that's a huge number of listings—unless you use the disc to develop mailing lists and databases (which is prohibited by the license anyway). The company offers services for creating lists and databases. The American Business Phone Book is very reasonably priced, and makes a good desktop resource.

HIGHLY RECOMMENDED

ProPhone National Business Directory

ProCD New Media Publishing	
Operating System:	DOS 3.3 or above
Class:	Business database, telephone listing
Search and Retrieval:	Proprietary
Updates:	Yearly
Subscription:	Yes
Purchase:	Yes
Licensing:	Single user and networks

FIGURE 7.5

The American Business Phone Book is a moderately priced compilation of over 10 million business phone numbers on one CD.

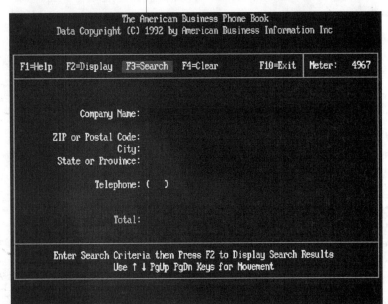

The National Business Directory is one of the best phone-disc series on the market (see fig. 7.6). Punch in a name, limit the search, and there's the number. Tag it. Tag a few others. You can print them, sort them, or save them to disc. The interface is easy to use, intuitive enough for any member of the office to work with after a few moment's training, and the speed of retrieval and searching is great.

As with all the phone discs on the market, you can also search the ProPhone National Business Directory by the industry-standard SIC business code. But with ProCD products, you can export the list searches to comma-delimited ASCII files so that you can quickly create databases, mailing lists, and labels.

The ProCD series is moderately priced: from the business disc to the comprehensive National Business Directory (a six-disc compilation of all residential and business listings from the US). The National Business Directory also allows you to export lists to disc files and to do unlimited searching of files—without any metering at all.

ProCD also sells network packages with prices for small to very large workgroups. With a minichanger CD-ROM drive on the net and the full national directory installed and loaded, an inside sales force can have a tremendous resource at their fingertips.

GPO (Government Publication Office) on Silver Platter

Silver Platter	
Operating System:	DOS 3.3 or above
Class:	Business and government database
Search and Retrieval:	PC-SPIRS (Silver Platter)
Updates:	Bimonthly
Subscription:	Yes
Purchase:	No
Licensing:	Single user and networks

If your company or business must rely on government documents for information; strategic figures; and data, maps, or other printed resources, you must license the GPO (Government Publication Office) on Silver Platter (see fig. 7.7). With an astounding bibliography of over 300,000 government documents, maps, and other printed materials, this comprehensive disc lets you search for any item back to 1986.

Despite the wealth of data here, the interface and search-and-retrieval engine make record searches painless. You can perform simple searches (such as word and phrase look-ups) from the main index by entering the term and combining it with others in a Boolean or nested-Boolean operation. For example, you can enter **highway AND construction AND legislation** to see publications about legislature funding of highway construction. And you can search the entire text of the database for references to a word or group of words. You can also do searches by author, simple subject, and identifiers.

Records in the GPO are extremely detailed; they list, among other facts, the title, the year published, where and from what government office or committee they came, where to obtain a copy of the publication, the publication's OCLC number, and much, much more. All citations include the document's SUDOCS (Superintendent of Documents Classification) number. Of course, you can search for documents by this number as well.

FIGURE 7.6

The ProPhone National Business Directory gives you all the convenience of its competitor's products with better features.

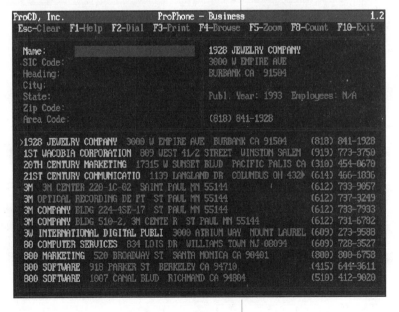

```
SilverPlatter 3.11    GPO on SilverPlatter (1976 - 2/93)   F10=Commands F1=Help
┌──────────────────────────────────────────────────────────────────────────┐
│                                                                 1 of 1124  │
│ AN: 3064952                                                                │
│ SU: NAS 1.15:104176                                                        │
│ SU: NAS115104176                                                           │
│ AU: Easley,-Wesley-C.                                                      │
│ CA: Langley Research Center.                                               │
│ TI: Expanded serial communication capability for the Transport Systems     │
│ Research Vehicle laptop computers.                                         │
│ SO: Hampton, Va. : National Aeronautics and Space Administration, Langley  │
│ Research Center ; [Springfield, Va.? : National Technical Information      │
│ Service [distributor], 1991].                                              │
│ PY: 1991                                                                   │
│ PD: 1 v                                                                    │
│ SE: NASA technical memorandum ; 104176.                                    │
│ NT: Distributed to depository libraries in microfiche.                     │
│  Shipping list no.: 92-1291-M.                                             │
│ IT: 0830-D (MF)                                                            │
│ DE: Aeronautics-Communication-systems.                                     │
│ PT: Monograph; Microfiche                                                  │
└──────────────────────────────────────────────────────────────────────────┘
MENU:  Mark Record   Select Search Term   Options   Find   Print   Download
Press ENTER to Mark records for PRINT or DOWNLOAD. Use PgDn and PgUp to scroll.
```

FIGURE 7.7

Short of living in the library, Silver Platter's GPO on Silver Platter is the best way to find the government document you need.

The GPO on Silver Platter is an invaluable CD-ROM for businesses and companies that do business with the government or need to track down relevant government publications that cover finance, business, health, agriculture, and so on.

Silver Platter

Silver Platter is the premiere CD-ROM publisher of bibliographic and abstract information. A representative sample of their products is scattered throughout this chapter. Take note of some other titles available from them:

➤ **COIN CD International.** Provides full text, world-wide company information: everything from earnings and credit ratings to strategy and business plans. Over 400,000 companies are listed with an additional 100,000 added each year.

➤ **ICC Key Notes.** Includes full text of over 220 market research reports covering 130 markets. Market size, trends, future developments, and much more are covered.

➤ **AGRISEARCH.** Contains five databases from African, European, Australian, US, and Canadian government offices for a complete bibliographic database on agriculture, food, and nutrition.

➤ **AGRICOLA.** Contains full bibliographic citations for US agriculture and life science; citations are from 1970 to the present.

➤ **Food Science and Technology.** Bibliographic citations on food products, food processing, and technology are compiled and updated quarterly. Over 1,800 journals are covered.

➤ **VETCD.** This comprehensive bibliography of veterinary science contains over 300,000 records from the last 20 years and is updated annually.

➤ **AV Online.** A complete database of educational audiovisual materials that includes video tapes, films, audio cassettes, filmstrips, and more. Over 380,000 items are indexed and it's updated annually.

➤ **OSH-ROM.** Databases of bibliographic citations concerning occupational health and safety are compiled from the US, the UK, and the United Nations. The databases are updated quarterly and contain over 350,000 citations.

➤ **Drugs and Pharmacology.** Contains over 1,382,000 abstracts and citations covering drugs and pharmacology from 1980 to the present. The disc is updated quarterly, and 145,000 records are added each year.

MarketPlace Business

MarketPlace	
Operating System:	Windows 3.1
Class:	Marketing database
Search and Retrieval:	Proprietary
Updates:	Annual
Subscription:	No
Purchase:	Yes
Licensing:	Single user

Imagine being able to key in all the characteristics for potential business clients and receive a customized list in a flash—complete with company biographies. That's exactly what MarketPlace Business delivers (see fig. 7.8). For example, your product—hand-held electronic order notebooks—may do well with businesses that have a large outside sales staff, selling over $20 million in product each year. With MarketPlace Business, all you have to do is input employee count and revenue thresholds, and up pop the numbers. You can isolate factors and generate lists according to SIC code (type of business), annual sales, number of employees, region of the country, public or private sector, and many other fields and combinations.

One thing that makes using MarketPlace Business so exciting is its ability to combine any of the fields for a truly customized result and then save the list to disk. These lists can be imported into databases for further refinement, printing of directories and reports, or output directly to printing labels for direct mailings.

Once a list is generated, you can work with a partial list so that you can experiment with a smaller set rather than the entire run.

MarketPlace Business is a direct marketer's and sales force's dream come true: lead generation. Because a product like this is only as good as its data, it's nice to know that the majority of MarketPlace's list is taken from Dunn and Bradstreet.

Compact d SEC

DisClosure Information Service	
Operating System:	DOS 3.3 or above
Class:	Financial database
Search and Retrieval:	DisClosure Spectrum
Updates:	Quarterly
Subscription:	Yes
Purchase:	No
Licensing:	Single user

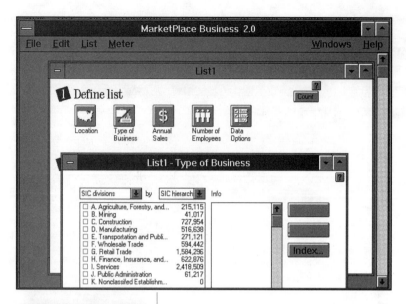

FIGURE 7.8

Create a direct-marketing database of leads in a hurry with MarketPlace Business.

HIGHLY RECOMMENDED

Suppose that you want to know who runs your competitor's business: vice presidents, president, and so on. Maybe even what their salaries are. Compact d SEC lets you pop up the pertinent information in a snap. The retrieval software is simple to use and lightening fast (see fig. 7.9). It's the kind of disc that's useful even during a phone conversation; all the info is immediately at your fingertips—including annual revenues, the stock ticker symbol, and corporate headquarters, addresses, and phone numbers. Virtually all companies filing with the SEC are on disc.

An indispensable reference for a sales and marketing department.

Predicasts F&S Index Plus Text

Silver Platter	
Operating System:	DOS 3.3 or above
Class:	General information database
Search and Retrieval:	SPIRS
Updates:	Monthly
Subscription:	Yes
Purchase:	No
Licensing:	Single user and networks

The wealth of information in Predicasts F&S Index Plus Text is staggering (see fig. 7.10). In one search session alone, we found references, abstracts, and full text from publications as diverse as the *Wall Street Journal*, *PC Week*, *Billboard Magazine*, and *Rubber and Plastics News*.

The search software is incredibly easy to use: the initial prompt is FIND; you type a word and refine the search with Boolean operands. The default display of the records is ALL, which gives you one article and citation after another. When you change the display to SOURCE, you can look through the search list by publication, marking and unmarking items for display, printing, or downloading to disk.

Virtually any topic—business, science, industry, finance—can be found on this disc. It's like having an entire business trade-publication library in the palm of your hand.

No amount of writing on our part can prove how powerful this information can be. With monthly updates, businesses can be instantly up to date on any number of vital issues, market trends, company strategies, and consumer research. When you buy a subscription to Predicasts F&S Index Plus Text, you buy valuable corporate information and a continuing business asset.

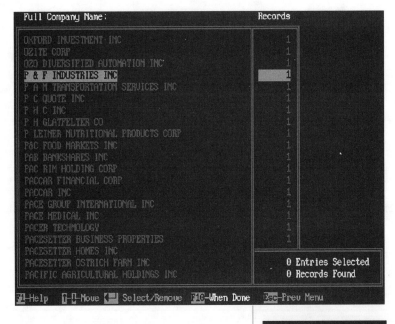

Map Expert

DeLorme Mapping	
Operating System:	Windows 3.1
Class:	Map and geographical information database
Search and Retrieval:	DeLorme Xmap
Updates:	N/A
Subscription:	N/A
Purchase:	Yes
Licensing:	Two-level scheme

If your business involves maps of US localities, chances are you can find a use for Map Expert. This application is a Windows-based computerized atlas. Its database contains just about every street in the US—even tiny little obscure ones. The program's interface lets you search by locations, by place name, by ZIP code, by area code or exchange, by street name, or by longitude/latitude.

Once you locate the desired location, you can annotate the map with a broad selection of cartographic tools that allow the addition of all standard map features. You then can print the map or export it for use in another program.

FIGURE 7.9

For a quick snapshot of the competition—or potential customers—DisClosure can't be beat.

AWARD OF EXCELLENCE

Map Expert

Map Expert is the culmination of DeLorme's Xmap technology development effort. Its extensive database allows quick retrieval of an enormous amount of information in a way far superior to its paper equivalent. When you add its reasonable price, you can see why Map expert clearly deserves special mention.

```
SilverPlatter 3.11     F&S INDEX PLUS TEXT U.S. 1992-3/93    F10=Commands F1=Help

  Tew Media: This memory module mfr will market PCMCIA-based fax/modem
cards
SO: Computer-Reseller-News. February 1, 1993, page 111
IS: 0893-8377.
TX: BY BRIAN GILLOOLY
  A manufacturer of memory modules is banking on the burgeoning acceptance
of PCMCIA technology by dedicating its entire business to the promotion of
PCMCIA-based products.
  New Media Corp., a 1-year-old venture based here, is plunging into the
PCMCIA market with new fax/modem and SCSI cards for use in both portables
and desktop computers.  Simon Harvey, vice president of worldwide sales and
marketing for New Media, said PCMCIA technology will provide 'as close to a
universal standard as this industry has ever had.'
  The vendor will soon bring to market a PCMCIA Level II fax/modem with
business-audio capability and a PCMCIA-based SCSI host adapter.  With the
fax/modem, users will be able to add voice annotation to downloaded files.
The SCSI adapter, which Harvey said will probably ship in April, will
provide easy CD-ROM, scanner or optical-drive capability to portables.
  The company is also developing Ethernet and wireless LAN cards, as well

MENU: Mark Record   Select Search Term   Options   Find   Print   Download

Press ENTER to Mark records for PRINT or DOWNLOAD. Use PgDn and PgUp to scroll.
```

Map Expert has many business uses, especially for organizations that deal in real estate or find themselves frequently drawing maps for customers or internal use. Instead of photocopying existing paper maps—probably in violation of copyright law—use Map Expert to provide a highly accurate, professional map. Further advantages are custom levels of detail and annotations that make the map even more useful.

Map Expert is one of our favorite products. If you use maps, take a look at it.

Law, Accounting, and Finance Discs

Law, accounting, and finance may seem a disparate group of professions to gather under a banner for our purposes, but the following applications have a great deal of crossover—especially for firms that deal with business taxes, business law involving taxes, and financial institutions heavily into investments and business partnerships. Let us emphatically state right here that the products described in the following sections are merely the tip of the CD-ROM iceberg when it comes to these areas of disc information. Check out The CD-ROM Directory on Disc, described earlier in this chapter, for other sources of professional applications.

Map Expert's licensing works on two levels. A limited-use license comes with the product and allows users to create an unlimited number of maps for internal use by the organization to which the software is licensed. With the second-tier license, users incur no additional cost: they just fill out a card included with the product. Once the card is completed and returned, users can create maps for limited publication and distribution. Additional rights are negotiable with DeLorme.

HIGHLY RECOMMENDED

SEC Online on Silver Platter

Silver Platter	
Operating System:	DOS 3.3 or above
Class:	Financial database
Search and Retrieval:	SPIRS
Updates:	Monthly
Subscription:	Yes
Purchase:	No
Licensing:	Single user and networks

SEC Online on Silver Platter is a financial institution's must-have application (see fig. 7.11). It's inconceivable that these CD-ROMs would not be in every stock brokerage, commodity trading house, investment firm, and bank or lending institution. The entire text—yes, the *entire* text of all SEC filings, including footnotes and related exhibits—is included on this set of CD-ROMs.

Silver Platter has added 22 search fields to the database to make searching for specifics as easy as inputting criteria in the fields. Annual reports, 10Ks, 10Qs, Proxy Statements, and 20Fs from virtually every publicly traded U.S. company are on this disc.

Among the facts you can find about companies are its *Fortune* ranking, the full text of its annual reports with full financial schedules, shareholder's equity, capitalization, and retained earnings.

In short, there is nothing you can't find out about the publicly filed information of these companies. You can search for the information in ways not possible in the paper filings. For example, you may want to search company records for specific officer's names or for specific states where companies were incorporated.

Once you find a company, you navigate the text through a Contents menu that gives you access to the Proxy, Form 10Q, Annual Reports, and Forms

```
SilverPlatter FT 1.11          SEC Online A-Z          F10=Commands F1=Help

SALOMON INC   ANNUAL REPORT (12/31/91)                        1 of 15

Salomon Brothers Precious Metals Inc ("SBPMI") trades gold, silver and
platinum group metals.  This entity also owns a 47% interest in a joint
venture formed in early 1991 with Almazjuvelirexport, a Russian-owned
entity, to market a portion of Russian production of platinum, palladium
and rhodium, primarily to North American industrial users.  SBPMI was
sold to Phibro Energy on February 1, 1992.


In the first quarter of 1991, Salomon Brothers relocated its New
York-based investment banking, sales, trading and research personnel
into facilities located at Seven World Trade Center in lower Manhattan,
New York.  Salomon Brothers' senior management as well as Salomon Inc's
headquarters, also relocated to the new facility.  During 1990, Salomon
Brothers moved its Tokyo-based operations to a new building in Tokyo's
downtown financial district.


Show: Contents   Mark   Select Search Term   Options   Find   Print   Download
           Top   Next hit   PReuious hit
Press ENTER to view the table of contents; TAB for other options
```

10K and 20F sections. You can mark sections of text or entire records for printing.

Costs savings are tremendous for companies that regularly use this information from print sources. Having this information electronically available at a moment's notice, with the ability to print what you need, when you need it, will pay for SEC Online on Silver Platter's subscription cost many times over.

FIGURE 7.11

SEC Online is the equivalent of having the SEC's resources at your disposal.

Federal Practice and Procedure, Wright and Miller

West Publishing, Inc.	
Operating System:	DOS 3.3 or above
Class:	Law database
Search and Retrieval:	Proprietary (Premise)
Updates:	Yes
Subscription:	Yes
Purchase:	No
Licensing:	Single user

HIGHLY RECOMMENDED

Law firms, law schools, and federal courthouses must all have the Federal Practice and Procedure disc by now (see fig. 7.12). It's inconceivable that such institutions would have this complex and highly detailed information in any form other than on CD-ROM. Segments can be marked, printed to disk—even in WordPerfect format—for use in word processors.

The software interface Premise uses for their legal CD-ROM discs is a logical and organized way to add numerous CD-ROM discs to the search interface of the application. You use the Premise software to add every CD to the Premise menu so that you can use one interface for all the CD-ROM applications: Bankruptcy, Federal Procedure, Tax Law, and so on. Then you select the database or book you want to work from. For example, the Bankruptcy and Federal Tax Law CD sets alone comprise 16 CDs, and you can search across all of them for specific data.

You can set a search for a topic or to retrieve a specific federal rule or related discussion once you know the specific title. You can search all federal procedures by areas such as main heading, title, text, footnotes, and index. The text and footnote searches alone prove the viability researching these materials on CD-ROM. To scan footnotes and full text of all federal civil and criminal procedures by hand, with printed material, would be impossible or extremely time-consuming in most cases. With the Premise interface, all you do is enter a term under the text heading, such as **jury dismissal**, and you see a list of the appropriate procedures where the term is used.

This one set of CD-ROMs replaces an entire law library of text, and with search capabilities unequaled.

Bankruptcy Law

West Publishing, Inc.	
Operating System:	DOS 3.3 or above
Class:	Bankruptcy-law database
Search and Retrieval:	Premise
Updates:	Yes
Subscription:	Yes
Purchase:	No
Licensing:	Single user

Bankruptcy law—from federal code to cases of interest—is comprehensively covered in West Publishing's five-CD set (see fig. 7.13). Among the separate items on these discs are the following:

➤ Bankruptcy Annotated Code, Rules, and Forms

➤ Federal Rules of Civil Procedure

➤ Federal Rules of Evidence

An adjunct to the civil procedures and code are a number of useful references, texts, and cases.

West Publishing's Bankruptcy Digest (part of the Bankruptcy Law set of discs) contains case summaries and titles of law-review articles. *Cowans Bankruptcy Law and Practice* is a guide to all aspects of bankruptcy practice. The *Bankruptcy Evidence Manual*, written by bankruptcy judge Barry Russell, is a full guide to evidentiary proceedings.

The discs' prime material are actual bankruptcy cases, in full text, decided by the United States Bankruptcy Courts, the United States District Courts, the United States Court of Appeals, and the United States Supreme Court. Headnotes and synopses are presented for many cases.

Each of the five bankruptcy CDs is called a *book*. Each book contains cases covering a three-to-four year period. When you want to use a CD, you select the appropriate book from the Premise menu and insert the proper CD.

You can retrieve cases based on issues, particular cases from citations, or from a particular court or jurisdiction. Searches can be combined to narrow search results. Search results may be printed or printed to disk for formatting.

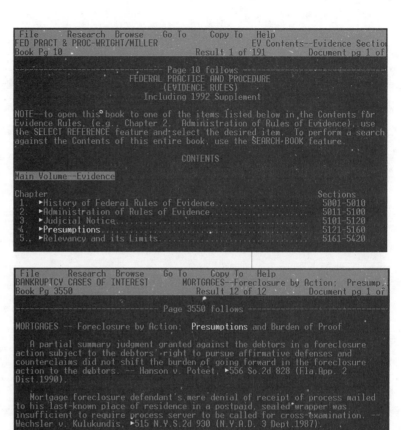

FIGURE 7.12, top

West Publishing's Federal Practice and Procedure is a complete guide to all aspects of federal, civil, and criminal law on one CD-ROM.

FIGURE 7.13, bottom

Bankruptcy cases dating back to 1979 are compiled on West Publishing's Bankruptcy Law disc.

Federal Taxation

West Publishing, Inc.

Operating System:	DOS 3.3 or above
Class:	Tax-law database
Search and Retrieval:	Premise
Updates:	Annual
Subscription:	Yes
Purchase:	No
Licensing:	Single user

FIGURE 7.14

West Publishing's Federal Taxation set is an 11-CD collection of federal tax regulations, codes, procedures, and cases from 1924 to the present.

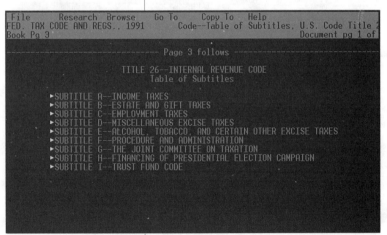

Leave it to the government to have the ability to fill CD-ROMs.... West Publishing's extensive, mind-boggling compilation on federal taxation consumes 11 CD-ROMs (see fig. 7.14). We have absolutely no estimate of how many volumes or how many bookshelves this set replaces. If any application can demonstrate the strength of CD-ROM technology, this one can.

At the center of the Federal Taxation set are the complete federal tax cases from 1924 to the present—from all federal courts: Claims Court through the Supreme Court. These cases can be searched by citation, title, or topic.

The other books—or discs—in this all-inclusive set contain a number of important volumes, including the following:

➤ **Federal Taxation Code and Regulations:** The current codes and regulations, in their entirety, as well as earlier versions dating back to 1984.

➤ **Digest of Cases and Administrative Materials:** Case annotations from 1940 to the present, as well as summaries of revenue rulings, revenue procedures, general-counsel memoranda, and actions on decisions issued by the IRS since January 1982. All summaries are produced by the Bureau of National Affairs.

➤ **Rules of the Tax Court and Claims Court:** All rules of procedure, pleading, pretrial motions, evidence, and appellate procedures for United States Tax Court and the United States Claims Court.

➤ **Federal Taxation Legislative History:** Contains the Bureau of National Affairs' Detailed Analysis, the House Ways and Means Committee Report, the Senate Finance Committee Report, the Conference Committee Report, and the Blue Book General Explanation of the Tax Reform Act of 1986; the Conference Report to TAMRA; descriptions of the

1987 and 1988 Technical Corrections Acts; the House Ways and Means Committee Report and the House Conference Report on the Revenue Reconciliation Act of 1989; and the House Ways and Means Committee Report on the Revenue Reconciliation Act of 1990.

➤ **Revenue Procedures:** Full-text descriptions of information releases issued by the IRS explaining the internal-management procedures of the IRS regarding tax matters, from 1954 to the present.

Other books include Actions on Decisions, General Counsel Memoranda, Letter Rulings, and a Taxation Table of Cases. Actually, it's a wonder it all fits on as *few* as 11 CD-ROMs.

Education and Library-Science Discs

The use of CD-ROM publications, research, and bibliographies in education can fill a book in itself. Everything from agriculture education to zoological bibliographies are available through specialized publishers, distributors, and colleges and universities. Regardless of your professional educational pursuit—the

preschool front to post-doctoral work—CD-ROM information on education and specialized resources for academic research are being published by the hundreds every month.

CD-ROMs won't make libraries obsolete, but they are the best hedge toward making them manageable as the information age fills shelf after shelf with new texts, periodicals, and research journals. Any library that wants to keep abreast of the books available, the books in print, and which periodicals contain what materials will use CDs. Only CD-ROM references can provide such easy-to-retrieve information and timely updates.

Reference materials, both general and professional, that once took up yards of shelf space have been reduced to inches of easily housed CD-ROMs. The ease with which you can search the electronic references is a good argument for their existence: how can you possibly search an entire dictionary's quotations for references to one word embedded in a print version? It's no surprise that CD-ROM technology has a firm foothold in the nation's libraries already. As keepers of information, libraries can readily see the awesome advantages and utility of using this technology to disseminate and store knowledge.

ERIC

Silver PlatterMLA Bibliography	
Operating System:	DOS 3.3 or above
Class:	Education professionals database
Search and Retrieval:	SPIRS
Updates:	Annual
Subscription:	Yes
Purchase:	No
Licensing:	Single user and networks

RECOMMENDED

This complete bibliographic database from the government-sponsored ERIC (Educational Resources Information Center) project covers over 775 periodicals on topics in education and education research. Journal, periodical, and book references are covered in detail (see fig. 7.15).

You can search by topic, title, author, publication year, and institution, among others. The detailed citations also indicate the audience for the cited material (preschool teachers, for example) and what type of material it is (with major and minor descriptors).

As with all Silver Platter software using their SPIRS interface, you can search for major headings or free text in the citations and perform nested Boolean operations to refine your results as you go along.

The single ERIC CD-ROM is a gateway, so to speak, to all the available educational resources available for teachers and educators. Armed with an ERIC CD-ROM, even teachers in remote areas can do research to find articles that they then can order.

School systems, all colleges and universities (especially those offering degrees and programs in education) must have this disc subscription; it's the best means for staying abreast of the current thought on education.

MLA Bibliography

Silver Platter	
Operating System:	DOS 3.3 or above
Class:	Education professionals database
Search and Retrieval:	SPIRS
Updates:	Annual
Subscription:	Yes
Purchase:	No
Licensing:	Single user and networks

Researching the literature on the topic of literature has always been productive with the Modern Language Association (MLA) Bibliography. But it's never been as easy as it is with CD-ROM (see fig. 7.16).

With over 500,000 citations from journals, books, articles, and reviews covering virtually every aspect of literature and poetry, the MLA Bibliography CD represents the entire body of thought in contemporary criticism from 1982 to the present. Most libraries cannot afford the space to keep volumes from that far back on the shelves—but this CD accomplishes the task nicely.

You can search the CD for free text and look for any occurrence of a word or words in the citation or its abstract. You can also search for article titles, periodical titles, and publication dates, among others. A search for author Toni Morrison, for example, turned up 249 separate book, journal, and article citations in just under three seconds.

You can print the results of a search to the printer or to disk. All ISBN and ISSN reference numbers are listed; securing the actual articles is a matter of finding a library that houses the materials.

The MLA Bibliography is the master-work bibliography of literary critical texts; the CD-ROM from Silver Platter makes it more accessible, available, and alive.

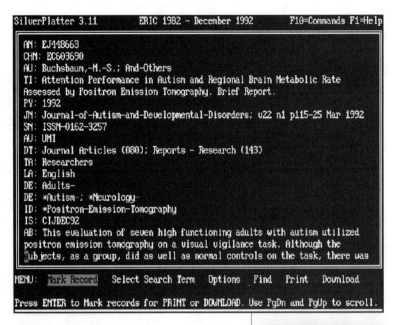

FIGURE 7.15

The complete ERIC bibliography on CD-ROMs has citations for virtually every article and resource on education from 1982 to the present.

Books In Print and Books In Print Plus

Bowker/Reed Publishing	
Operating System:	DOS 3.3 or above
Class:	Publication database
Search and Retrieval:	Proprietary
Updates:	Monthly
Subscription:	Yes
Purchase:	No
Licensing:	Single user

If you own or manage a book store that doesn't already employ this amazing CD-ROM, your competition is going to eat you alive. All educational institutions should be required to have the Books In Print/Books In Print Plus disc on-hand at all times (see fig. 7.17).

Regardless of the book, if it's in print, it's contained somewhere on this disc. When you install it, you can choose which default search criteria come up on your search list; author, title, subject, original language, publication date, and many others. By searching with

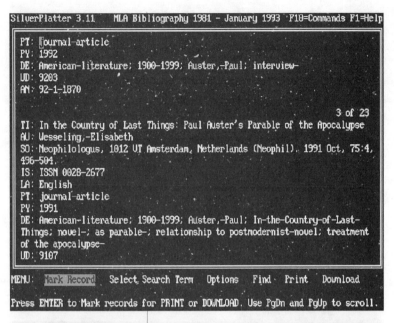

these criteria, you can find almost anything instantly: from books on Antarctica to novels by Gilbert Sorrentino. As a tribute to its timeliness, Books In Print listed an anthology that Steve edited—*South Side Stories*—and the listing appeared in the monthly edition in which the book first saw print.

Searches can be combined, printed to disk, or sent to the printer. For example, you can search for all books that have Portuguese as the original language and that were printed after 1991; the result is an extensive list of contemporary Portuguese books in English translation.

The Books In Print Plus edition gives you capsule reviews of selected books—nearly all the books, as far as we can tell—and you can print these as well. Scholars will love the ability to print an entire search session to disk for later formatting, making bibliographical work a far less tiresome chore.

Of course, all ISBN, publisher, and publication information is included. As a fabulous side benefit, the Books In Print CD can be configured to automatically dial any electronic book-order-processing computer and submit orders from your search lists, either live or from searches saved to disk.

A useful tool in its own right in printed format, Books In Print on CD-ROM is indispensable to bookstores, libraries, and educational institutions.

FIGURE 7.16, top

The MLA Bibliography makes language research as easy as pressing a few keys.

FIGURE 7.17, bottom

Books In Print and Books In Print Plus from Bowker/ Reed Publishing revolutionizes the art of finding books.

Ulrich's Plus

Bowker/Reed Publishing	
Operating System:	DOS 3.3 or above
Class:	Publication database
Search and Retrieval:	Proprietary
Updates:	Monthly
Subscription:	Yes
Purchase:	No
Licensing:	Single user

Also from Bowker/Reed Publishing and utilizing the same interface as Books in Print, Ulrich's Plus does the job for periodical and irregularly released publications. Ulrich's Plus is another product that leverages the amazing storage capacity of CD-ROM to offer a huge, searchable database that must be updated frequently to remain useful.

Ulrich's database contains about 200,000 entries, covering publications from 67,000 publishers in 200 countries. For some additional impressive numbers try these:

➤ 127,000 periodicals
➤ 700 subjects
➤ 60,000 serials
➤ 50,000 annotations

As you can see, this is a massive database. In addition to the information you expect (things like title, subject, editor, and the like), Ulrich's Plus offers information on advertising rates and contact names.

If you work with periodicals—as a librarian, ad agency, or publisher—you'll find Ulrich's Plus an unprecedented asset to your business.

Children's Reference Plus

Bowker/Reed Publishing	
Operating System:	DOS 3.3 or above
Class:	Publications database
Search and Retrieval:	Proprietary
Updates:	Monthly
Subscription:	Yes
Purchase:	No
Licensing:	Single user

Children's Reference Plus is a resource for teachers, librarians, and bookstores to guarantee you stay up-to-date on anything published for children. Children's Reference Plus is yet another Bowker/Reed Publishing title that offers an amazingly extensive database of publications for a particular market. In this case, the database provides bibliographic and qualitative information on just about anything relating to children that is available as a book, computer software, audio, or video.

Children's Reference Plus provides the following information:

➤ **Books in Print:** more than 84,000 titles

➤ **Books Out of Print:** 47,000 additional titles

➤ **Textbooks in Print:** 37,000 items in 21 categories

➤ **Fiction, Folklore, Fantasy, and Poetry for Children:** for the years 1876 to 1985

➤ **Ulrich's:** 3000 periodicals

➤ **Bowkers Complete Video Directory:** 18,000 videos

➤ **Words on Cassette:** 5700 tapes

Any educator or librarian serious about seeking out materials for children will, no doubt, find this reference a marvelous resource.

Video Directory

Bowker/Reed Publishing	
Operating System:	DOS 3.3 or above
Class:	Publication database (video)
Search and Retrieval:	Proprietary
Updates:	Yes
Subscription:	Yes
Purchase:	N/A
Licensing:	N/A

Although there is only one kind of business that can use the Video Directory, it is certainly on the "must have" list for anyone involved in the entertainment video business.

With Video Directory, you can search through more than 90,000 citations in a variety of ways. The database is divided into 575 subject headings that you can browse or search by a number of categories:

➤ Title, including the use of wildcards

➤ Keyword in title, including Boolean operations

➤ Performer/director

➤ Other contributor credits

➤ Awards, including breakdown of Academy Award categories

➤ Keyword searches most of the citation

➤ Manufacturer/distributor

➤ Order number/UPC

➤ Price, with mathematical-value operations

➤ Subject/genre

➤ Year produced

➤ Year released

As you can see, the database is searchable enough to satisfy almost any demand. Citations include a great deal of information. The standard view of an entry includes the following:

➤ Title and year released

➤ Genre

➤ Color or black-and-white and length

➤ Cast

➤ Description

➤ Awards

➤ Manufacturer/distributor

➤ Rights

➤ Format/price/ISBN

➤ Status

The rights information is a relatively new addition. This field contains one of the following:

➤ Home

➤ Group

➤ Closed circuit

➤ Cable

➤ Broadcast

➤ Nonprofit

➤ MRA

As if all this wasn't enough, the disc contains over 1500 full text reviews gleaned from *Variety* magazine. What a resource for the video operator! We cannot imagine doing business without this product.

The Oxford English Dictionary, Second Edition

Oxford University Press	
Operating System:	Windows 3.1
Class:	Language database
Search and Retrieval:	Proprietary
Updates:	No
Subscription:	No
Purchase:	Yes
Licensing:	Single user and networks

This one application has done quite a lot to popularize CD-ROM technology. Even the most computer-illiterate, when told that the entire text of the venerable *Oxford English Dictionary* can be squeezed onto one disc, can see that CD-ROM technology is truly amazing. The people at Oxford painstakingly transferred the entire text, including its foreign and phonetic characters, to the Windows-based Oxford English Dictionary, Second Edition disc (see fig. 7.18). They then surrounded the dictionary with an extremely flexible and powerful search engine and topped it off with excellent export and printing capabilities.

You can searches for words—either headwords or words in the entire text—phrases, quotations, or authors of quotations. Etymological searches can be performed as well. You can save the results of searches to disk for later use or exported them to disk files. Printing from the program is also supported, and you even have the option of changing the font in which characters are printed.

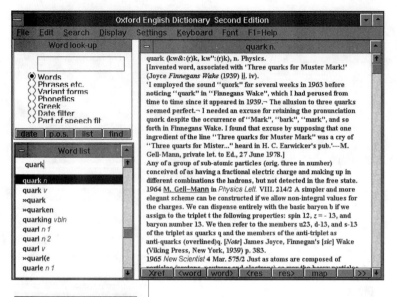

The Oxford English Dictionary is more malleable and usable than its printed cousin—not to mention over 10 pounds lighter.

RECOMMENDED

The searches don't stop with the interface, however. You can build extremely complex Boolean nested searches, save them into editable scripts, and even submit the scripts to the search engine. These scripts can be saved;

if you ever have to perform similar searches, it's an easy matter to edit the old script and submit the new one.

This scripting power allows you to perform such tasks as finding all references to Mars within any quotation by any author before 1900 but after 1600 and only if the quote also contains the word *heaven*.

For all its power, grace, and utility, the Oxford English Dictionary is not for everyone, however. The price is steep, so only serious professionals need apply. Although the cost of developing the disc must have been high, Oxford University Press would do well to cut the price—to perhaps half its current list—to sell many more of them and recoup the initial investment many times over.

We suspect that other extremely comprehensive dictionaries are in development now, and that, despite its honorable lineage, the Oxford English Dictionary may have some competition on CD-ROM.

Beacon: The Multimedia Guidance Resource

Macmillan New Media	
Operating System:	DOS 3.3 or above
Class:	Career database
Search and Retrieval:	Proprietary
Updates:	Annual
Subscription:	No
Purchase:	Yes
Licensing:	Single user

The Multimedia Guidance Resource is more than a resource for selecting colleges. The guide is a computer-assisted tutor for helping students select an appropriate college or university (see fig. 7.19). The Beacon set comes with a video of instruction on how to use the CD-ROM application, a pair of headphones, and the CD-ROM itself. After watching the video, students can easily boot up the software and be on their way to choosing a college.

After perusing an initial set of menus, the software can ask a variety of questions concerning students' preferences in attending college: do they want to attend a two-year or four-year institution? Public or private? What size school will they feel most comfortable in?

From these and scores of other questions, Beacon gradually narrows the search through its database and arrives at a suitable list for the student to consider. Once the list is made, the student can print it or browse through detailed descriptions of each of the candidates.

In addition to a thorough description of each institution's resources, emphases, locale, and atmosphere, the database contains valuable admission information, guidelines, and deadlines.

Beacon is the perfect high-school guidance counselor's friend; it almost eliminates the need for the countless catalogs, brochures, and bulletins that crowd counseling offices. Students find the impartial and impersonal computer program less threatening or pressuring, perhaps, than their counselor or parents.

Barron's Profiles of American Colleges

LRI	
Operating System:	Windows 3.1
Class:	Academic institution database
Search and Retrieval:	Viewer
Updates:	Annual
Subscription:	No
Purchase:	Yes
Licensing:	Single user

**HIGHLY
RECOMMENDED**

LRI's Profiles of American Colleges disc is excellent. Although not as much of a guided tour as the Beacon disc, LRI excels in search and browsing features. The Windows-based Viewer interface makes quick work of copying and pasting relevant information into a word processor or to a printer (see fig. 7.20).

Barron's outline format lends itself to free-form searches. A student or counselor can easily navigate the sections of the disc.

Barron's Profiles of American Colleges includes tips on selecting a school, factors that most schools consider during the application process, and detailed information on each of the more than 1,500 colleges and universities included on the disc. When you click on the map icon, you pop up a map with the location of the college. A few of the major colleges have photos on disc too. Some university-approved admissions forms are also included.

Because this application doesn't tie itself too tightly to a particular format, students, teachers, and even parents find Barron's Profiles of American Colleges an extremely helpful and informative disc. Its reasonable price (less than $100) makes it very attractive to the home and school environments.

Healthcare Discs

The single entry in this category is a comprehensive resource for physicians. Whether they own and operate their own small practices or are part of a large medical center, physicians will find that this timely database makes quick references and research an easy task.

Physician's MEDLINE is an informative bibliographic disc that allows physicians to keep up

**HIGHLY
RECOMMENDED**

Physician's MEDLINE

Macmillan New Media	
Operating System:	DOS 3.3 or above
Class:	Medical database
Search and Retrieval:	BRS
Updates:	Quarterly
Subscription:	Yes
Purchase:	No
Licensing:	Single user

on all current medical techniques, discoveries, and research from dozens of journals (see fig. 7.21).

The Physician's MEDLINE disc is updated quarterly. You can search the disc by author, publication date, keywords, or any text. You can browse through compiled lists of search results, print them to disk, or send them to the printer.

An affordable way for doctors to search for the information they need—without subscribing to all that they don't need—Physician's MEDLINE is a great resource for small or large practices.

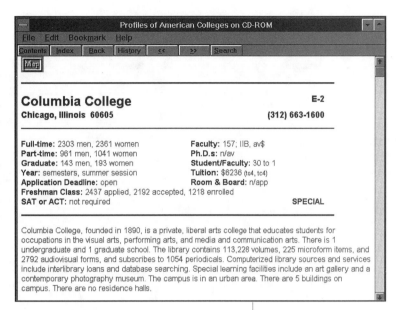

FIGURE 7.20, top

Barron's Profiles of American Colleges is a perfect home or school program: it's thorough and very affordable.

FIGURE 7.21, bottom

Physician's MEDLINE keeps any practice up to date with the click of a keyboard.

Chapter 8

CD-ROM for Home Reference and Education

Without a doubt, the revolution of CD-ROM technology will have its greatest impact where you live—at home. With a CD-ROM drive and a modest investment in software titles, you can equip your family with resource, reference, and educational tools unheard of a few years ago. Your library of discs, in a physical span of no more than 6 or 8 inches, can hold materials that rival—or surpass—the holdings at your local library. Regardless of your interests or educational requirements, CD-ROM titles are now available to enrich your home-based work and your children's education.

This chapter explores some of the latest applications and gives you an idea of the merits and capabilities we found in installing, testing, and using the following CD applications for your home.

About This Chapter

This chapter provides an overview of the capabilities of home and educational software. The variety of products available for home and educational use is great—as you can see from the sheer length of this chapter, which presents only a sample of the titles out there. This chapter takes you on a tour of some of the better applications available. **For information about additional home and educational titles, start by looking at Appendix C, "Additional CD-ROM Software Titles."**

EXPLANATION
MPC

MPC is an acronym for Multimedia PC and refers to a specification for multimedia-capable personal computers that was written by a consortium led by Microsoft. This specification describes the minimum performance levels and equipment a PC must have to run an MPC application correctly. The original spec called for an 80286 processor, which was widely regarded as a mistake by those not involved in drafting the standard. The latest revision requires a minimum of an 80386SX processor. MPC machines and applications can be distinguished by the MPC logo—the letters *MPC* with the image of a CD in the center of the *M*.

Encyclopedia Discs

The encyclopedia is a natural for CD-ROM, and to be expected, more than a few are already on the market. Look at the advantages of an electronic encyclopedia:

➤ Occupies a mere 1/4 inch of bookshelf space, as opposed to 2 to 4 feet for the bound and printed version.

➤ Contains hypertext links to any document or related term.

➤ Documents, pictures, and maps can be printed and carried anywhere.

➤ Provides sound and video in addition to photographs.

➤ Searches take seconds rather than minutes.

➤ There are no multiple volumes to deal with.

➤ Has virtually limitless search capabilities. You should closely scrutinize the capabilities and operating system requirements of these valuable reference materials to determine which best suits your needs. Make sure that you buy an encyclopedia for the environment you and your family work in the most. For example, if you do all your word processing and most of your computing in Windows, an **MPC** encyclopedia makes the most sense. If you use your machine mostly for DOS applications, look more closely at DOS multimedia encyclopedias.

Like printed encyclopedias, CD-ROM encyclopedias have a wide range of content and depth of coverage. Some are best suited for families with younger children (there are fewer articles than are contained in a full-blown set of encyclopedias but they cover the basics very well). Others rank up there with their printed counterparts and contain tens of thousands of full-length articles, complete with maps, charts, and illustrations.

Compton's Interactive Encyclopedia

Compton's New Media	
Operating System:	Windows 3.1
Interface:	Compton's Smartrieve, Windows-based mouse, and text
Multimedia:	Video, animation, sound, color graphics
Audience:	12 years and up
System Requirements:	MPC-compatible machine

HIGHLY RECOMMENDED

Compton's Interactive Encyclopedia is virtually all an encyclopedia on CD-ROM should be. Its interface is easy for children to use, yet powerful enough for adult-strength searches and retrievals (see fig. 8.1). Button bars along the right side of the screen enable you to open indexes to graphics, sounds, atlases, slide shows, animation, videos, and more; a search box lets you specify any phrase or word for easy access to articles. Search results are presented in an indexed list; you merely highlight the appropriate article, click on it, and off you go.

Articles are displayed in great-looking, easy-to-read, Windows-based fonts, with margin icons that represent pictures, charts, maps, and videos. Clicking on an icon displays the multimedia element. Also in the margins are useful related-article icons for easy cross-references. Words with **hypertext** links or extensive cross-references to other segments of the encyclopedia are highlighted. Click on the word and away you go to the cross-referenced material.

One of the handiest features in Compton's Interactive Encyclopedia is its virtual Workspace. A miniature representation of open windows in a grid appears in the lower-right corner of the application. You can add multiple searches, videos, and articles to these miniature windows and skip back and forth among

FIGURE 8.1

Compton's encyclopedia has all the multimedia bells and whistles, including full-motion video and sound—as well as over 32,000 in-depth entries.

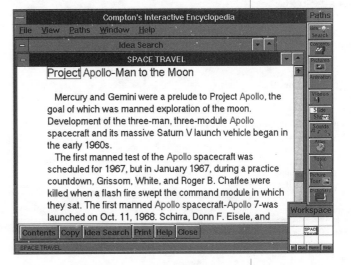

Hypertext

A hypertext document is an electronic document that attempts to overcome the inherently linear nature of the written word. The traditional problem with printed documents is that a cross-reference—say, to another chapter—requires you to interrupt your reading and search it out. With a hypertext link, you need only click on a highlighted word to instantly display the cross-reference. In the book you are now reading, this very margin note is an attempt to provide something similar in a printed format.

The New Grolier Multimedia Encyclopedia

Let's face it—all CD-ROM encyclopedias are good. Grolier's, however, stood out when we took into consideration a few key points. The interface was easy to use and very fast when compared to the other applications. This one encyclopedia can be used by adults and children with equal utility—we didn't find that to be true with some of the other encyclopedias. This encyclopedia is for the entire family.

them by clicking on the grid. This feature is especially useful when you are researching a number of different—or related—topics and want to go back and forth quickly without resorting to menus or searches. The number of virtual windows you can keep open is limited to the amount of memory you have on the machine. If you exit Compton's Interactive Encyclopedia with any virtual windows open, it asks whether you want to save the Workspaces—an excellent way to resume work right where you left off.

The Workspaces are also ideal for multiple users. You, your spouse, and the kids can all keep your own searches and articles in separate Workspaces, each saved and ready to resume when the application is fired up again.

This product's article depth and quality are superb. To give you an example, the encyclopedia contains an article on manned space flight that is well over 16 pages—not including its many pictures, videos, and sound bites.

The full-motion video is handled through Video for Windows and runs without a hitch on small or large screens attached to a 486-33 machine. Slower systems produce smaller video windows, but should reproduce just fine. A handy index of videos and animations makes it easy to browse through these exciting features with the click of a mouse.

If you have a diverse group of reference hounds in your household, this multimedia encyclopedia is the best one around. It's easy for children in junior high and above to use and powerful enough to be a constant reference for adults.

The New Grolier Multimedia Encyclopedia

Grolier Publishing	
Operating System:	DOS 3.1 or above, Windows 3.1, Macintosh
Interface:	Text, menus, mouse
Multimedia:	Video, animation, sound, and color graphics
Audience:	12 years and up
System Requirements:	
For Windows:	MPC-compatible machine
For DOS:	VGA or better display and sound card

The depth of the Grolier encyclopedia is equal to that of Compton's and may even surpass it in some technical areas (see fig. 8.2). The interface is extremely easy to use. Particularly impressive are its search capabilities: it stands head and shoulders above the competition. With three-level Boolean search support and adjustable word-proximities searches, virtually everything in the book is a mere keystroke or two away. The ability to search for captions and pictures is another rare bonus among multimedia encyclopedias.

The New Grolier Multimedia Encyclopedia contains over 33,000 articles, making it a full-fledged electronic brother to the bound volumes you may be used to. In the latest version, over 7,000 articles are new or revised, covering all the major events in the former Soviet Union and Eastern Europe.

Maps, charts, animation, and full-motion video are also bountiful and easily accessible through a toolbar across the top of the screen. The video sequences run smoothly in the Video for Windows screen, and a handy icon indicates where related articles exist throughout the text, pictures, and videos.

Other major features in this package are its new Knowledge Tree and Timeline features. With Knowledge Tree, you are presented with a gradually narrowing hierarchy of knowledge that lets you browse the encyclopedia in ways you've never before been able to do. For example, the initial "tree" lists Arts, Science, History, and so on. Clicking on Arts takes you to a subgroup: Architecture, Literature, and so on. The Timeline feature lets you walk through the encyclopedia according to time segments, beginning at thousands of years B.C. Once you click on a time segment in the time line, articles relating to that period are listed.

A Bookmark feature makes it easy to leave numerous marks for related articles or to resume work later. When you choose Bookmark

from the menu, you see a list of available bookmarks; a simple click takes you there. Although the Bookmark feature is not as useful as Compton's virtual Workspace feature, it certainly is a handy and well-designed plus to this application.

The DOS version of this encyclopedia carries over many of the features of the Windows version by using menu selections rather than icons. The DOS version is nearly on par with the Windows version as far as its usability and implementation of sound and video goes. This DOS-based encyclopedia is definitely the one to get—no second thoughts required. Only one caveat: animation is not available in the DOS version.

Grolier has delivered a top-notch encyclopedia here. Its features don't overwhelm the user, yet are available whenever you need them. The articles are well written and plentiful, and the use of pictures and animation is well implemented. The speed of this application is also impressive: searches for individual articles and cross-links are noticeably faster

FIGURE 8.2

The Grolier encyclopedia comes in a number of "flavors": DOS, Macintosh, and Windows MPC versions are available.

than with other multimedia encyclopedias. Its support for a variety of operating systems is admirable; virtually any home computer, therefore, has access to this great encyclopedia.

Encarta

RECOMMENDED

Microsoft Corporation	
Operating System:	Windows 3.1
Interface:	Text, menus, mouse
Multimedia:	Video, animation, sound, color graphics
Audience:	12 years and up
System Requirements:	MPC-compatible machine

FIGURE 8.3

Microsoft's Encarta is a visually impressive multimedia exploration of the encyclopedia.

Microsoft's Encarta is an ambitious entry in the CD-ROM encyclopedia race (see fig. 8.3). Of all the encyclopedias tested, Encarta has, by far, the most extensive multimedia displays—sound, video, animation, and graphics are virtually everywhere you turn in this book. The Viewer-based front-end is easy to use and handy for searching; hypertext cross-references throughout the book make browsing for extensive knowledge easy.

The only problem with Encarta is the quality of its contents. It appears that Encarta has fewer entries and shorter and less complete articles than do many competing encyclopedias. This will, no doubt, be remedied in later editions. Still, the use of multimedia and its superior interface make Encarta a strong contender for your home-reference purchase.

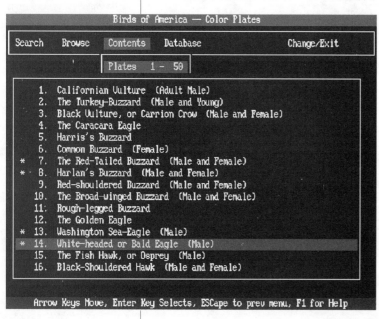

Software Toolworks Multimedia Encyclopedia and MPC Encyclopedia

Software Toolworks	
Operating System:	DOS 3.1 or above, Windows 3.1
Interface:	Menus, text
Multimedia:	Video, animation, sound, and color graphics
Audience:	12 years and up
System Requirements:	
For DOS:	VGA or better display
For Windows:	MPC-compatible machine

For the bulk of the features and usability of the Software Toolworks Multimedia Encyclopedia—either the DOS or Windows version—refer to the description of the Grolier encyclopedia, earlier in this chapter. Essentially, Toolworks is distributing earlier versions of the Grolier product under their name; you'll frequently see this package bundled with MPC upgrade kits and made available by drive distributors that offer low-cost software titles when you buy CD-ROM hardware (see fig. 8.4).

Although the price is right, the Software Toolworks Multimedia Encyclopedia is probably not the most current Grolier version available. Check with a distributor or Software Toolworks to find out precisely how their version measures up with the current Grolier title. This product is an excellent value, however, whether the package comes bundled with a drive or comes directly from the distributor.

FIGURE 8.4

The Software Toolworks Multimedia Encyclopedia.

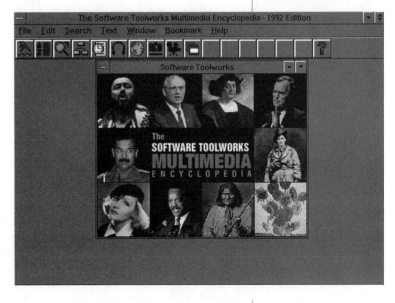

Desktop Libraries and General-Reference Discs

If you find yourself groping for dictionaries, almanacs, and other far-flung reference works while you're involved in your work, you might want to keep one of these discs permanently parked in your CD-ROM drive. By exploiting the full capacity of CD-ROM discs, publishers can pack whole collections of reference works onto one CD, making desktop libraries and general-reference applications a perfect companion to business, scholarly, and everyday writing.

Software Toolworks Reference Library

RECOMMENDED

Software Toolworks	
Operating System:	DOS 3.1 or above (also runs under Windows)
Interface:	Text, menus
Multimedia:	
Audience:	14 years and up
System Requirements:	640K memory

The Software Toolworks Reference Library is a virtual powerhouse of useful references, all on one CD. Look what's included:
➤ *Webster's New World Dictionary of Quotable Definitions*
➤ *Webster's New World Dictionary*
➤ *Webster's New World Thesaurus*
➤ *The New York Times Public Library Desk Reference*
➤ *Dictionary of 20th Century History*
➤ *The National Directory*
➤ *Lasser's Legal and Corporation Forms for the Small Business*

That's a lot, and all of it is top-notch. You select which domain—or book—you want to access through a handy menu system. Once inside a book, you can use wild-card and Boolean searches to retrieve material. The interface allows you to print items to disk or to the printer and to cut and paste into your word processor; there's a configuration option that tells the application where you keep your word processor.

The New York Times Public Library Desk Reference is always handy: you can settle disputes, such as how many home runs Babe Ruth hit in his career, and you can find mundane but useful information, such as how to remove oil stains from silk.

What makes this disc a real standout for small businesses is its legal-forms segment. Virtually all small-business contracts are included; all you need to do is fill in the particulars and go. *The National Directory* is also a great minireference to have: within seconds you can search the database for addresses and phone numbers of all major businesses, institutions, and government offices.

The disc's interface also keeps a running, saved tally of your session searches, making it easy to skip back and forth with ease. You can mark entire texts, segments of texts, or lists for printing or cutting and pasting.

This reference is indispensable for the small businessperson and is also handy around the house. The almanac and dictionary are some of the best, and these alone may be worth the price. The Software Toolworks Reference Library was very well-behaved in a DOS window under Windows 3.1, and its DOS-alone performance was outstanding. This product is particularly great if you mainly use DOS applications and it coexists wonderfully in a Windows environment, too.

Multimedia Bookshelf '93

Microsoft Corporation	
Operating System:	Windows 3.1
Interface:	Windows Viewer 2.0, text, and menus
Multimedia:	Sound, animation
Audience:	12 years and up
System Requirements:	MPC-compatible machine

Microsoft's Multimedia Bookshelf is a perfect complement to your home-based office (see fig. 8.5). If you work in Windows, you need this CD. Microsoft has packed this one disc with all of these pieces:

➤ *The American Heritage Dictionary*
➤ *The Concise Columbia Encyclopedia*
➤ *Bartlett's Familiar Quotations*
➤ *Roget's II Thesaurus*
➤ *The Hammond Atlas*
➤ *World Almanac*

If you're writing a speech, business proposal, or presentation or one of the children is working on a term paper, tuck the Multimedia Bookshelf into your CD-ROM drive. The volumes included on the disc are some of the best references available today—and Microsoft made them one step better than their printed counterparts by including multimedia aspects in all volumes. *The American Heritage Dictionary*, for example, includes a pronunciation icon—simply click on the icon to hear the word pronounced. *The Concise Columbia Encyclopedia* has animations of biological and natural processes such as the life-cycle of volcanoes and the workings of the human heart.

Using sound to its advantage is exploited in *Bartlett's Familiar Quotations* where some poetry and verse is spoken—in many cases by the authors themselves. Sample musical-instrument sounds grace the dictionary as well, and the almanac contains narrative in appropriate places.

Because Microsoft's Multimedia Bookshelf is a Windows program, you can cut from the

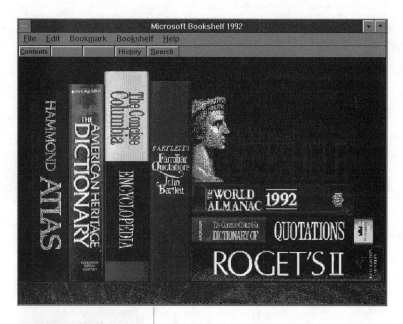

ponents from any Window application is just a hotkey away.

The 1993 edition has been updated to include events in Eastern Europe and the former Soviet Union—from brand-new maps in the atlas to almanac and encyclopedia articles.

Don't expect the encyclopedia to compete with the full-blown versions (such as Grolier's and Compton's) described earlier in this chapter, but it's a serviceable and useful companion piece in this suite of reference materials; it'll answer most everyday questions you might need when covering general topics.

This is a must-buy for Windows users.

Other Reference Discs

This section introduces a grab-bag of discs that can be useful—provided that you have an interest in the discs' topics. Film, magazine articles, consumer information, and a multimedia children's dictionary fill out the miscellaneous discs covered in the following sections.

FIGURE 8.5

Microsoft's Multimedia Bookshelf '93 is the perfect Windows sidekick as you plow through your work at home—or in the office.

RECOMMENDED

references and paste into your documents; you can also export clips of dictionary and encyclopedia graphics elements simply by pointing and clicking them into your work document. And with the convenient Viewer Quickeys installed, calling up any of the com-

Roger Ebert's Home Movie Companion

Quanta Press	
Operating System:	DOS 3.1 or above (also runs under Windows)
Interface:	Folio (text, menus)
Multimedia:	N/A
Audience:	Secondary school and up
System Requirements:	VGA or better display

So you're about to make yet another trek to the video store, but you've run out of rental ideas. Pop Roger Ebert's Home Movie Companion into your CD-ROM drive to get the lowdown on films from every genre, period, and category (see fig. 8.6).

What makes this application better than a reference—and it's great for that, too—are Ebert's reviews, reprinted on the disc. Before you rent *Plan Nine from Outer Space*, get Ebert's capsule review. The CD-ROM contains all the printed material of Ebert's popular book and, like its printed counterpart, updates are issued every year.

Also included are a number of Ebert's essays and interviews in full text. Print them and enjoy at your leisure (remember that you print them to disk and retrieve them into your word processor to change their formatting or typeface).

The Folio interface, a menuing system and front-end, is the best there is for DOS; The Home Movie Companion disc is easy to search because it uses the Folio interface. For example, you can combine search criteria to narrow down your selections.

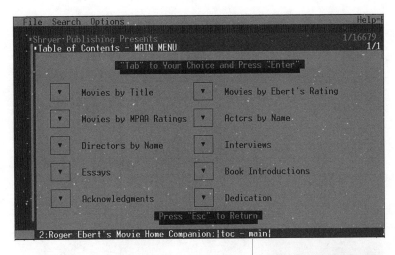

The initial menu presents you with choices such as Essays, Interviews, and Movies by Ebert's Rating; you take it from there. Although a mouse isn't required, it's helpful, especially if you want to mark blocks of texts or sections of interviews and essays.

This is a great CD just to browse—as much for Roger's reviews as for unearthing overlooked movies and avoiding some potential rental disasters. The movie-phile in your family will not want to be without this disc.

Cinemania

Microsoft Corporation	
Operating System:	Windows 3.1
Interface:	Viewer
Multimedia:	Sound, color photos
Audience:	Secondary school and up
System Requirements:	MPC-compatible machine for sound

FIGURE 8.6

Check out Roger Ebert's Home Movie Companion before you check out another video.

HIGHLY RECOMMENDED

MultiMedia Gallery

Gary Lockwood and Keir Dullea plot, while HAL watches in the background, in 2001: A SPACE ODYSSEY.

© 1968 Turner Entertainment Co. All rights reserved.

Although Microsoft's Cinemania can't compare to Roger Ebert's movie-lover's guide in-depth reviews or search capabilities, this Windows application gets high marks for a great interface and the inclusion of some nice multimedia touches (see fig. 8.7).

Cinemania has a tremendous bibliography of films available. You can search by title, genre, actors, directors, or in some cases, screenwriters. By using a "list function," you can browse a category and tag films to add to a list; multiple lists are supported. This function makes it easy, for example, to compile a quick hit list of science-fiction movies and then print it out.

Other sections of the application are biographies of important actors, actresses, directors, and other movie notables; the *Baseline Encyclopedia of Film* contains articles on studios, specific Hollywood trends and trend-setters, and essays on particular films. The Glossary option explains movie terminology; if you've always wondered what *film noir* means, the glossary can help you out.

The Gallery portion is a multimedia compendium of still photos from key films and sound bites of dialogue. Stills are represented by a movie camera, and sound by a microphone icon. When accessing any of these items, you can hyperlink to related articles by clicking on highlighted text areas. And using the Walkman-like control box that has radio buttons makes navigation easy for even the most computer-phobic.

Although the sum of Cinemania's parts make up an impressive whole, this application could benefit from more detailed reviews and better search capabilities—like those found in Roger Ebert's Home Movie Companion. If future upgrades expand the areas of coverage a bit and update the database regularly, this could be the only movie and video guide you ever need. For now, Cinemania and the Home Movie Companion together make the ultimate in movie reference.

Consumer Information

Quanta Press	
Operating System:	Windows 3.1
Interface:	Menus, text
Multimedia:	Sound
Audience:	College and up
System Requirements:	MPC-compatible machine for sound

This is the entire Pueblo Colorado Consumer Information pamphlet collection straight from Uncle Sam to CD-ROM (see fig 8.8) Quanta Press has done a good job compiling the data onto one CD with a very usable interface. Searches are limited, however, to browsing through the index or searching for keywords.

Key articles contain narrated introductions, accessed by clicking on the sound icons where appropriate. Not all articles contain narration, however, and few of the articles are entirely narrated. If you've wondered about the best life-insurance plan for your needs, for example, this CD can call it up for you in seconds. Other topics include health, conservation, consumer rights, and gardening tips. Here are some other highlights, particularly useful to small businesses:

➤ Patent procedures and rights
➤ How to incorporate a business
➤ Business insurance
➤ Credit protection and rights
➤ Retirement annuities explained and compared
➤ Tax advice on a variety of topics
➤ Buying surplus government properties

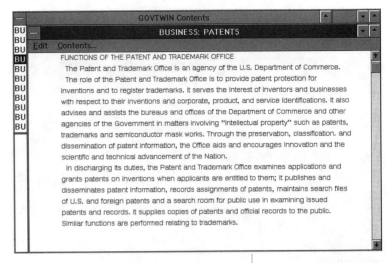

An extensive section on child care and education—nearly 50 pamphlets—focuses on everything from early childhood development to stimulating a child's creativity and learning abilities.

If you've ever been tempted to send away for the catalog and want the best in free government information, save the postage and aggravation of sending away for individual pamphlets; this CD-ROM has them all.

FIGURE 8.8

The Government's Consumer Information pamphlets debut on Quanta's Windows-based CD-ROM.

Sports Illustrated CD-ROM Sports Almanac

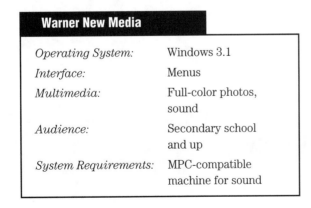

Warner New Media	
Operating System:	Windows 3.1
Interface:	Menus
Multimedia:	Full-color photos, sound
Audience:	Secondary school and up
System Requirements:	MPC-compatible machine for sound

HIGHLY RECOMMENDED

For The Record • Year by Year

Scorecard | Find | Again | Table of Contents

FIGURE 8.9

Relive a year's worth of sports on the Sports Illustrated CD-ROM Sports Almanac.

The main table of contents gives you plenty of options: NCAA basketball and football; pro baseball, basketball, hockey, and football; horse and motor racing—the list goes on. Each option branches off to the year's review of the selected sport. Within that sport subsection, you can perform keyword searches to look up favorite teams, players, coaches, and so on.

Another main-menu choice brings you to the statistics section where you can search or browse through the complete statistics for any given sport. The Profiles menu option contains full biographies on over 500 important sports figures. The Awards section is a comprehensive database of major sports awards dating back to 1931. Who won the third Superbowl? It's just a mouse click away.

Other main-menu items include a picture gallery of the year's best *Sports Illustrated* photos, obituaries for the year, and a section covering miscellaneous sports, such as bicycling and marathons.

Sound adds a dimension that the paperbound version obviously lacks, and the CD requires no installation whatsoever—simply click on the start-up batch file and go.

If you have a sports fanatic in the house, this is a perfect gift CD—all the quality, information, and excitement of *Sports Illustrated* without the paper.

This CD is better than a full year's subscription to *Sports Illustrated* in many ways. How could you possibly look up all the photos and articles of Michael Jordon in a matter of seconds with all those printed back issues? Although not all the articles or pictures from the previous year are on the CD (the swimsuit edition isn't included, for example), many are—particularly those concerning key sporting events—and the full-color photos look great on a VGA monitor (see fig. 8.9).

Macmillan Dictionary for Children

Macmillan New Media	
Operating System:	Windows 3.1
Interface:	Toolbook
Multimedia:	Animation, color graphics, sound
Audience:	Kindergarten through grammar school
System Requirements:	MPC-compatible machine

HIGHLY RECOMMENDED

Only a CD-ROM product can pull off this wonderful version of the old reference essential, the dictionary. The Macmillan Dictionary for Children, written and produced especially for children with help from Public Broadcasting Service (PBS) and Macmillan, demonstrates the pure utility—and fun—that CD-ROM can deliver to the learning experience (see fig. 8.10).

The dictionary's interface is clean and unconfusing—a must for the younger computer users in the house—and the variety of ways you can search for words can't be found in its printed counterpart. Children use the Go To function by typing a word or part of a word to go directly to that section of the dictionary. Guide List and Word List menu choices make for easy browsing and narrowing of word choices, providing users with alphabetized lists.

The multimedia aspects of this product really make it shine. Not only is the word in question pronounced when you click on it, but nearly every word in that word's definition can be pronounced as well, helping your child build his or her vocabulary even further. In addition, words with alternative pronuncia-

tions are spoken one after the other, in order of preferred pronunciation.

Children have over 12,000 words at their disposal, and they'll have fun just browsing and clicking on unfamiliar words. Some words, where appropriate, have sound effects; for example, you hear a *beep* when you click on

FIGURE 8.10

Children use an animated icon—Zak—to navigate the Macmillan Dictionary for Children.

Dictionary for Children

Multimedia

Macmillan

Dictionary

the word *beep*. Visual illustrations are plentiful as well, with 1,000 full-color pieces of artwork and not merely drawings.

If all that weren't enough to get your child more interested in language, the Macmillan Dictionary for Children contains three dictionary games: a spelling bee, hangman, and word search. Zak, the dictionary's ever-available tour guide and game partner, adds a playful touch whenever possible. Zak directs children to further explore aspects of the book they might overlook; Zak is like having a fun-loving teacher at your child's call.

If you have young ones in the house and have wondered how you can get them to become more comfortable with the computer, the Macmillan Dictionary for Children gives you the perfect "excuse" to teach them some basic computing skills.

This product is a sure winner. What better way to heighten your children's interest in language?

Health Discs

Ever since Dr. Spock's baby-care book entered the households of America (and probably well before that), home health books have been perennial bestsellers. No doubt that CD-ROM health books will also do well: they're crammed with information, explanation, and in most cases, are heavily illustrated and animated.

RECOMMENDED

Mayo Clinic Family Health Book, Interactive Edition

Interactive Ventures	
Operating System:	Windows 3.1
Interface:	Hypertext
Multimedia:	Sound, pictures
Audience:	12 years and up
System Requirements:	MPC-compatible machine

This CD-ROM is just what its title says: a book. It's the hypertext version of the Mayo Clinic Family Health Book; the text of the book has been made into a hypertext document (see fig. 8.11). In hypertext, references to other material in a document are made with hot links—that is, you click on specially highlighted text to "pop up" definitions, illustrations, or other information.

The Mayo book, in paper form, is an excellent reference. The hypertext, multimedia version adds the versatility of a computer database to the high quality of the basic information. Unlike paper books with their limited indexes, computerized books have unlimited search capabilities. Finding references to any particular word is as simple as typing it in a dialog box.

The book covers basic health issues from infancy to late adulthood. It also covers diseases, first aid, and how to stay healthy. The heaviest use of multimedia is a narrated guide of the human anatomy.

The Mayo Clinic Family Health Book is an excellent example of the power of computerized books—and it is still just a first-generation attempt.

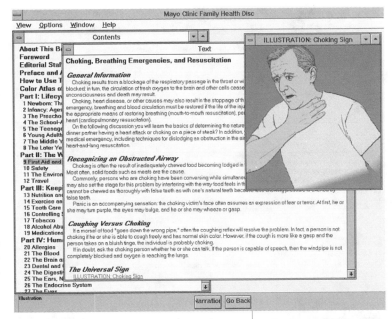

The Family Doctor

FIGURE 8.11

The Mayo Clinic Family Health Book by Interactive Ventures.

RECOMMENDED

Creative Multimedia Corporation

Operating System:	Windows 3.1, DOS 3.3 or above, and Macintosh (on same disc)
Interface:	Toolbook
Multimedia:	Color graphics, sound
Audience:	Secondary school and up
System Requirements:	VGA or better display

The Family Doctor is a good general reference for the average family (see fig. 8.12). When you want just the quick facts and don't want to get bogged down in excessive detail, the Family Doctor is a perfect health reference to have around. It's an updated and expanded version of Dr. Allen Bruckheim's popular printed book: most topics are handled in a question-and-answer format.

From the main menu, you can search for topics by using a three-level Boolean search capability—three levels of IF, THEN, NOR,

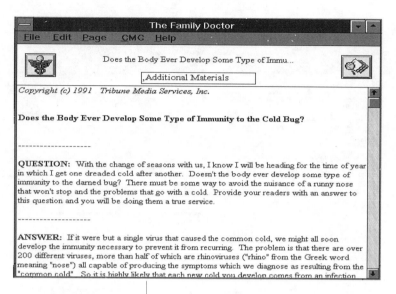

The Family Doctor
File Edit Page CMC Help

Does the Body Ever Develop Some Type of Immu...

,Additional Materials

Copyright (c) 1991 Tribune Media Services, Inc.

Does the Body Ever Develop Some Type of Immunity to the Cold Bug?

QUESTION: With the change of seasons with us, I know I will be heading for the time of year in which I get one dreaded cold after another. Doesn't the body ever develop some type of immunity to the darned bug? There must be some way to avoid the nuisance of a runny nose that won't stop and the problems that go with a cold. Provide your readers with an answer to this question and you will be doing them a true service.

ANSWER: If it were but a single virus that caused the common cold, we might all soon develop the immunity necessary to prevent it from recurring. The problem is that there are over 200 different viruses, more than half of which are rhinoviruses ("rhino" from the Greek word meaning "nose") all capable of producing the symptoms which we diagnose as resulting from the "common cold." So it is highly likely that each new cold you develop comes from an infection

tedious. The writing is clear, informative, and easy to digest.

Also from the main menu, you can access the gallery of illustrations that accompanies the articles. All illustrations are high-resolution color bitmaps that reproduce well on-screen and on the printer. Over 300 such illustrations appear throughout the book—a useful visual aid for explaining complicated procedures and diseases.

The main menu also gives you access to a prescription drugs database. With data on over 1,600 prescription drugs, this section is valuable to all patients.

Medical terms—often tongue twisters—are pronounced for you with the MPC version (DOS and Mac versions do not provide pronunciations). To round out its features, the CD has an extensive human-anatomy guide, updated health booklets, and listings for national health resources such as support groups and information agencies and institutions.

FIGURE 8.12

The Family Doctor takes a question-and-answer approach to health information.

AND, and OR conditions. Your search results are presented in list format—simply click on the ones you want to view. All full-text articles and illustrations are done in an easy-to-read font, and none of the articles is overly long or

Vital Signs

Texas Caviar	
Operating System:	Windows 3.1
Interface:	Menus, text
Multimedia:	Sound
Audience:	Preschool children and up
System Requirements:	MPC-compatible machine

The Vital Signs application tries to bring the whole family into the picture. For example, you'll find segments that range from how to brush your teeth to how to perform a breast examination. Unlike the other CD-ROM health references described in this section, this disc places much of its emphasis on preventative medicine and education, and although its information is useful, this CD is not a complete home medical guide for that reason.

The main menu consists of iconic representations of a man, woman, child, baby, and an elderly person. As you expect, you can search the indexes of these gender-specific and age-specific categories; you also can perform global searches for information.

Sound accompanies many of the well-produced instructional segments. The segments for smaller children make this a good disc to buy for them alone.

Another great feature of Vital Signs is its bilingual narration and text; when you install this disc, you choose between Spanish and English. Besides making vital information available for the Spanish-speaking population, budding Spanish students will get some valuable practice by using Vital Signs in its Spanish format.

History and Current-Events Discs

For researching history and current events, powerful indexing and cross-referencing tools are a must; CD-ROM technology frees you from the restraint of paper and offers full-text searches impossible with traditional books and reference sources. The representative CD-ROMs described in the following sections range from a history of the world to a photo pictorial of President Clinton.

History of the World
Bureau Development's product is a spectacular example of what CD-ROM can do for historical research. Containing thousands of original documents, History of the World places no restraints on how information can be searched. Bureau Development provided more than just a collection of documents and a search engine: they licensed documents not in the public domain and provided analysis to make understanding the results of your search easier.

History of the World

Bureau Development, Inc.	
Operating System:	DOS 3.3 or above, Macintosh
Interface:	Menus
Multimedia:	Pictures, CD audio
Audience:	12 years and up
System Requirements:	VGA or better display

The History of the World CD-ROM is an excellent example of Bureau Development's forte: the compilation of hundreds of public-domain documents into a usable database on a single disc (see fig. 8.13). The History of the World organizes more than 1,000 diverse documents, pictures, maps, and sounds into six different databases:

➤ **Titles.** This database allows you to access documents by title and includes two

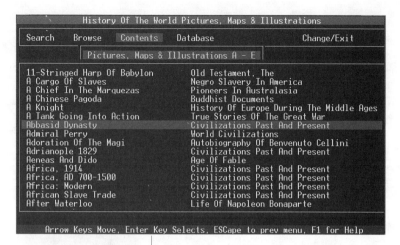

FIGURE 8.13

History of the World is a masterful example of how to best use CD-ROMs in reference applications.

copyrighted text books from Harper Collins Publishers: *Civilization: Past and Present* and *Civilization: A World Phenomenon.*

➤ **Themes.** This arrangement of titles provides thematic access and is divided into ten categories:

  Economics
  Exploration, Discovery, and Travel
  Overviews and Narratives
  People and Letters
  Philosophy
  Politics
  Religion
  Science, Technology, and Inventions
  Society, Culture, and the Arts
  War, Conquests, and Battles

➤ **Regions.** This database arranges titles according to parts of the world, including the following:

  Global
  Africa
  The Americas
  Asia
  Europe
  The Pacific Region

➤ **Time Periods.** The editors of this database chose seven time periods that they felt arose naturally from history:

  Origins of Civilization: 0 to 500 BC
  The Classical Period: 500 BC to 500 AD
  The Post-Classical Period: 500 AD to 1450
  The World Shrinks: 1450 to 1750
  The Industrial Period: 1750 to 1900
  The Twentieth Century: 1900 to today

➤ **Pictures, Maps, and Illustrations.** History of the World offers more than 600 illustrations, including photos and maps. You can view all of them on any VGA adapter. Political cartoons supplement articles concerning political history, and photos document historical events.

➤ **Speeches and Eyewitness Accounts.** Thanks to the CD-ROM's capability to store audio, Bureau Development has included speeches and eyewitness accounts gleaned from the national archives in Washington, D.C. These historical sound clips range from portions of a speech by Adolph Hitler to audio from the first landing on the moon. You can hear the audio by connecting speakers or headphones to the audio output of any CD-ROM drive.

Although the majority of the material on this CD-ROM is in the public domain, the editors of this disc did not just lump a bunch of material together and give it a title. It is well organized and includes useful introductory material that enhances the value of the raw data.

History of the World uses Disc Passage as its retrieval software, and although it is not the most sophisticated retrieval software in terms of search capability, it has enough capacity to do some decent searches on the huge collection of documents stored on the CD.

Although the History of the World has a list price in excess of $700, it is a must-have item for libraries, serious home schoolers, and anyone who needs to do historical research.

CD Sourcebook of American History

Infobases International	
Operating System:	DOS 3.3 or above (also runs under Windows)
Interface:	Menus and mouse
Multimedia:	Pictures
Audience:	12 years and up
System Requirements:	VGA or better display for images

CD Sourcebook of American History will probably become one of your favorites. Not only does this disc provide access to a library of nearly 1,000 source documents, it provides a very sophisticated menu and search system that performs complex searches very quickly.

Any student of American history will salivate over this disc. Titles include such pivotal documents as *The Federalist Papers*, de Toqueville's *Democracy in America*, Franklin's autobiography, and other complete texts. Also on this disc are hundreds of source documents such as treaties, founding documents, first-person accounts from historical figures like Revere and Columbus, inaugural addresses of all the presidents, and famous speeches. In all, almost 20,000 pages of material are at your fingertips.

The CD Sourcebook of American History also includes VGA images of important documents, political cartoons, photographs, broadsheets, and the like. These images are accessible through a separate viewer (included)—the only part of the program that cannot run in a DOS box under Windows.

This volume is the first of two to be released and covers up to World War I. Anyone researching or interested in American history is missing out on a great opportunity without this disc.

The Presidents: It All Started with George

National Geographic, Educational Media Division	
Operating System:	DOS 3.1 or above (also runs under Windows)
Interface:	IBM Linkway
Multimedia:	Color graphics, sound
Audience:	Primary-school children through high-school students
System Requirements:	Sound card

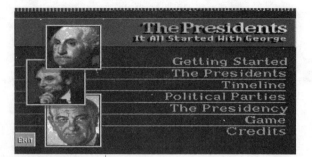

FIGURE 8.14

National Geographic's The Presidents is a great learning tool for American history.

Each president is introduced with a brief quotation and vital statistics such as his home state and election percentages. Under the president's portrait are options for further articles on his term, and pictures or videos with informative captions and narrations. The disc contains over 1,000 photographs and portraits and 33 video clips. Famous presidential speeches are recorded on the disc as well. Other narrations explain the process of elections, government, and the office of the president itself. The electoral college is explained, for example, by a series of graphics, charts, maps, and step-by-step narration.

If your children are studying the presidency, the national election process, or just need to get interested in this country's history, The Presidents: It All Started with George is an excellent hook into our past (see fig. 8.14). Clearly designed for children—and well done for this audience—the easy interface and visually stimulating photos, videos, and timelines make learning about the presidential office a joy for kids.

The main menu lets you choose from presidential portraits, a presidential timeline that highlights events in each president's term, explanations of the national electoral process, and even a presidential trivia game designed to test your knowledge and researching capabilities.

The trivia game included on the disc isn't just a rote question-and-answer game. You can go off to do research on the disc to find the right answer and return once you find the proper information.

Clearly designed for students, this CD-ROM provides a painless and enjoyable way for children to learn about this country's forefathers—from George Washington to George Bush. You'll be looking over your kids' shoulders and will even find the trivia game a challenge for yourself.

Time Table of History: Business, Politics, and Media

Xiphias	
Operating System:	DOS 3.1 or above (also runs under Windows)
Interface:	Menus
Multimedia:	Color graphics
Audience:	Secondary school and up
System Requirements:	VGA or better display

The Xiphias series of time tables isn't what you'd call a tremendous resource for full-text research, but it does an excellent job teaching the chronology and basic histories of certain knowledge areas. The Business, Politics, and Media disc, for example, has all major historical events laid out in either timeline or timebase format. The timebase format is an event-by-event walk-through of history; the timeline format allows you to view segments of time with all events laid out along the segment (fig. 8.15 shows the timeline format).

Navigation is easy, the interface is very easy to use and learn, and the ability to view separate timelines gives you a unique perspective on history. You can choose an advertising timeline, for example, that shows the appearance of the first classified ad, the first advertising agency, and other advertising milestones.

Xiphias has other Time Table discs besides the Business, Politics, and Media one described here, including a science and technology disc.

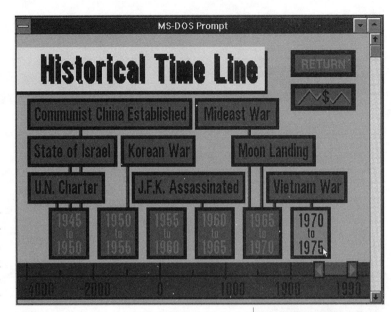

The Twelve Roads to Gettysburg

Ebook, Inc.	
Operating System:	Windows 3.1
Interface:	MacroMind Windows Player
Multimedia:	Color graphics, photography, sound
Audience:	Secondary school and up
System Requirements:	MPC-compatible machine

FIGURE 8.15

Timelines make history more accessible, and Xiphias' Time Table of History is a great CD-ROM adaptation of a popular history-teaching concept.

RECOMMENDED

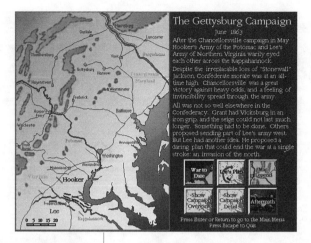

FIGURE 8.16

Ebook's excellent Civil War disc, the Twelve Roads to Gettysburg, uses multimedia to its best advantage.

Ebook, Inc. has a whole series of great multimedia titles, and Twelve Roads to Gettysburg is among the best (see fig. 8.16). Students can get a look at this momentous turning point in our nation's history with this in-depth study of Gettysburg—before, during, and well after the battle. The information on this disc is worthy of any full textbook on the topic.

The main menu of this multimedia excursion allows you to examine these options: Campaigns and Strategies, The Battle, Gettysburg Today, and the Armies and Individuals of both the Confederate and the Union.

The Campaign segment gives you an over-view of the Civil War up to the time of the Battle of Gettysburg, where the forces stood before the battle, and what each general had planned for the ensuing battle. Detailed maps of the area pinpoint troops and geographical features of the surrounding terrain.

The Battle option, the most impressive in the entire series, walks you through the battle day by day with animated troop movements depicted on the topographical maps. Each battle segment is expertly narrated.

The Gettysburg Today section is a tour of the present memorial battlefield site. The Armies and Individuals segment gives you a detailed account of troop strength, armaments, and profiles of key officers.

The entire disc is lavishly embellished with daguerreotypes, photos, and portraits set against background music from the period. Histories of the compositions are included too.

This CD-ROM is an expertly orchestrated application. Even if you have little initial interest in the Civil War or Gettysburg, the compelling presentation made with this CD will have you riveted in no time at all. It's an excellent introduction—or review—to an important segment of this nation's past.

Time Almanac 1992

HIGHLY RECOMMENDED

Compact Publishing	
Operating System:	DOS 3.3 or above, Windows 3.1
Interface:	Menus, text
Multimedia:	Video, color graphics, sound
Audience:	Secondary school and up
System Requirements:	VGA or better display, sound card

Time Almanac 1992 is an excellent representation of *Time Magazine*, the most popular news magazine ever published (see fig. 8.17). You can browse through weekly editions of *Time Magazine* that go back four years, which makes this disc a great alternative to your local library's microfilm collection. With the application's search feature, you can search the entire text database for weekly articles and for milestone events captured in the disc's Decades section.

The magazine's reputation for great maps, charts, and illustrations is carefully preserved here with stunning clarity on a VGA monitor. Even the video clips play smoothly, and there is great narration and live sound from actual events that take the printed version one or two steps better. All text articles include links that let you jump to related articles, charts, or illustrations. While searching, you can list up to 255 results. Utilities from the menu bar let you mark blocks of text, take notes, list your notes, print items to disk, or send items to the printer.

As if its full-text articles and videos weren't enough, the disc also includes world and United States almanacs with statistics, maps, and important organizations and political events.

The NewsQuest game included on this disc is a great challenge, putting all other current-

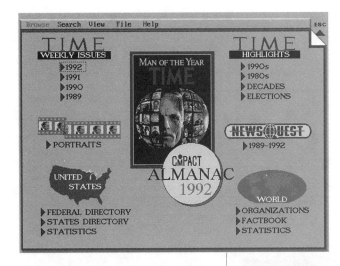

events trivia games to shame. You can perform searches from within the game (that is, you can "cheat" by researching the disc's contents). Although you may use the disc for reference, the game portion is a tool for giving your kids a more thorough education in current events. Registered users receive special upgrade pricing on new editions.

By the time you read this, Compact Publishing will be shipping a Windows MPC version of the Time Almanac 1992. For DOS or Windows, this CD-ROM is an invaluable addition to your home library.

FIGURE 8.17

Time Almanac 1992 gives you all the top events from 1992—and many in the past—in full multimedia.

Desert Storm: The War in the Persian Gulf

Warner New Media	
Operating System:	Windows 3.1 with MPC extensions
Interface:	Toolbook
Multimedia:	Color graphics, sound
Audience:	Secondary school and up
System Requirements:	MPC-compatible machine

RECOMMENDED

ToolBook - DSTORM.TBK

FIGURE 8.18

Desert Storm: The War in the Persian Gulf takes you step by step through the war with dramatic photos, text, and narration.

Admit it. You—like all Americans—were glued to the TV for as many waking minutes as possible during the Persian Gulf War. If you missed anything major, it's on this CD in text, sound, charts, maps, history, and background. Desert Storm: The War in the Persian Gulf

walks you through the entire campaign, day by day, from military, political, and media perspectives (see fig. 8.18).

From the main menu, you're presented with a week-by-week timeline of the war. Select a week, and you have choices of listening to audio clips, reading *Time Magazine* coverage of the war, examining a selected editorial, or studying public-opinion polls and other timely aspects from that segment of the war, including battle preparations, strategies, maps, and charts.

Pay particular note to the photo galleries presented for each week. The *Time* photographers took some of the most spectacular shots of the war, and the best of the best are included on this disc. Audio clips range from SCUD missile attacks to political briefings to Arab protests.

If you want a record of the war, purchasing this disc is far better than collecting newspapers and magazines. The information here is well-organized, concise, and easy to use.

Clinton: A Portrait of Victory

Warner New Media	
Operating System:	DOS 3.1 or above
Interface:	Menus
Multimedia:	Color graphics, sound
Audience:	Secondary school and up
System Requirements:	VGA to Super VGA display, sound card

Essentially a pictorial record of the 1992 election from the Clinton camp's perspective, Warner New Media's Clinton: A Portrait of Victory presents black-and-white pictures accompanied by stereo narration of key events during Clinton's campaign, nomination, and election.

No mouse or fancy menus are needed; you merely press keys to navigate a series of high-quality photos and unfolding stories. This product was turned out in record time: a few short months after the election. This may foreshadow the things to come in multimedia applications—instant multimedia news and portraits. If prices are kept reasonable, and this one is, these miniature CD-ROM documentaries may prove extremely popular in years to come.

Space Adventure

Knowledge Adventure, Inc.	
Operating System:	DOS 3.1 or above
Interface:	Menus
Multimedia:	Video, color graphics, sound
Audience:	Primary through secondary school
System Requirements:	VGA or better display, sound card

Science Discs

You'd think that science CDs would be flying out of developer's doors at this time. What better medium could possibly exist for reference and instruction in topics such as astronomy, physics, chemistry, and the like? As of this writing, however, few general-reference and educational CDs are available in this topic area. The ones that are available, however, are mighty impressive, particularly those developed by Knowledge Adventure, Inc., who have spent great development effort putting together some of the most engaging CD-ROM applications seen in *any* category.

AWARD OF EXCELLENCE

Space Adventure

Knowledge Adventure's use of animation, video, sound—and most importantly, solid historical facts and figures—make this application a spellbinding adventure for any child interested in US manned space flight. Multiple screens and cross-references give children an excellent way to discover and learn new information about space and space exploration.

SATURN
  Beyond Jupiter comes Saturn, a giant planet famous for its brilliant rings. Saturn is similar to Jupiter, but 16 percent smaller in diameter and one-third as massive. It has many moons, but only one of them, Titan, is large. Titan is especially noteworthy because it's

Saturn and Satellites

If it relates to space, it's probably on this disc. From Stonehenge to space colonies, kids can track topics, branch off to interesting related articles, watch videos, and hear narration nearly every step of the way.

The main screen allows kids to choose from a variety of topics or to search for their own keywords or phrases. Among some of the main-menu icons they can choose from are a reference library, an overview of our solar system, the galaxy, our planets, and moons and space exploration.

A rotating globe lets kids zoom in on geographical areas, such as Germany, and click on various sites related to space, such as the development of the V-2 rocket. Animations concerning everything from the big bang to space stations are viewed in a VCR-like controlled window, with test links to other subjects. A timeline at the bottom of the screen lets kids explore space in history as well, giving them a bird's-eye view of the creation of the solar system, for example.

The narration is great, the animation is top-notch, and the videos and games captivate even the most computer-wary kid. If you have kids, buy this disc.

FIGURE 8.19

Your kids can blast off into the cosmos with Knowledge Adventure's Space Adventure multimedia learning disc.

Knowledge Adventure stakes out some important education turf with its Space Adventure title (see fig. 8.19). The videos, the interface, and the sheer fun of learning are captured in all their titles, but their talents are put to particularly good use in Space Adventure.

Dinosaur Adventure

HIGHLY RECOMMENDED

Knowledge Adventure, Inc.	
Operating System:	DOS 3.1 or above
Interface:	Menus
Multimedia:	Video, animation, color graphics, sound
Audience:	Primary through secondary school
System Requirements:	VGA or better display, sound card

Dinosaurs are popular with kids. The Dinosaur Adventure disc will be a smash hit (see fig. 8.20). From the opening video of dinosaurs clashing to the incredibly detailed reference section off the main menu, this adventure gives kids more dinosaur than they can handle in one sitting.

What's particularly impressive about this disc is its multilevel layout: there are games, reference materials, and articles for nearly every age level. The narrations for the indepth animations and color graphics are excellent—even a first-grade student can get a lot from these articles.

The main menu allows kids to use a reference guide to look up their favorite topics, examine varieties of dinosaurs, hunt for fossils, or view a timeline of dinosaur history, including theories on their extinction.

Most kids, regardless of age, are enthralled with the dinosaur videos. Knowledge Adventure "hired" full-scale robotic dinosaurs for these segments and filmed them on various locations in California. The results are impressive, right down to the tyrannosaurus roars.

A particularly fascinating section of the program lets you examine the globe for fossil digs: click on one and get a picture and history of the site, the fossils found there, or both.

You and your kids will be impressed with the quality of this and other Knowledge Adventure products. They do things right and

seem to understand what many educators have forgotten—the sheer joy of learning. This disc will keep your kids engaged for hours, and they'll return to it many times, each time exploring yet another facet of the program.

All Knowledge Adventure products come with a guarantee that if you or your child are not fully satisfied with the product, you can return it for a refund—a guarantee that probably hasn't had any takers.

FIGURE 8.20

Dinosaur Adventure gives kids more dinosaur than they can handle in one sitting.

Murmurs of Earth

AWARD OF EXCELLENCE

Murmurs of Earth

Warner New Media combines print, audio, and data to produce a unique offering in the form of Murmurs of Earth. This title presents the information that appeared on the side of the Voyager space probe. When Voyager was launched, an optical disc—similar to a CD—went with it to educate anyone who might encounter the probe about the people and practices of Earth. Carl Sagan and others wrote the book accompanying the Murmurs of Earth disc to explain and describe Voyager's interstellar record. This is a great collector's item for any space fan.

Warner New Media.	
Operating System:	DOS 3.3 or above, Macintosh
Interface:	Canned presentation
Multimedia:	Audio, images
Audience:	12 years and up
System Requirements:	VGA or better display

Murmurs of the Earth is a record of the information sent into interstellar space with the Voyager space vehicle. It was sent in the form of a laser-disc plaque, along with what were hoped to be universally decodeable instructions for decoding the disc. The instructions started with a hydrogen atom and ended with a diagram of the timing characteristics of the disc's signals (assuming that some very intelligent extraterrestrials would find this probe).

Encoded on the plaque was an array of images, sounds, and messages from the people of Earth. These items fell into ten categories:

Pictures (118)
Some Beethoven
Greetings from then president, Jimmy Carter
A list of members of the United States Congress
Greetings from the secretary general of the United Nations
Greetings in 54 languages
Greetings from the United Nations
Greetings from whales
Sounds of Earth
Music of the world

The CD-ROM portion of Murmurs of Earth is just a small portion of this product. This product is really a multimedia book/CD set. Murmurs comes in a box designed to keep. It holds a 270-page book, *Murmurs of Earth*, published by Random House; a small book of images sent back by the Voyager space probe; and a 2-CD jewel box. This presentation provides a unique combination of traditional printed text, CD audio, and CD-ROM. It is a must-have item for space and technology aficionados and is worth having even if you can't take advantage of the CD-ROM data portion of the product. This may be the first "coffee-table" CD-ROM.

The View from Earth

Time-Life	
Operating System:	Windows 3.1 with MPC extensions
Interface:	Menus
Multimedia:	Pictures, sounds, animations
Audience:	7 years and up
System Requirements:	MPC-compatible machine

HIGHLY RECOMMENDED

On July 11, 1991, the most closely scrutinized solar eclipse in history darkened the mountaintops of Hawaii. Time-Life's View from Earth is a nicely done MPC-based multimedia presentation about the eclipse and each of its players: earth, moon, and sun (see fig. 8.21).

After a television-style introductory segment, you can choose a presentation from one of the four topics (Earth, Moon, Sun, and Eclipse). The presentations are professionally presented and narrated. Also available are a glossary and an extensive library of information.

This disc is worth having if you're interested in its contents. It also is an excellent example of a well-done MPC application—smooth and nice to look at.

Creation Stories

Warner New Media	
Operating System:	Windows 3.1 or above
Interface:	Menus
Multimedia:	Color graphics, sound
Audience:	Primary school and up
System Requirements:	MPC-compatible machine

RECOMMENDED

FIGURE 8.21

This Time-Life look at our solar system and a day-in-the-life of an eclipse is a great source for exploring space.

The Creation Stories multimedia CD from Warner New Media does more than fascinate with its compellingly narrated stories; it's also a reference book on creation myths and facts. From cultural myths to examples in fiction, this world tour of the many faces of our genesis is much more entertaining than you might at first imagine (see fig. 8.22).

Tales from Mozambique to the Old Testament are narrated against a background of full-color photographs and original and historic artwork. The accompanying music adds the right atmosphere to each story. In addition to the narrated stories is a fine collection of text-only stories you can read.

The only complaint you may have about Creation Stories is that it copies many of its pictures to an available hard drive during play, taking up disk space you thought wasn't needed. However, it is a well-produced and unique work of artistry.

Adult-Literature Discs

Despite all the high-tech computer paraphernalia, jargon, and chipsets in your life, you probably still enjoy some old-fashioned plea-sures, like reading a good book. You may not want to hear this, but CD-ROMs have invaded that formerly hallowed turf too; now you can read a good "text file" of Sherlock Holmes, Dickens, Aristotle, or Shakespeare, all in the comfort of your favorite Super VGA monitor. The truly conservative can print out the text files and continue reading in the traditional manner. But like it or not, these CD-ROM versions of some of the world's classics have a number of distinct advantages, for both casual readers and serious scholars:

➤ Less than 1/2,000 of the shelf space is required for the disc as for housing the same amount of text in bound paper form.

➤ Pages aren't subject to tearing or disfigurement.

➤ You can choose the typeface, spacing, and type size you want—excellent for visually impaired readers.

➤ You can search, index, and compare text for a variety of investigative pursuits into author style, language anomalies, syntactical patterns, and usage.

And if all that isn't enough, the CD-ROM versions of collected works are often a fraction of what printed editions can cost. Like them or hate them, CD-ROM collections of literature are growing quickly, for a number of economical and marketing reasons.

First, the publication of collected classics on CD-ROM is a low-cost proposition from a copyright standpoint. Dickens and members of his estate are long gone, and his work has passed into the public domain—as is the case with virtually every author collected on popular classics sets of CDs. That's not to say that the CD is cost-free; there is still the enormous burden of scanning in and carefully proofreading the electronic version of the text to ensure that it matches the author's original published version. But only a compendium of public-domain literature is feasible to publish on one CD-ROM. Imagine the cost, for example, of securing the rights to and publishing the entire works of major American writers from the 1950s and 1960s. If costs could be brought down somehow, both scholars and avid readers would be ecstatic at the prospect of receiving contemporary works on CD. Some efforts are already in the works to do just that. Byron Priess, a new multimedia publishing firm in Brooklyn, has begun to "adapt" some popular works to the CD medium, with stunning results.

Second, other marketing strategies recognize that many works that can be collected and published on CD-ROM have a wide and lasting appeal, both for the sheer joy of reading them and their invaluable use in research and education. Shakespeare's plays, for example, have lasted not simply because the works are deemed literature, but because their themes, characters, and drama still enlighten our human condition today. An illuminating examination of the human spirit and our common dilemmas is the true measure of a work's lasting value.

You can only wonder what William Shakespeare would have thought of having his voluminous handwritten scripts—his entire life's work—reduced to a string of zeros and ones across a disc no bigger than the palm of his hand. But forget the technology; his work does still exist—whether it's in printer's ink or bits and bytes—and that, after all, is what matters.

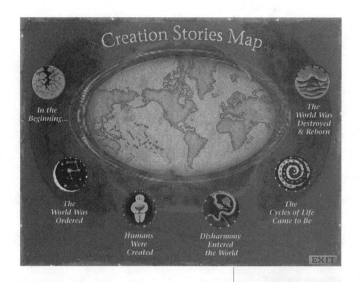

FIGURE 8.22

A world full of world-creation stories are told on Warner New Media's Creation Stories.

AWARD OF EXCELLENCE

Library of the Future, 2nd Edition

World Library's Windows-based version of the Library of the Future is a literature buff's dream come true. Extensive cross-referencing of over 600 megabytes of the world's greatest literature, Windows cut-and-paste features, and the ability to mark and retrieve text at a later time make this a hypertext version of your own personal classics library.

Library of the Future, 2nd Edition

World Library	
Operating System:	DOS 3.1 or above, Windows 3.0 or above
Interface: Menus	
Multimedia:	VGA graphics illustrations
Audience:	Secondary school and up
System Requirements:	VGA or better display

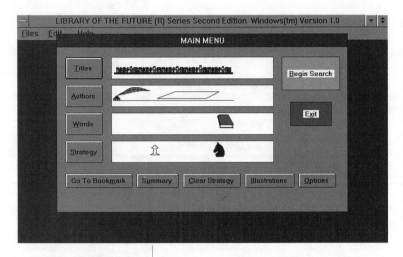

FIGURE 8.23

Library of the Future, Second Edition, in either DOS or Windows, is the literature buff's dream come true.

Library of the Future, Second Edition is amazing, whether you use DOS or Windows (both are included on one disc). It is one thing to compile one of the greatest collections of literature, science, philosophy, drama, and history onto one disc, but World Library didn't stop there; their search-and-retrieval engine is a sheer joy to use and opens up a world of possibilities for both the serious scholar and the casual reader (see fig. 8.23).

First things first. This CD-ROM houses a ton of good stuff: over 2,000 full novels, books, poems, plays—the list goes on and on. In fact, the listing in the CD's pamphlet takes up the most paper for the product (in small type) because there is just so much to list. Try some of these on for size:

➤ All of Shakespeare's plays and sonnets
➤ All of Edgar Allen Poe's works, including critical essays
➤ The works of Aristotle, Plato, Kant, and many more
➤ Frank Baum's Oz trilogy
➤ All of Lewis Carroll's works, including original illustrations

This bulleted list is paltry and doesn't come close to doing justice to the contents of the

disc. But if that were all the disc did—compile some of the greatest works in Western civilization—it would be a mess to find anything properly. Where this application really shines is World Library's Instant Access search-and-retrieval software. You can search by word, subject, phrase, and date in a four-level Boolean search; the search also allows searches for exact phrases, for words a definable number of words apart, or even for words that are whole pages apart. Other search possibilities include searching by category (such as biology, drama, philosophy, and so on), searching by region (such as Asia, North America, and other continents and subcontinents), searching by ages and eras, and searching by country. You can combine any and all of these categories. For example, a search of the category Literature, the region North America, the country USA, and the era 1869 to Present produces a list of authors such as Mark Twain, Herman Melville, and Henry James, as well as their works.

But the search possibilities do not end with the initial interface, as good as that is by itself. After you select a work from a list and begin reading it, you can highlight any word or string of words and perform a hypertext search of the entire disc—and this doesn't take long at all. For example, while reading Poe's "Cask of Amontillado," Steve thought he'd seen a reference to Amontillado wine in one of Poe's lesser-known works, predating this more famous and successful work. By highlighting Amontillado and performing a hypertext search, Steve discovered that, sure enough, *Amontillado* is mentioned in dialogue in Poe's short piece "Lionizing." After you select a title and specify the word you want to find, the hypertext search takes you right to the section where that word is used.

As you might expect, you can mark and print blocks, whole pages, or entire texts. Printing to an ASCII text file enables you to import the work into your favorite word processor and change the typeface and spacing before printing.

If you're a true computerphile, you can read the text on-screen. For those who are truly lazy, you can set the text to scroll automatically as you control the rate. Imagine: you don't even have to turn pages anymore. The Windows version allows you to display up to eight separate works in different windows, making comparisons and multiple text marking nearly effortless.

An additional amenity is the multiple-bookmarks feature: drop a bookmark in a work and pick up where you left off later. The notepad feature lets you mark text with "invisible" margin notes—imagine, truly guilt-free book annotations.

One final touch: World Library includes all original illustrations from printed editions. These images are invaluable in works such as Carroll's *Through the Looking Glass*, Darwin's *The Origins of Man*, and Poe's *Narrative of Arthur Gordon Pym*.

World Library produces a number of other fine titles as well, including the first edition of the Library of the Future, a subset of the works in this second edition; the Electronic Home Library disc, which has 250 titles; and the Murder, Mystery, Magic, and Terror disc, containing 171 horror, science fiction, and occult stories.

The Library of the Future, Second Edition, has something for everyone: history, biology, philosophy, poetry, and on and on. Buy this disc. It's what CD-ROM technology is all about.

Great Literature: Personal Library Series

RECOMMENDED

Bureau Development, Inc.	
Operating System:	DOS 3.1 or above, Macintosh
Interface:	DiscPassage
Multimedia:	VGA graphics, sound
Audience:	Secondary school and up
System Requirements:	VGA or better display

Bureau Development's Great Literature disc takes almost the same approach as the World Library application. Both discs have hundreds of works of literature, many of them overlapping, but this disc has many more poets and poetry selections (see fig. 8.24). If you want more literature—drama, poetry, and fiction—

and less philosophy, this disc may be the right choice.

Great Literature uses the DOS DiscPassage interface, which enables you to search by word, author, subject, or title. You can perform Boolean searches from a submenu, with great flexibility for narrowing your search

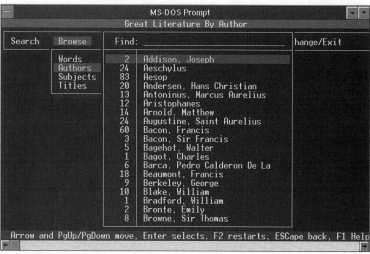

```
─  ┌──────────────── MS-DOS Prompt ────────────────┐ ▼ ▲
   │           Great Literature By Author            │
 ┌─────────┬──────────┬────────────────────────────┬───────────┐
 │ Search  │ Browse   │ Find:                      │ hange/Exit│
 ├─────────┼──────────┼────────────────────────────┼───────────┤
 │         │ Words    │    2  Addison, Joseph       │           │
 │         │ Authors  │   24  Aeschylus             │           │
 │         │ Subjects │   83  Aesop                 │           │
 │         │ Titles   │   20  Andersen, Hans Christian          │
 │         │          │   13  Antoninus, Marcus Aurelius        │
 │         │          │   12  Aristophanes          │           │
 │         │          │   14  Arnold, Matthew       │           │
 │         │          │   24  Augustine, Saint Aurelius         │
 │         │          │   60  Bacon, Francis        │           │
 │         │          │    3  Bacon, Sir Francis    │           │
 │         │          │    5  Bagehot, Walter       │           │
 │         │          │    1  Bagot, Charles        │           │
 │         │          │    6  Barca, Pedro Calderon De La       │
 │         │          │   18  Beaumont, Francis     │           │
 │         │          │    9  Berkeley, George      │           │
 │         │          │   10  Blake, William        │           │
 │         │          │    1  Bradford, William     │           │
 │         │          │    2  Bronte, Emily         │           │
 │         │          │    8  Browne, Sir Thomas    │           │
 ├─────────┴──────────┴────────────────────────────┴───────────┤
 │ Arrow and PgUp/PgDown move, Enter selects, F2 restarts, ESCape back, F1 Help│
 └─────────────────────────────────────────────────────────────┘
```

FIGURE 8.24

Enjoy 1,896 great works of literature on one CD from Bureau Development, Inc.

The main menu also gives you access to the Browse function, which lets you review lists of words, authors, subjects, or titles. The Contents option on the main menu lists all the titles, and you can scroll through and view the list. Because the literature is kept in three databases, the main-menu Database option lets you select the title, author, or type of literature you want to browse.

You can mark blocks of text or tag entire articles for printing. Printing to a text file is supported—just import the ASCII text file into your favorite word processor to change formatting before printing.

Some great features of the Great Literature disc are the VGA illustrations, narration, and musical scores provided for some of the more notable titles.

results by using up to seven search terms. Then you choose the article you want to view from the search results list.

Shakespeare

Creative Multimedia Corporation	
Operating System:	DOS 3.1 or above, Macintosh
Interface:	DiscPassage
Multimedia:	N/A
Audience:	Secondary school and up
System Requirements:	N/A

This disc houses the complete Shakespeare. Absolutely complete. And the plays are in both American and Queen's English, making "translation" or comparison very easy to do. The entire text is indexed—excluding noise words—so looking up any word or phrase in the works is a snap. Seven-level Boolean searches are supported, and you can search from the menu for titles, subjects, or, curiously, the author (see fig. 8.25).

Being able to switch back and forth between American and English versions and to mark and print passages make this CD-ROM a valuable learning tool for students. An extensive glossary in the back of the CD book explains unfamiliar terms, words, and phrases; of course, you can print the entire list.

Shakespeare buffs will love this disc; any student taking a literature course with a Shakespeare component will surely benefit from this application. Besides, the disc is many times less expensive than some of the printed Shakespeare volumes, not to mention that the type isn't too small to read.

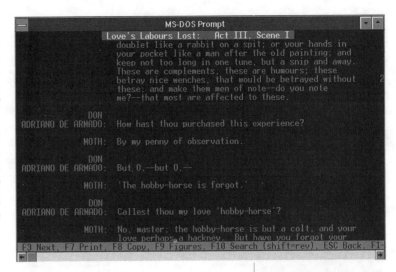

FIGURE 8.25

You can read the entire works of Shakespeare in either the Queen's English or in American English on this CD-ROM from Creative Multimedia Corporation.

Sherlock Holmes on Disc!

Creative Multimedia Corporation	
Operating System:	DOS 3.1 or above, Macintosh
Interface:	DiscPassage
Multimedia:	
Audience:	Secondary school and up
System Requirements:	

RECOMMENDED

Take all of Sir Arthur Conan Doyle's Sherlock Holmes stories—every last one of them—toss in block prints from the earliest editions of the Doyle works, top it off with the complete text of *The Medical Casebook of Doctor Arthur Conan Doyle*, and you have a Holmes-fanatic's dream. Sherlock Holmes on Disc! from Creative Multimedia Corporation is great for printing selected stories, browsing through titles, and discovering how many Holmes stories you've probably missed reading (see fig. 8.26).

What makes this a recommended disc is the *Medical Casebook*—an extensive bibliography and history of the author, presented by

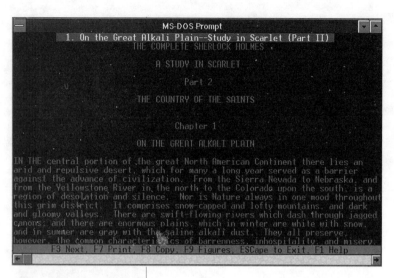

Sherlock Holmes on Disc! presents every Sherlock Holmes story that Arthur Conan Doyle ever published.

RECOMMENDED

Alvin E. Rodin and Jack D. Key. It is a definitive source of information on Doyle's life.

The DiscPassage interface for this disc is similar to other literature titles that use this engine: it allows seven-level Boolean searches; title, word, and subject retrieval; and searches of the individual databases.

The CD-ROM version of these texts is at least as expensive as the printed version, but the printed version doesn't give you the search capabilities or flexibility. Get this as a gift for the mystery-lover in your family.

Monarch Notes

Bureau Development, Inc.	
Operating System:	DOS 3.1 or above, Macintosh
Interface:	DiscPassage
Multimedia:	N/A
Audience:	Secondary school and up
System Requirements:	N/A

All English and literature teachers probably should skip this section. Your biggest nightmare has come true: this one CD contains the complete collection of Monarch Notes—the scourge of literature-class book reports and essay exams. That's right, everything from Chinua Achebe's "Things Fall Apart" to Emile Zola's *Germinal* is faithfully outlined, explicated, and summarized, complete with discussions and essays of major thematic elements (see fig. 8.27).

Professors take heart, though. These guides are not just used for cribbing notes for a book report. The conservative, thoughtful explanations and summaries of some of the greatest literature can be used—truly!—as a great study guide for beginners. And packaging all this literary concentrate on a CD-ROM makes it possible to examine common themes, motifs, and plots across a decade of work.

The DiscPassage software (must all literature programs use DiscPassage?) gives you seven levels of Boolean searches; title, author, and subject queries; and searches on separate databases.

As Jerry Pournelle said when discussing this application in one of his columns in *Byte* magazine, "English teachers and literature professors everywhere will want to get this disc—if only for self defense."

Discs about Animals and Such

What better topic for multimedia CD-ROMs than animals? They're colorful, we love to watch them move, and the range of sounds they produce is amazing. Throw into the mix that most kids simply love the little critters (and the large ones), and you have the basis for a perfect home CD-ROM application.

This section only scratches the surface of this topic. There are dozens of animal and wildlife applications to choose from, with more coming out every day. Some take a traditional reference approach; others use multimedia in a creative and original manner, organizing and presenting materials in a way that only multimedia can.

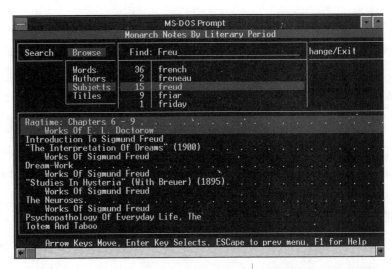

Dictionary of the Living World

Compton's New Media	
Operating System:	Windows 3.1
Interface:	Menus
Multimedia:	Video, color graphics, sound
Audience:	Late grammar school and up
System Requirements:	MPC-compatible machine

FIGURE 8.27

Your English professor should have had this CD—Monarch Notes on CD-ROM.

HIGHLY RECOMMENDED

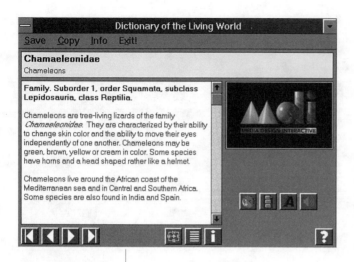

FIGURE 8.28

The Dictionary of the Living World is a thoughtful and successful use of multimedia to illustrate science in nature.

HIGHLY RECOMMENDED

Although its initial menus are a bit disorienting, the Dictionary of the Living World is a superior CD-ROM application (see fig. 8.28). It isn't just a broad zoological overview of animals, it's an entire biological and entomological examination of life on the planet in multimedia format.

The initial index lists the disc's contents in alphabetical order. The list is long—over 5,000 species are covered. You can browse through the list or pull up a search interface that supports four levels of Boolean searches as well as searches for animations, photos, sounds, and videos. The search engine is fast and efficient; even children in mid-grammar school can learn to perform simple searches with little difficulty. Search results are kept in a list you can conveniently return to again and again, or you can erase the search and start over.

This disc's use of multimedia elements is magnificent. Sounds of various fish, fowl, animals, and insects accompany their photos; clicking on the speaker icon gives you a sample. Videos are displayed in a similar way. Videos display well on a VGA monitor, with synchronized sound in some cases. The animations, however, are the most productive. The developers of this application know when to use the proper elements: the animations are instructive and easy to understand, everything that a visual aid is supposed to accomplish. The explanation of chameleon skin-color changes is a fascinating experience.

This disc takes you way beyond a simple visit with our furry friends. The Dictionary of the Living World is a serious—and valuable—learning tool.

The San Diego Zoo Presents...The Animals!

Software Toolworks	
Operating System:	Windows 3.1
Interface:	Menus
Multimedia:	Video, color graphics, sound
Audience:	Late preschool through primary school
System Requirements:	MPC-compatible machine

The San Diego Zoo Presents...The Animals! provides a great trip to the San Diego zoo without the expense of plane fares or wearing out your shoes. The organization of this disc owes its originality to the developers' keen use of multimedia. The main menu is a visual representation of the zoo; you see Rain Forest, Mountains, Temperate Forest, and other habitats (see fig. 8.29). By clicking on a "zone," you are transported to that part of the zoo to examine the animals and their habitats for that region. Videos and still photography are plentiful—with the best quality on our VGA monitor being 320 by 240 pixel resolution. Full-screen videos and photos, although available on a 486 PC, are too grainy, but the smaller sizes look gorgeous.

Of course with animals come sounds, and this disc is full of them, including ambient sounds. When you enter the rain forest section, for example, you hear it drip and echo as a rain forest should. Besides the tours of the various habitats, children can watch and listen to two dozen informative essays concerning the zoo, including visits with zoo veterinarians and a photo essay on the founding of the zoo in 1922.

Packed onto this disc are 2-1/2 hours of audio, in addition to the text, graphics, 1,300 color photographs, and 82 video clips. This CD must be stuffed to the very edges. In fact, more facts, figures, and text are available here than you can find on an unguided tour of the actual zoo itself; over 2,500 articles, descriptions, and scientific data are a mouse click away. The zoo has over 200 animals to visit, so it's a good thing they're captured on CD: you can return as many times as you like, and the gate is always open.

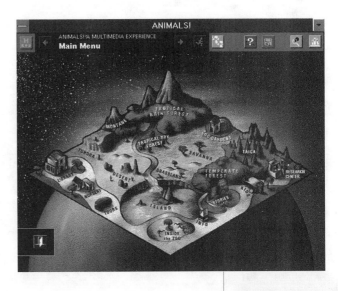

FIGURE 8.29

Although seeing the zoo in person is the best, this disc gives you a great way to visit the San Diego Zoo without leaving your home.

Multimedia Animals Encyclopedia

Applied Optical Media Corporation	
Operating System:	Windows 3.1
Interface:	Menus
Multimedia:	Color graphics, sound
Audience:	Late primary through secondary school
System Requirements:	MPC-compatible machine

The Multimedia Animals Encyclopedia from Applied Optical is long on organization and use of sound for the pronunciation of Latin and popular names of animals, the species, and genus. The interface is easy to use: you can select databases that deal with animal diet, habitat, range, or the animals themselves (see fig. 8.30).

After you've studied a particular animal, you can tag it and assign it to your own personal zoo. Fill up your zoo with the animals you want to revisit and examine them in more detail later.

The program displays animals in full-color VGA illustrations, with extensive descriptions and facts concerning feeding habits, natural habitat, and range of habitation.

FIGURE 8.30

The Multimedia Animals Encyclopedia is thorough, uses sound to great effect, and is easy for young children to use.

RECOMMENDED

Mammals: A Multimedia Encyclopedia

National Geographic Society, Educational Media Division	
Operating System:	DOS 3.3 or above
Interface:	IBM Linkway (menus)
Multimedia:	Video, color graphics, sound
Audience:	Late preschool and up
System Requirements:	VGA or better display

Mammals: A Multimedia Encyclopedia is based on National Geographic's award-winning two-volume *Book of Mammals*. The menu-driven interface is easy to navigate, even for four-to-five-year olds, and the multiple layers of detail and text are a great reference guide for much-older children.

According to the disc's developers, this application includes the equivalent of 600 pages of text and more than 700 full-screen, full-color photos. The photos and videos are the centerpiece of this production, all taken from National Geographic's extensive photo library and numerous nature documentaries. Maps, charts, and quick-fact sheets on animals and their habitats round out an informative and fun-to-use package.

Multimedia Audubon's Birds and Multimedia Audubon's Mammals

Creative Multimedia Corporation	
Operating System:	DOS 3.1 or above
Interface:	DiscPassage
Multimedia:	Color graphics, sound
Audience:	Grammar school and up
System Requirements:	Sound card

Short of spending a fortune for a set of Audubon's original color paintings of the birds and mammals of North America, the two discs, Multimedia Audubon's Birds and Multimedia Audubon's Mammals, sold separately, are a faithful reproduction of the paintings and full text of the original works. In fact, the editor claims that the high-quality VGA images on the discs are taken directly from original first-edition printings of Audubon's work. The book and its color plates are in the exact order in which they originally appeared (see fig. 8.31).

Of course, CD-ROM lets you search by any term or word used in the text, making this collection more than a linear slide show of the Audubon masterpieces. You can browse through the color plates one volume at a time or search for individual species.

The multimedia twist is the addition of bird calls and mammal sounds from a fairly large sample of the book's subjects. Although owning printed versions of these incredible images—in oversized stock, of course—would be preferable to viewing them on a tiny computer screen, these discs are an elegant presentation of John Audubon's artistry.

Children's Literature Discs

The most important things you can do for your children's education is to get them to read and to improve their reading skills. Whether they

FIGURE 8.31

The Audubon series from Creative Multimedia faithfully reproduces the printed versions of these classic nature texts, with a few multimedia extras.

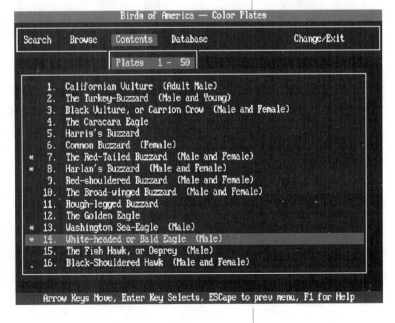

get their information from a hard-bound text, a paperback book, or a CD-ROM database, they'll still be reading. And in this age of information explosion, words are where the information is.

Whatever the medium, look for stories and books that sufficiently challenge your children's skills. Watch their reading progress and suggest books appropriately. Let them explore a number of different types of books—fairy tales, science, contemporary children's stories, and so on. Above all, don't let reading become a chore for them.

About Ebook

The next four applications are produced by Ebook, Inc., a relatively new company in the software business. Their title list is impressive already and is growing each day. As proven with Knowledge Adventure (described earlier in this chapter), Ebook is a company that delivers consistently great products for the home-education audience. Virtually every Ebook title is presented handsomely and uses multimedia effectively; most importantly, Ebook is committed to delivering quality content through their entire product line. Following is a sample of their products, but you should write to the company for a full catalog. As of this writing, the company also was shipping the following titles:

> Aesop's Multimedia Tales
> The Star Child, by Oscar Wild
> Peter and the Wolf

RECOMMENDED

The White Horse Child

Ebook, Inc.

Operating System:	Windows 3.1
Interface:	Modified Viewer
Multimedia:	Color graphics, sound
Audience:	Grammar school
System Requirements:	MPC-compatible machine

This engaging story by Greg Bear is about a young boy and the conflict within his family when his imagination and creativity are awakened by a mysterious elderly couple. The story is told in the first person, from the boy's point of view, and you follow him through a difficult dilemma. There are numerous fairy tales and folks tales and scary tales folded into the overall story, with animations illustrating some of the imbedded tales (see fig. 8.32).

As with all Ebook titles, this one has a table of contents at the beginning. You can go directly to the story, search the story for key words or phrases, watch a short interview with the author, or view the animations.

The disc's interface is extremely easy to use. As your child reads through the story, words that might be unfamiliar are highlighted; clicking on a highlighted word pops open a brief definition box. Your child can read the story from the "page" (the screen) or simultaneously read and listen to the story being narrated by the author.

There's nothing too fancy about *The White Horse Child*, but that's actually one of its strengths. The multimedia elements—the animation and narration—do not detract from the story, which your children will find amusing, thought provoking, and a charm to read. Peppered throughout are enough words and phrases to make reading the book a challenge.

Don Quixote

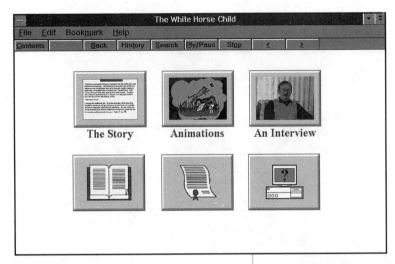

Depending on your child's reading skills, this story should fall into the age range of 8 to 12 years.

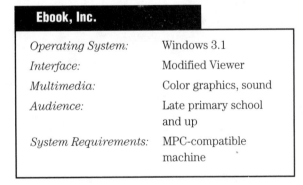

Ebook, Inc.	
Operating System:	Windows 3.1
Interface:	Modified Viewer
Multimedia:	Color graphics, sound
Audience:	Late primary school and up
System Requirements:	MPC-compatible machine

FIGURE 8.32

The White Horse Child, by Greg Bear, is one of nearly a dozen of Ebook's excellent multimedia book products.

At that moment a slight wind rose up and the great blades began to turn. "I don't care how many arms you have!" Don Quixote roared. Commending his soul to his lady Dulcinea, he raised his shield and lunged head-on, striking his lance against the lowest blade of the first windmill. But the blade, gathering speed as it rose, dashed his lance to pieces, lifting both horse and rider high in the air, then hurling them down onto the plain.

Sancho Panza rushed to help them. "Good God!" he cried when he saw that neither Don Quixote nor his horse could move. "I told you they were windmills."

You'll love this full-text multimedia presentation of Cervantes' *Don Quixote* (see fig. 8.33). The text is presented in easy-to-read typefaces, and the illustrations—all in full color—are an imaginative addition to this classic tale. The narration is a professional rendition of Quixote's journey, given with the appropriate flare.

If you've never read Cervantes' *Don Quixote*, this disc provides an excellent way to introduce yourself and your children to this fabulous and hilarious work of literature. Your children will find the "definitions on demand"—pop-up definitions of selected words in the text—a bonus in understanding and enjoying the tale.

A Christmas Carol

Ebook, Inc.

Operating System:	Windows 3.1
Interface:	Modified Viewer
Multimedia:	Color graphics, sound
Audience:	Late grammar school and up
System Requirements:	MPC-compatible machine

One of the primary reasons books endure despite the onslaught of film and video is that readers still respect and admire a well-turned phrase and the idiosyncratic voices of individual writers. To see a film rendition of Charles Dickens' *A Christmas Carol* is one thing—and a good thing—but to read this classic as Dickens wrote it is to experience the story in a totally new way (see fig. 8.34).

Ebook's presentation is superb. You can elect to read the text, read with narration, or read with both narration and period music. You'll also find a picture and music gallery, so that you and your family can replay the holiday carols or view the illustrations.

The best way to use this multimedia application, however, is simply to read the story. Dickens is considered a great author—and for good reason. His wit, irony, and deft storytelling skills are as apparent and enjoyable today as they were in his own time.

As with all Ebook titles, you can perform searches of the text, skip to particular pages and chapters, click on archaic or difficult words to get a pop-up definition, and page through the text at your own pace.

Buy this disc as holiday entertainment for the whole family. By reading along with the text or simply listening to the deft narration, you and your family will undoubtedly find Ebook's adaptation of *A Christmas Carol* thoroughly entertaining and a learning experience.

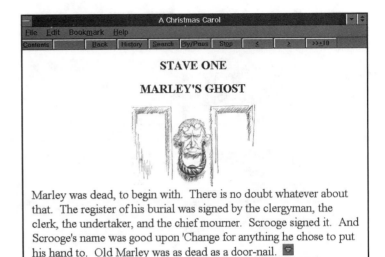

Sleeping Beauty

Ebook, Inc.

Operating System:	Windows 3.1
Interface:	Modified Viewer
Multimedia:	Color graphics, sound
Audience:	Late preschool to mid-grammar school
System Requirements:	MPC-compatible machine

This one Ebook title will do more to entice your child to read than any amount of bribery or cajoling. The lavish layout of the text, the full-color illustrations, and the wonderful musical score from Dean Samuels provide a perfect backdrop for reading this children's fairy-tale classic (see fig. 8.35).

This story—like all Ebook titles—features pop-up definitions of unfamiliar words and the capability to search for words and phrases, making it easy for children to find their favorite parts of this story once they've read it. Judith Jones' narration is wonderful; if you have an early reader, the narration provides

FIGURE 8.34

Charles Dickens' holiday favorite, *A Christmas Carol*, is lovingly presented in this multimedia book adaptation from Ebook.

RECOMMENDED

the perfect way to introduce new vocabulary words and increase reading skills: your child can read along with the narrator.

The illustrations are fantastic—some of them are even animated—and they never detract from the importance of the text. The music is a big plus; the score has the quality of a medieval, wandering minstrel band, which heightens the atmosphere set by the story.

Buy this disc to challenge your early readers. They'll love you for it.

FIGURE 8.35

Children love Ebook's presentation of the fairy tale Sleeping Beauty, in which the multimedia additions are never a distraction from the written text.

HIGHLY RECOMMENDED

Annabel's Dream of Ancient Egypt

Texas Caviar	
Operating System:	Windows 3.1
Interface:	Menus
Multimedia:	Color graphics, sound
Audience:	Late preschool through grammar school
System Requirements:	MPC-compatible machine

Telling a story is one thing, but using it to both entertain and educate is quite another. Texas Caviar's Annabel's Dream of Ancient Egypt is a delightful and educational multimedia trip for your children.

The secret of this story's success is that it operates on many different levels—from the engaging story line of Annabel the cat's difficulties with her sister cats, to the games, puzzles, and history cleverly tucked away into every nook and cranny of this adventure story.

Texas Caviar has done a superb job of mixing fun with learning, and your children will be fascinated with the variety of activities associated with Annabel's story. Among the things children can do is explore the world of Egypt and hieroglyphs, learn about opera, and play with and print hieroglyphic messages.

Many different age and learning levels are covered. In fact, this is a story-game children will return to again and again, building their vocabulary and their listening and learning skills each time.

The great music, animation, and multimedia tools make Annabel's Dream of Ancient Egypt a must for your children's CD-ROM library.

Just Grandma and Me

Operating System:	Windows 3.1
Interface:	Menus
Multimedia:	Animated color graphics, sound
Audience:	Late preschool through grammar school
System Requirements:	MPC-compatible machine

HIGHLY RECOMMENDED

Brøderbund calls their list of children's titles the *Living Book* series—an accurate description. Children interact with the characters, the story, and objects in the animated graphics for a full and fun multimedia learning story. Although Brøderbund advises that Just Grandma and Me is for ages 6 through 10, bright late preschoolers get an enormous benefit from interacting with the pictures, characters, and unique vocabulary-building interface too.

You can set up the story with no narration, allowing advanced readers to read at their own pace, or you can set up the program to narrate the story one page at a time. The story's words are highlighted as the narrator reads, enforcing vocabulary. At any time, the child can click on any word to hear it pronounced—a real boon to teaching reading.

The fun rests not only in the clever and fun writing in this Mercer Mayer story, but also in all the surprises hidden in each frame of the story. Clicking on a bucket at the beach, for example, causes a fish to leap out and splash back into the water; clicking on a tree makes an animated bluebird dive-bomb the roadway and then return to its perch.

This disc also contains an interesting option: you can play it in English, Japanese, or Spanish.

The illustrations, animations, music, and story all combine for a tremendous multimedia storybook. This disc is great fun and a tremendous learning-to-read tool. Buy it for your early readers and let them loose on this brilliant reading adventure.

Arthur's Teacher Trouble

Brøderbund	
Operating System:	Windows 3.1
Interface:	Menus
Multimedia:	Animated color graphics, sound
Audience:	Grammar school
System Requirements:	MPC-compatible machine

Brøderbund does it again: this second title in the *Living Book* series is just as engaging and educational as Just Grandma and Me. Built for a slightly older crowd, Arthur's Teacher Trouble has the same easy-to-use interface and wonderful interactive narration as the other *Living Book* titles.

Your child can run the story as a continuous, narrated animation or in the more fun—and educational—interactive mode. Whether the child chooses to have the story narrated or not, he or she can click on any word in the story to hear it pronounced.

This Marc Brown story of a student with a particularly demanding teacher is funny, instructive, and raises questions many children have about their own classroom experiences. Beautifully illustrated and animated, this Broderbund title is another "must have" for your beginning readers.

Mixed-Up Mother Goose

Sierra Online	
Operating System:	Windows 3.0 or above
Interface:	Menus
Multimedia:	Animated color graphics, sound
Audience:	Preschool through early grammar school
System Requirements:	MPC-compatible machine

Sierra Online is most famous for their adventure games, but they should place a continued emphasis on learning games such as Mixed-Up Mother Goose. This highly successful and imaginative romp through nursery rhyme favorites is a wonderful learning experience for young children (see fig. 8.36). Hopefully, Sierra is developing other titles like this one.

In the opening, the child picks the character who will represent him or her in this adventure to unscramble and assemble the nursery rhymes of Mother Goose.

The animation, narration, and music are all very good, and the oversized icons and easy interface make this learning game easy for very young grammar-school children to play on their own. But you'll want to be there to join in the fun as well.

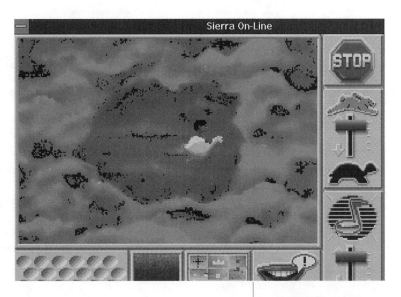

The Tale of Peter Rabbit

Discis Knowledge Research	
Operating System:	Windows 3.1, DOS 3.3 or above, and Macintosh (on one disc)
Interface:	Menus
Multimedia:	Color graphics, sound
Audience:	Preschool
System Requirements:	MPC-compatible machine

It's easy to see why The Tale of Peter Rabbit has won so many awards and recommendations in the short time since its release. Not only is the original story faithfully reproduced in storybook fashion, but this highly customizable storybook telling of Peter Rabbit is an educational dream come true.

First of all, parents can set up the program for a variety of options, depending on the child's experience and reading level. You can set the pace of the narration, for example, allowing very early readers to follow each word at a more suitable pace. Words can be pronounced by syllable, too, making early pronunciation of more difficult words easier to master. Other levels allow you to include designations for the parts of speech, determine whether sound effects should be included, and set the story so that it is read in Spanish.

The original illustrations are reproduced with great effect in 256-color VGA, and the narration is perfect. When readers click on words and objects in the illustrations, the words are pronounced.

Because this storybook is a classic, the multimedia elements make it an even stronger learning tool. The Discis series is great. Please consider all their titles for your home learning and reading library.

HIGHLY RECOMMENDED

Heather Hits Her First Home Run

Discis Knowledge Research	
Operating System:	Windows 3.1, DOS 3.3 or above, and Macintosh (on one disc)
Interface:	Menus
Multimedia:	Color graphics, sound
Audience:	Late preschool through early grammar school
System Requirements:	MPC-compatible machine

Built for a slightly older crowd than the audience of Discis' Peter Rabbit, Heather Hits Her First Home Run includes all the highly customizable options of the other discs in the Kids Can Read series. Those options include syllabic and adjustable rate pronunciation and narration, interactive sound effects, and the capability for parents to save all the options they've customized for their children.

Heather's struggle to make it as a good player on her neighborhood baseball team provides an entertaining and instructional story designed to motivate children. As with all discs

in this series, your child can point to an object, see the word associated with it, and hear the word pronounced.

When a child clicks on a word for pronunciation, that word is automatically added to a recall list. The child can then review this list—and the pronunciations—at any time.

Discis has other discs in the series, including Really Scary Poems for Rotten Kids. After reviewing any of these books, you will look forward to more titles in this innovative and superlative series of children's books.

Language-Instruction Discs

Here's a perfect case for CD-ROM multimedia. How better to learn a language than to hear it being spoken? How better to navigate foreign vocabulary than at your own pace? The two multimedia foreign-language systems discussed in this section are good examples of what's possible with this technology, especially for the foreign-language student in your home. If your children need additional work on their foreign-language skills, these products can help them more quickly assimilate a second tongue.

Learn To Speak...

RECOMMENDED

Hyperglot	
Operating System:	Windows 3.1
Interface:	Menus
Multimedia:	Color graphics, sound
Audience:	Late grammar school and up
System Requirements:	MPC-compatible machine

FIGURE 8.37

The Learn To Speak series from Hyperglot is a great home-study disc for virtually any intermediate learner.

Hyperglot publishes a series of these CD-ROM-based language tutors that are as comprehensive as any intermediate-level language text (see fig. 8.37). You can view or use the CD by starting with its table of contents, which features a parts-of-speech tutorial and a conversational tutorial. You can skip back and forth between the tutorials if you want. For example, you can read up on the common verb forms in French and then take a hyperlink to a narrated conversation that employs many of these constructions.

The depth of coverage is great. The tutorials and conversations are well done, and the use of the CD technology—hyperlinks, search capabilities, and audio narration—is super.

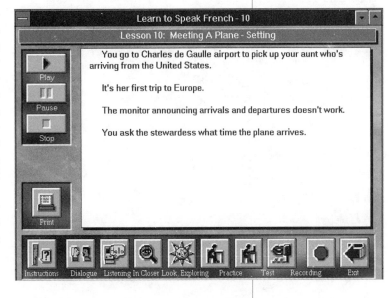

This series is a recommended supplement to any language student's arsenal to become fluent—or conversant—in any of the major languages. The Hyperglot series features language courses in French, German, Spanish, and Italian.

Playing with Language

RECOMMENDED

Syracuse Language Systems	
Operating System:	Windows 3.1
Interface:	Menus
Multimedia:	Color graphics, sound
Audience:	Early primary through beginning secondary school
System Requirements:	MPC-compatible machine

FIGURE 8.38

The Playing with Language series takes an interactive approach to learning, using graphics-based games for positive reinforcement.

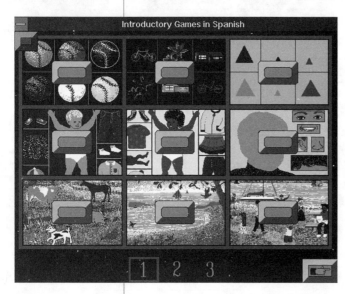

Syracuse Language Systems takes a novel approach to using multimedia to its fullest in this series of language discs. Not meant as a comprehensive, "from the ground up" way to learn a language, this series focuses on improving literacy and cognition in the language your student is mastering (see fig. 8.38).

The games are completely narrated in the foreign language, with instructions and questions spoken in a normal manner; in other words, the narrator doesn't slow down his or her speech for the sake of comprehension. The games themselves are a series of graphic scenarios. For example, a park near a lake shows a number of children in different activities. Speaking in the foreign language, the narrator asks the student which child is sleeping. When the student clicks on the correct child in the picture, he or she is congratulated; if the student misses, the activity of the incorrect choice is narrated, and the original question is asked again.

This disc provides an entirely natural way to learn a language, and when you think about it, it's the way we all learned our native speech. This series of discs is not intended to replace basic language-learning courses; it reinforces and broadens the student's cognitive skills in using a foreign language. Its aim is to remove the word *foreign* from foreign-language learning, and it does a superlative job.

The discs come in a variety of languages, including Spanish, French, and German. In addition, there are various levels of difficulty within each language. You can start out with the disc Introductory Games in Spanish, for example, and then move up to the intermediate and advanced discs, each sold separately.

Music Discs

What a natural! Music instruction, history, and education on CD—the predominate media for music distribution. Of course, the multimedia CD-ROM delivers graphics, stereo sound, and tons of text to round out the music it can deliver. The following CD titles are some of the best music education and reference CDs you can find; in the coming year, look for reference and entertainment CDs of the Beatles, Stravinsky, Mozart, and many others. This segment of the multimedia CD-ROM marketplace might be the fastest growing and most creative of all.

AWARD OF EXCELLENCE

Musical Instruments

Microsoft's Musical Instruments CD may be the most beautiful presentation of any of the software titles we looked at. This encyclopedia includes the pictures and sounds of an enormous collection of musical instruments—from the common penny whistle to the obscure nose flute. The interface, illustrations, and high-fidelity musical samples are superb. You *need* this CD.

Musical Instruments

Microsoft Corporation	
Operating System:	Windows 3.1 with MPC extensions
Interface:	Full Windows interface
Multimedia:	Picture, sound
Audience:	Preschool to adult
System Requirements:	MPC-compatible machine

The beautiful pictures in this CD-ROM presentation come from a very well-done picture book originally published in England—and they translate well to the computer screen (see fig. 8.39). Examples of music and musical timbres cover instruments from the everyday instruments familiar to everyone, to instruments

whose names and sounds you might never hear anywhere other than this CD-ROM.

The information is organized into four formats:

➤ **Families of Instruments.** This section of the disc includes these categories: Brass, Strings, Woodwinds, Keyboards, and Percussion. Each category includes instruments not

normally encountered but classed with the rest in their group.

➤ **Musical Ensembles.** Orchestras, rock bands, wind bands, chamber groups, jazz bands, steel bands, and gamelans are covered, with descriptions of the groups, their instruments, and musical examples.

➤ **Instruments of the World.** Laid out on a world map, this section groups instruments by region. You click on a region and then on an instrument to get detailed information about your choice.

➤ **A–Z of Instruments.** Just what it says– an alphabetical listing of all the instruments on the disc.

If you have children, or any interest in musical instruments yourself, put this disc on your required list. You'll not be disappointed.

FIGURE 8.39

Microsoft's Musical Instruments CD-ROM provides one of the most engaging MPC presentations available.

HIGHLY RECOMMENDED

Composer Quest

Doctor T's Music Software	
Operating System:	Windows 3.0 or above
Interface:	Menus
Multimedia:	Color graphics, sound
Audience:	Late grammar school and up
System Requirements:	MPC-compatible machine

The premise behind Composer Quest is good fun: you're given a fragment of music to listen to and then you're supposed to jump back in time to identify its composer.

The time-machine interface allows you to jump to particular musical periods—Romantic, Classical, Jazz, and so on. Once in the selected period, you can "interrogate" composers, who give you clues about the whereabouts in time of the composer of the mystery piece. These clues are biographical, musical, and historical facts about the era, the composer, and musical history. So although the clues are useful in helping you win the game, you learn a lot about music in the process as well.

The game never takes itself too seriously, and children of all ages will be entertained and challenged at the same time. Besides the game, you can play the music tracks alone or skip along the timelines for interesting biographies and musical history. Music students of all ages will find this disc amusing and informative.

RECOMMENDED

Jazz: A Multimedia History

Compton's New Media	
Operating System:	Windows 3.1
Interface:	Modified Viewer
Multimedia:	Video, color graphics, sound
Audience:	Secondary school and up
System Requirements:	MPC-compatible machine

FIGURE 8.40

Video, live jazz recordings, and hundreds of photos and illustrations make Compton's Jazz: A Multimedia History a demonstration of multimedia at its best.

From the beginnings of jazz in the late 19th century through fusion and avant garde in the 1970s and 1980s, Jazz: A Multimedia History from Compton's New Media takes you on a visual, historical, and music-filled tour of the greatest influences in America's native musical form (see fig. 8.40).

The text, brilliantly written by Lewis Parker and Michael Ullman, traces the great movements in jazz throughout this century. Text is highlighted with musical scores and hundreds of still photos and video clips. Among the clips are a rare television appearance of Billie Holiday on CBS television in the '50s, and Miles

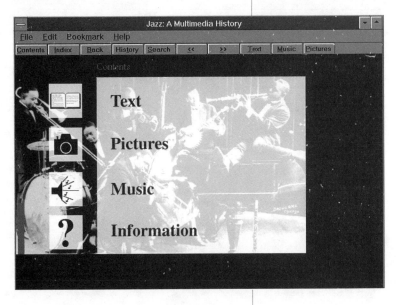

Davis and John Coltrane. Many of the photos from the '20s, '30s, and '40s are from the Rutgers Institute for Jazz Studies and reproduce well on a VGA screen.

Music lovers will appreciate the numerous live music cuts on this disc, many of which have long been out of circulation. The presentation finishes up with an extensive bibliography, discography, and an interview with the authors.

Music lovers, especially jazz aficionados, will want this disc as a complement to their collection; the bibliography alone may be worth the price of this disc.

Geography, Atlases, and Travel Discs

What better place to store full-color graphics images of maps than on CD-ROM? This genre of CD-ROM publishing is growing more popular every day, with atlases, mapping programs, world tours, and travelogues finding a natural home on the ample storage medium of CD-ROM and today's full-color, high-resolution PC monitors. And that's key: the better your graphics card and display, the more utility you'll get out of these geography, mapping, and travel programs.

Global Explorer

HIGHLY RECOMMENDED

DeLorme Mapping	
Operating System:	Windows 3.1
Interface:	Full Windows interface
Multimedia:	
Audience:	7 years and up
System Requirements:	VGA or better display

Global Explorer is an outstanding use of CD-ROM (see fig. 8.41). It brings a staple reference document—the world atlas—into the computer age. Global Explorer is an atlas of unprecedented detail that offers an aggregate map unavailable elsewhere.

Global Explorer's feature list is impressive:
➤ 100,000 gazetteer items—points of interest and information
➤ 100 detailed city street maps from around the world
➤ National and provincial boundaries

➤ Bodies of water
➤ Urban areas
➤ Major highways
➤ Elevation data
➤ Terrain types, including wetlands, oil fields, and other types

As if this isn't enough, Global Explorer also has a unique interface that allows you to simulate air travel along commercial routes among the major cities of the world. This application would be impossible if not for the power of the computer, and it's one that's worth owning.

HIGHLY RECOMMENDED

Street Atlas USA

DeLorme Mapping	
Operating System:	Windows 3.1
Interface:	Full Windows interface
Multimedia:	
Audience:	7 years and up
System Requirements:	VGA or better display

FIGURE 8.41

Global Explorer is DeLorme's world atlas on CD-ROM.

The low end of DeLorme's atlas products, Street Atlas USA is a marvel, particularly considering its low price. Street Atlas is a searchable street atlas, much like a paper, with two important differences. First, the searches are computerized and can be made by place name, street name, ZIP code, and area code/exchange. The second difference is the startling fact that just about every street in the U.S. is in this atlas (see fig. 8.42).

You'll have a tough time trying to stump Street Atlas USA, even when you search for obscure streets gleaned from your friends' hometowns—and this isn't just a marketing claim. What makes these searches possible is the combination of CD-ROM technology and DeLorme's Xmap technology, which allows the compact storage and quick retrieval of all those streets and other map features.

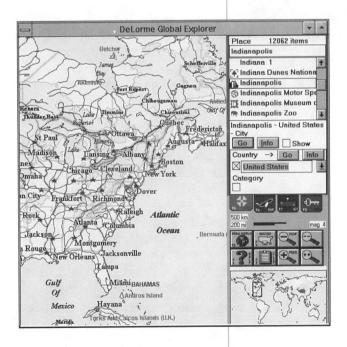

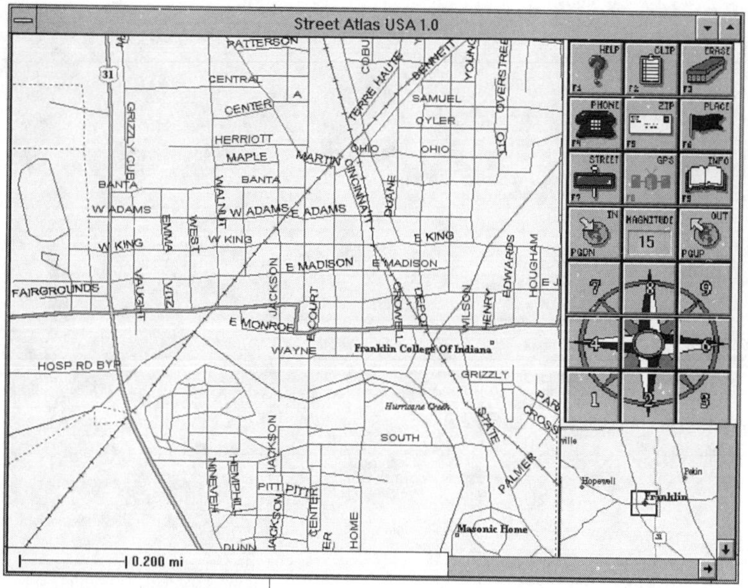

FIGURE 8.42

Street Atlas USA contains virtually every street in the nation, all on one disc.

Street Atlas USA is essentially a stripped-down version of another DeLorme product, Map Expert, described in Chapter 7, "CD-ROM in Business." Compared to Map Expert, Street Atlas USA is "crippled." It is missing some features that professional map users may prefer to have, such as high-resolution export of maps and longitude/latitude data. This product's reduced capabilities, however, are offset by its reduced price, putting this disc in the reach of the home user.

Street Atlas is great for the research, travel planning, and just plain fun. Put this disc on your want list.

Chapter 9

CD-ROM for After Hours

You've spent a long hard day at your home computer researching tax code or assembling a bibliography of articles concerning your company's competition. And your children just want to do something on a rainy day besides watching even more TV. A CD-ROM game can be just the answer; after all, we all have to have some fun. And CD-ROM games are the best entertainment values going right now.

In this chapter, we've done our best to round up the latest and greatest CD-ROM gaming titles. The disc included with this book has short demos of some of these titles. These demos provide a better taste of the programs than the simple screen captures accompanying each review. In each review, we'll give you a thumbnail sketch of the game's objectives and play as well as a handy specification checklist to make it easier to determine which are compatible with your system. Where possible, we've grouped games according to developer or distributor. We've also estimated the audience level for each, with tips on content where appropriate.

Today's Game Technology

If you've been following PC game technology for the last several years, you've noticed a significant change. Games are more sophisticated, employing 3D graphics and animation lavishly rendered in full color; sound has evolved from simple *blip*s and *beep*s to full-stereo MIDI orchestration, accompanied by speech; and game complexity has grown accordingly, with engaging storylines, plots, and characters. PC games have traditionally installed on the hard drive of your computer; but all these advances and improvements in sound, graphics, and story eat tons of disk space. For example, Origin's Wing Commander II—the most advanced space shoot-'em-up ever produced—needs over 25 megabytes of hard drive real estate when fully installed—without the speech modules!

It's easy to see why game producers have embraced CD-ROM technology as the development medium of choice. No longer hamstrung by the limited and valuable space of customer's hard drives, they now have over 600 megabytes of development elbow-room to let their creations run wild. The only restriction imposed on the game producers when moving to CD-ROM is the drive's relatively slow speed. Remember, the best CD-ROM drives have access rates (that is, the time it takes to find data) in the 200-to-280 millisecond range; most hard drives can access data under 20 milliseconds. Transfer rates (that is, the time it takes to move data), of course, are also much slower for CD-ROM and contribute to the challenge of delivering the game in a format that is not distracting or annoyingly slow. The most ingenious developers have cleverly minimized the effects of slow CD-ROM drive speed by **caching** significant portions of their games in computer memory just before playback.

Pauses for drawing data from the CD into cache are timed to occur between scenes or game levels, where they are less noticeable and don't affect the playability of the game. Other developers use a disk cache or copy bit-intensive files to the hard disk, which is a less desirable but understandable alternative for some action-packed games that need many megabytes of data on faster media.

There's good news on both fronts—CD-ROM technology and game development. First, CD-ROM access and transfer rates are improving steadily. And game developers are getting more adept at porting existing games or developing new games to accommodate the new technology. As a consumer, you'll do well to keep one thing in mind: because games and other multimedia applications require the most horsepower you can provide, you'll see the best possible results—and enjoy your play all the more—if you purchase the fastest

CD-ROM drive you can afford. **See Chapter 3, "How To Select CD-ROM Drives," for a full run-down on current CD-ROM drives and their specifications.** If you already own a CD-ROM drive and want to increase its performance, you can include more caching buffers on the drive or consider a commercial CD-ROM-caching program.

The Current State of the Gaming Art—and What's Next

The sound, animation, and graphics capabilities of your system determine whether you get the optimum use of the multimedia technology that has been exploited to its fullest by today's game producers. We've already mentioned the need for a fast CD-ROM drive—MPC compliance might not be enough in the future as video becomes more important. But even your graphics adapter, sound card, and speaker systems must be up-to-date to get the full effect of some of the latest gaming thrills. For example, speech recorded to CD in 16-bits becomes gravelly and scratchy when played on an 8-bit card; through inferior speakers, the mellow tones of Don Pardo doing voice-overs in Space Quest IV, for example, become a tinny representation of his voice. Similarly, music takes a heavy hit in quality when played over 8-bit systems. Animations run faster and more smoothly if your system is at least a 386-25 MHz and has a solid accelerated graphics card. That's not to say that slower systems can't run the latest CD-ROM software—developers must be careful not to go too far, too fast, and leave behind an installed system base that can still benefit from their latest software. But the industry—and games in particular—are

EXPLANATION

Caching

The useful concept of caching is used in most computer technology. Caching leverages a smaller amount of faster, more expensive storage for dynamic use; the slower, cheaper media provides mass storage. Caching works like this: data that is needed now—or that a program guesses will be needed soon—is moved from slower storage (CD-ROM, disk, and so on) to faster "storage" (RAM, fast disk, and so on). This process allows the required data to be retrieved in a timely fashion. Caching is especially useful to games where the goal is smooth animation or sound, and a still or silent pause moving toward this type of configuration for the best results in gaming and multimedia performance:

➤ A 386-25 MHz or better processor

➤ 4 megabytes or more of RAM

➤ Accelerated Super VGA adapter

➤ 16-bit sound card with DAC (Digital-to-Analog Converter)

➤ Amplified speakers with bass boost or subwoofers

➤ 300 millisecond CD-ROM drive with 64KB buffer and double-speed transfer rate or better

Speech and Sound

Most games on CD-ROM now incorporate some speech. Sierra Online (one of the most innovative game producers and one of the first to incorporate speech into their games) has gone so far as to develop lip-syncing technology into their speech-enhanced games. Characters actually look as though they are mouthing the words rather than moving their lips in some poorly dubbed Godzilla-like movie. In earlier disk-based versions of games, speech was used sparingly—or not at all—because of space limitations. (Remember that one minute of speech takes several megabytes of disk space). As a result, disk-based versions of games relegated all story narration and instruction to text boxes floating amid the graphics panels. With speech-enhanced CD-ROM games, the panels are gone, giving the player an unobstructed view of the action or story.

Most high-end games incorporate MIDI (Musical Instrument Digital Interface) or Red Book audio (audio stored on the CD) music as background for their games now. Only a true 16-bit sound card can reproduce these effects accurately. Cards that incorporate sampled sounds do an even better job and may become increasingly affordable and prevalent in the months to come. Most game developers maintain installation options for 8-bit sound card users because they realize that 16-bit cards are relatively new and haven't garnered a large share of market yet.

Graphics and Animation

Most games—even those on CD-ROM—have been limited to EGA and VGA resolutions. The technology exists to use higher resolution and provide more detailed graphics, but developers must create their games for a home market where the predominant display adapter has been a standard VGA—or even an EGA. That's changing. A handful of titles now support Super VGA displays up to 800 by 600 pixels and over 35,000 colors, nearly doubling the resolution of graphics and adding a 16-fold increase to the number of colors artists can paint with. For an eye-popping look at what's possible in Super VGA graphics and animation, look at a recent software release by Virgin Games: The 7th Guest features lush, realistic detailing and smooth animation as you move from room to spooky room in a haunted house; this type of realism can be rendered only with a high-resolution video card. Increasingly, game developers will move to the higher-resolution platforms; most no longer support EGA displays or adapters.

Some developers are beginning to experiment with full-motion video as well. Interplay, Virgin, CMC, and Sierra Online have all released or are about to release game titles that incorporate some elements of video through custom overlay, Video for Windows, or through Micromind's Projector technologies.

Computer gaming is an art form where some developers are concerned. Those in the forefront, as mentioned, are already utilizing the best in sound, graphics, and animation. They prefer to offer products with the best animation, graphics, video, and sound that technology allows. And more and more users are upgrading their systems—which is good news. Once a significant number of systems have higher-end displays and sound capabilities, software developers can begin to fully exploit the capacity of CD-ROM and the latest generation of 16-bit audio cards.

> **How To Use This Chapter**
>
> The description of each product in this chapter begins with a chart; these charts provide consistent at-a-glance information.
>
> Two special icons are used to mark products that are especially noteworthy: Recommended and Highly Recommended. In addition, a few superlative products have been given an Award of Excellence (we explain why these titles are cream of the crop in the margin-note text accompanying the award icon).

About This Chapter

This chapter describes some of the most innovate game titles available on CD-ROM. Most game titles in this chapter are grouped by manufacturer. Although this chapter describes several dozen titles, hundreds more are available. **For information about additional game titles, look at Appendix C, "Additional CD-ROM Software Titles," which lists hundreds of CD-ROMs.**

Sierra Online

Sierra Online is one of the most prolific, innovative, and successful PC game developers around. Unlike some game developers that produce products for everything from 8-bit Nintendo to 486 MPC systems, Sierra focuses on computer-based adventure game development. Its specialization pays off.

HIGHLY RECOMMENDED

King's Quest V

Operating System:	DOS 3.3 or above, Windows 3.1 with MPC extensions
Interface:	Point-and-click, text
Pointing Devices:	Mouse, keyboard
Sound:	All major cards
Graphics:	VGA
Audience:	Ages 7 and up

It's no wonder that Roberta William's King's Quest series has lasted to a fifth and sixth sequel: the storylines, characters, and graphics make them the most engaging role-playing adventure games available (see fig. 9.1).

Although King's Quest VI has just been released on floppy disk, the fifth installment is the first to make CD-ROM. All the characters—from the dashing prince to his owl sidekick—are narrated by actors. As with earlier King's Quest games, you play the hero and are involved in many dangerous treks and missions. Here, the princess has been abducted by an evil sorcerer, and you must find and free her. The puzzles and tasks are often tricky, which makes it a perfect game for adults to play with their children. For example, at one point our hero finds a hidden vault in the desert—only to discover he needs a special staff to open the door. After exploring the desert wastelands—be careful you don't die of thirst!—he happens upon a caravan of thieves who possess the staff he needs. Only cunning and trickery can get the staff.

Because this is a problem-solving game, many of the puzzle parts can be solved separately, allowing you to roam freely throughout the various lands within the gamescape: towns, deserts, gypsy wagons, vast seas inhabited with sea creatures, and icy mountain castles are just some of the lands you visit.

Collect anything you can—loaves of bread, rope, old shoes—you never know what you'll need on your explorations. Save the game frequently—evil sorcerers, beasts, and sudden disasters may lurk around every corner.

The Sierra interface, common to all its software, is a convenient way to play games. A menu is hidden at the top: move the cursor to the top edge of the picture and pop-up icons appear that represent game options (an eye for examine, a hand for take, and so on). Other options include saving and restoring games, adjusting the speed of the animation, and separate volume controls for speech and music.

FIGURE 9.1

King's Quest V was the first CD-ROM game to incorporate extensive speech. The 256-color VGA graphics and stereo music score add to its allure.

This isn't a game younger children can play on their own—but it makes for an interesting and challenging group endeavor. Children over nine years old can get very far in the game without adult help—but why let them have all the fun? There are enough strategy and surprises here to keep most adults enthralled; helping with the puzzles and the taking in the entertaining characters and voices keep children riveted for hours. The game is a long one—both in actual playing time and in the areas you explore. Because of all its fine storytelling, imagination, and painstaking care in details, King's Quest V is highly recommended.

Sierra Online's Space Quest series is another long-lasting success story. The main character in all the titles is Roger Wilco; he began the series as a janitor aboard an intergalactic garbage scow, only to have fate step in and launch him through a series of adventures throughout the known—and unknown—universe. The series is decidedly tongue-in-cheek, and the hero is as reluctant as he is unlucky. You guide Roger through his exploits, and hopefully, to victory (see fig. 9.2).

Space Quest IV

Operating System:	DOS 3.3 or above, Windows 3.1 with MPC extensions
Interface:	Point-and-click
Pointing Devices:	Mouse, keyboard, joystick
Sound:	All major cards
Graphics:	256-color VGA
Audience:	Ages 15 and up

In this fourth installment—Alien Time Rippers—Roger finds himself chased out of a back-galaxy dive by a cadre of storm troopers. While making his escape, he's rescued by a stranger who has, as Roger puts it, "an overgrown hair dryer" that rips open an escape hatch. Roger leaps through, only to find himself back on his home planet—Xenon—many decades into the future. Stand in the main square long enough, and you'll see an innocuous yet familiar figure stroll across the screen. And here's the only hint we'll give you—the visitor isn't merely a sight gag; he plays an important part in your escape.

The puzzles, conundrums, and scavenger hunts in the game are difficult. You may find yourself stuck in a number places—but the challenge is worth it. Roger is as sarcastic and hapless as ever, and there are even a number of interesting arcade-style hurdles to leap as you progress through the many levels.

Getting Help

If you get so frustrated you can't stand it anymore, hints and tips are available for many popular games—CD-ROM-based or otherwise—on CompuServe's Games forum. You'll probably need a Universal Hint viewer for the hint files (also available on the forum). Type **GO GAMERS** at the CIS prompt.

Did we mention that Space Quest IV is funny? For example, when Roger finds himself suddenly transported back to an episode from Space Quest I, the scenery looks odd: it's in 16-color EGA graphics. One of the characters quips, "That's all we had back then." Narrated asides, goofy characters, and the most unlikely juxtapositions in time and space—along with Roger's cutting remarks—make the entire Space Quest series more fun than just its challenging puzzles.

FIGURE 9.2

Space Quest IV on CD-ROM is campier than ever with narration and voice-overs adding new dimension to an old favorite.

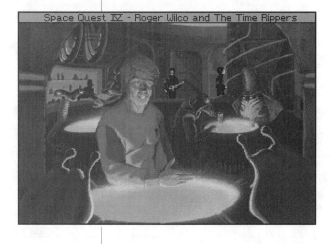

The narration—done with the pizzazz and aplomb that only Don Pardo can provide—reinforce the campy, off-beat storyline. Sound effects, music, and additional voices round out an excellent sound track for this mis-adventure. In the graphics department, Sierra has never done better. The 256-color VGA backgrounds and animation make this a game-playing pleasure.

This is definitely a teens-and-up kind of game, if for nothing else than the quips, situations, and level of difficulty. The humor, we're sure, may not be for everyone, but then neither are role-playing games. This kind of CD-ROM game, however, really shows what the technology—and creative developers—can do.

EcoQuest: The Search for Cetus

RECOMMENDED

Operating System:	DOS 3.3 or above, Windows 3.1 with MPC extensions
Interface:	Point-and-click, text
Pointing Devices:	Mouse, keyboard, joystick
Sound:	All Major Sound Cards
Graphics:	256-color VGA
Audience:	Ages 12 and up

FIGURE 9.3

Kids help Adam and Dolphinius the dolphin save an underwater world in EcoQuest.

With the EcoQuest: The Search for Cetus role-playing game, Sierra Online takes you on an adventure under the sea (see fig. 9.3). The hero is Adam, son of a marine biologist who helps his father nurse a dolphin back to health after it's trapped and nearly killed in a drift net. As he plays with the recuperating dolphin, Adam discovers it has surprising powers. He learns that the dolphin was on a mission when it was nearly killed and determines to let it go.

Adam joins his new-found sea-friend Dolphinius on an ocean trek through ancient ruins, an underwater sea-life city, and an abandoned ocean-floor oil-drilling rig. Adam—and

you—get points for helping sea creatures, picking up trash, and bettering the ocean environment. And, of course, you get points for solving the many puzzles and hunts along the ocean floor.

As you can tell, EcoQuest has a decidedly proenvironment bent. There's much here about the way toxins, garbage, and other wastes affect plant and animal life in the oceans. According to Sierra Online, the facts have been checked with oceanographers; the game does a good job of imparting facts about marine biology and ocean ecosystems. To further the point, a copy of *I Helped Save the Earth: 55 Fun Ways Kids Can Make a Difference* is included in the game box (a kid's sticker book

of household conservation hints such as turning out lights when you leave a room, using less hot water, and so on).

The familiar Sierra Online interface is intact—with one small addition: the cursor is shaped like a dolphin. The MIDI music score and underwater sound special-effects are great, and the voices of the narrators and characters in this adventure game are some of the best.

The game is definitely geared to an older child (some of the puzzles are be too difficult for younger players to solve on their own). The theme, story, and characters are well-suited for children under 12 and adults to play together, however.

Jones in the Fast Lane

Operating System:	DOS 3.3 or above, Windows 3.1 with MPC extensions
Interface:	Point-and-click, text
Pointing Devices:	Mouse, keyboard
Sound:	All major cards
Graphics:	256-color VGA
Audience:	Ages 12 and up

If you don't get enough of trying to make it in the big city, Jones in the Fast lane is for you. This computerized board game challenges you to take your choice of character (two female, two male) from destitute poverty—no job, no place to live, not even decent clothes—to the top of the corporate ladder.

The game begins by choosing goals in each of four iconically represented areas: money (dollar bill), happiness (smiley face), educa-

tion (diploma), and success (briefcase). Each move takes one "Jones" week. During each week—elapsed time is displayed on a clock at the bottom of the board—you must move your character from place to place and make choices about how to spend your money and time.

At each stop along the way, you hear and see characters, from the rent-office manager—who somehow seems to dislike you even as she thanks you for the rent—to the professor at

"Hi Tech University," who is reminiscent of a Three Stooges character.

Jones in the Fast Lane is a relatively easy game to play and is definitely more fun with multiple players—the game supports up to four. The software provides the game's namesake, Jones, if you are without human companionship.

Jones in the Fast Lane runs under DOS or in an MPC window—and does the MPC job quite well. It expects a 640x480x256 color display driver for Windows, but runs under higher resolution with no problem.

Jones in the Fast Lane is definitely not designed for young children (who would not understand its basic premises). There is nothing objectionable in the game, however.

LucasFilm Games

A division of LucasArts, LucasFilm Games has begun to enhance some of their more popular diskette-based by moving them to CD-ROM. As is true with Sierra Online products, LucasFilm Games enhanced its titles by including improved music and speech support.

The Secret of Monkey Island

Operating System:	DOS 3.3 or above
Interface:	Point-and-click, text
Pointing Devices:	Mouse, keyboard
Sound:	All major cards
Graphics:	256-color VGA
Audience:	Ages 12 and up

Ever wonder what it was like to be a pirate? Wonder no more and climb onboard with Guybush Threepwood as he does battle with pirates, ghosts, ghouls, and monkeys to discover the hidden treasures of a legendary pirate-ghost in The Secret of Monkey Island (see fig. 9.4).
This LucasFilm Games title is filled with jokes, puns, and tons of puzzles. Unlike other adventure and role-playing games, you aren't in danger of being bumped off or forced to start over.

Guybush starts his adventure on Melee Island, a backwater Caribbean seaport filled with grog-sloshing pirates and pirate-wannabes. Guybush would like to qualify as a pirate himself—but he doesn't have the skills or money to do so. Only by completing a series of tasks and solving a few island mysteries is he

The Secret of Monkey Island is loads of fun for the entire family—chock full of games, jokes, puns, and pirate lore.

able to gain piratehood and go in pursuit of the secret of Monkey Island.

The graphics in this game are stunning—hand-painted backdrops and character portraits make playing the game a visually exciting experience—and the sound track is chock-full of foot-tapping calypso and reggae. Kids—and adults—find Guybush's adventure fun to solve, and the game keeps both groups busy for hours. This one was so much fun, one of Steve's kids was marking a calendar to keep track of when the next installment in the series would be on the software shelves.

Another nice touch to the CD-ROM Secret of Monkey Island is the inclusion of French, Italian, German, and Spanish versions of the game. These additions make the Secret of Monkey Island a multinational game—or a tool for teaching a foreign language. What is the word for *grog* in Spanish anyway?

Secret Weapons of the Luftwaffe

Operating System:	DOS 3.3 or above
Interface:	Menus
Pointing Devices:	Joystick, mouse, keyboard
Sound:	All major cards
Graphics:	256-color graphics
Audience:	Ages 12 and up

World War II over England, France, and Germany during aerial bombing raids, dogfights, and emergency landings is the action-packed backdrop for this flight-and-war simulator. In Secret Weapons of the Luftwaffe, you choose the plane and armaments for your missions, take your briefings in the ready room, and hit the skies (see fig. 9.5).

The animation and graphics here are better than average, and the missions are challenging—particularly the bombing runs. You may do well to stick to a few training flights before taking on the more complicated missions. Racking up downed enemy planes and completing your missions successfully are the only ways to move up in the ranks, however.

The CD-ROM version of this game contains more missions and more planes than the diskette version. (The additional missions and planes are extras you have to purchase and add on later if you buy the diskette version.) Among some of the World War II combat planes you can fly, both real and fabricated, are the Messerschmidt 262 jet fighter, the P-47 Thunderbolt, the Gotha 229 flying wing, and the P-80 Shooting Star jet fighter.

FIGURE 9.5

Secret Weapons of the Luftwaffe sends you into the flak-heavy skies of WWII in a variety of missions and planes.

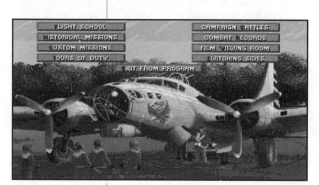

Secret Weapons of the Luftwaffe, as you can tell, plays fast and loose with history, so if you are a history fanatic, this game may not appeal to you. The flying simulations and graphics are good, though, and the sound effects play well over a good sound card and speakers. The array of missions you can fly is staggering; one level lets you fly historic missions—recreations of actual air battles and bombing runs; another level allows you to customize your own mission, from choosing a target to picking your flight path; yet another module allows you to orchestrate large-scale campaigns—from either the Allied or Axis side. With all the missions on this one disc, it'll take days to fly and master them all. If you love flight simulators and general shoot-'em-ups, Secret Weapons of the Luftwaffe will make a good addition to your games gallery.

Loom

Operating System:	DOS 3.3 or above
Interface:	Point-and-click
Pointing Devices:	Mouse, keyboard
Sound:	All major cards
Graphics:	256-color VGA
Audience:	Ages 10 and up

Loom is an adventure game with a musical twist. As the hero of this game, you must collect magical spells and powers by weaving musical passages—the more you collect, the more power you receive. Spells include Invisibility, Terror, Healing, and Night Vision. As a novice spellweaver, you must collect as many spells as possible because your journey to restore the master loom is fraught with obstacles and puzzles (see fig. 9.6).

The graphics here are a great lure to children of virtually any age. The gathering of spells from musical notes is a tricky—and fun—way for children to learn notation: they must assemble the spells by writing the notes on staffs within the Book of Patterns, a booklet included with the game.

The sound effects and music are great, and the narration is suitably other-worldly. If your child likes music and puzzle-solving, this is a good game, though not as challenging as some other titles in the LucasFilm Games list.

FIGURE 9.6

Gather spells, power and musical ability with LucasFilm Games' Loom.

Origin

Origin's motto is "We Create Worlds," and it's a good description of their product direction. Animation, sound, and speech all come together nicely with the Origin products on CD-ROM, whether it's a fantasy world of knights, might, and magic or a deep-space shoot-'em-up.

Wing Commander/Ultima VI: The False Prophet

In Wing Commander/Ultima VI: The False Prophet, Origin has combined two of its most

popular titles on one CD-ROM (two games for the price of one on this two-CD set that takes up only a fraction of the shelf space of the disk-based version). Nothing has been enhanced from the diskette-distributed version, but if you don't own either and want a good Origin sampler, this is a good disc to start with.

One of the programs on this combo-CD is the ground-breaking Wing Commander. Its use of detailed graphics and animation upped the ante in the PC game industry and competitors have been trying to catch up since (see fig. 9.7).

HIGHLY RECOMMENDED

Wing Commander

Operating System:	DOS 3.3 or above
Interface:	Menu
Pointing Devices:	Joystick, mouse
Sound:	All major cards
Graphics:	256-color MCGA
Audience:	Ages 12 and up

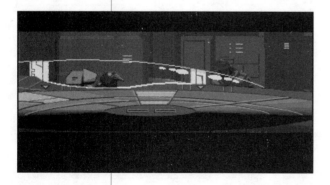

In this role-playing action game, you're a pilot aboard a space station behind the battle lines. The Kilrathi, a lion-like race of aliens, is bent on destroying the human race and occupying its worlds. A routine escort mission to the front gets you wrapped up in the heat of battle—despite the objections of one of your former superior officers. Subsequent missions get more furious and heated, with as many as 12 high-speed enemy fighters involved in the fray.

Flying a variety of ships and missions, Wing Commander is tricky to master—but a built-in flight simulator or trainer and advice from the more seasoned pilots in the lounge are enough to help you rack up kills on subsequent missions. Before each mission, you're briefed and sent out. You control the ship's path and all armaments. Often you fly in formation with one or more pilots—with communication between ships a must in coordinating a successful mission. Surviving a mission is tough, and when you die—and you will—you have the option of replaying the mission until you come out unscratched. And if living through a Kilrathi cat-fight isn't enough, you can vaporize yourself redocking your craft improperly, so handle your landing with finesse as well.

The missions, the graphics, and even the sounds are great. It's easy to see why the hard-drive version of this game was so popular—even when it ate up 15 megabytes of precious disk space. Packing this and Ultima VI on one disc is worth the price.

Ultima VI: The False Prophet

Operating System:	DOS 3.3 or above
Interface:	Menu
Pointing Devices:	Mouse, keyboard
Sound:	All major cards
Graphics:	256-color VGA
Audience:	Ages 12 and up

The Ultima series may never die—through time, interplanetary travel, and underground, its various permutations and storyline just keep going. Each new chapter, it should be mentioned, gains a more sophisticated interface, richer graphics, and better stories.

Ultima VI: The False Prophet is the sixth in the series and is included with Wing Commander on one CD. This time, you are taken once again to Britannia—a medieval world of knights, villains, supernatural powers, and magic (see fig. 9.8). The hero—Avatar—must take on the hordes of Gargoyles who have escaped from the underworld to threaten all of Britannia. The Gargoyles lay siege to important Britannia strongholds and places of knowledge, so it's imperative that you, Avatar, come to the rescue. Hints are given that the Gargoyles have risen in search of something that can make them even more powerful, so your fight is one against time as well.

FIGURE 9.8

Ultima VI and going strong; this favorite among role-playing games gets more sophisticated with each installment.

Kneeling, the hordes sway and chant as a stately winged nightmare steps forward.

The Ultima interface is easy to use: you move your band of collected characters around the countryside and through village and city by clicking the mouse. You can rearm or use items any member is carrying by selecting their character. Like most role-playing games, you amass a small band of multitalented assistants and find a way to defeat the enemy by collecting armor, money, and jewels; most importantly, you must build your strengths and spell-casting abilities.

HIGHLY RECOMMENDED

Wing Commander II Deluxe Edition

Operating System:	DOS 3.3 or above
Interface:	Menu
Pointing Devices:	Joystick (recommended), mouse
Sound:	All major cards
Graphics:	256-color MCGA
Audience:	Ages 12 and up

FIGURE 9.9

Wing Commander II, complete with 80 missions, great stereo sound, and full speech, is the best space game on the shelves.

If the missions in Wing Commander I weren't enough, slip this CD into the drive and hang onto your joystick (see fig. 9.9). This CD contains over 80 missions, all of Wing Commander II, the optional Special Operations I and II packages, and the Speech Accessory Pack—all of which can overwhelm the average home-based PC hard drive. There are, in fact, more missions here than on all the diskette-based versions.

After a near-disaster at the end of Wing Commander I, you are court-martialed and relieved of your combat status. Renewed fighting and a quirk of fate push you back into the battle—against a superior officer's wish. You're fighting many of your own crew members as well as the Kilrathi in this episode.

The formula here is the same as the original—more briefings and more space battles. The addition of speech and a more complex storyline, however, make this a superior game to the original Wing Commander. The action is just as tough to master, with the addition of a few unexpected enemy wrinkles to keep even the best fliers from getting too cocky. If you want to see high-speed action at its best, test out this CD.

Creative Multimedia Corporation

Creative Multimedia Corporation is a company that's making a multimedia statement in a number of areas. Not only does CMC produce some fine games and entertainments, their family reference and education CDs are some of the best in the CD software industry. CMC and ICOM Simulations are the only game producers whose products are strictly CD based.

Beyond the Wall of Stars

Operating System:	Windows 3.1 with MPC extensions, Macintosh
Interface:	Menu
Pointing Devices:	Mouse
Sound:	All major cards
Graphics:	VGA
Audience:	Ages 12 and up

CMC bills Beyond the Wall of Stars as an interactive multimedia adventure story; although that's quite a mouthful, it's an apt description. A science-fiction story set on a dying planet named Caledon, from which a delegation of galactic travelers set out to find Taran—a world fabled to be habitable and capable of helping the dying race. As a participant in the storyline, you choose the captain of the mission from eligible crew members. You also make key decisions throughout the story, such as whether to answer a distress signal coming from a nearby planet or continue with your rescue mission. Each decision, of course, alters the ultimate outcome of the story. And each twist adds new subplots and characters to the story's roster (see fig. 9.10).

FIGURE 9.10

Beyond the Wall of Stars is an interactive novel—you choose among the many plot alternatives.

The interface is easy to work with and, unlike some games and stories, the sound track for this adventure is perfect for its purposes. (Some scores become as irritating as off-key humming after prolonged play.) Although the animation isn't very sophisticated, that's not why you bought this ticket to begin with. Here it's all story—and it's a full story, too: you won't be able to finish it in one sitting. The interface includes a bookmark feature for just that reason. You can place multiple bookmarks within the story so that you can explore different branches of the storyline or more than one person can read the story.

Who Killed Sam Rupert?

Operating System:	Windows 3.1 with MPC extensions
Interface:	Menu, point-and-click
Pointing Devices:	Mouse
Sound:	All major cards
Graphics:	256-color VGA
Audience:	Ages 12 and up

Test your sleuthing skills in the multimedia game Who Killed Sam Rupert?

If just watching *Perry Mason* or *Murder She Wrote* isn't enough, Who Killed Sam Rupert? may appease the budding gumshoe in you (see fig. 9.11). As the story opens, you arrive on the scene of the murder of Sam Rupert in the wine cellar of his popular and elegant restaurant, Sam's. Your assistant gives you a run-down on the initial crime scene and then you're left to investigate. By picking various menu options, you can search the entire restaurant, perform careful forensic examinations of the actual murder scene and body, interview various suspects, and read Sam's appointment books and phone messages. Suspect interviews are QuickTime for Windows videos that pop onto the screen; all other options are VGA photos you can examine in some detail. Printed records of alibis, Sam's guest reservations, and recordings of his phone messages are also available to sift for clues.

Once you determine which suspects you want to interview in depth, you must pass a press conference. There, reporters ask you questions about the crime scene, possible suspects, and events leading up to Sam's death. If you don't answer at least seven of the ten questions correctly, you're sent back for more investigation.

Once you choose your suspects for interviewing, you select the questions you want to ask. You also have access to the full autopsy report and forensic analysis you performed at the crime scene. Based on the interviews, the analysis, and the autopsy, you can swear out a warrant. The suspect is arrested and your case is analyzed—if it's correct, the suspect is locked up and you win. If you're wrong, the suspect is set free and you have to go back to your other suspects.

The sound and video make this game an interesting, interactive whodunnit.

Goferwinkel's Adventures

Operating System:	Windows 3.1 with MPC extensions
Interface:	Menu
Pointing Devices:	Mouse
Sound:	All major cards
Graphics:	256-color VGA
Audience:	Ages 5 to 11

With the most eye-popping color in any CD-ROM we've seen, Goferwinkel's Adventures is a multimedia comic book that is especially good fun for the younger set. It's a comic book they can control, playing or replaying scenes in Goferwinkel's struggle to get safely to the Lavender Land.

The sound and voices are a great addition to a snappily drawn cartoon. Preschoolers will especially love this game, which also helps them learn to use a mouse and get used to using computers.

ICOM Simulations

ICOM Simulations is an innovative company. Although their only CD-ROM based games to date are Sherlock Holmes Volumes I, II, and III, these games are ground-breakers in the use of video and CD-ROM. In addition to CD-ROM Holmes for the PC, ICOM has ported many of the volumes to Sega Genesis, the Macintosh, and the Tandy VIS system. There are no diskette-based game titles for ICOM—they stick strictly to CD-ROM.

Sherlock Holmes

If the use of video and sound weren't innovative enough, ICOM's genuinely challenging Sherlock Holmes adventures will keep you sleuthing for hours.

Sherlock Holmes, Volumes I, II, and III

Operating System:	DOS 3.3 or above
Interface:	Menu
Pointing Devices:	Mouse
Sound:	All major cards
Graphics:	256-color VGA
Audience:	Ages 12 and up

It's almost unfair to lump all three Sherlock Holmes volumes together, but they all follow the exact same format and interface (see fig. 9.12). At the start, you choose from three separate cases and then are given a brief video introduction to the current case. From there, you—as Holmes—must find the murderer. From a convenient interface, you select addresses to visit (such as Scotland Yard, the Coroner, and other official—and unofficial—establishments). At each venue, you see a short video clip of your interview. Make sure that you take careful notes—each scene contains valuable clues to the solution of the mystery.

Each interview may lead you to yet another interview or establishment. You have other valuable allies you can count on as well: the Baker Street Irregulars are your snitches in the street who can make preliminary visits for you to gather information. A crime reporter for the *London Times* often has valuable insights into characters that you can't obtain anywhere else.

Other resources for sleuthing include Holmes' personal files of notable personages in London and copies of the *London Times*—in both print and electronic format—which you can browse for the off-beat clue or connection.

Once you believe you've gathered enough clues to make an arrest, you can appear before a judge. Be careful—he'll want to know many things before putting your suspect on trial, and he's impatient with detectives who waste his time with half-baked theories.

Although all the fun is in the solving, you can rate your effectiveness by Watson's summary of your work at the end of each case—the higher the score, the worse you've done.

FIGURE 9.12

Sherlock Holmes Volume III: High-quality video and genuinely tough murder cases send you through Arthur Conan Doyle's London.

Watson lets you know what the perfect number of moves would have been. We're not sure even the "real" Holmes is that effective.

This is a thoroughly enjoyable game, much more sophisticated than any other whodunnit on the market—either diskette-based or disc-based titles. If you love mysteries and a great challenge, get Volume I. We're sure you'll be become an ICOM-Holmes addict and pick up the other volumes as well.

Mantis Experimental Fighter

Operating System:	DOS 3.3 or above
Interface:	Menu
Pointing Devices:	Joystick (recommended), mouse
Sound:	All major cards
Graphics:	256-color VGA
Audience:	Ages 12 and up

Because Microprose has virtually every other type of simulator available, it was only a matter of time before they took to outer space. Although the diskette-based version of Mantis Experimental Fighter was released six months before the CD version, the CD is well worth the wait.

The animation and graphics are smooth, the sound is superb, and the speech enhancements make this a great CD game. The theme is a familiar one among space-arcade games: the Earth has been invaded by insect-like aliens that use human bodies as hosts. A united force of Earth pilots—FIST—has grouped in space to head off a new wave of aliens coming in for the kill.

You pilot a Mantis fighter (the most advanced in the fleet) against a variety of alien ships. The action during the flight sequences is smooth and sure, and it takes little time to get adjusted to piloting the simulator.

Microprose

Microprose is a powerhouse in the PC gaming business and has plane, tank, and war simulators that are among the best in the business. Microprose has only recently begun exploring the CD-ROM as gaming media. Expect many more of their titles to show up on silver platters in the near future.

RECOMMENDED

The CD version has speech and animation that the diskette version lacks—making this a superior product. You'll recognize the briefing-and-mission-flying story style used in other games (such as Wing Commander), but Mantis Experimental Fighter has a totally different feel. This game, in fact, gears you up gradually to rougher and tougher missions, allowing you to gain some expertise with the craft before taking on heavier battles. If you've tried Wing Commander and found it difficult to work with, Mantis Experimental Fighter may be a better space-arcade battle for you to fight.

The initial animation sequences are tremendous—even though they require a large cache on your hard drive; if you have that temporary space available, they're not to be missed.

Based on the success of Mantis, Microprose is sure to introduce other CD titles and, possibly, a sequel to the Mantis story.

Interplay

Although we were only able to review one Interplay CD at the time this book went to print, a spokesperson for the company confirmed that they would be shipping a number of new CDs in 1993, including a CD version of *Lord of the Rings* that features over 20 minutes of video from the movie *The Hobbit*. Also in production is Buzz Aldrin's Race to Space.

HIGHLY RECOMMENDED

FIGURE 9.13

Willie Beamish is for kids—especially for those over 18 years old.

Dynamix

Dynamix has recently become a subsidiary of Sierra Online, who knows a good company to buy when they see one. Dynamix CD titles have been announced for other CD formats recently, including Tandy VIS and Sega Genesis.

The Adventures of Willie Beamish is a pure joy to play with older kids. It's an adventure game with a twist: everything is cartoons and you play the part of Willie Beamish, a preteen boy with energy, mischief, and problems to spare (see fig. 9.13).

The Adventures of Willie Beamish

Operating System:	DOS 3.3 or above
Interface:	Menu
Pointing Devices:	Mouse (recommended), keyboard
Sound:	All major cards
Graphics:	256-color VGA
Audience:	Ages 12 and up

Willie's biggest dream is to enter the Nintari Video Game Championship—but the competition requires money, which Willie doesn't have. With his friends and his pet frog, Willie devises a way to earn his way to the games: enter the frog-jumping contest and win first prize.

As Willie struggles to get his frog ready for competition, other storylines develop—the town is plagued by a mysterious sludge, workers are laid off, and Willie's father, we discover, is in for trouble. Only Willie can save the town and his Dad.

Throughout this gorgeously painted cartoon, you control Willie's actions, help him solve the puzzles he needs to get ahead in the game, and ultimately triumph over evil. Many of the game's puzzles are arcade-action based; others require pure gray-matter skills, striking a good balance for both of this game's potential audiences.

The sound, music, and voices are superb and enhance the wacky, Saturday-morning cartoon atmosphere of Willie's world. We hope Dynamix doesn't stop with one Willie under its belt. Willie is a fresh concept that older kids will enjoy playing with their parents—a welcome way to bridge a computer generation gap. Let the kids handle the arcade action, and you help out with the brain teasers.

Swfte

As far as we know, the Bicycle CD-ROM Collection is the only CD-ROM game collection published by Swfte—but what more could a card lover ask for?

If you like cards, get the Bicycle CD-ROM Collection collection. Poker, cribbage, bridge, and solitaire are all here on one moderately priced disc (see fig. 9.14).

Bicycle CD-ROM Collection

Operating System:	DOS 3.3 or above
Interface:	Menu
Pointing Devices:	Mouse (recommended), keyboard
Sound:	None
Graphics:	CGA, EGA, MCGA, and VGA
Audience:	Ages 12 and up

The cards are sharp and clear in VGA resolution, and using the cribbage board was far easier with a mouse than not. Play against the computer—if you dare—and be prepared for a real challenge.

The solitaire module includes seven different varieties of solo cards, including Canfield, Klondike, and Little Spider. The poker segment allows for stud and draw, both of which can have wildcard play as well.

The documentation is top-notch, and the back of the book even has a quirky collection of card trivia, card-making lore, and various anecdotes about Bicycle's long history. The price is very reasonable, and all the cards you'd care to play are all on one disc.

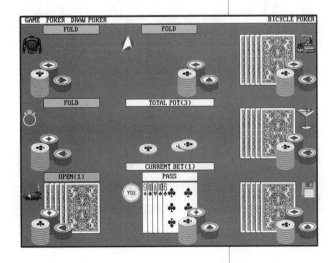

FIGURE 9.14

The Bicycle poker game is one of four in this collection's deck.

Brøderbund

Most people associate Brøderbund with educational software, and most people will also make a case for including the following title in the "educational" category. But let's face it—Carmen San Diego is more fun than education for most kids.

Where in the World Is Carmen San Diego Deluxe

Operating System:	DOS 3.3 or above
Interface:	Menu
Pointing Devices:	Mouse, keyboard
Sound:	All major cards
Graphics:	VGA
Audience:	Ages 12 and up

The *Deluxe* in Where in the World Is Carmen San Diego Deluxe stands for more sound, more voices, more of everything than the original program (which was released nearly three years ago). The interface is vastly improved as well, making navigation around the world and through the clue lists much easier (see fig. 9.15).

The premise of Where in the World Is Carmen San Diego is that you play a rookie gumshoe for the Acme Detective Agency—dedicated to foiling the evil band of Carmen San Diego's world-wide network of art and jewel thieves. Once you're assigned a case by headquarters over your communicator, you must select a spot on the globe to jet to for clue searching. When you land somewhere that plays a part in the criminal's crime or flight, you receive valuable additional information on their whereabouts. Clues are, of course, tied to geography, language, religion, and cuisine of various countries throughout the world.

The voices—of the chief, your travel agent Shirley, and various witnesses—make this game a lot more fun than the original. Actual still-life photos of representative landmarks and clips of native music—from the banjoes of the US to the Irish harp—are used when you arrive in each country.

The cases are a challenge for most kids, and the clues may send them immediately to your multimedia CD-ROM encyclopedia for answers.

FIGURE 9.15

Your global pursuit of master criminals in Where in the World Is Carmen San Diego is controlled with your Acme Communicator.

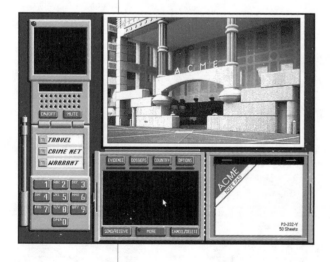

Virgin

Virgin has recently committed themselves to CD-ROM by releasing three titles, two of which, Conan and Spirit of Excalibur, are variations of diskette-based titles released earlier. The big news from this smaller developer in the games market is its CD-ROM title The 7th Guest, which we've saved as the last title in this section—and the last is truly the best in this chapter.

Conan the Cimmerian

Operating System:	DOS 3.3 or above
Interface:	Point-and-click, text
Pointing Devices:	Mouse, keyboard
Sound:	Adlib and Roland only
Graphics:	MCGA and VGA
Audience:	Ages 12 and up

If you like your adventures set in the past and like to do your battles with maces, swords, and shields, Conan the Cimmerian is a great little game. Replete with sorcerers, demons, and supernatural enemies, Conan's journeys take him from crowded cities to underground labyrinths (see fig. 9.16).

The story begins with the massacre of Conan's entire village. He sets out to avenge the deaths of his loved ones, roaming the hills and towns of Hyborea to collect spells, magic, and secrets to aide him in his quest.

The graphics are good, the interface easy to use, and the sound—if you have one of the two supported sound cards—is CD quality. This is a good adaptation of the diskette-based game, but we wonder why Virgin decided to go with such limited sound-card support. Most systems run Sound Blaster or compatible cards (of which there are scores) and tying the game to so few sound options may drastically limit the sales of the Conan title.

FIGURE 9.16

Swashbuckling adventures with Conan in the land of Hyborea.

The Spirit of Excalibur

Operating System:	DOS 3.3 or above
Interface:	Point-and-click
Pointing Devices:	Mouse, keyboard, joystick
Sound:	Roland, Adlib, or CD audio
Graphics:	MCGA and VGA
Audience:	Ages 12 and up

As the Spirit of Excalibur opens, Arthur has died in battle and you play his successor, the Head Knight of the Round Table. Your only problem is travelling from York to Camelot to take control of the realm. Among your many enemies are Mordred, Arthur's illegitimate son, and Lancelot and his followers, who do not acknowledge your leadership (see fig. 9.17).

FIGURE 9.17

Arthurian legends are played out in Virgin's Spirit of Excalibur.

Your journey—and victory—depends on battle strategy, the training of your troops, and the defeat of supernatural forces allied against you. As with most adventure games, you and your loyal knights accumulate strength, wisdom, and other attributes through survival of battles and the discovery of secrets in the countryside. The game's map and scene views are useful for navigating the medieval terrain and preparing for challenges ahead.

The game has five levels, or episodes, and you must triumph in all five to win the game. Each episode is progressively more difficult, and an unimproved band of knights may find it difficult to survive.

The audio is of great quality when played over the CD, but again, we wonder about the lack of sound-card support. Graphics and the game interface are fine, and the level of play was challenging, with many surprises along the route.

7th Guest

Operating System:	DOS 3.3 or above
Interface:	Point-and-click
Pointing Devices:	Mouse (recommended), keyboard
Sound:	All major cards
Graphics:	256-color MCGA, SVGA
Audience:	Ages 12 and up

AWARD OF EXCELLENCE

7th Guest

If you buy only one CD-ROM-based game, get this one. The graphics, sound, animation, and full-motion video all push the envelope of current technology. If all that weren't enough, the game is engaging and full of challenging logic puzzles. A must have!

Wow! That's the first and only word out of your mouth after starting 7th Guest. This game is so far ahead of the pack in graphics, sound, and animation it leaves you nearly speechless.

Before we even attempt to describe the game itself, we must point out that this game is, in all earnestness, in a class by itself. Using high-resolution 3D modeling software to develop the realistic interiors of the haunted Stouf Mansion, Virgin has produced the only game on the market that approaches the full meaning of the phrase *interactive adventure*. Because of its astounding graphics clarity, you feel as though you're in the corridors of a real house. A trip down a spider-clogged drainpipe, playing chess, and looking through telescopes and microscopes take on unparalleled realism. The house sets, the sound effects, and music are all a boost to the game as well. Live video of ghosts—and an extensive introduction to the house's past and that of its builder, Stouf—add yet another layer of complexity. When you consider the wealth of graphics, sound, and video, it should come as no surprise that the program is shipped on two CDs.

The setting is a small New England town; you visit the reputedly haunted Stouf mansion in search of clues to the murder of a journalist and the secrets the house is supposed to guard.

You have a booklet of clippings collected on the house and its builder (the toymaker Stouf) and related articles about the town, including a mysterious virus that killed a dozen children before the disease just as mysteriously disappeared.

As you wander the mansion, you're beckoned or warned off available directions of travel by an animated skeletal hand—the cursor changes according to function. A rolling, disembodied eye indicates one of Stouf's many puzzles left behind in the house; a skull with a pulsating brain indicates the location of the puzzles; and a mask shows where a ghostly vignette may be played out.

All the rooms in the Stouf mansion are not immediately available. Solving Stouf puzzles opens rooms, each of which contains valuable clues about the many mysteries of Stouf and his mansion. You'll enjoy the puzzles as much as the animation.

The game's cover says that this is the future of interactive games. For once, marketing hype comes up square with the truth. If you have the equipment needed to play this game, buy it. You won't regret it—even if you're a confirmed game snob.

Chapter 10

Copyright Laws

As you've seen in the preceding chapters, CD-ROM publishers are distributing tens of megabytes of art, sound files, photography, and film clips on each of their CD-ROMs. How you use these files depends solely on the publisher's agreement with the owners of the source material. Unfortunately, the owner of the source material is often not the publisher; therein lies the complication.

Copyrights

The Congress shall have Power...To promote the Progress of Science and useful Arts, by securing for limited Times to Authors and Inventors the exclusive Right to their respective Writings and Discoveries....

—Article II, Section 8
Constitution of the United States

In the simplest of terms, copyrighted material on a CD-ROM is owned by another party—an individual artist, a news organization, or an estate. The distribution of the material does not mean that it belongs to the purchaser. This concept is one you're familiar with: when you purchase the latest Stephen King novel, you don't dash to the nearest copy machine to run off copies for your friends and family. The book is a copyrighted work, with rights belonging to the author of the book. Only with the author's and publisher's permission can you run off a copy for your brother—and you'll find it very difficult to secure that permission. The livelihood of the author, publisher, and even the bookstores that carry King's works all depend on adherence to copyright laws.

Without copyrights, the publishing business could not survive. This idea is so fundamental that its roots appear in the Constitution of the United States. Without it, cheap copies of printed works would turn up everywhere, with no royalty or profit for the author, the publisher, or their distributors. Works would be altered without regard to the original, changing the intent of a work. Finally, the quality of the work would suffer, injuring the reputation of the author and the publisher, making future products unmarketable.

CAUTION

Seek Legal Advice

Because of the intricacies and ambiguities involved in copyright law, you are advised to contact a lawyer if you are protecting a work of value.

CAUTION

User Beware

Just because a work does not bear a copyright notice does not mean that it is a public-domain item. If you are unsure of a work's status and you cannot contact the owner, it's probably best not to make use of it.

CAUTION

Don't Lose Control

If you would like to make one of your own works available, it is best to do so by first copyrighting the work and then offering it for use with no fee. If you place the work into the public domain, you have no control over it whatsoever and you may regret it later.

For these reasons, **copyrighted** works are always designated as such. The copyright symbol (©) and words describing the extent and scope of the copyright appear at the beginning of the text, alerting purchasers to their obligations when buying the work.

Copyright Notices

Because the US is a signatory to the Berne convention, it is no longer necessary for an explicit notice to appear on a work for that work to be protected. Instead, an implied copyright exists for all original works. This doesn't mean that you can find yourself in trouble for using a work with no copyright notice; rather, the originator can notify you and tell you to stop using the work. The ultimate protection is registration of a copyright, which costs about $10 and provides evidence that an individual or corporation is the originator.

Taken to its extremes, a world without copyrights would gradually grind to a halt—authors would refuse to produce, publishers would stop the presses, and bookstores would close shop. In essence, copyrights provide the incentive to produce new works in an environment protected from theft. Copyrights control and ensure quality and accurate representation.

It's easy to see that the authors, publishers, and distributors benefit from copyright law, but what about the consumer? As we explained, the alternative—no copyright protection—virtually eliminates the incentive to publish, making new works scarce or nonexistent. But copyrights, paradoxically, protect the consumer in a variety of ways:

➤ Copyrights ensure that the product you purchase is in the form and content intended by the author and publisher; what you get is what they wanted you to get—the decision to purchase is left to you.

➤ Copyrights make it less likely that undeserving works are brought out as products. With the work itself protected, the publisher then invests in paper, printing presses, ware-houses, delivery trucks, and marketing campaigns to get the product in front of the consumer. No business can long survive delivering products no one will purchase. Publishers, therefore, secure the rights to works that are marketable. A certain level of quality is virtually ensured.

➤ Copyrights make publishing a competitive business. Rights to the most marketable materials go to the publishers that pay the best price. These publishers, in turn, spend time and money marketing the works to recoup their investment. In this environment, works are more visible and subjected to greater scrutiny, and the public is more informed on the quality of individual products.

Public Domain

Once a work of art no longer has rights assigned to it, it becomes what is known as **public domain**. A work may be in the public domain if any of these conditions arise:

➤ The work's copyright has run out and is no longer in effect.

➤ The **holder** of the copyright has released the work into the public domain and relinquishes all rights.

➤ No rights were ever assigned or claimed for the work and its use has been widespread.

Copyrights do run out. The length of the copyright depends on the type of work produced, how the creator of the work copyrighted the material to begin with, and what types of rights might survive the creator and be passed to heirs.

Work created before copyright law was enforced or work created long ago and no longer copyrighted fall into the public domain. Shakespeare's plays and Nathaniel Hawthorn's novels, for example, fall into this category. The plays and the novels may be reproduced at will, with no royalties or fees paid to anyone.

Anyone can use public-domain materials for whatever purpose without obligation to any other party. No fees, royalties, or permissions must be paid or secured for the use of public-domain materials, nor are there restrictions on how they can be used—a scene from Macbeth, for example, can be used to sell sleeping pills.

Fair Use

Life under copyright law has become complicated, however. The introduction of VCRs, tape recorders, computer media, and duplicating machines has made enforcement of copyrights difficult and has deadened the public's sensitivity to copyright law.

When it is so easy to reproduce copyrighted material, the consumer may feel that no law is being broken. This is not the case. Technically, any reproduction of a copyrighted work—in any form—is an infringement on the holder's rights. If you use a copyrighted photograph in a sales brochure without securing the holder's permission, you've violated the law. If you copy a film clip and use it in a marketing presentation without permission, you're liable under the law.

These cases of infringement are easy for most of us to determine. Other areas are less definitive. What if you use that same photograph on an invitation to a New Year's Eve party and distribute it to a select group of friends? Or you use that film clip to illustrate script-writing techniques in your high-school English class?

To address this issue of personal use, the courts have produced what is known as The Fair Use Doctrine. This doctrine covers four points—or criteria—for determining whether use of a copyrighted work can be claimed as "fair use" rather than falling under the strict terms of copyright law. These criteria are as follows:

1. The purpose and character of the use, including whether such use is of a commercial nature or is for nonprofit educational purposes.

2. The nature of the copyrighted work.

3. The amount and substantiality of the portion used in relationship to the copyrighted work as a whole.

4. The effect of the use on the potential market of value of the copyrighted work.

In a nutshell, the doctrine protects your personal use of a copyrighted product if:

1. You will not profit from the reproduction.

2. The work's individual copyright protection is taken into consideration—for example, laws covering printed text differ from those protecting music.

3. You use only a portion of a work.

4. Your use does not adversely affect the profit to be made by the holder of the copyright.

The first example—using a commercial, copyrighted photograph on invitations to a New Year's Eve party—hits some of the fair-use criteria and violates others. For example, you are using the work in its entirety, making your use a clear violation of point number three. Copyright laws governing photography insist on a per-use basis as well: you must pay a sliding-scale fee for a work depending on the number of appearances the photo will make. Yet you clearly are not affecting the market value of the photo or using it for profit. Your potential for breaking the law here, seems evenly split.

The second example is more easy to determine. First, your intent is non-profit and educational in nature; showing a high-school English class a film clip does not make anyone any money—unless you charge admission. Second, the nature of film copyrights allows the use of brief segments for criticism. Third, your clip constitutes only a brief segment of the entire work. And finally, your presentation of the clip in no way lessens the market value of the entire film. In fact, such a "tease" of a clip may cause the entire class to rent the film on videotape after viewing the segment in class.

The bottom line with fair use is not simple to determine, but you should keep a few things in mind. If the use is non-commercial in nature—that is, it promotes a non-profit enterprise—it may fall under fair-use protection. If your use does not constitute a loss in profit for the copyright holder, and especially if you use only a small portion of the work, you should be protected by the fair-use provision. The courts have a long way to go on this issue, however.

In a suit brought before the US Supreme Court (Sony vs. Universal Studios), the court ruled that taping a TV show for personal use at a later date did not constitute a copyright infringement. The reasoning was that the consumer would tape the show for viewing later, and had no intention of distributing the product for profit. But look at the number of fair-use clauses the ruling violates!

Furthermore, software companies instruct individual users (for good reason) to make backup copies of distribution diskettes in the event that an original diskette is damaged.

All these ambiguities make copyright law and fair use an affair potentially fraught with confusion and liability for consumers and small businesses.

CD-ROM and Copyright Law

Materials contained on a CD-ROM are subject to the same copyright laws as other media. What may confuse the issue, however, is that CD-ROMs may not contain only one form of original work. Text files, of course, are subject to the laws pertaining to written works. Music files fall under the laws protecting recorded materials, and film clips and photos have laws

protecting them as well. In effect, CD-ROMs can carry virtually every known type of copyrightable material.

A CD-ROM can include all the forms of copyrighted materials, making the publishing of CD-ROMs particularly tricky. Publishers may find themselves in need of securing rights from a number of different sources, adding to production costs. But securing the rights to publish or republish on a CD-ROM is just the beginning of a CD-ROM publisher's duties. The materials may fall into different categories and be subjected to different laws. For example, the use of a copy-protected photograph on a CD may be subject to royalty payments only if the consumer uses the particular photo in a commercial enterprise, such as a printed advertisement; all the text on the disc may be subject to author royalties based on the number of discs sold to customers.

For this reason, copyright clearinghouses have emerged as an important catalyst in the CD-ROM publishing business, helping CD-ROM publishers and copyright holders more efficiently secure and sell rights to works in a timely fashion. By using such clearinghouses, the publishers spend less time internally negotiating rights and more time producing and distributing products. Copyright holders are ensured that their rights are protected in a uniform manner, and they don't lose royalties or spend significant time in negotiation. Authors can even submit materials and their standard copyright terms to such clearing houses for publishers to choose from.

Your Copyright Responsibilities

As discussed, the capability of CD-ROM to contain a variety of different media makes it susceptible to all types of copyright law. The

CAUTION

Beware the Lack of Notice

Some publishers are not nearly as forthright as they should be. You'll be surprised to find, for example, that purchasing a certain commercial series of photographs on CD does not give you the right to reproduce the photos in any form without permission. You find that out, however, only after you open the disc package—making a refund of your money nearly impossible. The outside of the disc case has no clear mention of this provision. Another vendor, however, makes it abundantly clear that you must pay fees for the use of any images contained on the enclosed disc. And you're alerted to this before you open the disc case.

potential for confusion and abuse—by both copyright holders and consumers—is as vast as the storage capacity of the disc itself.

Let's take a seemingly innocuous example. You purchase a CD containing a huge database of sound effects and music files. One of the files is a recording of the opening of the popular TV show *Star Trek*: "Space. The final frontier..." intones William Shatner, with the familiar theme from Star Trek playing under his voice over.

If you use this music/voice clip in a multimedia presentation to promote the more spacious interior of a new minivan at a trade show, are you violating copyright law? Probably. The music is, without a doubt, copyrighted. The excerpted words of the opening may also constitute an infringement. And furthermore, using Star Trek to promote a new car model clearly violates the fair-use doctrine of infringement (using the Star Trek identification to profitably market a vehicle). But it came on a disc with so many other effects, who would know what is in the public domain and what is not?

Most CD-ROM publishers are extremely responsible when they market their discs and **clearly state**—on the outside packaging—that the contents are either public domain or copyright-protected materials. There should be further warnings in the software program itself that tell you precisely what you can—or cannot—do with the materials.

Protect Yourself

When using clip media from any CD-ROM—either for fair use or commercial purposes—read all the fine print included with the disc and in the software itself. Take your cues from this information.

For example, the copyright use for Digital Directory Assistance's PhoneDisc USA is clear, concise, and unambiguous:

> This product a) may be used only by the purchasing end-user and may not be made available for any other use by loan, rental, service bureau, or other arrangement; b) may only be used for reference purposes; use for commercial direct mail or telemarketing of more than 100 listings per month is strictly prohibited; c) may only be used with a single microcomputer permitting access by one individual at one time; d) may not be made available to multiple users at one time through networking or any other means without obtaining a separate networking license from DDA.

This is the first paragraph on the back of the PhoneDisc USA case; it gives the business user very clear guidelines for the use of the product. According to Digital Directory Assistance, in a nutshell, you can't do these things with the disc:

➤ Use the disc for mailing lists
➤ Allow more than one person to use the disc at one time, or loan it to any other person
➤ Use the disc for extensive telemarketing

Most importantly, you make your purchasing decisions about this CD accordingly. If you need a disc for telemarketing, you know this is not the product for you.

Other publishers are not as clear in their copyright notices. If you have questions regarding fair use or copyrights of a particular piece of media, call the publisher before you use the media in a commercial enterprise. Get the use restrictions or copyright guidelines in writing—for example, have them fax this information and explanation.

When determining whether your use of clip media falls under the fair-use doctrine, make certain that you are covered in at least two of the four areas of the guidelines—making absolutely certain that your use does not infringe on profits to the copyright holder.

Make no assumptions about public domain. Never use entire works or substantial portions of works unless they are clearly and irrevocably presented as public-domain property. Use of an entire chapter from Herman Melville's *Typee* from the Library of the Future disc may seem perfectly acceptable—Melville's work is in the public domain, after all. But the notice on World Library's disc—stamped on the disc itself, the outside package, and in the title screen of the software—clearly states: "Unauthorized reproduction, lending, or distribution of text or programs contained on this disc is strictly prohibited." Fair use would be applicable, however. Because of the collision of copyright law and the licensing of software databases like the Library of the Future, the application of a concept like "fair use" is not clear cut.

An Editorial on the Future of Copyright Law

For CD-ROM publishing to truly flourish, new rules must be set. Copyright laws must become more uniform, universal, and, above all, understandable. Most infringements today are probably caused by confusion and the wide distribution of copyrighted materials. Laws must reflect this wider distribution and make compliance an easier—and not a more difficult—feat for the average business and consumer.

The current copyright laws are out of date. The current laws never anticipated the explosion in the information industry, nor could they anticipate the technologies that make information so readily available. Congress needs to revamp laws to reflect the use of media clips, text, and information in an age where dissemination of copyrighted materials should be opened up—and not hamstrung—by copyright law. Make certain that copyright holders are fairly compensated, but make compliance less bothersome and confusing.

Some proponents of reform suggest that an industry-wide tariff be placed on each CD-ROM sale, provided that the use of the information on the disc is for limited commercial application; the proceeds would go to a common copyright-royalty fund. In this scenario, you in essence comply the moment you make your CD-ROM purchase. Opponents of this measure believe that the tariff penalizes those users who never intend to use the products for any commercial reproduction.

Until copyright laws are streamlined or reformed, we need to be vigilant. Individuals, finally, must be educated and responsible for the use of CD-ROM-based materials; intentional abuse of the laws will only restrict the number and nature of materials available for distribution on CD-ROM. Companies publishing CD-ROM materials need to follow the lead of vendors who supply clear, concise, and easy-to-follow instructions regarding the nature of the copyrighted material contained on the discs.

Chapter 11

Beyond the Basics

So your business has a CD-ROM drive or two installed, and some employees are finding information faster than ever before. Productivity is increasing, cost of research is dropping, but the hassles of adding a CD-ROM drive to every employee's desk who could benefit from the technology is getting a bit much. The demand for CD-ROM information is increasing. Even your outside sales force is requesting access to the company database. Thankfully, there are ways to ensure that your use of CD-ROM is more cost-effective and efficient.

When Enough Discs Aren't Enough Any More

If you want to network large numbers of CD-ROM discs, consider CD-ROM drive arrays or a CD-ROM changer. These technologies have distinct benefits in networked environments, and you need to evaluate them separately. Each has its own advantages and disadvantages for distributing data across a network, whether it's a large, multiserver Novell NetWare network or a smaller peer-to-peer environment such as Windows for Workgroups.

For compiling and publishing your own in-house databases or other CD-ROM materials, consider mastering or recording your own CDs. The technology for in-house production of CDs has advanced enormously, making production a mere question of budget rather than expertise. Corporate databases, inventories, and archives can be recorded, distributed, or put in vaults for safekeeping. **CD-R drives** make distribution of massive amounts of data throughout a company cost-effective.

This chapter introduces you to the following kinds of advanced CD-ROM hardware:

➤ **CD-ROM changers.** A **changer** is a CD-ROM drive that accepts up to six discs in a cartridge. Each disc is usually assigned a separate drive letter (for example, the game CD can be drive G, the encyclopedia CD can be drive H, and so on), although you can "combine" all the discs in the changer and refer to them by a single drive letter.

EXPLANATION

Record Your Own

There exist CD-ROM drives that can create CDs. These CD-R (or CD-recordable) drives use special blank media for the recording of data in standard CD formats such as CD and CD-ROM-XA.

> ➤ **CD-ROM jukeboxes.** A jukebox is similar to a changer except that it can have multiple CD-ROM drives and uses a robotic-arm mechanism to change discs.
>
> ➤ **CD-ROM arrays.** An **array** is a string of disc drives chained together. Arrays are usually fixed; that is, if there are four disc drives chained together in an array, you cannot add a fifth drive to the chain.
>
> ➤ **CD-ROM towers.** Tower systems offer all the benefits of arrays and go one further: they are expandable. Manufactures offer tower systems that can accommodate up to 18 disc drives. You can start with three drives and add drives whenever you need more power.

In addition, the second part of the chapter explains how to make "master" (or original) discs that then can be copied and used in the drive devices described in the first part of the chapter.

CD-ROM Changers

You're already very familiar with the technology used to stack a number of CDs on a network even if you've never seen a CD-ROM changer. The most popular CD changers are the Pioneer series of CD minichangers that use the same **cartridge** found in the Pioneer audio CD players. The similarities don't end there, either. Changers assign drive letters to every CD held in the cartridge. When a user on the network or on a standalone PC requests data from one of these "drives," the changer loads the appropriate disc into the CD-ROM reader. There is only one physical drive, but the drive designations are assigned to the individual discs for identification purposes: users, or their applications, know that drive K, for example, holds the corporate customer database and drive L holds the company's product literature.

Changers also can be programmed to treat all the discs as one massive database, allowing the search and retrieval of data to span all the CD-ROMs in the **magazine**. A company with enormous databases on discs can then "publish" them on the network as one dataset; the users and their applications need not know that the actual data resides on many different platters.

The CD-ROM changer is especially useful when organizations have to keep massive amounts of infrequently used data available at all times. Because there is only one physical drive, a user requesting a single bit of data can access the changer at any given time. Requests from other users looking for data on another disc loaded in the changer's magazine must wait, or retry their request later when the changer is available.

Changers are especially useful to individual users who must keep massive databases or research resources at their fingertips. Without a changer, the user must sift through a stack of CDs, unload the current CD from the drive, and then load the CD with the appropriate data. With a changer, this activity is unnecessary. Applications can be configured to expect to find data on a given CD with an assigned drive letter. Multiple magazines of CDs can also be configured. For example, a librarian can load one magazine of CDs containing all literature and language databases, another magazine full of CDs with biology and chemistry abstracts, and yet another magazine with general-reference CD-ROM applications. Each magazine is a self-contained and defined library of information.

A law firm can pack one changer with bankruptcy CD databases, another with tax law CDs, another with state statutes, and yet another with an archive of the firm's past legal briefs.

TIP

Changers and Arrays

For single users who need massive CD collections at their disposal or for a disc collection that is infrequently used, a changer is an ideal, cost-effective solution. If you expect even moderate traffic to the disc collection, however, consider a CD-ROM array.

EXPLANATION

Magazines and Cartridges

A magazine (also known as a cartridge) is a special case that holds up to six CD-ROM discs for use in a changer. It allows the changer to mechanically "change" discs as they are needed.

The advantages of a CD changer are simple. The cost for changers is significantly less than buying the equivalent of that number of drives. For example, the Pioneer DRM-600A, a six-disc changer, sells for about $900 through some distributors. The price of six stand-alone drives is considerably more—nearly four times as much, in fact.

The disadvantages relate mainly to networked CD environments. The minichanger is, in fact, one drive. If you expect access to the changer by a large number of people across the network, a changer cannot get the job done. Speed is another consideration. Although the disc-swapping speed is greatly improved in the newer changer models, users can expect a 6-to-15-second delay between their request for data and the actual loading and access of the CD.

Pioneer

Pioneer was the first to manufacture CD-ROM changers. Their minichanger series is the most affordable solution around. The drive accepts, as we've said, standard Pioneer CD cartridges, available where Pioneer audio CD drives are sold.

Pioneer DRM-600-A

Interface:	SCSI
Access time:	600 ms
Data transfer rate:	153 KB/s
CD-ROM formats supported:	ISO 9660, High Sierra, CD-DA
Suggested list price:	$1,250

The DRM-600-A is Pioneer's first changer, and is still very popular. As does the DRM-604x (described in the following section), the DRM-600-A holds a standard six-disc magazine. The back of the unit has standard RCA audio output jacks, dual SCSI ports for easy daisy-chaining of SCSI devices either before or after the changer, a grounded power input, and a SCSI ID switch.

The front of the unit has a disc-eject button; headphone jack with volume control; power, drive busy, and audio indicator lights; and an AC power switch.

Because the DRM-600-A has a relatively high access time, this drive may not be suitable for multimedia applications that make extensive use of video; the sustained transfer rate does match the MPC specification, however. For cost-effective access to text databases or information in earlier CD-ROM formats that doesn't depend on high transfer rates, however, the drive can't be beat.

The DRM-600-A has a standard SCSI interface that makes it ideal for users who have already installed SCSI devices. Using CorelSCSI!, the drive tested just fine on a variety of Adaptec, Future Domain, and Bus-Tek controllers.

Pioneer DRM-604x	
Interface:	SCSI, SCSI-2
Access time:	300 ms
Data buffer:	128KB
CD-ROM formats supported:	ISO 9660, High Sierra, CD-DA, CD- CD-ROM-XA (Mode 2, Form 1 and 2), Rock Ridge, CD-R mastered discs
Data transfer rate:	612 KB/s
Suggested list price:	$1,795

EXPLANATION

QuadSpin

A number of vendors, including NEC, Texel, Toshiba, and Chinon, supply high-speed versions of their drives. The Pioneer minichanger offers what the company calls *QuadSpin*—speeds up to four times the base delivery rate for data.

EXPLANATION

Jukeboxes

CD-ROM jukeboxes are the functional equivalent of the jukeboxes you know from Pop's Soda Shoppe. They use a robotic arm to change compact discs in a standard CD-ROM drive, much the way the 45 rpm records were placed on a normal turntable.

The DRM-604X **QuadSpin** minichanger has all the front-panel and back-panel features of the DRM-600-A. An additional LED on the front panel of the DRM-604x indicates when the drive is in QuadSpin mode.

The DRM-604x is, without a doubt, a killer CD-ROM configuration. The transfer rate is unexcelled at the time of this printing, making the QuadSpin the best drive around for accessing massive data chunks—from archived, scanned photos to full-motion video. The number of formats supported also make this a good all-around CD-ROM reader, regardless of your data types.

This changer also boasts a quick five-second disc-swapping mechanism, making delays to disc far less bothersome than earlier versions. Using CorelSCSI!, it's a simple matter to hook the QuadSpin onto an Adaptec, Future Domain, or other supported controller.

Although the price may seem high, look what you get with the DRM-604x in terms of functionality: virtually all CD formats are supported; the drive has the highest transfer rate available; its SCSI-2 interface makes it a snap to configure; and you have the equivalent of six CD-ROM drives in one case.

This drive is highly recommended for power CD-users, small businesses with extensive reference requirements, and networks in which archived data is needed at a moment's notice. The DRM-604x is a great CD-ROM product that has no competition in its class.

CD-ROM Jukeboxes

Changers generally use a mechanism that holds all the discs in a turntable, cassette, or magazine. Another technology—the **jukebox**—uses an array of discs in a "library." The jukebox is so named because of its similarity to the familiar machines that play 45 rpm records in restaurants and bars.

TAC Systems

Although Pioneer has led the way in six-disc magazine technology, other companies and OEMs are providing higher-end jukebox solutions that may be more applicable to large law firms or sites that require access to more than six CDs at one time. One such company is TAC Systems.

TAC JukeDrive	
Interface:	SCSI-2
Access time:	300 ms
Data buffer:	64KB
CD-ROM formats supported:	CD-DA, High Sierra
Data transfer rate:	153 KB/s
Suggested list price:	From $10,595 to $18,595

The TAC JukeDrive comes in 50-, 100-, and 200-disc configurations. The 50-disc configuration lets two drives operate off the same unit so that two users can simultaneously access the 50-disc library (provided that both users do not request the same disc). The 200-disc JukeDrive can accommodate four drives, increasing the number of simultaneous accesses.

In all the TAC JukeDrive systems, the software loads each CD at its disposal and catalogs the disc labels, adding them to a menu that can be accessed by networked users. TAC Systems claims that these JukeDrives can be daisy-chained for a maximum of over 11,000 online CDs. All the TAC systems use Hitachi drives and support most CD-ROM formats, with the exception of CD-ROM-XA.

Users of TAC JukeDrive systems tend to be government agencies, communications companies, large law firms, procurement companies, and research institutions that generate a lot of in-house data.

Other Vendors

Companies and government institutions and agencies are finding it economical to archive data with CD-R technology and then make the recorded data available to certain users over a network with jukeboxes. Other vendors of jukebox solutions are also delivering products now, most based on third-party drive and robotic mechanisms.

CD-ROM Arrays

CD-ROM arrays are a cost-effective way to "publish" CD-ROM data across a network so that a large number of users can simultaneously access discs. In essence, arrays or towers (towers are described later in this chapter) are a series of connected, individual drives. Each drive can hold a unique data disc; the array allows multiple users to access the CD library at the same time. In fact, text-based discs can accommodate three or four users on one disc with little degradation in performance across the network.

Arrays are ideal for high-traffic data. If many users need to access your company's disc library, an array is the most economical solution.

Arrays come in a variety of configurations, depending on the manufacturer. Four-disc arrays are common. Some OEM vendors supply *towers*—expandable array systems to which the user can add drives as budget and expansion of data CDs demand.

For example, you can buy a 12-bay tower system with only three or four drives installed. As your system grows, you can plug in additional drives and make minor configuration modifications to the software.

Fixed arrays allow only the number of drives for which the cabinet was originally configured. But fixed arrays can be daisy-chained, providing a way to add drives in four-drive or six-drive increments.

If you anticipate that four drives, for example, is the maximum needed for a given segment of your network, a fixed array is sufficient. If you know that expansion of your datasets is only a matter of time, an expandable tower configuration is not only more economical, but also entails far fewer installation and configuration hassles.

Toshiba TXM-3401A4	
Interface:	SCSI-2
Access time:	200 ms
Data buffer:	64KB
CD-ROM formats supported:	CD-DA, CD-ROM-XA
Data transfer rate:	300 KB/s
Drives in array:	4
Suggested list price:	$3,575

The Toshiba TXM-3401A4 is a four-drive fixed-array system that packs four Toshiba double-speed CD-ROM drives in one compact enclosure. The unit has a good cooling-fan system and standard SCSI ports on the back, allowing you to daisy-chain units or add the TXM-3401A4 to an existing SCSI chain of devices.

Because the drives are based on the standard Toshiba drive mechanisms, there is support for CD-DA, ISO 9660, CD-ROM-XA, and PhotoCD formats.

The industry-high 200 ms average access rate makes this array system fast at getting to data and certainly out-performs most other arrays in a networked environment.

Other Arrays

JVC, Todd Systems, and other manufacturers and OEMs make fixed-array systems. **See Appendix G, "Miscellaneous Hardware and Software Vendors," for company information.**

CD-ROM Towers

Tower systems are expandable versions of arrays that allow you to start out small—with two or three drives—and add as demand grows. Many third-party OEMs have begun putting together comprehensive network tower systems, using off-the-shelf CD-ROM drives in custom-designed cabinets. The clear differentiating factors among tower systems are these:

➤ Ease of expansion
➤ Software
➤ Drives used

TAC Systems

TAC Systems offers a full line of tower systems. You can purchase towers with any number of Hitachi drives installed and add more

drives as your needs expand. The maximum tower configuration available for TAC Systems is 18 separate drives in one enclosure. In addition to manufacturing a wide variety of tower systems, TAC can build custom towers to fill your specific needs.

Todd Systems

Todd Systems offers a veritable buffet of array, fixed-array, and tower systems that are limited only by your imagination and budget. Todd was one of the first companies to offer tower solutions in networked environments and has the experience to custom-build systems for almost any CD-ROM requirement.

How To Master Your Own CD-ROM Data Discs

Many companies are finding that archiving data or publishing company databases on CD-ROM discs is an affordable and productive way to get information quickly to customers, employees, and the public. The major drawback to recording your own CDs in the past has been cost: initial CD-R drives typically cost $15,000 or more. Prices have plummeted in recent months, however.

The dye-based recordable media used in CD-R drives has also come down substantially in price, with single blank discs selling for as little as $30 to $40. By the fall of 1993, media costs may be half that price.

CD-R makes a lot of sense for organizations that have large sets of data that must be periodically distributed to a wide audience. Catalogs, transaction records, and the like can require large amounts of storage, making them difficult and costly to distribute by conventional means. CD, however offers a simple, low-cost alternative.

Understanding the Premastering Process

The best CD-R drives in the world are useless without **premastering and mastering software**. Without these important tools, the recorded CD-R discs are not compatible—or readable—by standard CD-ROM drives. Although you can write data to CD-R drives with many software packages, only full-featured premastering systems allow you to record in industry-standard formats and offer a variety of other features.

Premastering, or logical formatting, is the process of converting your data—a company database, archival data, or scanned images—into a format that is accepted by the standard CD-ROM drive. Chapter 2, "CD-ROM Specifications Explained," describes many of these formats, such as ISO 9660, PhotoCD, and CD-ROM-XA.

When you use software to premaster data, it accepts your DOS-based data as input and produces as output a disc image of the data in the logical format that will be transferred to the blank CD. For this reason, premastering software needs massive amounts of hard drive storage space to record the disc image—up to 640 megabytes, or the equivalent of the final CD.

Because hard drives are expensive, the best premastering software supports large-capacity tape drives—4mm and 8mm drives are the most popular and have capacities in the 2-to-6-gigabyte range. The premastering software can then take your finished data or data application and store it in logical format on inexpensive tape. An added benefit of using

tape as an intermediary storage point for premastering is that you can make multiple, different masters, store them on a tape or tapes, and then run a series of CD-R discs from one tape session.

There are pros and cons to the use of tape in the mastering process, however. The tape drives themselves are $2000 to $7000, even though the tape itself is cheap. If you don't anticipate mastering a large number of different discs at one time, a large hard drive, devoted strictly to storing the premastered disc image, may be more economical. Hard drives in the 600-megabyte range are currently going for about $800. If your network or workstation needs tape backup, on the other hand, consider a 4mm tape drive that can serve as both a backup for the system and as a premastering facility for disc production.

All premastering software is not created equal. Beyond the CD-ROM formats it supports, a number of other factors must be accounted for. For example, because of the unique, spiraling track of the CD-ROM's recorded surface, data recorded on the inner tracks of the disc are more quickly accessed than those on the outer rim. Premastering software should allow you to determine where datasets, or files, are placed on the disc—reserving the most frequently accessed files for the inner tracks and relegating the least-used data to the farther reaches of the disc. Organizing your data in such a way increases the disc's performance.

In addition to optimizing the placement of data, the software should conserve space—that is, it should recognize blank areas within an image and eliminate them. When dumping a disc image to tape, for example, the software may read blank sectors of the hard drive and transfer them intact to the disc image, resulting in wasted CD-ROM disc space.

EXPLANATION

Premastering and Mastering Software

Premastering is the process of formatting the data on the PC in the way it will be placed on the disc; mastering is the process of copying the data onto an actual CD. Premastering can occur in the computer's RAM (if there is enough) but is usually done on the hard drive or on a tape drive.

Simulation of the finished product from the hard disk is also a key ingredient in good premastering software. It's best to run data from its disc image to see whether everything runs smoothly and the data is properly accessible before you make the expensive commitment to record the data on a blank disc. Recording to a CD-ROM is an expense in not only media, but valuable time: CDs take anywhere from a half hour to an hour to write. Some premastering software even simulates CD-ROM access times in test mode, allowing you to better determine how optimized your data is for the end user or the end user's application.

In general, you'll want to record your own CDs in the ISO 9660 format, which makes them compatible with the widest possible range of CD-ROM drives. Specialty applications (such as multimedia and PhotoCD) may mean you have to use different formats, however. For storing text-based or simple image-based databases, the ISO 9660 format is more than adequate.

Once the disc image of your data is saved and tested, the simple task of mastering begins. The mastering software reads the disc image from the hard drive or tape and transfers it to the CD-R drive, imprinting your data on a standard CD-ROM-format recordable disc. The recorded discs can be accessed, copied, or sent to a mastering facility where multiple copies can be mass-produced after making a production master from the CD-R disc.

Looking at Premastering and Mastering Software

One of the factors fueling the expansion of CD-R use is the availability of a number of top-notch premastering/mastering software packages. Earlier mastering software was difficult

to use and required a great deal of formatting knowledge to use effectively; most mastering software is now turnkey in nature and is compatible with virtually all the standard **CD-R** drives on the market.

There are two ways to premaster a disc. In the first, you build an actual image on a physical disk or tape. In the second (as is done with some titles described later in this chapter), you create "virtual disc images" on the fly. In other words, the software builds the image directly from the DOS files and transfers the image to the recordable disc as it goes along, eliminating the need for large hard drives or auxiliary tape systems. However, virtual-image software also prevents you from testing your data's viability and usability before committing it to CD-R disc. You can test your data, however, with the first method, and using a staged area for disc images makes multiple copies of one image relatively painless.

Note that most CD-R drives now come with at least some premastering software bundled in. Although this software may be less sophisticated than more full-featured—and full-priced—premastering packages, for most data-storage purposes, the bundled software may be just fine. The following sections describe just a few stand-alone premastering programs.

Tempra CD Maker

The Windows-based Tempra CD Maker mastering software from Mathmatica has a number of features to recommend it:

➤ Files, directories, and partitions to be recorded can be individually tagged

➤ Has a selection of ISO 9660 or High Sierra formats

➤ Provides simulation of CD for data testing

The Tempra CD Maker supports the Philips CD recorder and retails for about $1495.

CD-R

The use of the term *CD-R* in this chapter refers to the recording of accessible data on a CD-ROM recordable disc.

Mathmatica also plans to sell a hardware/software package that includes a Philips CD-R drive and a full range of Mathmatica authoring and animation tools.

Make Disc and Media Master

A longtime leader in the use of CD-ROM in the UNIX marketplace, Young Minds has recently released a Windows-based version of their Make Disc and Media Master software. Together, both components have a suggested list price of $1495.

Make Disc is the premastering and mastering component that allows you to select files, directories, and partitions for transfer to a disc image in ISO 9660 format. Media Master is also Windows-based and allows you to test-drive the data before committing it to disc.

CD-Prepare and CD-Record

Like Young Minds, DataWare Technology has two premastering and mastering software components: CD-Prepare and CD-Record. These software titles are pretty self-explanatory: The Prepare product produces a disc image—not virtual—that it stores on disk or tape. The disc image can be tested before you use CD-Record to send it to the recorder.

CD-GEN

The CD-GEN software from CD-ROM Strategies, Inc., supports most CD-ROM file structures and formats and has many additional features. It allows simple ordering of data for dataset optimization on the CD-ROM disc, provides support for all major CD-R recorders (including the Sony CDW-900E and the Philips CDD 521).

CD-GEN allows you to perform premaster-ing in multiple sessions to tape—

a godsend for those who are tight on hard drive space or for those who want to create discs over a period of time.

The simulation portion of the program allows you to test data access from a disc image. You can even tweak the simulated CD-ROM drive's specifications to see, for example, how the data reacts on a 600ms versus a 200ms CD-ROM drive.

As a bonus, the CD-GEN software can also perform on-the-fly CD-R images, bypassing the creation of the disc or tape image.

Although many software developers have taken premastering and mastering software and broken them into separate, complimentary packages, CD-ROM Strategies has delivered a full-function, all-in-one solution to recording CD-R data.

Looking at CD-R Drives

Large manufacturers have begun releasing CD-R drives, making prices very competitive. Bare drives—just the CD-R mechanism itself—run in the $4000 to $7000 range. Premastering and mastering software add from $1200 to $3000 to the final cost. Many companies are beginning to offer CD-R hardware/software bundles that slash costs even further. As competition heats up, look for continued price drops.

JVC, Philips, Sony, Ricoh, Pinnacle Micro, and Meridian Data all have competitively priced systems shipping now. Other systems have been announced but are not yet shipping. Keep in mind that CD-R may be the single-fastest growing segment in the CD-ROM industry; prices should fall and capabilities should increase dramatically over the next 12 months.

The hardware/software packages described in the following sections provide entire solutions to moving data onto CD-R discs.

Pinnacle Micro RCD-202	
Compatibility:	PC, Macintosh, or MPC-compliant
Interface:	SCSI, SCSI-2, or Proprietary
Formats supported:	CD-DA, ISO 9660, High Sierra, CD-ROM-XA
Average Access time:	3000 ms
Transfer rate:	153 KB/s
Data buffer:	64KB
Software included:	Premastering, mastering
Suggested list price:	$4095

FIGURE 11.1

The Pinnacle Micro RCD-202.

The RCD-202 from Pinnacle Micro supports the recording of virtually all CD-ROM formats with the exception of CD-I and CD-ROM-XA: CD-DA, PhotoCD, and mixed audio/data formats are supported. The drive has a standard SCSI interface and RCA jacks (see fig. 11.1). The Pinnacle Micro internal, half-height unit is an exceptional value at $4095.

Meridian Data Personal SCRIBE	
Compatibility:	PC, Macintosh, or MPC-compliant
Interface:	SCSI-2
Formats supported:	CD-DA, ISO 9660, High Sierra, CD-ROM-XA
Average Access time:	350 ms
Transfer rate:	153 KB/s
Data buffer:	64KB
Software included:	Premastering, mastering
Suggested list price:	$7995

The Meridian Data Personal SCRIBE 500.

Meridian ships a whole system—drive, software for mastering, and SCSI adapter and cables. The Meridian Data Personal SCRIBE 500 supports ISO 9660, CD-DA, and PhotoCD formats (see fig. 11.2).

The Meridian package includes the following:

➤ Personal SCRIBE software for CD mastering

➤ CD-ROM recorder, cable, and interface card

➤ One blank CD

Personal SCRIBE 500 is an affordable, highly versatile system that should be at the top of any list for consideration. Meridian Data has a strong presence in the optical field (the company claims that nearly 75 percent of all published CD-ROM titles originated on a Meridian hardware/software system). For in-house data duplication, archiving, or distribution, the Personal SCRIBE 500 is a perfect solution.

Philips 521WR

Compatibility:	PC, Macintosh, or MPC-compliant
Interface:	SCSI-2
Formats supported:	CD-DA, ISO 9660, High Sierra, CD-ROM-XA
Average Access time:	350 ms
Transfer rate:	153 KB/s
Data buffer:	64KB
Software included:	Premastering, mastering
Suggested list price:	$8995

Other Meridian Data Innovations

Meridian also sells a networked CD-R and has announced a joint venture with Kodak to provide multi-session PhotoCD capabilities across a network. The NETSCRIBE 1000, like the Personal SCRIBE 500, packs all hardware and software into one bundle. The basic NETSCRIBE 1000 package also has NetWare support for up to five users. A networked CD-R enables multiple users to archive valuable data and images to the CD-R for off-site storage or use in an array for publishing the finished data to the company network. The five-user NETSCRIBE 1000, including all hardware and software, is $13,995.

Meridian Data is best known for its CD-ROM networking software: CD-Net. CD-Net is used to network multiple CD-ROM drives under the Novell NetWare operating system. When considering array systems or jukeboxes for use across the network, Meridian CD-Net may be the best software solution available.

Philips recently announced full CD-R publishing packages running under Microsoft Windows and for the Macintosh System 7. Not only does the publishing system include all the necessary hardware for mastering CDs, the Windows-based mastering software handles ISO 9660, High Sierra, CD-DA, and PhotoCD formats. Software upgrades allow the 521WR to record CD-ROM-XA and CD-I format discs as well.

The complete bundled solution has a suggested list price of $8995.

JVC Personal RomMaker	
Compatibility:	PC, Macintosh, or MPC-compliant
Interface:	SCSI-2
Formats supported:	CD-DA, ISO 9660, High Sierra, CD-ROM-XA
Average Access time:	300 ms
Transfer rate:	153 KB/s
Data buffer:	128KB
Software included:	Premastering, mastering
Suggested list price:	$12,799

FIGURE 11.3

The JVC Personal Archiver is a new, low-cost, CD-ROM archiving system that supports Macintosh and DOS machines.

JVC offers premastering software and hardware solutions for both Macintosh and DOS machines (see fig. 11.3). The system's software creates a disc image on a hard drive that is a part of the JVC system. Once the disc image is created, you can test the data in its disc-image format. From the hard drive, the JVC software can then move the data to a CD-R.

The JVC system includes everything you need to create CD-R discs, including a large hard drive for data-disc images and CD-ROM image testing.

Sony CDW-900E	
Compatibility:	PC, UNIX, Macintosh, or MPC-compliant
Interface:	SCSI-2
Formats supported:	CD-DA, ISO 9660, High Sierra, CD-ROM-XA, MMCD
Average Access time:	350 ms
Transfer rate:	154 KB/s
Data buffer:	64KB
Software included:	Premastering, mastering
Suggested list price:	Not available

Sony's CDW-900E is a double-speed transfer-rate drive that supports all major CD-ROM formats (ISO 9660 and High Sierra) as well as Sony's format for its **MMCD** player. Unlike other CD-R drives on the market, the Sony cannot read standard CD-ROM discs.

When used with the recently announced Sony Multimedia Authoring software, the CDW-900E makes an ideal system for producing prototype CD-ROM-XA application titles. It is not good for standard CD-ROM distribution of data, however. The drive and software are sold primarily to application developers. Pricing was not available.

How To Develop CD-ROM Applications

When it comes to CD-ROM applications, data isn't everything. To produce a usable, stand-alone CD-ROM application, there's a lot more to do than dump the contents of your company's customer list onto a disc and turn it loose on the sales force. For example, although 99 percent of Prophone's excellent business phone-number CD-ROM is just that—names and phone numbers—it would be a useless lump of data without its fine search-and-retrieval software.

That's the bottom line in producing high-quality CD-ROM applications: the interface. Big databases require elegant front ends. Multimedia applications with mounds of sound, video, and text need a system for pulling it into a useful tool.

Although you won't be able to build your own multimedia CD-ROM by the time you finish this chapter, we guarantee you'll have a good understanding of the hard work that goes into producing all the fine CD titles we've described in this book.

The first (and perhaps the only obvious) decision a CD-ROM developer must make is what form the application will take. That is, will the application be primarily text or primarily other media, such as graphics, video, or

EXPLANATION
Executive CDs

Sony's MMCD (multimedia CD) player uses standard CDs written in a proprietary format to provide a platform for multimedia applications in a portable package. The software offerings for this player are mostly targeted at the traveling business executive; titles include foreign-language instruction and business-database applications.

sound. Multimedia and text-based applications share some similarities in the development process, but tools for creating the two basic types of CD-ROM applications are vastly different. Each application type poses a different set of challenges for the developer.

Multimedia development adds another layer of complexity to the development process. Not only must text and graphic elements be indexed for later retrieval, but sound, video, and animation may also play a large part in the finished product. Fortunately, a number of multimedia development products are now on the market, easing the construction of complex software titles.

Text-based applications are usually databases of information from which users need to extract and compile data. The applications may include graphic images, but their primary purpose is to communicate text information.

Because the meat of the application is the database's text, two factors are critical in molding the lump of textual data into a solid application: the indexing of the text and the software that performs the searches.

First of all, the text must be in a format that the indexing software can read. For example, Microsoft's Viewer can read only Microsoft Word files. Other indexing software accepts only ASCII text or RTF (Rich Text Format) files. Fortunately, the better packages can import a variety of standard word processing formats for the indexing process.

Indexing Applications

Text-based CD-ROM authoring software includes utilities for indexing the database of text. A thorough indexing of a volume of history, for example, would compile all references to every word—and its location in the volume. The compiled index serves as the gateway for the user front end.

To continue with the example of a history volume, assume that the indexing software found all occurrences of the name *Richard Nixon* in your 2,000-page history volume. The compiled index has *Richard Nixon* pointers and cross-listings to specific sections of the volume that contain references to the former President. When a user queries the application for "Richard Nixon," the software goes to the index and provides the user with a list of chapters or articles that contain the queried text. This list comes from the stored, compiled index.

Indexing, then, plays a critical role in an application's performance—whether it is text-based or multimedia-based. For example, you would never want a complete index of all the text in a database: indexing words such as *the* and *and* serves no purpose. These words are called *noise words*; good indexing software provides a way to exclude such words from the index-building process. You can usually submit such a list to the software before indexing. Here's a partial list of typical noise words:

> a
> an
> and
> that
> the
> there
> which
> would

You get the picture. Unless you're doing textual analysis concerning an author's writing style, indexing noise words is a waste of CD-ROM space.

Other irrelevant words may not be as readily apparent as noise words. For example, it would be similarly useless to index all the occurrences of the word *CD-ROM* in this book—you'd be presented with a list of nearly every page in this book. In the development of text-based applications, proper and economical indexing is the key to building a good end product.

Aside from the exclusion of noise words, indexing must also mirror the uses the data will be put to in the application. For example, *Bowker's Books in Print* on CD-ROM allows you to search the contents of the database for given predefined fields. No other indexing is necessary in this application. To simplify the search interface in *Books in Print*, you can search by any of the following fields:

> Author
> Title
> Publisher
> ISBN
> Audience

(Other fields are available in the application; these are just some examples.) When searching for a book in this database, why would any user need a text that is 100-percent indexed? The developer, in constructing the application, indexes only those elements that the application (and therefore the user) would want to search for. The result is a faster application, a less confusing interface for the user, and a vast conservation of the CD-ROM disc space used to hold the compiled indexes. Not to mention a time-saver in the initial indexing and preparation process.

Unless the developer is submitting an entire text for thorough indexing to the software, the indexing process can be a tedious one—a trained operator or the developer must make decisions about what gets indexed, what can be left out, and what categories various words or fields fall into. This is a necessary and time-consuming evil of building text-based CD-ROM applications. But the effort pays off in the finished product.

We'll say it again: in application development, the index is the key to a successful CD-ROM.

Using Search-and-Retrieval Software

If you've ever looked at text-based CD-ROM applications, you've noted that they all basically allow you to search for items or citations by submitting a request to the application. Most are menu based, offering a variety of options for requesting data; others merely present you with a stark and uninviting question mark.

Welcome to the user interface and search-and-retrieval engines. Search-and-retrieval front ends are available to developers as a tool kit—the indexing software puts tags in the text; the search-and-retrieval software uses the compiled index to find citations, present choices to the user, and go to and retrieve the chosen text or field.

Obviously, not all search-and-retrieval engines are created equal. And not all are suitable to every type of application task. Before we go into the features of search-and-retrieval software, let's look at the individual components of this application front end.

Text-based search software usually incorporates a text menu from which the user chooses various options and actions. The menus may be as simple as "Search" and "Print" options or as complex as a multilayered, pull-down menu of Boolean operands, clipboards for marked text, and printer configurations. In some search-and-retrieval software development kits, the search interfaces are not customizable and offer the developers little freedom to add their own items or menu choices. Other development kits allow a complete customization of the interface. But despite interfaces with limited customization, you'll begin to recognize similar interfaces if you use a variety of CD titles from different developers. You'll also begin to favor—and

Good Data, Bad Interface

Based on our experience, the contents of a CD-ROM application may not be enough to persuade us to use it if it has a search-and-retrieval engine we've grown to dislike. All the data in the world is not worth the aggravation of certain limitations.

FIGURE 11.4

Roger Ebert's Home Movie Companion, published by Quantas Press, uses the popular Folio View search-and-retrieval software.

detest, perhaps—the capabilities or short-comings of the various engines.

There's good reason for the use of standard interfaces. Unless the application is so unique in the presentation of its material that it needs a custom search-and-retrieval engine, a ready-made interface allows the CD publisher to more quickly produce the application and bring it to market. Why reinvent the wheel when there are a number of great packages available?

The interface is intimately tied to the capabilities of the search-and-retrieval software that lies beneath the surface. Menu items and options, then, are often based in large part on the underlying capabilities of the software. Take a look at the interface for *Roger Ebert's Home Movie Companion*, for example (see fig. 11.4).

Note that the primary areas of search are clearly defined for the user at the outset—no other options are allowed at this stage. The Movies by Titles and Essays options are menu items; you must branch to these areas before continuing. This arrangement may be a plus—users are guided to areas in which the developer expects they may have an interest. The

downside of this menu system is a limited view of the entire database; options for wider searches open up only after a category has been selected. This particular interface allows the developer to program the initial menu choices—but that is all. From a development standpoint, this particular engine is extremely easy to implement and produces highly effective full-text applications. The look and feel of the interface during the searches (as is true for most search-and-retrieval engines) is identical for all applications that use this software for development.

Flexibility and logic are key in the choice of an interface front-end. For a video guide, the Folio front end with its main-menu choices is a better interface than providing the user with a cryptic search option. The individual who will browse a video database expects a simpler approach to finding information.

Looking at Search-and-Retrieval Engines

As you might expect, the search-and-retrieval engines that lie underneath the interfaces have different capabilities as well. Some search engines provide you with a list of choices you then can view one at a time; you return to the list after each viewing. Other engines require you to perform the search each time you view a listing. Still others allow you to compile a list of citations and print the entire set—to the screen, to a disk, or to a printer. Again, the purpose of the application determines the best type of retrieval. For most applications, however, the more options available to the user for retrieval, the better. And unless the developer anticipates fundamental confusion in using search techniques, the broadest possible search capabilities should be provided.

Aside from how the citations are retrieved—to the screen, the printer, or to disk files—

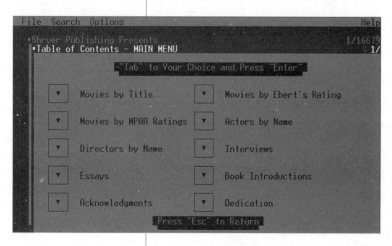

another consideration in retrieval software is the way text is displayed. In World Library's *Library of the Future*, for example, you can display text in full screen, partial screen, and with automatic scrolling (see fig. 11.5). The Folio engine used in *Roger Ebert's Home Video Companion* layers the screen with window on top of window of retrieved text when you retrieve more than one item, allowing you to skip back and forth between retrieved citations at will. But note: a retrieval engine that piles up cross-references on the screen for an electronic software manual would be completely inappropriate for reading Dickens' *Bleak House* on a monitor. The *Bleak House* application—and its ultimate use: reading—require a totally different interface design to make it useful.

Understanding Search Terms and Operations

Depending on the search-and-retrieval engine in the developer's application, you may or may not be able to do a large number of types of searches. Here are some of the types of searches that may be allowed, based on the search-and-retrieval software:

➤ **Wildcard.** Just as you use wildcard operations in DOS, some search engines allow you to use wildcards when searching databases. For example, if you use ***ball** in a search of the *Compton's Interactive Encyclopedia*, you get the results shown in figure 11.6.

➤ **Boolean.** Boolean searches—or Boolean logic—are a series of search techniques in which inclusion or exclusion of a combination of elements produces a set of results. For example, a search of our history text with the Boolean expression **Nixon AND Vietnam** results in a list of all articles that contain mentions of both Nixon *and* Vietnam. Here are other examples of Boolean operation:

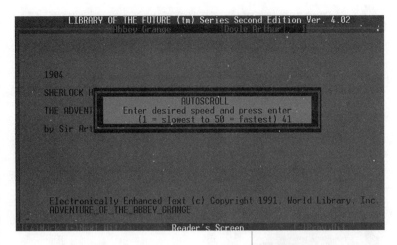

OR: automobile OR car

NOT: automobile NOT Ford

Good search software allows *nested* Boolean operations. For example, **automobile AND car NOT Ford** produces references to any article that contains the words *automobile* and *car* but not if the word *Ford* is also mentioned.

In addition to nesting, some search software allows Boolean *proximity* searches. If a word falls within the same sentence, paragraph, or page, it is a candidate for the **proximity** search. The search **automobile AND Ford SENTENCE** produces all citations in which *automobile* and *Ford* fall in the same sentence.

➤ **Phrase.** Search software that allows phrase look-ups is especially useful in full-text documents. You input the exact phrase you are looking for, and the search engine finds the text string within the database of text. Entering **Four score and seven years ago** for our history CD-ROM, for example, takes you to Lincoln's Gettysburg Address.

Phrase searches are also useful for finding all occurrences of phrases in a collection of texts in one database. Entering **Oedipus complex**, for example, calls up all the references

Proximity: How Close Is "Close"?

Proximity searches in some software allow proximity values, expressed in numbers, for determining hits or misses. Using **automobiles AND Ford > 5**, for example, ensures that all text that includes the words *automobile* and *Ford* within five words or less of each other is a hit; any other condition is a miss.

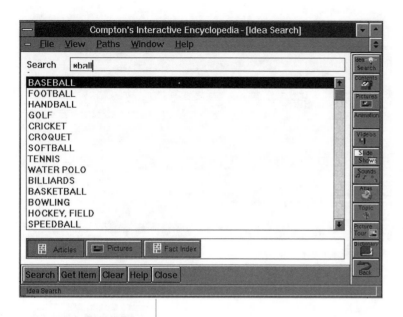

photos in the CD-ROM application, and the scanning software only supports certain graphics formats, the developer must convert the art and photo scans to one of the retrieval software's supported formats. Developers must also take into consideration what resolutions the application-development software supports; it makes no sense to scan or create high-resolution elements if the intended platform does not support the higher resolutions or the retrieval software cannot display it properly.

FIGURE 11.6.

The use of the wildcard asterisk (*) before the word *ball* in the search calls up all articles in the encyclopedia that end in *ball* as well as any article that contains *ball* as part of the text (or any part of any word in the text).

to this Freudian term in Quanta's *Monarch Notes*. Any application that uses full text should allow phrase searches.

➤ **Field.** Applications based primarily on fixed-field databases (that is, databases in which data exists exclusively in one strictly defined field or another) provide searches within any given field; they may also allow the addition of wildcard searching within any given field. A search for **Morris*** in the Last Name field in a phone-directory database should result in a list of all last names beginning with the letters *morris*: Morris, Morrison, Morrisey, and so on.

Indexing Graphics

Most development packages (although not all) allow the indexing and retrieval of standard graphic elements such as PCX files. And some development packages support only a limited number of graphics formats. If a developer wants to use scanned art work or product

SGML

To help provide a basis for standard transmission of text from one operating system and application to another without massive reformatting, the SGML (Standard General Markup Language) has been adopted by a number of software application and publishing groups. This language, originally intended for publishing text electronically in a number of desktop publishing and document archiving applications, is already in use in a number of CD-ROM application-development packages. Although it is not an indexing convention, SGML allows any SGML-aware application to format and display text in a uniform manner, despite the text's origin or the platform on which it is used (DOS, Mac, UNIX, and so on). CD-ROM authoring programs that accept SGML-formatted text can easily import documents for use in applications across platforms, regardless of the source of the document. Features of the SGML format also allow for some indexing, making the data preparation and indexing procedure even less complicated.

SGML tags, on the highest level, identify types of documents, which is useful in a many-faceted database. Descriptive tags are used for incorporated elements, such as charts, graphs, or graphics files. Finer-level tags are used for definitions of headings, subheadings, and other subdivisions and special-case text-handling and formatting conventions.

Use of SGML in the data-preparation stage of development smooths the integration of text retrieval and display in the final stages of development. And as we said, many data-preparation programs accept text with SGML tags—and many add-on packages for popular word processors can add SGML tags to existing word processor documents.

Indexing and Search-and-Retrieval Software

There are dozens of indexing and search-and-retrieval packages available now. All provide developers with tools to index data and provide an interface to the search-and-retrieval engine. These packages permit the developer—for a fee (usually by royalty on a bulk basis)—to include the software on the disc as a part of the application. Other packages charge only for the development software; some allow the developer to include **run-time modules** free of charge.

In addition, some development packages allow a full range of search capabilities—from limited field searches to nested Boolean operations and a full complement of graphics indexing and display capabilities—and may also be useful in developing products across different platforms. The trend in development packages, in fact, is toward cross-platform development in which database and multimedia objects are usable in nearly identical formats in any operating system.

This multiplatform strategy lets publishers drastically reduce production costs, and, hopefully, pass on these savings to consumers.

ROMware

Nimbus' ROMware development search-and-retrieval package allows DOS, Windows, and multimedia options. The package is strong on full-text indexing and use of graphics in a DOS environment. The company also makes ROMview, a Windows-based equivalent of the DOS-based ROMware.

The interface is customizable, and searches can be compiled. Searching by phrase and nested Boolean operations is possible; text blocking is also supported. Toolkits for further customization (such as BookFace) allow creation of various display characteristics for specific applications.

Here's an added bonus for developers: Nimbus is also a full-service CD-ROM production facility that provides everything from project consultation to warehousing of finished products.

KAware

The KAware DOS-based development package allows for extensive interface customization. For an excellent example of the flexibility KAware has—particularly with fixed-field databases—see the TFPL *CD-ROM Directory*, which lists thousands of CD-ROM titles, software distributors, hardware manufacturers and much, much more. The TFPL disc has an extensive array of searchable fields—made possible by the KAware indexing and search-and-retrieval engine. Searches can be further refined within fields or sub-fields, making it easy for searches to zero-in on specific results.

Another of KAware's retrieval features is its ability to combine previous searches into a printable or disk file. You can also omit certain searches from the compiled list, making misses and mistakes easy to prune from your finished work.

Folio Views and Folio Views for Windows

Although Folio got its biggest boost in the development of online technical manuals and software troubleshooting guides, users with little experience also can index and build a standard interface for a text database. One of the best examples of the use of Folio outside

EXPLANATION
Run-Time Versions

Run-time versions of software (in this case, of search-and-retrieval packages) are free-standing engines that run independently of the development software on the disc and are usually provided free of charge or for a small royalty fee (charged to the developer).

the software-manual arena is in Infobases' *American History* CD. The Folio interface allows for extremely flexible searches on full-text databases. Text is compressed after conversion to the Folio database; a wide variety of word processing formats are supported.

Add-in modules allow developers to scan and perform optical character recognition on text, and then import the text directly into Folio. Applications created with Folio let users create annotations, bookmarks, and shadow files that can be saved for later reference.

The DOS version of Folio has support for graphics files that are stored and viewed separately.

The Folio system is, perhaps, the easiest for the uninitiated to use. The straightforward way in which Folio imports and indexes full-text databases is a painless process. The newer OCR and graphics features make it a perfect development tool for businesses that want to distribute data in stand-alone format in a hurry, and that want to spend as little time as possible making subsequent updates.

The Windows-based version of Folio adds font and screen configurations to Folio's excellent basic search-and-retrieval engine. All the ease-of-use in the DOS product is preserved, and there are the additional WYSIWYG features of Windows fonts and formatting. Another great feature for the Windows version is support for OLE: graphics, sound, and even video objects can be imbedded anywhere in Folio Views once they're named and stored.

Font, hierarchy, and highlighting styles can be set as well. Folio text databases developed under DOS can be used with the Windows version, and vice-versa. Print versions of any Folio Views retain all formatting.

CD Author/CD Answer and CD Author/CD Answer for Windows

Dataware has been in the CD-ROM development business since there was a CD-ROM development business. Their popular authoring and retrieval development systems are available for every platform from DOS to Windows to the Macintosh. CD Author has utilities that convert and index data; the package also allows users to customize menus from a library of predefined interfaces. The retrieval package, CD Answer, supports a variety of searches, all selectively available during application development: the developer decides how much—or how little—the application will be able to search.

Dataware recently announced multiplatform support for their authoring system, allowing one application to be ported to UNIX, DOS, Apple, Windows, MMCD, and other formats. This flexibility allows developers to quickly deliver products to a number of operating systems and CD formats in a short development cycle. The CD Author/CD Answer system also supports multiple formats recorded to one disc, allowing data on a single disc to be shared by UNIX, DOS, and all other platforms. According to Dataware, over 400 CD-ROM titles have been developed to date using their software.

Dataware's Windows-based package has all the features of the DOS package as well as Windows-based customizable menus, dialog boxes, and buttons. The Windows version supports many of the Windows MCI extensions, allowing the inclusion of graphics and sound objects.

Windows-Based Multimedia Application Development Software

Because Windows multimedia development may involve text, graphics, video, and sound, the multimedia development tools described in the following sections are often more akin to storyboards for the production of films rather than systems for retrieving data. Some of these development tools (most notably Asymetrix's Toolbook) have data-query functions; others only allow selection of prewritten scripts or menu choices and have little opportunity for branching or searching. It's important to note that most of these systems are primarily used for other multimedia presentations rather than CD-ROM-based applications; disk-based and kiosk-based presentations are the most prevalent. There's one exception in this group: a number of commercial applications have been developed using Toolbook.

Smartrieve

Compton's Smartrieve would easily fall into the multimedia authoring category were it not for its extensive search-and-retrieve capabilities. Actually a set of tools, the Compton package allows developers to index a variety of text, graphics, and sound files and formats for use with Compton's search-and-retrieval engine. SMARTBUILD, naturally, is the database indexing and building software; SMARTDR is the retrieval engine that allows the simultaneous search of multiple databases (sound, graphics, or text). A library of user-customizable subroutines for interfaces is included in the SMARTAPI utilities. Another feature of the Smartrieve system is that it allows Compton to build in their Virtual Workspace windows to all applications, giving users a thumbnail view of previous searches, available merely by clicking on the representation. Within workspaces, text and graphics can be cut and pasted.

Compton is using these development tools to provide software titles on a variety of platforms including Apple, Tandy, VIS, and MMCD.

Toolbook

Asymetrix's Toolbook was one of the first multimedia authoring tools available and is still one of the most favored. Unlike some other development tools, Toolbook is easy to use and extremely versatile in creating text-links and hypertext cross-references.

What makes Toolbook so easy to use is the extensive set of templates included in the basic software package. Users can plug text and graphics into predefined panels and easily customize a wide range of dialog boxes, radio buttons, and menus.

Video and animations in any of the Windows-supported formats can be included as well; OLE support lets you add sound and other objects from a number of Windows-based applications (from spreadsheets to paint programs to word processors).

A number of multimedia publishers have developed titles using Toolbook, and for good reason. Development is straightforward and developers can use off-the-shelf Windows applications to develop all the necessary multimedia elements. Perhaps the biggest reason for its popularity is that Toolbook includes a royalty-free run-time module with its already reasonably priced development kit. Developers both large and small can put together an application and distribute it freely. Examples of Toolbook-developed CD-ROMs include

Warner New Media's *Desert Storm* and EduQuest's *National Parks*.

The only drawback to Toolbook is its reliance on a page philosophy; in other words, screens full of data are presented one at a time and must be linked by scripts to produce more than one contiguous page of information.

To be fair, however, the scripting capabilities in Toolbook are powerful; if developers take the relatively short time to learn the Toolbook language, they can construct incredibly detailed, linked, hypertext creations. Toolbook's level of hypertext creation and maintenance is more difficult to achieve with other packages, even with the object-oriented application-development tools.

IconAuthor

IconAuthor, the multifaceted authoring toolkit from AIMtech, is one of the most feature rich of any Windows-based multimedia development software available.

The latest version of IconAuthor supports OLE and DDL, making it possible to include any and all Windows-based graphics, sound, text, and video elements from standard Windows applications.

IconAuthor uses a flow-chart approach to application development. A toolbar running along the side of the development space allows the developer to select, in icon format, any type of supported element. The developer then assigns the appropriate text, animation, or other object to the icon and moves down the flow chart, building the application one element at a time.

The program uses extensive branching, and can attach many conditions to events. For example, if a mouse is clicked during the play of an animation, the application can ask whether the user wants to see the animation full screen, to continue playing it, or quit. In addition, the branching supports extensive database management of multimedia elements and allows extensive conditional use of objects in many layers.

With its easy-to-understand objects, flowchart construction, and extensive support of video and branching capabilities, IconAuthor is a full toolbelt for creating the most complex—and exciting—multimedia presentations.

HSC Interactive

HSC Interactive is a trimmed-back version of its big-brother application, IconAuthor. Interactive supports fewer branching elements and has fewer predefined object elements that you can use in the flow-chart builds for finished applications than does IconAuthor.

Other capabilities missing from HSC Interactive, when compared to IconAuthor, are the database management of elements and some graphics-format support. The presentations you develop with Interactive may not be as complex as those possible with IconAuthor, but Interactive is also more than five times less expensive than AIMtech's high-end product.

Authorware

Macromedia's multimedia development package is the top in its class—and the most expensive. Run-time version royalties, similarly, are also top of the heap in terms of price.

But with the price comes a variety of features and performance that many of the other development packages lack. The Authorware system is similar to IconAuthor in its icon-based, flow-chart approach to building applications.

Branching and conditions for branching to other events are even more extensive than those available in other packages, and the latest version of Authorware allows multiple events to occur simultaneously—providing for multitasking multimedia, as it were. For example, while viewing a Video for Windows clip about the first moon landing, you can hit the *A* text button to pop up a related text article or a biography and still photo of Neal Armstrong.

The video formats supported by Authorware include DVI, Video for Windows, and QuickTime for Windows, making it the most video-intensive multimedia development kit available today. OLE and DDL support allow the use of any Windows-based element.

Completely customizable button bars, menus, and dialog boxes round out this one-stop multimedia authoring solution.

StudioXA

Mammoth Micro recently released this cross-platform development tool for producing MMCD (CD-ROM-XA), OS/2, and MPC multimedia titles. The StudioXA authoring system does everything from capturing and storing audio, video, and graphics elements to formatting the data for true XA interleaving of audio and video. Toolkits for sizing video and touching up graphics elements are also included. Video can be captured at rates up to 15 frames per second.

Most importantly, the developer can preview the multimedia production at any time during its creation; alternatively, any portion of the production can be viewed and edited. Developers can create screen layouts as well as button bars, radio buttons, hot spots, and scroll bars, all without any programming knowledge. Buttons can be scripted to any element or action within the presentation.

Most importantly, StudioXA formats the finished piece in the XA disc format, ready to

be recorded onto any CD-R that supports the XA specification. XA-formatted files, of course, can also be premastered onto tape. Developers can preview the finished CD in simulation of a CD-ROM XA. Most important to developers, Mammoth's companion software, PlayerXA, allows applications created with StudioXA to be played on MPC, OS/2, or MMCD formats with no modification to the original application.

User-Tested, Author-Recommended

Before we leave the discussion of application development tools, we'd like to express our preferences. After reviewing and using well over 150 CD-ROM titles for this book—and in our professions—we've come up with a few favorite user interfaces:

Text-based: Folio Views

Windows-based: Microsoft Viewer

Multimedia-based: Authorware

How To Master, Produce, and Print CD-ROM Applications

Once developers have completed and debugged the CD-ROM application, the premastering and mastering process begins. If developers use premastering software that simulates CD-ROM usage, they can even test the application's performance and make adjustments accordingly.

After debugging and premastering, developers can record the final CD-ROM application on a CD-R disc to produce a formatted CD-ROM disc that can be used to produce a *one-off*.

What's a One-Off?

A *one-off* is a single production copy of a CD-ROM made for testing purposes. The developer sends the CD-R disc or tape master to a one-off facility or full-production house to have a production disc made. This disc is used for extensive testing of the application before a full production run is made. Major developers use multiple one-offs for field testing before making the costly commitment to a full production run.

A number of one-off companies have started up over the last two years; many of them are not even attached to full-production facilities. Their sole reason for existence is to offer one-off test discs and limited-run production CDs. In many cases, these small shops are better suited to providing discs for limited-use CD developers; as a rule, larger full-service facilities don't consider taking project with very small production runs.

CD-ROM Production Facilities

A number of independent and large commercial facilities are available to the CD-ROM developer for mass production of the final application. Most facilities in this competitive environment offer complete one-stop CD-ROM production.

One successful independent, Nimbus Corporation, offers a full gamut of CD-ROM-production services from data conversion all the way to warehousing. Nimbus, and other full-service facilities, can provide these services:

➤ Prepare and convert data

➤ Premaster and master data

➤ Create master discs and one-off productions

➤ Take care of full production runs, including quality control

➤ Provide disc and jewel-case imprinting and packaging

➤ Arrange shipping and warehousing

Other services available through some facilities include drop shipment of orders to distributors and order fulfillment. In some cases, the last developers may see of their code before it arrives shrink-wrapped is the CD-R or tape sent to the facility.

The Optical Publishers Association

Independent publishers, in particular, are advised to join the Optical Publishers Association. This Ohio-based professional organization is a clearinghouse of information for CD-ROM application developers. The association provides members with industry updates on a quarterly basis concerning the latest in hardware, software, and production technologies and techniques; a monthly publication, "Digital Publishing Business," focuses on the business aspects of CD-ROM development and production. The association's founder, Richard Bowers, compiles an extensive bibliography of background and technical books and papers on the CD-ROM industry.

Association members also receive information regarding related technical associations, trade shows, and technical seminars and workshops.

Aside from member benefits, the Optical Publisher's Association has taken a proactive role in such issues as multimedia standards development and standards in the interpretability of search-and-retrieval software.

The Optical Publisher's Association may be reached at the following address:

PO Box 212668

Columbus, Ohio 43221

Or contact the OPA on CompuServe; just type **GO CDROM VENDORS.**

Chapter 12

CD-ROM on the Road: Going Portable

For those of you whose work keeps you on the go, the notebook computer and its liberating portability have been the answer to a prayer. Yet if you adopt CD-ROM technology, are you going to be tied to a desk again?

The answer, thankfully, is a resounding *no*. Although still in its infancy, portable CD-ROM technology is mature enough for consideration. The small but competent selection of portable, battery-powered drives, integrated notebook machines, portable computers with CD-ROM capability, and specialized CD-player hardware offers enough choice to get you going in this emerging field.

Choosing Your Poison

The decision about what sort of portable CD-ROM hardware to buy is made easier by the somewhat limited selection available. However, you still must decide just what you hope to accomplish with your portable CD-ROM before you can make a choice. Let's take a look at the four classes of hardware—portable drives, integrated notebook systems, integrated lunchbox systems, and dedicated portable readers—and what they offer.

Portable Drives

Portable CD-ROM drives are built using the same technology as Sony Corporation's ubiquitous Discman portable CD player. Portable CD-ROM drives are relatively lightweight and battery powered. Unfortunately, they are also noticeably slower than their desktop counterparts. This is because the sled that moves the laser pickup is not designed to move quickly—a relatively unimportant thing when you use the drive for music, but very noticeable when you use the drive to access data.

Although the slow-moving sled affects **seek time** (the time it takes the drive to find the next item), it does not hurt the data transfer rate, another important speed specification.

There are two basic reasons you may want to buy a portable CD-ROM drive. If you already own a notebook or portable computer and

TIP

Small but Slow

If you intend to use a portable drive for things like multimedia presentations—where sluggish seek times may interfere with a smooth result—you may want to look at other possibilities.

don't look forward to investing in another, a portable drive can add CD-ROM capability to your existing computer. Most portable drives connect to the parallel port of your machine, using either a parallel-to-SCSI adapter or some proprietary adapter. A CD-ROM drive that uses the SCSI scheme is clearly the preference.

The other reason you may choose a portable drive is cost. No, portable drives are not inherently cheaper than packages with integrated CD-ROM drives; but if you intend to use CD-ROM at your desk as well as on the road, the portable drive can pull double duty and save you hundreds of dollars.

The following sections describe some of the portable drives currently available. The list is not intended to be exhaustive. Because of the nature of portables—they require a state-of-the-art design just to make them work—there are really no bad ones on the market. Base your choice on specifications and price.

CD Porta-Drive Model T3401

External (Portable)	
[x] PC compatible	
[x] Macintosh compatible	
[x] MPC compliant	
[x] PhotoCD, single session	
[x] PhotoCD, multi-session	
Interface:	
[x] SCSI	
[x] SCSI-2	
[ ] Proprietary	
Average access time	200 ms
Transfer rate	330 KB/s
Buffer	256KB
Audio:	
[x] Standard RCA jacks	
[x] Headphones	
[x] 4-pin CD audio out	
Suggested list price:	$850

The price of the CD Porta-Drive Model T3401 includes drive, caddy, power supply, enclosure, and instructions. SCSI cards are sold separately by the company, but Adaptec, Future Domain, and Procom SCSI adapters should be fine if you use the appropriate Toshiba drivers.

The company also sells a parallel-to-SCSI adapter—a SCSI-on-the-printer-port solution for the external drive. This adapter makes it possible to easily attach the drive to a notebook computer that has no slot available for a SCSI card. It is also an ideal solution for those who are squeamish about opening up PCs and messing with SCSI interface cards.

NEC MultiSpin-38

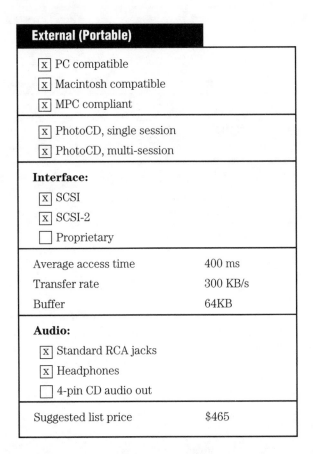

External (Portable)

[x] PC compatible	
[x] Macintosh compatible	
[x] MPC compliant	
[x] PhotoCD, single session	
[x] PhotoCD, multi-session	
Interface:	
[x] SCSI	
[x] SCSI-2	
[ ] Proprietary	
Average access time	400 ms
Transfer rate	300 KB/s
Buffer	64KB
Audio:	
[x] Standard RCA jacks	
[x] Headphones	
[ ] 4-pin CD audio out	
Suggested list price	$465

Notice that the NEC MultiSpin-38 portable has a higher access time and less of a buffer than the NEC MultiSpin-74 or MultiSpin-84 drives. Still, this is an amazing price for a portable CD-ROM drive that uses double-speed technology. This MultiSpin drive is more than adequate for multimedia tasks, including full-motion video in QuickTime for the Mac or Video for Windows.

Liberty 115 Series

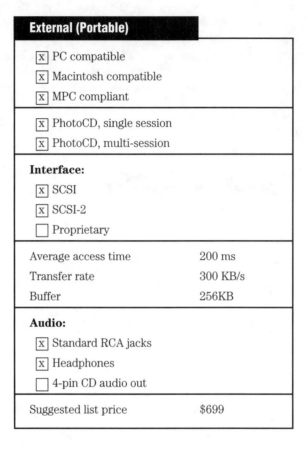

External (Portable)	
☒ PC compatible	
☒ Macintosh compatible	
☒ MPC compliant	
☒ PhotoCD, single session	
☒ PhotoCD, multi-session	
Interface:	
☒ SCSI	
☒ SCSI-2	
☐ Proprietary	
Average access time	200 ms
Transfer rate	300 KB/s
Buffer	256KB
Audio:	
☒ Standard RCA jacks	
☒ Headphones	
☐ 4-pin CD audio out	
Suggested list price	$699

Liberty Systems

Liberty Systems is best known for bundling a variety of mass-storage devices with SCSI and parallel-to-SCSI interfaces. The company specializes in removable-media drives such as Syquest systems and high-end optical products. Their 115CD-P portable CD-ROM reader is a Toshiba drive in a Liberty enclosure with parallel-to SCSI, Macintosh, and standard PC SCSI connection options. It prices out much lower than the CD-Technology portable (described in the preceding section), which is based on the same Toshiba XM-301 drive mechanism. If you want a solid portable at an attractive price, take a look at the Liberty drive.

The **Liberty** model 115CD-P has a parallel-port SCSI adapter and a price of $799. All systems—Macintosh, PC with host adapter, or PC with parallel port—ship with cable, power cord, and software for drive installation. An optional padded carrying case is $29.

Toshiba TXM-3401P

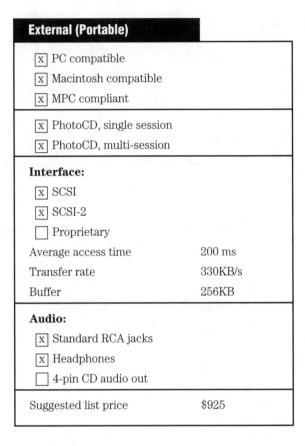

External (Portable)	
☒ PC compatible	
☒ Macintosh compatible	
☒ MPC compliant	
☒ PhotoCD, single session	
☒ PhotoCD, multi-session	
Interface:	
☒ SCSI	
☒ SCSI-2	
☐ Proprietary	
Average access time	200 ms
Transfer rate	330KB/s
Buffer	256KB
Audio:	
☒ Standard RCA jacks	
☒ Headphones	
☐ 4-pin CD audio out	
Suggested list price	$925

The TXM-3401P is Toshiba's portable version of their double-speed drive, identical in specs to their internal (XM-3401B) and external (XM-3401E) models.

The Notebook Solution

If you don't already own a notebook computer, or if ease of transportation is a key requirement, an integrated notebook solution may be the answer for you. These machines are standard notebook computers with CD-ROM drives somehow directly adapted to the case of the machine. There are not many choices in this market, and the clear leader is the DynaVision—manufactured by Scenario.

The DynaVision looks like a normal notebook computer—in fact, it is a top-end Texas Instruments model—except that the bottom half contains a CD-ROM drive. The drive is a standard Philips drive with excellent performance. The drive manages to turn in a 350 ms average seek time—well within most needs—and a full 150 KB/s transfer rate for good multimedia performance. If the Scenario machine has a downside, it may be its weight.

Extra batteries, the portable CD-ROM drive, charger, and case (and the DynaVision requires all of these) make this nonintegrated system fairly hefty. In other words, don't think just because the DynaVision is a notebook computer that carrying it won't be a burden. Outfitted for the road, a DynaVision machine tips the scales at more than 15 pounds, so keep this in mind while dreaming about your new machine.

The DynaVision line has more than one model, although they are all the same size. Following is a quick run-through of the line.

DynaVision III

Processor:	80386SX
Display:	Gray-scale LCD
Hard drive capacity:	80MB or 120MB
Battery life:	About 4 hours
Weight:	10.3 pounds

The DynaVision III is the entry-level system based on a Texas Instruments TravelMate 3000 WinSX. This basic machine has been well reviewed and is designed to run Microsoft Windows—an advantage for multimedia users.

DynaVision IV

Processor:	80486
Display:	Gray-scale LCD
Hard drive capacity:	80MB, 120MB, or 200MB
Battery life:	About 4 hours
Weight:	10.3 pounds

The DynaVision IV is essentially the same machine as the DynaVision III but uses the much more powerful 486 processor.

DynaVision IIIC

Processor:	80386SL
Display:	Active-matrix color
Battery life:	About 2 hours
Weight:	11.5 pounds

The DynaVision IIIc adds the splash of an active-matrix color LCD display by building the machine on the Sharp PC-6881 notebook computer. The Sharp PC-6881 is known for its exceptional display quality. The trade-off—except for higher cost, of course—comes in battery life. Active-matrix displays are very power hungry. Add this to the hefty requirements for spinning the CD-ROM drive and you can see why the poor little laptop battery has trouble with this arrangement. In its favor is the fact that the DynaVision IIIc is based on an Intel SL processor which has onboard power management to dramatically reduce the power used by system components when they are idle.

Lunchbox Options

Portable machines using desktop components in a "luggable" case are often referred to as *lunchbox* machines. This name derives from the form of the box itself: it is reminiscent of an oversized lunch box. Many lunchbox options are available because it does not require much sophistication to integrate a CD-ROM into one—thanks to the fact that the lunchbox case accepts standard components. As you may expect, the standard components become a double-edged sword: quality of components and construction are extremely variable in this market.

If you don't need battery power or exceptionally small size, and you think you want an expansion slot or two for special hardware, the lunchbox machine may be just what you are looking for. If you do intend to buy a lunchbox from a local or mail-order clone dealer, please do a lot of research first! You may easily find yourself with a machine that doesn't work quite right, and a dealer who can't—or won't—fix it. Get references from the company and call the users; ask about durability and solidity of the product and the quality of service from the seller. Call at least three vendors of lunchbox systems, then decide.

The Dolch Mach from Dolch Computer Systems

One company we can unequivocally recommend in the lunchbox-computer market is Dolch. These guys have been making high-end portable systems since it was possible. Although they also offer a line of traditional-style systems, their latest product is truly state-of-the-art for portable equipment.

The newest technology from Dolch is called the Mach. It is a scalable, liquid-cooled, rubberized, multimedia machine—please don't slobber on the book. Let's look at that in slow motion.

➤ **Scalable.** Unlike other transportable machines, the Mach is built in layers called *MultiSlice modules*. Each two-inch-thick module offers four slots and a drive bay. The slices plug into a passive backplane that connects them to the CPU. This means you can add to the capacity of the Mach—with either drives or slots—and even change the CPU, right up to the capacity of the power supply.

➤ **Liquid cooled.** One of the things that makes traditional lunchbox machines larger than they might otherwise be is the need to circulate air through the case. Even with the provided air space, these machines can get hotter than you like. Dolch got around this problem—and greatly reduced the machine size—by employing a more efficient liquid-cooling technology. Liquid cooling enables Dolch to equip a Mach with processors as powerful—and as hot—as the 80486 DX2/66. This is a serious advantage.

➤ **Rubberized.** The enclosure for the Mach is made from a metallic alloy and then covered with a sexy black silicone rubber. This makes it one of the most rugged machines around—in addition to its other virtues.

➤ **Multimedia machine.** The Mach is certainly no slouch in the multimedia arena. It is, of course, available with a CD-ROM drive, but it also sports an active-matrix color display and a hi-fi audio system good enough to make a presentation to a large room.

Clearly, the Dolch is a superior machine. But, as you expect, it is not a cheap machine. The price varies along with the very flexible configuration options, but you can expect to see a retail list price of about $20,000 on a well-outfitted multimedia presentation machine (street prices are less, of course). On the other hand, if you need what the Mach can do to get your work done—or you have lots of money to burn—the price may be worth paying: there is nothing else like it on the market. If seeing that price tag almost killed you, look at Dolch's more traditional lunchbox systems, which share the commitment to quality that the company applied to the Mach.

Dedicated Drives

One of the largest potential applications for CD-ROM is in the arena of portable, dedicated drives. These drives allow the average person to carry unprecedented quantities of information for easy reference. Described here is the Sony PIX-100, one of the early offerings in this area; other manufacturers will undoubtedly produce similar drives in the near future.

Sony PIX-100

Sony's MultiMedia CD (MMCD) player is a battery-powered unit that uses specially formatted CD-ROMs. These CDs are written on standard discs—but with a proprietary format. The Sony PIX-100 MMCD player itself has a small LCD display and a (very) small—but functional—speaker for audio. It also has output jacks for headphones and for NTSC (standard) video that enables the player to use a monitor and display in color.

The PIX-100 player we looked at has a small QWERTY keyboard for text input and a four-way cursor-control key for navigation. Also included are five function keys and a pair of large Yes and No buttons. The player is easy to use; the titles we looked at were impressive, given the limitations of the hardware.

Sony now offers a large catalog of titles, many focusing on business. The travelling executive seems to be a primary target for this portable unit. Here are the two titles we got a look at:

➤ **Newsweek Interactive's Unfinished Business.** This offering, subtitled "Mending the Earth," is an ecological propaganda disc presenting a case for thinking "green." It uses an animated narrative backed up by charts and a database of written materials that can be searched by the user. The title is nicely done.

➤ **Fodor's The Wall Street Guide to Business Travel.** This disc is a talking database covering 31 major US cities. It provides information on lodging, entertainment, and general trivia about each city. It is a nice reference for the frequent traveler.

The MMCD player is a product on its evolutionary way up. Take a look at one in a nearby electronics store to see whether it's for you. Pay particular attention to the titles available; remember that the discs are proprietary. One nice side benefit of these machines is that they play audio CDs as well.

Chapter 13

CD-ROM in the Family Room

You may already have a Sega Genesis or Super Nintendo video game system in your home. These second-generation game systems are nearly as plentiful and popular as VCRs in this country. Within the next three years, these seemingly innocuous, mindless game machines will begin to mature into full-fledged computer systems. The key to the expansion of these game platforms lies in CD-ROM.

Although the main focus of this book is the enormous impact CD-ROM technology has on your PC, CDs are invading your family room as well. A number of home-entertainment and education systems are shipping now—or will ship very shortly—which will drastically alter perceptions about standard video game systems. With the storage capacity of CDs added to existing systems or as a part of wholly new home systems, video games, entertainment, and education in the family room will take a bold new direction.

The Future of Home-Entertainment Systems

Although you may already be accustomed to the *zaps*, *zings*, and animations of video-arcade action blaring from your TV set, soon you can hear and see a guided museum tour, preschool phonics lessons, or the illustrated text of one of your favorite novels. In short, your preteen video-game fanatics may have to compete with the rest of the family for access to the new and expanded systems.

Like all evolving technology, though, there's good news and bad news. The good news is obvious: game systems add education and reference sources to the mix of offerings, making these complete family systems. The bad news is that these systems require an investment in hardware and CDs above and beyond what you may already have invested in your PC-based

More Terms

For the purposes of this chapter, when we refer to *home-system CDs*, we are describing those entertainment and game systems that hook up to your TV.

CD-ROM setup. **Home-system CDs,** with a few exceptions, are incompatible with your PC CD-ROM drive (and with each other), and there is little likelihood that this will change.

The high-tech home in the next few years might have a PC with reference, education, and entertainment CDs in the den and a different set of similar CDs for the family-room system. Many people will choose one system over the other—a PC or home-entertainment system—and for good reason. Building a library for two competing CD formats can get expensive in a hurry, and you may find yourself analyzing which system makes the most sense for your home.

Keep a few things in mind: PC-based CD-ROM reference and business applications have a tremendous head-start on the evolving home systems. A PC armed with a CD-ROM drive is a formidable business and research tool that home-based systems will never quite rival. The home systems, on the other hand, will be simpler to use, and their CD titles will be aimed at broader, more consumer-oriented topics. You won't see a comprehensive US history CD on a Sega Genesis system anytime soon—quite possibly never.

So you may have no choice: your PC may have a CD-ROM for reference, research, and occasional education or game CDs, and your family-room system may have a collection of entertainment, light education, and many game CDs. There's no denying the two types of systems have their own niches for home use—but no one can predict which will dominate the home market.

Purchasing any of these systems requires some caution. Many are in direct competition with each other and offer no compatibility. A disc for the Tandy VIS system, for example, is useless on the Philips CD-I, and vice-versa. Who'll win? Who'll survive? Atari and Magnavox

home-game systems were once all the rage in American homes; today they're all but forgotten in the wake of Nintendo and Sega. Buying a Philips CD-I, Tandy VIS, or even a Sega CD player is, in may ways, an unprotected investment. Although they offer a significant library of CD titles now, there is no guarantee that software developers will continue to support any of these platforms in the future.

Just as software drove the PC marketplace, so too will software development grow or stall the acceptance of home-based entertainment systems. CD-ROM makes the expansion of these systems practical, but the creativity, usefulness, and mass appeal of home-system CD titles are the only factor that can ensure their success.

CD-ROM Upgrades to Current Game Systems

The big three home-game systems—Sega, TurboGraphx, and Nintendo—have all shipped or announced CD-ROM drive upgrades to their current products. As expected, the CD titles for these systems will remain predominantly games. The storage capacity of CD enables software developers the chance to expand their use of graphics, music, and—in some cases—actual video in their products, making video games more sophisticated than ever.

In the past, game developers for these systems packed their software onto ROM-based memory contained in the plug-in game cartridges. There's a limited amount of space for these ROMs in the cartridge cases, however, and the ROM chips themselves, despite price decreases, are many times more expensive than the pressing and production costs of a single CD-ROM disc.

Consider the real estate as well: The most ambitious game cartridge has, at the high end, 40 megabytes of ROM storage. As you know, the CD-ROM disc can accommodate over 600 megabytes of data. Even luxuriously scored and painstakingly animated video games have elbow room to spare when developed for a CD-ROM attached to the game system.

It's no wonder that these home systems, in competition with one another and other emerging technologies, have stepped up the pace by introducing CD-ROM drive add-ons for their basic systems.

TurboGraphx

A division of NEC, TurboGraphx was the first video-game system with a CD-ROM add-on. The basic system is 16 bit—meaning its internal processor uses a 16-bit-wide data path, allowing faster refreshes and more complex video manipulation and sound reproduction than earlier 8-bit game systems.

The TurboGraphx CD add-on includes a set of sample CD game titles, cables for attaching it to the basic TurboGraphx system, and outputs for amplified stereo sound hookup to your home stereo.

The TurboGraphx system—even though it is one of the first CD systems—has had disappointing sales despite its relatively reasonable $599 price tag. In many areas, it is difficult to find, and software titles for this machine—in either cartridge or CD format—are on the wane as a result. Although the system is technically on a par with Sega or Super Nintendo in its use of graphics and sound, it hasn't had the market success of its rivals.

It's unclear whether the parent company, NEC, will continue to push the system aggressively enough in the face of stiff competition with Sega and Nintendo. The dwindling num-

ber of titles for the system by third-party developers is also an indication that this platform may be in deep trouble. To give you an indication of development interest, only four or five new TurboGraphx CD titles were announced at the winter Consumer Electronics Show in 1993; dozens of Sega CDs were announced at the same show.

Sega CD

Sega rolled out their CD system for the 1992 Christmas buying season and was in for a shock: the initial production run of the Sega Genesis CD add-on sold out in a matter of days. The demand for the CD-ROM unit surpassed all the company's early predictions. A number of big-name software developers have come on board to roll out software CDs for the Sega CD—Electronic Arts, Sony, and Konami, to name a few—and others are already producing titles for this brand-new system. Although the Sega is less than a year old, there are over 20 game CDs available already and dozens more are expected for the 1993 Christmas buying season.

The Sega CD unit plugs into the top of the existing Sega Genesis system and is literally held fast by the plug and a bracket, making the unit connect solidly to the Genesis base. Plugs in the back allow you to connect the unit directly to a stereo unit or to your TV's stereo jacks for CD-quality sound effects and music.

Sega got ambitious with the CD unit. Although the base Genesis system already uses a 16-bit microprocessor, an additional processor was added to the CD unit for faster graphics. The CD also carries an on-board memory chip for storing game scores or game place markers.

The CD unit ships with a number of CD software titles, including ICOM Simulations' popular Sherlock Holmes, an interactive, live-video mystery game (also available for the PC) in which the player helps Holmes solve one of three mysteries. The point-and-click interface of the Holmes title is controlled with the standard Genesis game pad. The live-video segments reproduce well on the home screen but not as crisply as on a PC-based Super VGA screen. Other titles that ship with the unit include titles previously released on cartridge: Battle Axe, Sol-Feace, and Shinobi. The entire package—CD-ROM drive plus bundled titles—has a suggested list price of $399.

With all that storage space to play with, a few early game titles prove the merit of using CD-ROM technology for gaming. Sony's CD-publishing division has produced Sewer Sharks, a full-motion video-arcade game set in the future. You play the part of a Sewer Jockey, piloting a super-fast subterranean craft that must sweep the sewers of assorted mutated vermin—everything from 100-pound sewer rats to the ultimate in sewer mutants: the dreaded ratagator.

The action on this game is fast and furious, with excellent music and voice overs. Only a storage technology like CD-ROM can give you this much video in an arcade-style game. If this game alone is any indication of what creative software developers can produce for the Sega CD system, the platform should be a continued success.

In addition to game CDs, a few **CD+G** discs are available for the Sega CD system. One CD+G title allows you to create your own music video, selecting a variety of still images to run in sequence with any of the music tracks on the disc.

Super Nintendo

Nintendo has announced the intention to produce a CD system add-on for their popular

Super Nintendo system for the 1993 Christmas buying season, but few details are available.

No doubt the system will be similar in function and capability to the Sega CD, allowing current Nintendo customers to simply plug in the new CD player to the existing system. Like Sega, the Nintendo system will no doubt include scratch memory for scores and an additional processor for improved graphics and sound capabilities.

Considering the enormous—and virtually dominating—success of the Nintendo system, the Nintendo CD add-on will probably be very successful. After all, their system has an estimated 20 million units installed in the US as of 1993. You can be assured that all major software developers will line up to deliver CD software titles for the new machine. Watch for a massive marketing and display blitz as the system rolls into virtually every sales outlet throughout the country.

In addition, it's a certainty that the new CD system will be released in conjunction with a number of CD software titles.

3DO

This company—and its yet-to-be-released product—is the dark horse in the game-system market right now. 3DO is a wholly new company with resources and cooperation formed from Electronic Arts, Time-Warner, and Matsushita. In fact, it's rumored that the three principal companies kicked in a total of $200 million to start up this home-entertainment newcomer.

At the 1993 Consumer Electronics Show in Las Vegas, the 3DO company released initial specifications for the 3DO platform to a number of third-party developers. These specs have no doubt sent a shock wave through corporate headquarters at Sega, Nintendo, and others.

EXPLANATION

CD+G Equals Karaoke

CD+G stands for CD audio plus graphics. This format provides the capability to play CD audio along with titles, still pictures, and song lyrics synchronized to the music. This CD format may be best suited for karaoke-style discs—music playing along with on-screen lyrics.

The proposed 3DO system, tentatively set to debut in the fall of 1993, includes the following:

➤ A 32-bit RISC processor

➤ A double-speed 300 KB/s CD-ROM drive

➤ CD-quality sound and 3D sound synthesis

The 32-bit RISC processor will provide an enormous boost in power over existing home systems. There is virtually no comparison—only high-end graphics workstations use this kind of raw processing power. The fast CD-ROM drive invites the use of extremely detailed 3D graphics and animations. The high-powered DSP (Digital Signal Processor) for sound allows the 3DO Multiplayer to produce 3D sound effects—the placement of sound around the listener at specific points in the room. At a demonstration at the Intermedia Multimedia trade show in San Jose in March 1993, demonstrations of the 3DO graphics and animation capabilities were, in a word, stunning.

Only a few technical drawbacks stand in 3DO's way to make a significant impact in home entertainment. The CD-ROM drive that will ship with the unit as an integral part of the system (not as an add-on) is not compatible with other CD-ROM disc formats. The ability to read Kodak PhotoCD discs is planned, however.

Full-motion video is handled in partial screen only—as it is in current game systems. According to developers, however, the shipping system will include a plug or slot for a future full-motion module. 3DO claims that they are waiting for full-motion standards to become formalized before committing to one technology. The plug-in support for full screen, full-motion video eliminates possible obsolescence.

If the hardware strengths of the 3DO system are not enough, the involvement of Electronic Arts guarantees a virtual landslide of software titles for this system right out of the starting gate. Electronic Arts is the top-producing software developer for a multitude of platforms, from the multimedia PC to Nintendo.

Other rumors flying about the introduction of this system include the possibility that the 3DO system may be, in part, designed as a front-end for interactive cable TV. If the rumor is true, it will be the gateway to couch-potato shopping, database searching, and town-hall meetings.

Initial pricing for the 3DO Multiplayer system is expected to be in the vicinity of $700—more expensive than its Sega and Nintendo rivals on the low end but in the same ballpark as the Tandy VIS and Philips CD-I players on the high end. If that price seems high, consider the processing power and the speed of the CD-ROM drive; the price may seem downright reasonable in today's market.

When you add education and reference materials to its video-game base, the 3DO system may be a big winner.

Tandy VIS

Tandy—the Radio Shack consumer electronics giant—entered the home-system market in August 1992 with the VIS CD-ROM-based system (see fig. 13.1). The Tandy unit has a number of things to recommend it. First and foremost, it is a **modular Windows-based system**—in other words, a subset of the popular PC-based Windows software forms the basis for the VIS operating system.

Tandy's system ships with a title that was originally released for PC-based Windows: Compton's Interactive Encyclopedia. The VIS title is nearly identical to its PC counterpart. Educational CDs are high on the Tandy software list, with most released titles catering to the education of children and adults. Here's an

Benefits of a Modular Windows-Based System

Why is having a Windows subset as Tandy's operating system a strength? It makes the development of VIS titles a snap for current Windows software developers. If, as a developer, you've already created a Windows-based multimedia encyclopedia, for example, you need only a moderate amount of redevelopment to create a VIS title.

The Tandy VIS system has an impressive library of available software titles, ranging from home education to games and entertainment.

overview of some of the currently, shipping titles for the VIS:

➤ **Just Grandma and Me.** The popular Brøderbund interactive story—also available for the PC—teaches children words and their pronunciations through a trip to the beach. Children point-and-click on objects to see the word for the object; then they click on the word to hear it pronounced.

➤ **Introductory Games for Learning Spanish.** Interactive games and stories teach children vocabulary, simple sentence structure, and pronunciations. This series is available for French, Japanese, and German as well.

➤ **Mutanoid Math Challenge.** The player can save Earth by defeating alien invaders only by solving math problems. Graphics, animation, and digitized speech and sound turn equations and deductive reasoning into an arcade-style game.

➤ **Our House.** Animated cartoon characters tour a home and its surroundings to an-

swer questions like "How does a radio work?" Among the many features are photos of homes from America's past.

➤ **Rick Ribbit's Adventure in Learning.** An animated frog aids children in learning numbers, letters, and words.

➤ **Whale's Tale.** While on an interactive adventure, children visit a whale museum, learn whale science and history, and view an actual video of whales (also available for the PC).

➤ **World Vista.** Detailed, full-color Rand McNally maps of over 220 nations and major cities are enhanced with statistical information, descriptions of countries, and representations of national flags and music (also available for the PC).

➤ **Compton's Interactive Encyclopedia.** Included in the basic VIS package, Compton's Interactive Encyclopedia includes the text of the full 26-volume printed edition as well as hundreds of photos, maps, and video (also available for the PC).

➤ **Links.** The most popular—and detailed—of all golf games for the PC is available for the VIS system as well.

Other game titles already available on the PC have been announced for the VIS system: Space Quest IV, 7th Guest, Loom, EcoQuest, Sherlock Holmes Consulting Detective, and the Micro League series of sports games (football, baseball, and basketball).

The Tandy VIS system ships with a controller pad, cables for hookup to regular or S-VHS TV, cords for stereo hookup, the Compton's Interactive Encyclopedia title, and one cartridge for saving game scores and book markers. Additional cartridges are available, and they can be labeled.

Tandy promises that they are 100 percent behind the VIS system and are not overly concerned by initial soft sales of the machines at their Radio Shack outlets. With broad software support and the ease with which developer's can convert existing Windows applications to the VIS platform, Tandy may, indeed, pull off a success with the VIS. It remains to be seen whether most people will go with Tandy, Philips, or the new 3DO system.

The Tandy VIS system with infra-red remote, one save cartridge, and Compton's Interactive Encyclopedia has a suggested list price of $699.

Philips CD-I

Philips took the lead with family-based education and entertainment systems with the introduction of the CD-I, or CD Interactive, in 1991 (see fig. 13.2). The CD-I is not positioned to compete with the game systems, although a number of game titles have appeared. The chief thrust of its software development has been in education and home reference—an area in which Philips has garnered a lot of third-party development support.

The CD-I system hooks up to the inputs of your TV or stereo. Connecting it to your stereo is the best bet, because the CD-I unit can also play audio CDs—after all, Philips was one of the inventors of the audio CD. Another plus for the Philips system is its ability to read Kodak PhotoCD discs. The system comes with an infra-red remote; an optional children's trackball (an oversized, brightly colored trackball and button pad that even small children can operate) is also available.

The Philips system is widely available at electronics and department stores and is heavily promoted in vertical markets as well. For example, a number of large businesses have developed CD-I discs for in-house training and point-of-sale kiosks for trade shows. With a dual-marketing strategy—business and

FIGURE 13.2

The Philips CD-I system, with over 150 software titles, has superior video and animation capabilities.

home use—Philips is keeping the CD-I system on its feet during a long, slow take-off period. Its strongest competitors are the Tandy VIS system and the yet-to-ship 3DO system.

The software titles for the Philips CD-I fill a 35-page catalog, and more have been announced for shipment in mid-to-late 1993. The current title count is near 100, and we'll take a quick look at a few titles here:

➤ **A Visit to Sesame Street: Numbers and A Visit to Sesame Street: Letters.** Two separate titles use the famous Sesame Street gang to interactively teach your preschooler numbers and letters through games and toys. Children explore a number of Sesame Street haunts including Big Bird's nest, the Count's castle, and Bert and Ernie's house.

➤ **Stickybear's Reading.** This program was a monster hit on the PC, and the CD-I version is more colorful, animated, and full of music. Stickybear helps children build sentences, learn words, and improve their use of language. The program can switch between English and Spanish, making this a useful early learning tool for Spanish.

➤ **Richard Scarry's Busiest Neighborhood and Richard Scarry's Best Neighborhood.** Sold separately, these two Scarry discs feature interactive visits to Busytown. Both discs are designed to aid preschoolers in a variety of prereading exercises.

➤ **Children's Musical Theater.** Various animal musicians help children put together their own music scores, with choices of instruments, musical styles, and lyrics.

➤ **Mother Goose: Hidden Pictures.** Objects are hidden in 26 pictures depicting Mother Goose fairy tales. Once children find all the hidden objects in a picture, an animated scene starts up.

➤ **Children's Bible Stories.** A series of discs with high-quality animation and music depict David and Goliath, Noah's Ark, the Story of Samson, and other Bible stories.

➤ **Tell Me Why, I and II.** These two discs adapt the popular *Tell Me Why* books to the CD-I format, answering in story and animation popular children's questions about how things work. Topic areas include the body, the zoo, and our world.

➤ **Story Machine: Star Dreams and Story Machine: Magic Tales.** Both these titles supply children with backgrounds, characters, and objects for creating their own stories. Once the characters are chosen, children can begin to write the story with screen text. Star Dreams is a space adventure; Magic Tales has a fairy-tale theme.

By building on the audio quality of the CD-I format, software developers have produced a number of graphically enhanced music CDs for the VIS system:

➤ **Louis Armstrong: An American Songbook.** Along with 12 Armstrong songs, this disc has illustrated profiles of composers, song lyrics, liner notes from Armstrong's albums, and a complete Louis Armstrong discography.

➤ **Jazz Giants: From Big Band to Bossa Nova.** Nineteen jazz hits from the likes of Count Bassie, Charlie Parker, Sarah Vaughn, Billy Holliday, Miles Davis, and Stan Getz. Biographies of each of the artists and liner notes are displayed.

➤ **You Sing Christmas Favorites.** This interactive Christmas album features 12 Christmas favorites accompanied by Christmas images and on-screen lyrics for a family sing-a-long.

➤ **Rembrandt: His Art and the Music of His Era.** Eighty of Rembrandt's best-known works are displayed, accompanied by music from the Baroque period. You select the art categories from religious, self-portrait, landscapes, and others. A visual tour of Rembrandt's birthplace is also included.

➤ **Private Lessons.** Here's a series of home CDs that really capitalizes on the word *interactive*. Rock, jazz, and classical guitar CDs teach you how to play the guitar with a tutor, interactively. Lessons are self paced and, obviously, repeatable.

➤ **The Great Art Series.** Renaissance, Impressionism, Van Gogh—nearly a dozen different CDs with superior-quality masterpieces are enhanced with classical soundtracks, maps, biographies, and more.

➤ **Treasures of the Smithsonian.** This interactive tour not only lets you walk around exhibits, it allows you to search our most famous American museum for items you're interested in. Detailed notes and descriptions accompany many items.

Aside from a wide base of software titles both shipping and announced, another indication of CD-I's health—despite soft sales—is Philips' recent announcement for add-on modules for the CD-I system.

Philips recently announced a **full-motion-video** upgrade cartridge for the CD-I system that allows CD-I titles to display up to 72 minutes of live-motion video and sound. The sample videos we saw at the Intermedia trade show in San Jose were laser-disc quality images—better than VCR in clarity—with full stereo soundtracks.

The new Philips cartridge carries an MPEG-I video-compression chipset that decompresses the CD-I disc-based video for display on your TV. The cartridge also has 1MB of memory for buffering sound and video, essential for the 30-frames-per-second of live-motion video and stereo sound. Philips maintains that the new cartridge also allows developers of CD-I titles to produce higher quality animations.

Pop-up VCR-like controls on-screen allow the user to freeze, rewind, or fast forward the video with a remote control. Philips will begin shipments of the add-on module in the fall of 1993, when it expects a number of titles that exploit the new video technology to be introduced.

Recently, Philips also introduced a portable version of the CD-I, which is targeted at business applications, sales presentations, and the interactive tutorial market. **Details on the portable CD-I are in Chapter 12, "CD-ROM on the Road: Going Portable."**

The Philips CD-I system with remote and Compton's Interactive Encyclopedia has a suggested list price of $699. Other CD-I titles range in price from $15 to $60.

Kodak PhotoCD

Some industry insiders joke that Kodak wanted out of the photo-developing business and that the Kodak PhotoCD was their ticket out. The PhotoCD format has already had clear and

overwhelming support from the CD-ROM industry. The Kodak PhotoCD unit for the home audience is targeted at customers who want to view their photographs on TV in full color. All Kodak PhotoCD units also play audio CDs (see fig. 13.3).

The PhotoCD scenario is this: you take a roll of exposed film to a neighborhood developer who ships the roll to a Kodak PhotoCD processing center. The film is developed and scanned at high resolution and imprinted on a special recordable CD disc. The finished product is shipped back to your developer. The key to the PhotoCD's success lies in its capability to record multiple photo sessions on one CD; you continue to bring in the same PhotoCD disc until it's filled up and then you start a new disc.

As a subset of the CD-ROM-XA specification, Kodak PhotoCDs can display photos along with titles and—it's promised—narration or audio soundtracks. Kodak now has three con-

FIGURE 13.3

Targeted at the photography hobbyist, the Kodak PhotoCD allows amateur and professional photogs to view their work on standard televisions.

 NOTE:

Do the Video Squeeze

What makes the full-motion video possible is the use of video-compression algorithms—special software that "squeezes" the digitized video images into a size that is practical to store.

sumer PhotoCD players on the market, all of which are multi-session:

➤ **PCD 270.** This is the lowest priced model, offering basic picture viewing and the ability to tag photos to be deleted from the playback session. The CD unit "remembers" which photos have been deleted, making it unnecessary to reprogram it each time the disc is used. The player also has an autoplay feature that cycles through selected photos. Suggested list price for the PCD 270 is $379.

➤ **PCD 870.** This model has advanced viewing features not available on the PCD 270. For example, users can select a portion of a photo for enlargement. Multiple-disc memory is also included, allowing you to create custom carousels of photos that the unit remembers for many discs. The suggested list price for the PCD 870 is $449.

➤ **PCD 5870.** This unit is identical in function to the PCD 870 but has a five-disc turntable that lets you play a series of photo or audio CDs. This player also has an on-screen display for programming photo series and numbering images. The suggested list price for the PCD 5870 is $549.

Compatibility

As you've read through the categories of home CD-ROM systems, you may have noticed that some systems are compatible, to a limited degree, with other systems. Let's run through the systems quickly to give you a run-down on these limited compatibilities. This information may sway your decision one way or another in selecting either a PC or home CD-ROM system. Please note: for the most part, game, education, and database applications developed for the PC are **not** usable in any home-game system.

➤ **PC CD-ROM Drives.** If your computer's CD-ROM drive is XA ready, and the manufacturer specifies that it has multi-session capabilities, you can read PhotoCDs on the drive if you add special PhotoCD-viewing software to the PC. (Some drives are only single session—they can read only the first recorded session on the PhotoCD.) Virtually all PC CD-ROM drives are capable of playing audio CDs.

➤ **Sega, Nintendo, 3DO.** The Sega, Nintendo, and 3DO systems are all incompatible. In addition, they cannot read any PC, PhotoCD, or CD-I formatted discs or applications. However, all three should play audio CDs.

➤ **Tandy VIS.** The Tandy VIS system is incompatible with PC, CD-I, Sega, Nintendo, and PhotoCD discs. The system does play audio CDs, however.

➤ **Philips CD-I.** The CD-I system is incompatible with PC, VIS, and game-system CD formats. The CD-I does play PhotoCDs and audio CDs, however.

➤ **Kodak Photo CDs.** The Kodak system is for photo and audio CDs only. The PhotoCDs are compatible with any multi-session PC CD-ROM drive, however.

What does all this incompatibility mean? Either you live in a two-CD environment—one set of CDs for your PC and yet another for your home—or you choose one over the other. If all you're interested in for your home is education, games, and very little reference, the VIS or CD-I system may be a perfect fit. Upgrading an existing home PC to a multimedia PC that uses CD-ROMs can easily cost more than your initial investment in the Philips or Kodak systems once you add a sound card, speakers, and the CD-ROM drive itself (provided you buy quality components). You may find a home-based multimedia PC worthwhile for business and reference work and may want to invest in the Sega, Nintendo, or the upcoming 3DO unit for games.

And if all that doesn't cause enough confusion, there are other factors entering the fray: Sony is rumored to be developing a home-system drive that is compatible with the Nintendo system. Philips may ship one of these drives as well. And if the 3DO Multiplayer is even a moderate success, look for other traditional CD-ROM drive manufacturers to jump on that wagon for one important reason: 3DO, unlike its home-system rivals, will not manufacture and sell the units themselves; they are in the process of licensing the technology to a number of third-party manufacturers.

We wish there was better news—that one system would fit all needs. At the very least, we wish a home-based system would take some PC-based CDs. After all, when the initial-investment dust settles, it's the cost of CD-ROM applications and software that run up the tab. Although that's good news for the software suppliers, it's bad news for the consumer.

Chapter 14

Video on Disc: CD-ROM and Full-Motion Video

We've spent the entire book lauding the storage capacity of CD-ROMs. By now, you probably have the impression that this technology is virtually inexhaustible when it comes to storing applications and sound. Not so. Emerging multimedia technologies have found a way to make even CD-ROM discs seem cramped for space. The introduction of full-motion video to commercial and limited-distribution applications has done more to fill CD-ROMs in the last year than all software applications combined.

Understanding Full-Motion Video

Photographs or still-images from motion video depend on the resolution at which they're captured and displayed; the amount of storage space required for a single image varies according to its resolution. Common television resolution, for example, contains approximately 480 horizontal lines—actually rows of dots or pixels—and up to 450 vertical lines. The most common PC standard for image processing and display is VGA—640 by 480 resolution. The multiple of this number—the horizontal by the vertical—yields the number of pixels in the image, which for VGA is 307,200.

That's fine for black-and-white images (you can store a black-and-white 640-by-480 resolution still image in 307,200 **bits**). But most video is color; to add "true color"—a representation of more than primary colors—you must compound your pixel storage requirements by a factor of 24. Each primary color is assigned a full byte—8 bits—for storage. This leap to 24-bit color multiplies the storage requirements for a single image by 24, bringing the total for a single frame of a full-color 640-by-480 resolution image to 921,600 bytes—nearly a megabyte!

EXPLANATION
Pixel

The term *pixel* is a contraction of two words: *picture* and *element*. A pixel is the "atomic" component of an image displayed on the computer.

But one image does not a video make. The standard frame rate that must be achieved for film and video to be considered "full-motion" is 30 frames per second (no PC-based animation even approaches this rate). Multiply, then, the storage space for a still image (921,600 bytes for a single full-color image) by 30 to get the storage requirements for a single second of video: the staggering number of 27,640,000 bytes! One second of video requires over 27 megabytes of storage space. A 30-second commercial, then, with absolutely no sound, cannot fit on a single CD-ROM.

Video Choices

Multimedia developers are presented with tough choices. They must either find a larger and more economical storage medium for the production and distribution of applications that contain full-motion video, or work with what's available. They've chosen the later because, at this point, no other storage medium can deliver as much for the money as CD-ROM. Shortcuts, technology, and creative development have all been deployed to deliver the best possible video in such a "cramped" space.

Compression

One way to reduce storage space is to compress the images before they are stored on the disc. A number of compression standards are available now, and we'll discuss some of them later. The best compression techniques employed today can reduce most frame sizes by a factor of 20. In other words, our original 27-megabyte 1-second video image can be stored in just over a megabyte of space using advanced compression techniques.

But it's not just the space requirements that necessitate compression. When pulling a multimegabyte file off a disk or disc for use as live video, the number of bytes that must be continuously transferred to display a smooth video is beyond current commonly available processor or disk subsystem speeds. Compression enables much more video information to be delivered in a short period of time, improving the flow of the video frame delivery.

Compressed data is not directly useful, however: it must be decompressed before it's sent off to an application for display. The compression and decompression must be performed by hardware or software by using the same type of compression standards, which further complicates widespread use of video in PC applications. As you may expect, competing compression techniques are currently being used. No single compression/decompression standard has emerged as the dominant standard.

Squeezing Data

You may wonder how it is possible to "compress" data. After all, a megabyte of data is a megabyte of information, isn't it? Well, not really. In the simplest terms, compression is easy to understand: it involves the removal of redundant information from the stored data.

Let's take a look a simple compression scheme called RLE (Run Length Encoding). With RLE, any time there are strings of the same value (for example 50 1s in a row), the value 1 is not stored 50 times. Instead, the value 1 is stored once with a note about the number of times it appears in a row. This technique works very well, particularly with simple images. Variations on this idea make up the more sophisticated schemes.

Compression comes in two varieties—hardware and software. Each, as you probably guessed, has advantages and disadvantages.

Hardware Compression

Hardware compression and decompression is performed by a specialized set of microprocessors called DSPs—Digital Signal Processors. These specialized chips contain software code for the compression algorithm used to compress incoming images. Most hardware compression also uses memory *buffers*—memory that stores the incoming frames before they are processed—so that the compression chipset can "keep up with" the flow of incoming data. Hardware-compression chips are found on hardware-compression boards that plug into the standard PC expansion bus.

Hardware decompression works in the opposite manner. When an application requests a compressed file from storage, the board accepts the compressed data in its buffer and, using the encoded algorithm, "replaces" the data that was removed from the compressed image. Once decompressed, the image is passed to the display through the application.

The chief advantage of hardware compression for video is computational power. The hardware performs the computer-intensive tasks of compression and decompression on the expansion card through the DSPs and related chips and buffers, saving the computer's main CPU and memory for the running of applications.

The obvious disadvantage is that computers must all have hardware compression cards conforming to the compression-board manufacturer's implementation of that particular compression algorithm. For this reason, video-compression boards have been expensive—hovering in the $1,000 range and scaring off all but the most ardent video-application developers and users.

Software Compression

Software implementation of decompression and compression is no different, in practice, than the hardware equivalent. Instead of using DSPs, coprocessors, and on-board memory to compress and decompress images as do hardware compression boards, software video compression uses the PC's main CPU and main RAM for all operations.

The important advantage of software compression is its portability: the PC need not have special hardware in place to use the video contained in the application. This arrangement allows application developers to write for a common platform of installed PCs and makes their applications instantly usable by a majority of users. The application must include a "run-time" version of the decompression software (a utility that reads and decompresses the video and passes it along to the display when necessary).

The chief disadvantage to software-based compression and decompression is the toll it takes on a PC's performance. Reading video off a CD-ROM causes some delay, and decompressing using the PC's CPU and memory causes further delays. Most systems with less than a 386-25 MHz processor will experience loss of frames and a jerky playback of video because of the resource-hungry nature of software decompression.

Other Video Economies

Compressing images is one way of making the most of storage space for video, but other techniques can be used as well. Although 30 frames-per-second is optimal for viewing motion video, a reduction in the number of frames-per-second can obviously cut the storage requirements. Video cut down to 15 frames-per-second is not uncommon in PC multimedia applications—but the results are noticeable. Further reductions can be made by reducing the pixel count. For example, our original 640-by-480-pixel window for images can be cut by 75 percent to 320 by 240, dramatically reducing storage requirements. The image is reduced in size, not in quality, so the PC displays a smaller version of the full-screen image. Similarly, reduction in the color depth from 24 to 16 or even to 8 bits trims down the size of video images considerably.

All these size-reduction techniques come at a cost. The image quality of a 15-frame-per-second video at 320-by-240 resolution is video, to be sure, but not the video you're used to seeing on your TV. For most current PC-based applications and presentations, such video may be just fine—but it lacks the realism of full-screen, truly full-motion video.

Video Application Development for CD-ROM

For software developers to incorporate video into CD-ROM applications, they need some additional hardware and software development tools. The process of including video in an application involves three steps.

1. The capture of video from an analog source, such as a camcorder, television, or VCR.

2. The processing of the image into the appropriate digitized format.

3. The incorporation of the video into the overall software application.

Capturing video from an analog source requires a video-capture board capable of processing 15-frames-per-second or more. A number of capture boards are on the market now. Most cards have standard RCA and S-VHS inputs that enable the easy hookup of a VCR, camcorder, or TV monitor directly to the PC card. The card processes the incoming analog signals, changes them to digital bits, and stores the incoming data on a hard drive or removable media device. Most capture boards do not employ compression or decompression techniques, so the digitized video is stored in its full, bloated state and can eat up a lot of storage in a short period of time. Other capture boards have hardware compression features and can save video files to the primary storage device in a proprietary compressed format.

Once the image is captured, it may have to be converted to the appropriate format for the application to use. Some capture boards include drivers that prepare the data, before storing it, for a number of video formats. Many multimedia authoring tools on the market today have extensive support for a variety of video formats; including video is just a matter of telling the application where the video clip is stored and when the multimedia presentation should use the clip. IconAuthor, Toolbook, and many other Windows and DOS-based authoring toolkits allow easy integration of video—and provide a number of more sophisticated uses, such as assigning video to hot spots, radio buttons, and menu items.

PC Video Standards

As we mentioned—and cautioned—a number of technologies are available for the compression, decompression, and digitization of video for PCs. Each has different features, strengths, and drawbacks. Some are strictly hardware based; others are software based. Many can be found implemented in both hardware and software. For the purposes of this book, we'll give you a thorough overview of the video standards currently available. It should be noted that all of the following **video standards** are currently very new and subject to modification and new implementations.

Indeo

Developed by Intel Corporation (the same folks that bring you the main CPU in your PC), the Indeo algorithm for compressing and decompressing video is independent of hardware or software. Intel incorporates the Indeo technology on all its DVI hardware compression/decompression boards; a slightly modified version of Indeo is incorporated in Microsoft's Video for Windows. Besides Microsoft, a number of third-party manufacturers have licensed the Indeo technology from Intel for use in their hardware and software products.

One of the chief advantages to Intel's Indeo compression/decompression algorithm (abbreviated as *codec*) is the inclusion of adaptive playback of Indeo-encoded clips. That is, the software dynamically adapts its playback for the platform it's running on. For example, a 386-based PC may play an Indeo file at perhaps one-quarter screen and a 15 frames-per-second rate; a 486 (because of its increased horsepower) may play the same video at half-screen and 25 frames-per-second. Intel has licensed the Indeo technology to Apple (for use with Apple's QuickTime video) and to IBM (for use with IBM's Ultimedia video).

Video for Windows

The addition of Video for Windows to the Microsoft Windows environment makes it possible

to use Intel's Indeo codec with Windows AVI (Audio Video Interleaved) files. What some people do not realize, however, is that the Video for Windows product also has built-in support for the new **MediaVision** Motive codec. To make things even more flexible for developers and users alike, the Video for Windows software can incorporate virtually any new codec that comes along—all users need to do is add the new codec module to Video for Windows.

Another strength of the Microsoft addition is its ability to take advantage of any available hardware assistance. For example, if the Video for Windows driver detects an Intel-based hardware codec, it dynamically adjusts to take full advantage of the hardware support, providing the application with full-screen, 30 frames-per-second video instead of using scaled-back windows in the applications.

> ### Microsoft's AVI
>
> Just as Sony developed and proposed the XA specification for CD-ROM drives to effectively interleave audio and video, Microsoft developed its own audio-video interleaving scheme (which it named with the simple acronym AVI). The AVI format does not depend on the data format of the drive but on the format of the data itself. Video is distributed on the disc in small segments by using files in the DIB (Device Independent Bitmaps) format. The DIB files contain compressed video frames. Audio is contained in separate WAVE or MIDI files. The Video for Windows player reads the appropriate DIB and WAVE files and synchronizes them appropriately during playback.
>
> Microsoft touts the AVI format as being platform independent. This arrangement makes it possible to move AVI applications to other operating systems and to store them on any current or yet-to-be developed media.

MPEG

The MPEG, or Motion Picture Experts Group, codec standard was developed before the Indeo standard. The MPEG specification adheres strictly to the 30 frames-per-second playback

Video Clips and Local Bus

In the course of testing CD-ROM applications that had multimedia video clips, we noted some incompatibilities with local bus video cards and some QuickTime and Video for Windows clips. We've had reports from other users as well. One vendor noted that video cards incorporating some local bus chipsets were, indeed, incompatible with some older implementations of video under Windows. At any rate, if you experience trouble playing back or capturing video through local bus VGA adapters, first contact the adapter's manufacturer—an updated driver may solve these problems.

MediaVision

MediaVision, makers of the popular Pro Audio Spectrum sound cards, recently announced a two-chip and decompression solution for full-motion video on 386 and above PCs. The chipset, called Motive, contains compression and decompression modules, each capable of 15-frame-per-second, 640-by-480 video. MediaVision is offering the chipset to third-party developers, in quantity, for $40 per set. If adopted by a large number of PC and add-on board manufacturers, this chipset could drastically reduce the cost of hardware compression for the PC industry.

rate, ensuring that video is smooth and free of lapses. (Lapses occur in other codec schemes when lesser frame counts are used.) All MPEG uses to date are hardware-based because of the enormous processing that must occur to decompress images at such a high frame rate and at full-screen resolutions.

Philips demonstrated full-motion MPEG video on its CD-I system at a recent trade show. The full-screen, full-motion video was impressive and had stop action and frame advance that is clearer than any other video technology now available. The MPEG II specification is so efficient that the CD-I demonstration disc used at the booth could store nearly 30 *minutes* of video on one CD-ROM. That might not sound like much—until you go though the math at the beginning of the chapter again.

Although MPEG shows the greatest long-term promise in delivering the most video in the least time and space, hardware platforms that use it are only now being delivered and costs have yet to come down significantly.

QuickTime for Windows

Apple has just released its QuickTime video player for use with Windows. Developers now can use any previously developed QuickTime for Macintosh videos on the Windows platform. The QuickTime Video for Windows format is already showing up in a number of multimedia PC-based applications; software developers that want to work with both Mac and Windows CD-ROM applications will probably prefer using QuickTime than any other video technology.

The QuickTime videos must be developed on the Macintosh; the end product is playable on QuickTime for Windows. There is no provision for developing QuickTime video under Windows. Intel recently announced support for QuickTime on the Mac through its Indeo algorithm, making Apple-to-Windows porting even less daunting.

Video Capture and Codec Boards

If development of video applications for CD-ROM is to be efficient, using a codec board or a software codec during video capture is a near requirement. Codec boards, as we mentioned, allow the developer to move the compression and decompression calculations from the main system CPU to the codec board itself, freeing the system for other application chores. Boards that support software codec—mostly those that have drivers compatible with Video for Windows—are a reasonable alternative to more expensive hardware codec systems. Following are some currently shipping video capture and codec boards for PCs.

MediaVision Pro Movie Spectrum

MediaVision's Pro Movie Spectrum is the lowest-priced Video for Windows-supported capture board. Compression of captured video is through the Motive hardware codec, located on the board. The board supports only 15 frames per second in a 160-by-120 window. Suggested list price is $349.

SuperMac Technology Video Spigot

The Video Spigot from SuperMac can capture video at 15 or 30 frames per second, but the frame rate depends on resolution—the higher the rate, the smaller the window. The highest resolution is 320 by 240. The Video Spigot uses its own proprietary hardware codec. Suggested list price is $499.

Creative Labs Video Blaster

The Video Blaster from Creative Labs uses the drivers in Video for Windows for capture compression. The Video Blaster also includes an audio mixer for the capture of audio files. The board supports 15 frames per second at 320-by-240 resolution. It's packaged with several multimedia presentation applications, including MacroMind's Action! and Mathmatica's Tempra. Suggested list price is $499.

IEV International ProMotion

ProMotion from IEV supports input up to a resolution of 1024 by 768 and comes with AVI drivers for Windows. The card is capable of 30 frames per second and permits editing and storage of individual video frames. Suggested list price is $995.

Cardinal Technologies SNAPlus

The SNAPlus card from Cardinal Technologies supports 30 frames per second through Video for Windows drivers that ship with the product. Standard video, S-VHS, and RGB input and outputs allow the SNAPlus to not only capture video for application development but allow video output from the PC to standard VCRs and camcorders. The Windows drivers allow direct manipulation of computer-interface controllable VCRs, such as the NEC PV-S98a, so that video tape can be controlled and edited through the SNAPlus software. Individual frames can be edited and stored in the DIB format. Live video can be displayed on-screen in true color in resolutions as high as 800 by 600. Captured video depends on Video for Windows for display resolutions 320 by 240. Suggested list price is $1,295.

Intel ActionMedia II

The ActionMedia II card from Intel features an on-board coprocessor and a hardware implementation of the Intel Indeo codec. The system is capable of 30 frames per second and full-screen or can scale back to 15 frames per second in a 320-by-240 window. The ActionMedia card includes audio capture as well, and has support for Microsoft Windows as well as DOS. Suggested list price is $1,295.

RECOMMENDED
Creative Labs Video Blaster

HIGHLY RECOMMENDED
IEV International Pro Motion

HIGHLY RECOMMENDED
Cardinal Technologies SNAPlus

RECOMMENDED
Intel ActionMedia II

Chapter 15

The Future of CD-ROM

You have to expect the obvious: a technology as hot and versatile as CD-ROM will continue to evolve and improve. In the next few years, we'll see enormous changes in CD-ROM drives and applications. Even though we're impressed—and rightfully so—with the technology as it stands today, increases in speed, capacity, standards, and application development will make many of these initial CD-ROM products seem quaint by comparison.

The good news is that we are not dealing with a "flash-in-the-pan" technology. Wide acceptance by consumers, developers, and major manufacturers ensure that CD-ROM technology will be a continued success. If you purchase CD-ROM technology now for your business or home, you're not buying into the next Edsel. Applications and standards will evolve in an orderly fashion, ensuring that what you buy today should be useful many years from now.

Engineers are working hard to make a good thing even better. In this chapter, we examine some of the impending advances in CD-ROM technology and application development. You can be assured that most of what we talk

about here is **not pure conjecture**—manufacturers and developers have gone on the record in announcing many of the future advancements that we discuss here. In other cases, a clear view of the current state of the market can give you an indication of what is to come. But that same marketplace can be cruel—a new, unexpected advance in one corner of the technology marketplace can change things overnight.

Increases in Performance

One constant you can count on in the computer world is this: if a new technology is developed, its main focus is on improving performance. Speed is nearly everything in computers. Faster video displays, hard drives, I/O busses, processors—you name it. CD-ROM drives are certainly not immune to these pressures. It's not enough to have video from CD-ROM, it's better to deliver it at 30 frames per second on a full screen. Accessing a data-

We're Not Making This Up

We stand by our discussions in this chapter as informed and reasonable opinions of the future state of the CD-ROM market, but offer no guarantees on our prognostications. In the computer marketplace, there's no such thing as sure bets or bug-free software—just change, constant change.

base of graphic images shouldn't require a pause from the drive, right? One of the clearest focuses of the CD-ROM manufacturers in the coming year will be speed and performance increases. Both initial access times and data transfer rates will improve in the next generation of CD-ROM drives.

Access Rates

As this book went to press, the fastest average access rate for any CD-ROM drive was Toshiba's basic production drive—clocking in at 200 milliseconds. Remember that access rate is the average time it takes the drive to position the read-beam on the disc and begin transferring data. When you compare CD-ROM access rates with hard drives, you get an idea of how much room there is for improvement: the typical hard drive nowadays has an average access rate of 15 to 20 milliseconds (ms).

The physical make-up of the CD-ROM drive itself contributes to its slow access time. The motor and tracking device that position the reading mechanism must seek across a spiral of data, positioning itself as closely as possible to a disc segment in front of the address of the requested data; the mechanism then reads through the initial data until it arrives at the location it needs. All this takes time, valuable time. Improvements in the speed of the positioning—or the stepper motors—as well as more precise initial reads will contribute to improved average access rates. There's some question about how fast—*reliably* fast, that is—the drives can be pushed. The physical distance and format of the data suggest that access rates will never approach that of hard drives. But as soon as you say something can't be done, someone'll go out and prove you wrong.

Drives with access rates below 200 milliseconds will begin shipping sometime in late 1993; by 1994, most major manufacturers will have drives in this class. This will put pricing pressures on the lower-end drives, and you'll see drives with perfectly acceptable 200-ms, 250-ms, and 300-ms access rates going for much less than they are now.

Transfer Rate

By increasing the spin rate and buffering of a drive, you can also increase its transfer rate. Remember: one of the keys to providing full-motion video is to increase the rate at which the computer—and its display—can receive the huge data files associated with video. Many manufacturers are shipping double-speed drives that adapt to the data task at hand. When Red Book audio is played, the double-speed disk slows to the speed required of CD-based audio, but when other data tasks are requested of the drive, it spins and reads at twice the speed of a normal CD player. **Refer to Chapter 2, "CD-ROM Specifications Explained," for more information about colored-book specifications.**

Pioneer's latest minichanger has quad-speed capabilities—four times the normal CD player transfer rate. If you want to use compressed, full-motion video in a full-screen display, the quad-speed transfer rate is ideal. Although compression and the computer's own memory and CPU resources can and will pick up much of the "slack" in such applications, the delivery of the data at a higher rate increases the overall performance of applications.

Look for other manufacturers to begin incorporating quad-speed capabilities in their drives in late 1993. But until applications that require and can utilize this higher speed become more widespread, transfer rate will not be a high priority. When Pentium-powered PCs and more sophisticated multimedia applications become more plentiful, quad-speed—and possibly higher—drives will gain popularity.

Increases in Capacity

Just when you thought 640 megabytes was enough storage to ship any imaginable software application, some hot-shot developer comes along and ruins the whole thing. Live video, stereo sound, and complex Super-VGA animations and graphics are already stretching the bounds of the once-unfathomable depths of CD-ROM storage. Developers are working now on increasing capacities, but a number of obstacles stand in the way.

The first obstacle is purely physical—there's only so much real estate on a CD-ROM disc. The only way to get more bits and bytes into that space is by cramming more information into the allotted space.

Compression

By compressing all forms of data used on the CD-ROM—sound, graphics, and text—developers can squeeze much more data into the same amount of space. The problem of *how* to squeeze the data is an issue, however. For every type of data, there are literally dozens of compression techniques available. Some are obviously more efficient and dominant than others, but so far, no one compression technology is a standard for any given data type. With a multiplicity of compression options available, software and application developers are at risk of choosing the "wrong" compression technology—that is, they may commit to a compression scheme that may not be sup-

ported in the long term by a large number of hardware manufacturers. **For more details about video-compression "standards" and technology, see Chapter 14, "Video on Disc: CD-ROM and Full-Motion Video."**

Compression—either through specialized microprocessor chips or through software that uses the PC's CPU and memory—offers a solution for getting more bits on the disc. Complications arise when applications need hardware compatibility or when using the PC's resources slow down the performance of the majority of today's installed computers.

As an example of the utility of compression techniques, an XA-encoded CD-ROM application can hold up to seven hours of audio—seven times the current, uncompressed capacity.

Audio Compression and Nonconformity Issues

The use of compression for audio is a perfect example of the utility of compression techniques. Sony proposed the CD-ROM-XA specification for the purpose of incorporating compressed audio in synchronized interleaving with graphics or video. This audio compression calls for the use of a specialized hardware chip to both encode the audio data during development and, most importantly, to decode and use the data on the application or playback end. This specialized code within the chipset is called ADPCM. For a drive to utilize XA-encoded audio, it must incorporate an ADPCM chip on the drive itself or, possibly, on the sound card the drive is patched to.

To further complicate the implementation of the XA specification in ADPCM hardware, there are compatibility issues with actually implementing the hardware—in other words, not all ADPCM chips are created alike. As a result, the XA format has not gained incredible momentum in the marketplace. Microsoft has developed its own interleaving and compression techniques for use with Windows, for example, with its DIB (Device Independent Bitmap) and AVI (Audio Visual Interleaved) file formats.

As a rule, software implementations of compression techniques are more portable and adaptable than hardware-based solutions. Software compression and decompression of data takes a heavy toll on the host system's resources, though; increasingly computational-intensive applications in combination with decompression tasks may force many systems to a noticeable crawl.

The important thing to remember is that compression and compression techniques are in a state of competition right now. Time, the marketplace, and continued advances in technology are the only factors that can push the competition into standardization. In the meantime, the designation *XA-ready*, for example, not only indicates that the drive is capable of being easily upgraded for audio compression in the XA specification, but that it also is multisession PhotoCD compatible. Of course, such a drive is backwards-compatible with all previous CD formats.

More Dots Per Inch: Blue-Light Lasers

Data compression is not the only answer to packing more bits on a disc. Why not pack the pits and lands—the basic CD-ROM data—closer together? Lasers used today in every CD-ROM are red-light lasers. They have distinct physical properties based on the wavelength of the light they project. This wavelength determines how precise and how small the pits of a CD-ROM's data can be. Blue-light lasers, under heavy research and development now, have a shorter wavelength than the current red-light lasers. With a shorter wavelength, data can be packed more tightly because the actual pits and lands can be much smaller and tracks can be packed more closely together.

There are a number of technological and marketing concerns for manufacturers to address. First, because of the greater density of the data, blue-light lasers will be more susceptible to disruption and corruption of data. Too,

the technology needed to mass-produce such mechanisms reliably does not exist today. This last hurdle has proved historically to be nearly insignificant: if there is sufficient demand, manufacturing develops accordingly.

Lastly—and perhaps most importantly—blue-light laser CD-ROM drives would, in all likelihood, be unable to read current CD-ROM discs. The data from the current generation of discs would be too widely dispersed, in effect, for the narrower beam to accurately read. Dual-light lasers could be produced, but at an enormous cost.

Although the blue-light laser CD-ROM is currently only in research and development, its capabilities may hasten both its demand and initial production. It's estimated that the capacity of a blue-light CD-ROM disc could be four to six times that of the current CD-ROM. A disc with nearly 2 gigabytes of room makes a multitude of video and sound applications practical and affordable.

Standards: A One-Size-Fits-All Future?

As popular and truly useful as CD-ROM technology is, its market base is severely fragmented. Even in its computer-based form, there are separate data and disc formats for DOS, Macintosh, and UNIX platforms. CD-ROM applications that are to have any sense of portability across different computer environments must currently be shipped with different operating-system interfaces and, in some cases, multiple-format discs (one-half of the disc may be in DOS and the remainder in Macintosh format, for example).

As if formatting for different operating systems were not enough, for CD-ROM applications to truly become a mass-market consumer item, the reconciliation of the remainder of the CD-ROM formats must happen. Remember that CD-ROM is incorporated into such home-use units as the Tandy VIS, the Philips CD-I, and even the Sega Genesis game system. Asking families to invest in CDs for their home-entertainment system and then reinvest in similar titles for the PC that sits in the den as a work tool is asking too much. The strategy is not geared to increasing acceptance and wide availability.

Rumors on the Standards Front

It's no surprise that some major manufacturers are eyeing the possibilities of increasing portability—especially across home-entertainment and PC-based systems. Companies are beginning to realize that a CD-ROM application that can be popped into a unit attached to the TV *and* in the PC in the den can increase the sales of both hardware platforms—as well as have a tremendous effect on software-application development. If the PC-based system and the home-entertainment system use compatible CDs, software developers can reach a larger market and focus on providing better titles, rather than waste development efforts porting similar applications to many different hardware platforms.

Rumors are strong that Sony is developing a CD-ROM-XA drive for use in both Nintendo's and Sega Genesis' newer systems due in 1994. If the drives are truly XA-compliant—to the Sony spec—information applications developed for one platform—say the PC—would be usable on the home-based Nintendo or Sega system, too. Besides giving the game developers a more expanded platform for zapping aliens and running mazes, it would effectively

allow many reference, educational, and business-oriented CD-ROM applications to migrate easily into consumer's family rooms.

As Tandy's VIS system, running a "portable" version of Microsoft Windows called Modular Windows, struggles to gain acceptance in the home, we wonder why extensive development efforts haven't been made to make Windows-based PC CD-ROM applications and VIS applications more interchangeable. Surely the development issues cannot be insurmountable, and if the Tandy system shows flagging sales and low-market penetration, its only savior may be the interchangeability of CD-ROM discs from PCs to the VIS platform.

Finally, the Sony CD-ROM-XA specification and Philips CD-I format are so close in actual details as to be virtually the same. Key elements are different, however, and those are enough to discourage computer-based developers from crossing the line into CD-I territory. If the Philips system could be modified in some way to use XA-compatible discs, Philips would instantly double the number of applications for the system and increase acceptance among users who have already invested—or are about to invest—in primarily PC-based CD-ROM applications.

And Yet Another Size

Sony recently announced the availability of yet another CD-ROM format—or rather, form factor. The latest is a 3.5-inch version of the current CD-ROM format. This scaled-back CD-ROM, according to the company, is perfect for laptop computers and can replace one of the floppy drives in larger PCs, much as the 3.5-inch floppy is gradually pushing out the 5.25-inch disks.

This small form-factor CD has a formatted capacity of nearly 200 megabytes, and Sony promises that will increase in the coming months. This new disc format—and the drives that use them—may have made developers a lot more nervous if the new drives had incorporated another file format as well. Fortunately, the new 3.5-inch discs and drives will use the standard CD-ROM High Sierra and XA formats.

Because the standard formats will be used on the smaller discs, CD-ROM software developers can ship products on both sizes of disc or make scaled-back versions of their products for the smaller drives. Truth be told, most CD-ROM applications that are primarily text-based consume barely a third of current CD-ROM discs—the rest is blank, unused space. Shipping sophisticated multimedia applications on dual media may be more troublesome because data may overrun the capacity of the smaller discs.

What's the Verdict?

What will come to pass? The introduction of other home-based systems, such as the 3DO

system, and the proliferation of PC-based drives may further fragment the market. On the other hand, these same pressures may force unlikely alliances, as in the Sony-Nintendo arrangement. The only outcome that benefits you as a consumer is increased compatibility and portability of CD-ROM formats and applications. Better titles—at more reasonable costs—will be the direct result of even a partial reconciliation between even a few of the competing formats.

Will we ever arrive at a one-drive-fits-all future? We doubt it. Some formats will simply disappear as that technology loses the fight to become a widely distributed product. Other formats will evolve into even more complex—and incompatible—technologies that address more sophisticated data applications.

In the meantime, buying, installing, and using a CD-ROM drive for your PC—whether at work or on your home PC—is a sound investment with a great future.

Drive Manufacturers in This Book

The following is a listing of CD-ROM drive manufacturers whose products are described in this book. Note that this is not a comprehensive, all-inclusive listing of CD-ROM drive manufacturers; a number of companies produce products that we thought were inappropriate for this book, and there were some companies who wished not to be included.

CD Technology, Inc.
766 San Aleso Avenue
Sunnyvale, CA 94086
Phone: (408) 752-8500
Fax: (408) 752-8501

Chinon America, Inc.
660 Maple Avenue
Torrance, CA 90503
Phone: (310) 533-0274 or (800) 441-0222
Fax: (310) 533-1727

Hitachi Multimedia Systems Division
3890 Steve Reynolds Blvd.
Norcross, GA 30093
Phone: (404) 279-5600
Fax: (404) 279-5699

Laser Magnetic Storage International Company
4425 ArrowsWest Drive
Colorado Springs, CO 80907-3489
Phone: (719) 593-7900
Fax: (719) 599-8713

Liberty Systems
160 Saratoga Ave.
Santa Clara, CA 95051
Phone: (408) 983-1127
Fax: (408) 243-2885

MicroSolutions Computer Products
132 W. Lincoln Highway
DeKalb, IL 60115
Phone: (815) 756-3411
Fax: (815) 756-2928

NEC Technologies, Inc.
1255 Michael Drive
Wood Dale, IL 60191-1094
Phone: (708) 860-9500

Philips Consumer Electronics Company
One Philips Drive
PO Box 14810
Knoxville, TN 37914-1810
Phone: (800) 845-7301

Procom Technology
2181 Dupont Drive
Irvine, CA 92715
Phone: (800) 800-8600 or (714) 852-1000
Fax: (714) 852-1221

Sony Corporation of America
1 Sony Drive
Park Ridge, NJ 07656
Phone: (201) 930-6432

Texel
1605 Wyatt Drive
Santa Clara, CA 95054
Phone: (408) 980-1838
Fax: (408) 980-1840

Toshiba America Information Systems, Inc.
Disk Products Division
9740 Irvine Boulevard
Irvine, CA 92718
Phone: (714) 583-3111
Fax: (714) 583-3133

Directory of CD-ROM Software Developers and Publishers Discussed in This Book

This appendix lists the names, addresses, and phone numbers of the main software manufacturers discussed in this book. Software developers include everyone from developers of search-and-retrieval software to database-compilation companies.

AimTech Corporation
20 Trafalgar Square
Nashua, NH 03063-1973
(603) 883-0220

ALDE Publishing
6520 Edenvale Boulevard
Eden Prairie, MN 55344
(612) 934-4239

American Business Information
5711 South 86th Circle
Omaha, NB 68127-0347
(402) 593-4565

Applied Optical Media Corp.
1450 Boot Road
West Chester, PA 19380
(215) 429-3701

Bowker Electronic Publishing
121 Chanlon Road
New Providence, NJ 07974
(908) 464-6800

Brøderbund
500 Redwood Blvd.
Novato, CA 94948
(415) 382-4400

Buckmaster Publishing
Route 4
Mineral, VA 23117
(703) 894-5777

Bureau of Electronic Publishing
141 New Road
Parsippany, NJ 07054
(201) 808-2700

Compact Publishing
PO Box 40310
Washington DC 20016
(202) 244-4770

Compton's New Media
2320 Camino Vida Roble
Carlsbad, CA 92009-1504
(619) 929-2500

Corel Systems Corporation
The Corel Building
1600 Carling Avenue
Ottawa, Ontario, Canada K1Z 8R7
(613) 728-8200

Creative Multimedia Corp.
514 NW 11th Avenue
Portland, OR 97209
(503) 241-4351

DeLorme Mapping
P.O. Box 298
Freeport, ME 04032
(207) 865-4171

Digital Directory Assistance
5161 River Road
Bethesda, MD 20816
(301) 657-8548

Discis Knowledge Research
45 Sheppard Avenue East
Suite 410
Toronto, Ontario, Canada M2N 5W9
(800) 567-4321

Disclosure Incorporated
5161 River Road
Bethesda, MD 20816
(800) 843-7747

Dr. T's Music Software
124 Crescent Road
Needham, MA 01294
(617) 455-1454 x226

Dun's Direct Access
Three Sylvan Way
Parsippany, NJ 07054
(800) 526-0651

Dynamix
1600 Mill Race Drive
Eugene, OR 97403
(800) 326-6654

Ebook Inc.
32970 Alvarado-Niles Road
Suite 704
Union City, CA 94587
(510) 429-1331

Eduquest
6269 B Variel Ave.
Woodland Hills, CA 91367
(818) 992-8484

Grolier Electronic Publishing
Sherman Turnpike
Danbury, CT 06816
(800) 356-5590

Healthcare Information Systems
2335 American River Drive
Suite 307
Sacramento, CA 95825
(916) 648-8075 or (800) 468-1128

HW Wilson
950 University Avenue
Bronx, NY 10452
(800) 367-6770 or (212) 588-8400

Hyperglot Software Company
5108-D Kingston Pike
Knoxville, TN 37939
(615) 558-8270

Icom Simulations
648 S. Wheeling Road
Wheeling, IL 60090
(708) 520-4440

Infobases International Inc.
1875 S. State Street
Suite 3100
Orem, UT 85058
(801) 224-2223

Information Access Company
367 Lakeside Drive
Foster City, CA 94404
(800) 227-8431 or (415) 378-5267

Interactive Ventures
2900 Lone Oak Parkway
Suite 122
Eagan, MN 55121
(612) 686-0779

InterOptica
300 Montgomery Street
San Francisco, CA 94104
(415) 788-8788

Interplay Productions
17922 Fitch Avenue
Irvine, CA 92714
(714) 553-6655

Knowledge Adventure
4502 Dyer Street
LaCrescenta, CA 91214
(800) 542-4240 or (818) 542-4200

Laser Resources, Inc.
20620 S. Leapwood Avenue
Carson, CA 90746
(310) 324-4444

LucasArts Entertainment
PO Box 10307
San Rafael, CA 94912
(415) 721-3300

Macmillan New Media
124 Mt. Auburn Street
Cambridge, MA 02138
(617) 661-2955

MarketPlace Information Corp.
Three University Office Park
Waltham, MA 02154
(617) 894-8371

Matthew Bender and Company
11 Penn Plaza
New York, NY 10001
(212) 216-8094

MicroProse Software
180 Lakefront Drive
Hunt Valley, MD 21030
(410) 771-0440

Microsoft
One Microsoft Way
Redmonds, WA 98052-6399
(206) 882-8080

National Geographic Society
1145 17th Street, NW
Washington DC 20036
(202) 775-6583

Oxford University Press
200 Madison Avenue, 9th Floor
New York, NY 10016
(212) 679-7300 ext. 7370

Pemberton Press
462 Danbury Road
Wilton, CT 06897-2126
(203) 761-1466

Penton Overseas Inc.
2740 Impala Drive
Carlsbad, CA 92008-7226
(619) 431-0060 or (800) 748-5804

ProCD New Media Publishing
8 Doaks Lane
Marblehead, MA 01945
(617) 631-9200

Quanta Press
1313 Fifth Street SE
Suite 223A
Minneapolis, MN 55414
(612) 379-3956

Random House Reference & Electronic Publishing
201 East 50th Street, 3rd Floor
New York, NY 10022
(212) 572-2750

Sierra On-Line
PO Box 485
Coarsegold, CA 93614
(800) 326-6654 or (209) 683-4468

Silver Platter Information
100 River Road Drive
Norwood, MA 02062-5026
(800) 343-0064 or (617) 769-2599

Software Toolworks
60 Leveroni Court
Novato, CA 94949
(415) 883-3000 ext. 566

Syracuse Language Systems
719 East Genesee Street
Syracuse, NY 13210
(315) 478-6729

Texas Caviar
3933 Steck Avenue
Suite B115
Austin, TX 78759
(512) 346-7887

Tiger Media
5801 East Slauson Avenue
Suite 200
Los Angeles, CA 90040
(213) 721-8282

Trilobyte
110 South 3rd
Jacksonville, OR 97530
(503) 899-1113

UMI
30 North Zeeb Road
Ann Arbor, MI 48106
(313) 761-4700 or (800) 521-0600

Virgin Enterprises
18061 Fitch Avenue
Irvine, CA 92714
(714) 833-8710

The Voyager Company
1351 Pacific Coast Highway
Santa Monica CA 90401
(310) 451-1383

Warner New Media
3500 W. Olive Ave
Suite 1050
Burbank, CA 91505
(818) 955-9999

West Publishing
610 Opperman Drive
Eagan, MN 55123
(800) 888-9907 or (612) 687-7450

World Library
12914 Haster Street
Garden Grove, CA 92640
(800) 443-0238 or (714) 748-7198

Ziff Communications Company
One Park Avenue
New York, NY 10016
(212) 503-5361

Additional CD-ROM Software Titles

This book and its accompanying CD are not sufficient to detail all the CD-ROM applications available today. For businesses, professionals, and institutions to keep abreast of what's available, we highly recommend a subscription to *The CD-ROM Directory*. The following list is arranged by categories; it is a compilation of additional CD-ROM titles—those not discussed in this book but that you may find useful.

Additional Business Titles

1987 Economic Censuses Report Series, Volume I
US Bureau of the Census

1991 IC MASTER CD-ROM Plus
Hearst Business Communications Inc.

AURA (All UK Registered Addresses)
Head Software International

Banker's Almanac
Silver Platter Information Inc.

Best Database Service - Life/Health Experience By State (By Line) Life Lines
A.M. Best Company

Best Database Service - Property/ Casualty Experience By State (By Line)
A.M. Best Company

BookFind-CD Business & Law
Book Data

BookFind-CD World Edition
Book Data

Business & Company Profile
Information Access Company

Business Calls Telephone Skills Training Course (CD-ROM-XA)
Xebec Multimedia Solutions

Business Dateline Ondisc
UMI (University Microfilms International)

Business Index
Information Access Company

Business Lists-on-Disc
American Business Information Inc. (ABI)

Business NewsBank
NewsBank

Business NewsBank PLUS
NewsBank

Business Periodicals Index
The H.W. Wilson Company

Business Periodicals Ondisc
UMI (University Microfilms International)

Business Systems Consulting Disc
Arthur Andersen & Company

Business Words
EuroTalk Limited

Business Yellow Pages of America
Innotech Inc.

Büro-Compact
Comunication GmbH

Canadian Business and Current Affairs (CBCA) - DIALOG OnDisc
DIALOG Information Services Inc.

CD News - The Arizona Republic
The Arizona Business Gazette

CD-EXPORT
Association Telexport

CD-SCAN
Kinokuniya Company Ltd.

CD/Europa
Lotus Development Corporation; Dun & Bradstreet Ltd.

Cfarbase for Global Investing
CIFAR - Center for International Financial Analysis & Research

Cfarbase for International Research
CIFAR - Center for International Financial Analysis & Research

COMLINE on Silver Platter
Silver Platter Information Inc.

Compact America
Compact Publications Inc.

Compact D/Canada
Disclosure Inc.

Compact D/SEC
Disclosure Inc.

Compact D/UK
Disclosure Inc.

COMPUSTAT PC Plus
Standard and Poor's Compustat Services Inc.

Comstock Desktop Photography CD-ROM Volume1
Comstock

Comstock Desktop Photography CD-ROM Volume2 Business
Comstock

Corporate Affiliations - DIALOG OnDisc
DIALOG Information Services Inc.

County and City Data Book 1988
US Bureau of the Census

County Business Patterns 1985
Space-Time Research Pty Ltd.

County Business Patterns 1986
Space-Time Research Pty Ltd.

County Business Patterns
Interactive Market Systems Inc. (IMS)

Current Data Bases (Media & Marketing Research Data)
Interactive Market Systems Inc. (IMS)

Custom CFR 13 - Business Credit and Assistance
CD Book Publishers

Custom CFR 16 - Commercial Practices
CD Book Publishers

DataDisc
INFO-ONE International Pty Ltd.

Detroit Free Press - DIALOG OnDisc
DIALOG Information Services Inc.

DigiSound Starter Disc
Presentation Graphics Group

Disclosure/Worldscope/Snapshots
Wright Investors' Service

Disclosure Corporate Snapshots
Disclosure Inc.

Discovery Preview - DIALOG OnDisc
DIALOG Information Services Inc.

DoD Contract/Procurement Locator
  Staff Directories Ltd.
Dun's BusinessLine
  Dun's Marketing Services; Donnelley
  Marketing Information Services (DMIS)
Dun's Million Dollar Disc
  Dun's Marketing Services
EDUCORP CD-ROM 6.0
  EDUCORP Computer Services
EDUCORP Clip-Art CD-ROM
  EDUCORP Computer Services
Electronic Book - International Business Guide (Asia-I)
  Nichigai Associates Inc.; Kinokuniya
  Company Ltd.
Electronic Book - International Business Guide (North America)
  Nichigai Associates Inc.; Kinokuniya
  Company Ltd.
Electronic Book - Key Person (Business Politics)
  EureCom AG
EureCom Business Database
  EureCom AG
EUROPAGES - The European Business Directory
  Euredit
EUROPAGES - The European Business Directory (CD-ROM-XA)
  Euredit
European Business Guide
  Business Information Publishers
European Corporations CD
  Silver Platter Information Inc.
EUROTRAVEL (Complete Travel Planner)
  Business Information Publishers B.V.
EXPLORE!
  DRI/McGraw-Hill
Exploria
  Infodidact

Farm Audience Readership Measurement Service
  Interactive Market Systems Inc. (IMS)
FBIS Electronic Index
  Readex
Federal Prime Contracts 1987-1989
  US Statistics Inc.
Fedstat
  US Statistics Inc.
Fedstat/Tiger - Digital Map Databases
  US Statistics Inc.
Fedstat ZIP-Industry
  US Statistics Inc.
Financial Times Graphics Source
  Zap Optical Ltd.
First Steps Towards Learning French
  Business Information Publishers
First Steps Towards Learning German
  Business Information Publishers
First Steps Towards Learning Italian
  Business Information Publishers
First Steps Towards Learning Spanish
  Business Information Publishers
Foods Intelligence on Compact Disc
  BIOSIS; Silver Platter Information Inc.
Foreign Trade Data - US Imports of Merchandise and US Exports of Merchandise
  US Bureau of the Census
Front-Page-News - plus Business
  Buckmaster Publishing
Front-Page-News plus Business 1991 (IBM)
  Wayzata Technology Inc.
Front-Page-News plus Business 1991 (Macintosh)
  Wayzata Technology Inc.
Functioning in Business
  Information Access Company
General Business File
  Information Access Company

General Periodicals Index (Academic Library Edition)
Information Access Company

General Periodicals Index (Public Library Edition)
Information Access Company

Health Index
Information Access Company

Healthy Life
Top Business System Co. Ltd.

HyperClips for Windows
The HyperMedia Group

IC/Discrete Parameter Database Service
Information Handling Services Inc.

ICP Software Information Database on CD-ROM (SID CD-ROM)
ICP (International Computer Programs)

Image Club ArtRoom 5.0 CD-ROM
Image Club Graphics Inc.

Image Gallery
NEC Technologies (USA) Inc.

Improving Your Job & Career Prospects
Queue Inc.

Infodirect - Canadian White Pages on CD-ROM
Telédirect Publications Inc.

Infomark Laser PC System
Equifax National Decision Systems

Interactive Business English
Information Access Company

Investext
Information Access Company

Japanese Corporate Profile
Nihon Keizai Shimbum Inc.

Japanese Language Learning for Business Travellers (CD-I)
UK Training Agency

Keep in Touch
Keep in Touch

Kompass CD
Kompass UK (Reed Information Services Ltd.)

Kompass Top 20
Disclosure Inc.

Laser D/International
Disclosure Inc.

Lists on Disc
International Data Computer Services Pty Ltd.

Lotus One Source
Lotus Development Corporation

Lotus One Source - CD/Banking - Bank Holding Companies
Lotus Development Corporation

Lotus One Source - CD/Corporate - Europe M&A
Lotus Development Corporation

Lotus One Source - CD/Corporate - International Public Companies
Lotus Development Corporation

Lotus One Source - CD/Corporate - UK Private+
Lotus Development Corporation

Lotus One Source - CD/Corporate - UK Public Companies
Lotus Development Corporation

Lotus One Source - CD/Corporate - US M&A
Lotus Development Corporation

Lotus One Source - CD/Corporate - US Private+
Lotus Development Corporation

Lotus One Source - CD/Corporate - US Public Companies
Lotus Development Corporation

Lotus One Source - CD/Investment - International Equities
Lotus Development Corporation

Lotus One Source - CD/Investment - US Equities
Lotus Development Corporation

Lotus One Source - CD/Networker
Lotus Development Corporation

Media Clips - Business Backgrounds
Aris Entertainment

Mediasource - General Topic Library - Volume1
Applied Optical Media Corporation

Miami Herald - DIALOG OnDisc
DIALOG Information Services Inc.

Middle East Diary
Quanta Press Inc.

Military Personnel/Base Locator (formerly DOD Phone Book/Defense Procurement)
Staff Directories Ltd.

Moody's Bank & Finance Manual & Disc
Moody's Investors Service

Moody's Industrial Manual & Disc
Moody's Investors Service

Moody's International Plus
Moody's Investors Service

Moody's OTC Industrial Manual & Disc
Moody's Investors Service

Moody's OTC Unlisted Manual & Disc
Moody's Investors Service

Moody's Transportation Manual & Disc
Moody's Investors Service

Movie Database and Software Potpourri
Bureau Development Inc.

National Economic
Boston Spa Training Ltd.

NEOMATICA
Boston Spa Training Ltd.

NewsBank Electronic Information System
NewsBank

NewsBank PLUS
NewsBank

NewsBank Reference Service
NewsBank

Newsday and New York Newsday - DIALOG OnDisc
DIALOG Information Services Inc.

PAIS on CD-ROM
Public Affairs Information Service (PAIS)

Pan European Study
Interactive Market Systems Inc. (IMS)

PC Plus/Global Vantage Stock Reports on CD-ROM
Standard and Poor's Compustat Services Inc.

PC Plus/S&P Stock Reports
Standard and Poor's Compustat Services Inc.

People in Business
Gazelle Technologies

Predicasts F&S Index Plus Text
Silver Platter Information Inc.

ProArt Professional Art Library - Trilogy 1
Multi-Ad Services Inc.

ProArt Professional Art Library - Trilogy 4
Multi-Ad Services Inc.

ProDirect (Canada)
UMI (University Microfilms International)

ProDirect (USA)
UMI (University Microfilms International)

Quantarc Electronic Library
Poulter Communications PLC

Quick Art Volume 1
Wheeler Arts

Readers Guide Abstracts
The H.W. Wilson Company

Readers Guide to Periodical Literature
The H.W. Wilson Company

Registry of Czechoslovak Companies on CD-ROM
Albertina Information Services Ltd.

Salescan
Dun & Bradstreet International

San Jose Mercury News - DIALOG OnDisc
DIALOG Information Services Inc.

SciTech Reference Plus
Bowker Electronic Publishing

SEC Online-10K
Silver Platter Information Inc.

SHIP Business Indicators
Slater Hall Information Products (SHIP)

Software CD - Descriptions & Reviews
Information Sources

Software Finder
Datapro Information Services Group

SpeedDial
Dataware Technologies

Standard & Poor's Corporations - DIALOG OnDisc
DIALOG Information Services Inc.

SuperCAT - Cataloging System
Gaylord Information Systems

Swedish Company Information
Bureau van Dijk S.A.; Soliditet - Esselte Info

Telecom Business Finder
Space-Time Research Pty Ltd.

Telefirm
Bureau van Dijk S.A.; Chambre de Commerce et d'Industrie de Paris (CCIP)

The Art of Visual Computing
Paracomp; The Company of Science and Art

The Business Collection
Micro Haus Ltd.

The Business File
CML Data

The Compendium of Australian Business
Westlink Data; Computer Audiographics Pty Ltd.

The Complete Manager (CD-I)
CD-I Training Ltd.

The Computer File
CML Data

The Dictionary of Law for Business
Jyukokumin-Sha Publishing Company Ltd.

The Dictionary of Law for Business (Data Discman)
Jyukokumin-Sha Publishing Company Ltd.

The International Graphics Library
Gazelle Technologies

The National Directory of Addresses and Telephone Numbers
Xiphias

The National Directory of Addresses and Telephone Numbers 1992
Omnigraphics Inc.

The North American Facsimile (FAX) Book
Quanta Press Inc.

The NTDB (National Trade Data Bank)
United States Department of Commerce

The Property File
CML Data

The Quebec Library/La Bibliotequé Quebecoisè
Inform II Microfor

The Retail Census of Australia - 1985/86 Release
Space-Time Research Pty Ltd.

The Software Users Year Book
VNU Business Publications

The Times and Sunday Times Compact Disc Edition
The Times Network Systems Limited

Thomas Register - DIALOG OnDisc
DIALOG Information Services Inc.

Toxic Release Inventory 1987
US Government Printing Office (GPO)

Trade Opportunities CD-ROM
Wayzata Technology Inc.

TRADEMARKSCAN (Federal) - DIALOG OnDisc
DIALOG Information Services Inc.

TRADEMARKSCAN (State) - DIALOG OnDisc
DIALOG Information Services Inc.

TSR - Company Information Files
Tokyo Shoko Research Ltd. (TSR)

Wilson Business Abstracts (WBA)
The H.W. Wilson Company

Women Partners in Development
CD Resources Inc.; EBSCO-CD

Work Room
EDUCORP Computer Services

World Fax Directory
Datamedia GmbH

World Travel Guide
Columbus Information

Additional Education Titles

800 College Boards
Queue Inc.

A+ French Tutor
Queue Inc.

A+ Spanish Tutor
Queue Inc.

A-V ONLINE
Access Innovations Inc.; Silver Platter Information Inc.

Academic Abstracts Full Text Elite
EBSCO Publishing

Academic Abstracts Full Text Select
EBSCO Publishing

Academic Index
Information Access Company

Access-Pennsylvania Statewide Database
Pennsylvania Department of Education, State Library

AIDS Information and Education Worldwide
CD Resources Inc.; EBSCO-CD

All About Science
Queue Inc.

American Family Physician 1985-1990
CMC - Creative Multimedia Corporation

American Government
Queue Inc.

An Introduction to Statistical Process Control
Iris Technology Ltd.

Anatomist 2.1
Folkstone Design Inc.

ASLIB Index to Theses - With Abstracts
Expert Information Ltd.; ASLIB - The Association for Information Management; Learned Information (Europe) Ltd.

AUSTROM - Australian Social Science, Law, and Education Database
INFORMIT, Royal Melbourne Institute of Technology Libraries

Authorware CD, Second Edition
Macromedia, Inc.

Avalanche Volume I
Apple Computer Australia

Bancos Bibliograficos Mexicanos (Mexican Bibliographic Database)
Universidad de Colima, Direccion General de Intercambio Academico Desarrollo Bibliotecario

Barney Bear Goes to School
Free Spirit Software

Battery CAI Course
Flysheet Information Services Inc.

Bibliography of Social Science and Educational Articles of the Henrietta Szold Institute
CDI - Compact Disc International Ltd.

BNI - British Newspaper Index on CD-ROM
Research Publications

BookFind-CD Children & Schools
Book Data

Brer Rabbit and the Wonderful Tar Baby (CD-I)
Philips Interactive Media of America (PIMA)

Britannica Family Choice
Compton's New Media

Business Calls Telephone Skills Training Course (CD-ROM-XA)
Xebec Multimedia Solutions

CAD VISION
Isvor-Fiat SpA

CAI on the Financial Commodities
NTT-LS; Dai Nippon Printing Company

Canadian Business and Current Affairs (CBCA) - DIALOG OnDisc
DIALOG Information Services Inc.

Canadian Register of Research and Researchers in the Social Sciences
University of Western Ontario

Career Opportunities
Quanta Press Inc.

CASPAR (Computer Aided Science Policy Analysis and Research)
Quantum Research Corporation

CD PLUS/ERIC (Educational Resources Information Center)
CD Plus Inc.

CD-Education
Micromedia Ltd.

CELL EBRATION
Science for Kids Inc.

Chemistry
Queue Inc.

Class Room
EDUCORP Computer Services

Clear Mind
CSK Research Institute Corporation (CRI)

College Blue Book on CD-ROM
Macmillan Publishing Company

Complete Maths Workshop
TopClass Technology

Comprehensive Review in Biology
Queue Inc.

Computers in Education
CDI - Compact Disc International Ltd.

Creepy Crawlies
Media Design Interactive Ltd.

Cross-Cultural CD
Silver Platter Information Inc.

Curriculum Resource Dissemination Project
INFO-ONE International Pty Ltd.

Custom CFR 34 - Education
CD Book Publishers

Desktop Music Creativity Kit
Passport Designs Inc.

Detroit Free Press - DIALOG OnDisc
DIALOG Information Services Inc.

Developing Writing Skills
Queue Inc.

Directory of Library and Information Professionals
American Library Association

Discis Book - A Long Hard Day on the Ranch, by Audrey Nelson
Discis Knowledge Research Inc.

Discis Book - Aesops Fables
Discis Knowledge Research Inc.

Discis Book - Cinderella
Discis Knowledge Research Inc.

Discis Book - Journeys - Emergent Level One CD-ROM
Discis Knowledge Research Inc.

Discis Book - Journeys - Emergent Level Two CD-ROM
Discis Knowledge Research Inc.

Discis Book - Moving Gives Me a Stomach Ache, by Heather McKend
Discis Knowledge Research Inc.

Discis Book - Mud Puddle, by Robert Munsch
Discis Knowledge Research Inc.

Discis Book - Scary Poems for Rotten Kids, by Sean O Huigin
Discis Knowledge Research Inc.

Discis Book - The Night Before Christmas CD-ROM
Discis Knowledge Research Inc.

Discis Book - The Paper Bag PrInc.ess, by Robert Munsch
Discis Knowledge Research Inc.

Discis Book - The Tale of Benjamin Bunny, by Beatrix Potter
Discis Knowledge Research Inc.

Discis Book - Thomas' Snowsuit, by Robert Munsch
Discis Knowledge Research Inc.

Discovery Training Toolkit - DIALOG OnDisc
DIALOG Information Services Inc.

Dissertation Abstracts Ondisc
UMI (University Microfilms International)

Distance Learning Database of Courses, Institutions, & Literature
International Centre for Distance Learning

Drawing (CD-I)
Philips Interactive Media of America (PIMA)

Dynamic English, Levels 1, 2, and 3
DynEd International Inc.

Dynamic Japanese, Levels 1, 2, and 3
DynEd International Inc.

Education Index
The H.W. Wilson Company

Educational Courseware
Jostens Learning Corporation

Educational Games for Young Children (IBM)
Queue Inc.

Educational Games for Young Children (Macintosh)
Queue Inc.

Educational Testing Database
Minnesota Department of Education

EDUCORP CD-ROM 6.0
EDUCORP Computer Services

EDUCORP Clip-Art CD-ROM
EDUCORP Computer Services

English Express CD-ROM Macintosh
Davidson and Associates Inc.

English Express CD-ROM MS-DOS
Davidson and Associates Inc.

English Vocabulary Learning Aid
CSK Research Institute Corporation (CRI)

ESC System
Educational Systems Corporation

Essay Writing
Victoria University of Technology (Footscray Institute of Technology)

Europe in the Round
Vocational Technologies Ltd.

Expanded Academic Index
Information Access Company

Exploring Mathematics with Mathematica
Addison-Wesley Publishing Company

First National Item Bank & Test Development System
Tescor Inc.

Flight 642 on CD-ROM
Innotech Inc.

Flysheet/China Dissertation Abstracts
Flysheet Information Services Inc.

Forces, Motion, & Work
Science for Kids Inc.; Europress Software Ltd.

Functioning in Business, Parts 1 and 2
DynEd International Inc.

Getting Ready for a Good Job
Interactive Knowledge Inc.

Green Energy CD-ROM
Djanogly City Technology College

Health & Nursing
Queue Inc.

Health For All - Primary Care and Consumer Information
CD Resources Inc.; EBSCO-CD

History of Western Civilization
Queue Inc.

How the Camel Got His Hump (CD-I)
Philips Interactive Media of America (PIMA)

How the Rhinoceros Got His Skin (CD-I)
Philips Interactive Media of America (PIMA)

I Can Read
Intechnica International Inc.

I Speak English (for Italian Speakers)
Editoria Elettronica Editel; Intechnica International

I Speak English (for Japanese Speakers)
Intechnica International Inc.

I Speak English (for Spanish Speakers)
Intechnica International Inc.

I Speak French
Intechnica International Inc.

I Speak German
Intechnica International Inc.

I Speak Japanese
Intechnica International Inc.

Improving Your Job & Career Prospects
Queue Inc.

Infomart on CD
Southam Electronic Publishing

Interactive Business English, Parts 1 and 2
DynEd International Inc.

Introduction to Potential Failure ModZ: Effect Analysis
Iris Technology Ltd.

IPL Series (Information Processing Lessons) 1: Learning Basic
Nippon Courseware Co Ltd.

IPL Series (Information Processing Lessons) 2: Learning Basic Algorithm
Nippon Courseware Co Ltd.

IPL Series (Information Processing Lessons) 3: Learning COBOL Basic Course
Nippon Courseware Co Ltd.

IPL Series (Information Processing Lessons) 4: Learning Fortran Basic Course
Nippon Courseware Co Ltd.

IPL Series (Information Processing Lessons) 5: Learning C Language Basic Course
Nippon Courseware Co Ltd.

IPL Series (Information Processing Lessons) 6: Learning OS Basic Course
Nippon Courseware Co Ltd.

IPL Series (Information Processing Lessons) 7: Learning UNIX Basic Course
Nippon Courseware Co Ltd.

IPL Series (Information Processing Lessons) 8: Learning Assembler (CASL) Basic Course
Nippon Courseware Co Ltd.

JILL (Jobs Illustrated)
INFO-ONE International Pty Ltd.

Joint Education Initiative - Earth Sciences Education
University of Maryland

Kaika
Bright Star Technology Inc.

Kids Room
EDUCORP Computer Services

Macademic
Quantum Leap Technologies

MacLife
HeartBeat Software Solutions

Magazine Article Summaries (MAS) Full Text Elite
EBSCO Publishing

Magazine Article Summaries Full Text Select
EBSCO Publishing

Mastering English Grammar
Queue Inc.

Mastering Math
Queue Inc.

Mastery Drill & Practice
HEC Software Inc.

Medicats
Big Time

Megastat Europe
ACT Multimedia; Nathan Logiciels

Miami Herald - DIALOG OnDisc
DIALOG Information Services Inc.

MIDEBANK
Minnesota Department of Education

Mother Goose Hidden Pictures (CD-I)
Philips Interactive Media of America (PIMA)

Mother Goose Rhymes to Color (CD-I)
Philips Interactive Media of America (PIMA)

MSSB
Innotech Inc.

Multimedia Beethoven - The Ninth Symphony
Microsoft Multimedia Division

Multimedia Training Disc - Repetitive Motion Injury
Canadian Centre for Occupational Health and Safety (CCOHS)

Multimedia Training Disc - Safe Use of Chemicals
Canadian Centre for Occupational Health and Safety (CCOHS)

My Fair Lady
CSK Research Institute Corporation (CRI)

My Fair Lady/CAN
CSK Research Institute Corporation (CRI)

NATASHA - National Archive on Sexuality, Health, & Adolescence
Sociometrics Corporation

National Economic, Social, and Environmental Data Bank (NESE-DB)
United States Department of Commerce, Office of Business Analysis

North Polar Expedition
Virgin Games

OAIP/Biology on CD-ROM
Innotech Inc.

OSH - A Collection of Training Packages
Canadian Centre for Occupational Health and Safety (CCOHS)

Pan European Study
Interactive Market Systems Inc. (IMS)

PC Blue
ALDE Publishing Inc.

Pecos Bill (CD-I)
Philips Interactive Media of America (PIMA)

Pediatrics in Review 1985-1991 and Redbook 1991
CMC - Creative Multimedia Corporation

Peterson's College Database
Silver Platter Information Inc.

Philadelphia Inquirer - DIALOG OnDisc
DIALOG Information Services Inc.

Primary Search
EBSCO Publishing

Private Lesson Series - Guitar One (CD-I)
Philips Interactive Media of America (PIMA)

ProArt Professional Art Library - Trilogy 4
Multi-Ad Services Inc.

ProDirect (Canada)
UMI (University Microfilms International)

ProDirect USA
UMI (University Microfilms International)

Quakie - Volcanoes and Earthquakes
NIAM Interactive Multimedia bv

Quick Art Deluxe (IBM)
Wayzata Technology Inc.

Quick Art Deluxe (Macintosh)
Wayzata Technology Inc.

R3 Room
EDUCORP Computer Services

Readers Guide Abstracts
The H.W. Wilson Company

Readers Guide to Periodical Literature
The H.W. Wilson Company

Reading for Children - Safety Learning Reading (CD-I)
Philips Interactive Media Systems

Reading Horizons, Learn To Read
HEC Software Inc.

Reasoning Skills
Queue Inc.

Richard Scarry's Best Neighbourhood Disc Ever (CD-I)
Philips Interactive Media of America (PIMA)

Richard Scarry's Busiest Neighbourhood Disc Ever (CD-I)
Philips Interactive Media of America (PIMA)

San Francisco Chronicle - DIALOG OnDisc
DIALOG Information Services Inc.

SchoolMatch
OCLC Online Computer Library Center Inc.

Schoolware on CD-ROM
Innotech Inc.

Science Helper K-8
PC-SIG Inc.

Shareware Express PC
Bureau Development Inc.

SHIP County and City Compendium
Slater Hall Information Products (SHIP)

SpaceTime and Art
Wayzata Technology Inc.

SPORT Discus
Silver Platter Information Inc.

Study Room
EDUCORP Computer Services

Talking Dictionary of Medical Terminology (Anatomy & Physiology for Nurses)
Victoria University of Technology (Footscray Institute of Technology)

Talking Jungle Safari
New Media Schoolhouse

Tell Me Why I (CD-I)
Philips Interactive Media of America (PIMA)

Tell Me Why II (CD-I)
Philips Interactive Media of America (PIMA)

The Best Literature Workbook Ever!
Queue Inc.

The College Handbook 1992 CD-ROM Edition
Maxwell Electronic Publishing

The Guinness Disc of Records 1991
UniDisc Inc.

The Gutenberg Project Series
Images + Data

The Heart - Its Functions and Disfunctions
CTU, University of Milan

The Independent on CD-ROM
FT PROFILE

The Must Know Words Disc
Interactive Knowledge Inc.

The New Reader Bookstore
Interactive Knowledge Inc.

The OCLC Education Library
Silver Platter Information Inc.

The PC-SIG Library
PC-SIG

The Pelican Creative Writing CD-ROM
Queue Inc.

The Philosopher's Index - DIALOG OnDisc
DIALOG Information Services Inc.

The Ready Course
Interactive Knowledge Inc.

The Toronto Star on CD-ROM
Southam Electronic Publishing

The World of Dinosaurs
Hary & Company

Third World Guide
Interaktiva Medier

Time (CD-I)
Quadrant Communicatie NV

Time Table of Arts and Entertainment
Xiphias

Time Table of Science and Innovation
Xiphias

Time Table of Science and Innovation
Xiphias

Time Traveller CD
New Media Schoolhouse

Unfamiliar Animals
CTU, University of Milan

US Civics/Citizenship (How To Become a US Citizen)
Quanta Press Inc.

Voila! The Interactive Audio French Tutor
Queue Inc.

Women Partners in Development
CD Resources Inc.; EBSCO-CD

Workplace Vocabulary
HEC Software Inc.

World Travel Guide
Columbus Information

Yo Hablo Español - Uno & Dos
Intechnica International Inc.

¡Ole! The Interactive Audio Spanish Tutor
Queue Inc.

Additional Science Research and Engineering Titles

ACEL Engineering Index Plus
ACEL Information Pty Ltd.

Active Library on Corrosion (ALC)
Elsevier Science Publishers B.V.

Agriculture and Human Resources Series - Agriculture
ALDE Publishing Inc.

Arctic & Antarctic Regions (Cold Regions)
National Information Services Corporation (NISC)

Bibliography of Mexican Research
Multiconsult SC

Biotechnology Abstracts on CD-ROM
Silver Platter Information Inc.

Biotechnology Engineering Citation Index
Institute for Scientific Information (ISI)

CABCD
Silver Platter Information Inc.

CADIS-Fasteners
CADIS Inc.

CADIS-Fluid Systems
CADIS Inc.

CAPS (Computer Aided Product Selection)
Cahners Technical Information Service

CASPAR (Computer Aided Science Policy Analysis and Research)
Quantum Research Corporation

CD-Code
Megalith Technologies Inc.

CD-GENE (Gene/Protein Sequence Database & Software)
Hitachi Software Engineering America Ltd.

CD-REEF
CSTB (Centre Scientifique et Technique du Bâtiment)

CD-STRAINS
Hitachi Software Engineering America Ltd.
Information Provider: American Type Culture Collection (ATCC); Hakko

CenBASE/Materials
Information Indexing, Inc.

Ceramic Abstracts
National Information Services Corporation (NISC)

CITIS
CITIS Ltd.

CONI (Construction Information)
CADIS Inc.

Construction Criteria Base (CCB)
National Institute of Building Sciences (NIBS)

Corps of Engineers Forms
US Army Corps of Engineers

Corps of Engineers Publications
US Army Corps of Engineers

CTI Plus
Bowker-Saur Ltd.

DNASIS-DBREF 50
Hitachi Software Engineering Co Ltd.

DOD Standardization Service on CD-ROM
Information Handling Services Inc.

DODISS Plus Service
Information Handling Services Inc.

EI CHEMDISC - DIALOG OnDisc
DIALOG Information Services Inc.

EI COMPENDEX PLUS - DIALOG OnDisc
DIALOG Information Services Inc.

EI EEDISC - DIALOG OnDisc
DIALOG Information Services Inc.

EI Energy and Environment Disc - DIALOG OnDisc
DIALOG Information Services Inc.

ElectriGuide - EPRI Research PowerDisc
Electric Power Research Institute (EPRI)

Electronic Book - Technical Terminology
Nichigai Associates Inc.; Kinokuniya Company Ltd.

EMF DATABASE
Information Ventures Inc.

Environment Canada HYDAT Surface Water
EarthInfo Inc.

FSTA
Silver Platter Information Inc.; IFIS (International Food Information Service)

GeoArchive
National Information Services Corporation (NISC)

GeoRef
Silver Platter Information Inc.

GLORIA Data - East Coast
US Geological Survey (USGS)

GLORIA Data - Gulf of Mexico
National Geophysical Data Center

GRASS 4.0 (Geographic Resources Analysis Support System)
Young Minds Inc.

HAP
Hamburg Educational Partnership

ICONDA
Silver Platter Information Inc.

IEEE/IEE Periodicals Ondisc (IPO)
UMI (University Microfilms International)

**INIS (International Nuclear Informa-
    tion System)**
Silver Platter Information Inc.; International Atomic Energy Agency (IAEA)

**INSPEC - Electronics and Computing
    Ondisc**
UMI (University Microfilms International)

INSPEC Ondisc
UMI (University Microfilms International)

International Frequency List (IFL)
International Telecommunications Union
(ITU)

Jane's Fighting Ships
Jane's Information Group

Jane's Naval Weapon Systems
Jane's Information Group

Materials Science Citation Index
Institute for Scientific Information (ISI)

MathSci Disc Set
Silver Platter Information Inc.

**McGraw-Hill Science and Technical
    Reference Set, Release 2.0**
McGraw-Hill Inc.

Meca CD
CETIM

MEDLINE - DIALOG OnDisc
DIALOG Information Services Inc.

**METADEX Collection (Metals, Poly-
    mers, Ceramics) - DIALOG OnDisc**
DIALOG Information Services Inc.

**MOVE (SAE Mobility Engineering
    Technology on CD-ROM)**
Society of Automotive Engineers Inc.

MOVE Plus
Society of Automotive Engineers Inc.

NTIS
Silver Platter Information Inc.

NTIS - DIALOG OnDisc
DIALOG Information Services Inc.

**Polymer Encyclopedia - DIALOG
    OnDisc**
DIALOG Information Services Inc.

**RCC literatuur informatie Verheer en
    Waterslaat**
RCC

RSWB
Information Centre for Regional Planning
and Building Construction (IRB) of the
Fraunhofer Society

Science Citation Index
Institute for Scientific Information (ISI)

SKF Equivalog
SKF Data Services

Specmaster Vendor Catalog
National Standards Association

SPECSystem
American Institute of Architects

Standards Search
Society of Automotive Engineers Inc.

Technical Literature Database
R.R. Donnelley & Sons Company

The BEST Disc
Longman Cartermill Ltd.

**The Forest Service Disc - An
    Engineering Sampler**
The Oxko Corporation

**The Mark Encyclopedia of Polymer
    Science and Engineering**
John Wiley & Sons Inc.

The OCLC Computer Library
Silver Platter Information Inc.

The OCLC Environment Library
Silver Platter Information Inc.

**US Coastguard Personnel and Naval
    Engineering Manuals**
US Coast Guard

VLIER-ENERPAC CAD Library
Norminfo

Water Resources Abstracts, Volume I
National Information Services
Corporation (NISC)

Additional Financial Titles

Agriculture and Human Resources Series - Agriculture
ALDE Publishing Inc.

Arthur Andersen Accounting Reference Library (ARL)
Arthur Andersen & Company

Audit Reference and Resource Disc (ARRD)
Arthur Andersen & Company

Bancbase I on CD-ROM
Newport Associates

Big CD-ROM
24 Ore Seme S.P.A - Divisione New Media

BookFind-CD BUSINESS & LAW
Book Data

Business Periodicals Index
The H.W. Wilson Company

CD PLUS/HEALTH
CD Plus Inc.

Cfarbase for Global Investing
CIFAR - Center for International Financial Analysis & Research

Cfarbase for International Research
CIFAR - Center for International Financial Analysis & Research

Compact D/Canada
Disclosure Inc.

Compact D/SEC
Disclosure Inc.

Compact D/UK
Disclosure Inc.

COMPUSTAT PC Plus Corporate Text
Standard and Poor's Compustat Services Inc.

Consu/Stats 1989
Hopkins Technology

Consu/Stats I
Hopkins Technology

Custom CFR 31 - Money & Finance: Treasury
CD Book Publishers

Directory of Public Servants (Japan)
Printing Bureau

Disclosure/Worldscope/Snapshots
Wright Investors' Service

Disclosure Corporate Snapshots
Disclosure Inc.

Duns Reference Plus
Dun & Bradstreet Information Services

Econ/Stats I
Hopkins Technology

European Corporations CD
Silver Platter Information Inc.

EXPLORE!
DRI/McGraw-Hill

Finance for Non-Finance Managers (provisional) (CD-I)
CD-I Training Ltd.

GPO on Silver Platter
Silver Platter Information Inc.

International Financial Statistics
International Monetary Fund (Bureau of Statistics)

IntlEc CD-ROM - The Index to International Economics
Information Access Company

Investext
Information Access Company

Lotus One Source - CD/Banking - Bank Holding Companies
Lotus Development Corporation

Lotus One Source - CD/Banking - Commercial Banks
Lotus Development Corporation

Lotus One Source - CD/Banking - Savings & Loans and Savings Banks
Lotus Development Corporation

Lotus One Source - CD/Corporate - US M&A
Lotus Development Corporation

Lotus One Source - CD/Investment -
  International Equities
  Lotus Development Corporation
**Lotus One Source - CD/Investment -
  US Equities**
  Lotus Development Corporation
Moody's Bank & Finance Manual & Disc
  Moody's Investors Service
Moody's Company Data
  Moody's Investors Service
Moody's Industrial Manual & Disc
  Moody's Investors Service
Moody's International Plus
  Moody's Investors Service
Moody's OTC Industrial Manual & Disc
  Moody's Investors Service
Moody's OTC Unlisted Manual & Disc
  Moody's Investors Service
Moody's Public Utility Manual & Disc
  Moody's Investors Service
Moody's Transportation Manual & Disc
  Moody's Investors Service
ORBASE
  Multimedia Publishing Ltd.
PAIS on CD-ROM
  Public Affairs Information Service (PAIS)
Photo Gallery
  NEC Technologies (USA) Inc.
photoBANK
  Wayzata Technology Inc.
**San Francisco Chronicle - DIALOG
  OnDisc**
  DIALOG Information Services Inc.
**Search Master Collier's Bankruptcy
  Library**
  Matthew Bender & Co Inc.
SEC Online on Silver Platter
  Silver Platter Information Inc.
SEC Online-10K
  Silver Platter Information Inc.
Securities Reports (Counter Stock)
  Printing Bureau

**Securities Reports (Foreign
  Companies)**
  Printing Bureau
Securities Reports (Listed Stock)
  Printing Bureau
Stockwatch Canada
  OSS Optical Storage Systems Inc.
The Economist on CD-ROM
  FT PROFILE
The Financial Times CD-ROM
  FT PROFILE
The Independent on CD-ROM
  FT PROFILE
The Intuition Expert
  Financial Courseware Ltd.
The NTDB (National Trade Data Bank)
  United States Department of Commerce
Wilson Business Abstracts (WBA)
  The H.W. Wilson Company
Winning Elections
  Wayzata Technology Inc.

Additional Law Titles

**Agent Orange - The Case Against
  America**
  Norman Ross Publishing Inc.
American Government
  Queue Inc.
**Aquatic Sciences and Fisheries
  Abstracts (ASFA)**
  Compact Cambridge
**Biographical Directory of the American
  Congress**
  Staff Directories Ltd.
BookFind-CD Business & Law
  Book Data
BookFind-CD World Edition
  Book Data
Canada Jurisprudence
  Inform II Microfor; Juris 2000

Canadian OHS Legislation
Canadian Centre for Occupational Health and Safety (CCOHS)

Canadian Register of Research and Researchers in the Social Sciences
University of Western Ontario

CASEBASE - The Arkansas Report
Law Office Information Systems

CASEBASE - The Connecticut Report
Law Office Information Systems

CASEBASE - The Rhode Island Report
Law Office Information Systems

Casetex
IBIS Service AG

CAT CD450 Law Cataloging Collection
OCLC Online Computer Library Center Inc.

CCINFOdisc - Series B1 - CanData (Canadian Occupational Health & Safety Databases)
Canadian Centre for Occupational Health and Safety (CCOHS)

Colorado Revised Statutes on CD-ROM
CD-ROM Resource Group Inc.

Commonwealth Corporations Law
DISKROM Australia

Commonwealth Statutes & Statutory Rules in Force
DISKROM Australia

Commonwealth Taxation Law
DISKROM Australia

Congressional Record - Proceedings and Debates of the 99th Congress (1985)
FD Inc.

Congressional Record on CD-ROM
FD Inc.

Current Law Yearbooks 1986-1990
Sweet & Maxwell Ltd.

Custom CFR 1 - General Provisions
CD Book Publishers

Custom CFR 10 - Energy
CD Book Publishers

Custom CFR 11 - Federal Elections
CD Book Publishers

Custom CFR 12 - Banks & Banking
CD Book Publishers

Custom CFR 13 - Business Credit and Assistance
CD Book Publishers

Custom CFR 14 - Aeronautics & Space Chapter Five Only
CD Book Publishers

Custom CFR 15 - Commerce & Foreign Trade
CD Book Publishers

Custom CFR 16 - Commercial Practices
CD Book Publishers

Custom CFR 17 - Commodity & Security Exchanges
CD Book Publishers

Custom CFR 18 - Conservation of Power and Water Resources
CD Book Publishers

Custom CFR 19 - Customs Duties
CD Book Publishers

Custom CFR 20 - Employees' Benefits
CD Book Publishers

Custom CFR 21 - Food & Drugs
CD Book Publishers

Custom CFR 22 - Foreign Relations
CD Book Publishers

Custom CFR 23 - Highways
CD Book Publishers

Custom CFR 24 - Housing & Urban Development
CD Book Publishers

Custom CFR 26 - Internal Revenue
CD Book Publishers

Custom CFR 27 - Alcohol
CD Book Publishers

Custom CFR 28 - Judicial Administration
CD Book Publishers

Custom CFR 29 - Labor
CD Book Publishers

Custom CFR 3 - The President
CD Book Publishers

Custom CFR 30 - Mineral Resources
CD Book Publishers

Custom CFR 31 - Money & Finance: Treasury
CD Book Publishers

Custom CFR 32 - National Defense
CD Book Publishers

Custom CFR 34 - Education
CD Book Publishers

Custom CFR 4 - Accounts
CD Book Publishers

Custom CFR 40 - Protection of Environment
CD Book Publishers

Custom CFR 41 - Public Contracts & Property Management
CD Book Publishers

Custom CFR 42 - Public Health
CD Book Publishers

Custom CFR 43 - Public Lands: Interior
CD Book Publishers

Custom CFR 44 - Emergency Management and Assistance
CD Book Publishers

Custom CFR 45 - Public Welfare
CD Book Publishers

Custom CFR 46 - Shipping
CD Book Publishers

Custom CFR 47 - Telecommunications
CD Book Publishers

Custom CFR 48 - Federal Acquisitions Regulations System
CD Book Publishers

Custom CFR 49 - Transportation
CD Book Publishers

Custom CFR 5 - Administrative Personnel
CD Book Publishers

Custom CFR 50 - Wildlife and Fisheries
CD Book Publishers

Custom CFR 7 - Agriculture
CD Book Publishers

Custom CFR 8 - Aliens & Nationality
CD Book Publishers

Custom CFR 9 - Animals & Animal Products
CD Book Publishers

Defense Library on Disc
Pentagon Library; National Defense University Library

ENFLEX INFO
ERM Computer Services Inc.

European Taxation Data Base
International Bureau of Fiscal Documentation (IBFD)

FDA on CD-ROM
FD Inc.

Federal Acquisition Regulations with Circulars; Federal Information Resources Management Regulations with Bulletins FAR/FIRMR
US Government Printing Office (GPO)

Georgia Law on Disc
The Michie Company

Government Documents Catalog Service (GDCS)
Auto-Graphics Inc.

HAZARD-MASTER
Technical Services Associates Inc.

HCFA on CD-ROM
FD Inc.

Hein's United States Treaties Index on CD-ROM
William S. Hein & Co Inc.

Index to Legal Periodicals
The H.W. Wilson Company

Iwanami Compact Legal Database
Iwanami Shoten Publishers; Dai Nippon Printing Company Ltd.

Labour Canada - Operations Program
Canadian Centre for Occupational Health and Safety (CCOHS)

Latin American Taxation Data Base
International Bureau of Fiscal Documentation (IBFD)

LAWBASE
IBIS Service AG

LAWDISC (California Civil Cases)
National Legal Databases Corporation

Lawmarc
Utlas International

LawSoft
IBIS Service AG

LegalBase
Nihon Horitsu Joho Center

LegalTrac
Information Access Company

Martindale-Hubbell Law Directory on CD-ROM
Martindale-Hubbell Electronic Publishing

Massachusetts Administrative Law Library
Social Law Library

Massachusetts Substantive Law Library
Social Law Library

Minnesota Statutes 1988
Minnesota State Revisor of Statutes Office; Innotech Inc.

Minnesota Statutes 1989
Innotech Inc.

Minnesota Statutes 1990
Innotech Inc.

Montana Statutes
Innotech Inc.

New England Law Library Consortium CD-ROM Union Catalog
New England Law Library Consortium (NELLCO)

New Mexico Law on Disc
The Michie Company

New South Wales Case Law 1973-1991
INFO-ONE International Pty Ltd.

NIJ Drugs and Crime CD-ROM Library
Abt Books Inc.

NSW Collectors Edition 1901-1972
INFO-ONE International Pty Ltd.

Nuova Fiscal Data
SEAT - Division Stet SPA; SIDAC SpA

Opal International Environmental Law Library
OPAL Publishing Corporation

Opal US Immigration Law Library
OPAL Publishing Corporation

ORBASE
Multimedia Publishing Ltd.

OSHA & DOT Regulations
Public Affairs Information Service (PAIS)

PAIS on CD-ROM
Public Affairs Information Service (PAIS)

POPLINE
Silver Platter Information Inc.

Public Law (PL) 94-171 Data (Census of Population and Housing 1990)
US Bureau of the Census

Revenue Rulings & Procedures
Prentice Hall Information Network

Search Master Business Commercial Library
Matthew Bender & Co Inc.

Search Master California Library
Matthew Bender & Co Inc.

Search Master Collier's Bankruptcy Library
Matthew Bender & Co Inc.

Search Master Federal Library
Matthew Bender & Co Inc.

Search Master Intellectual Property Library
Matthew Bender & Co Inc.

Search Master New York Library
Matthew Bender & Co Inc.

Search Master Personal Injury Library
Matthew Bender & Co Inc.

Search Master Tax Library
Matthew Bender & Co Inc.

Search Master Texas Library
Matthew Bender & Co Inc.
Securities Reports (Counter Stock)
Printing Bureau
Securities Reports (Foreign Companies)
Printing Bureau
Securities Reports (Listed Stock)
Printing Bureau
SI-CD
HMSO New Media Publishing; Context Ltd.
softbase
IBIS Service AG
softlaw
IBIS Service AG
Tax Disc
HMSO New Media Publishing; CLS (UK) Ltd.
Terrorist Group Profiles
Quanta Press Inc.
The Banking Library
IHS Regulatory Products Inc.
The Commonwealth Numbered Acts Disc
DISKROM Australia
The Constitution Papers
Reflective Arts Publishing
The Dictionary of Law for Business
Jyukokumin-Sha Publishing Company Ltd.
The Dictionary of Law for Business (Data Discman)
Jyukokumin-Sha Publishing Company Ltd.
Toxic Release Inventory 1987
US Government Printing Office (GPO)
Unreported Judgments on CD-ROM
INFO-ONE International Pty Ltd.
Utah Law on Disc
The Michie Company

Victoria Case Law 1957-1991
INFO-ONE International Pty Ltd.
Virginia Law on Disc
The Michie Company
Voter Lists on Compact Disc
Aristotle Industries
West CD-ROM Federal Securities Library
West Publishing Company
West CD-ROM Federal Tax Library
West Publishing Company
West CD-ROM Government Contracts Library
West Publishing Company
West Military Justice Library
West Publishing Company

Additional Medical Titles

AIDS Compact Library CD-ROM
Maxwell Electronic Publishing
AIDS Information and Education Worldwide
CD Resources Inc.; EBSCO-CD
AIDSLINE
Silver Platter Information Inc.
American Family Physician 1985-1990
CMC - Creative Multimedia Corporation
American Journal of Public Health CD-ROM
Maxwell Electronic Publishing
Annals of Internal Medicine CD-ROM
Maxwell Electronic Publishing
ASSIA Plus
Bowker-Saur Ltd.
BiblioMed Cardiology Series
Healthcare Information Services Inc.
BiblioMed Citation Series
Healthcare Information Services Inc.

BiblioMed Gastroenterology Series
Healthcare Information Services Inc.

BiblioMed Infectious Diseases
Healthcare Information Services Inc.

BiblioMed Professional Series
Healthcare Information Services Inc.

Biological & Agricultural Index
The H.W. Wilson Company

Biological Abstracts on Compact Disc (BA on CD)
BIOSIS; Silver Platter Information Inc.

Biological Abstracts/RRM (BA/RRM on CD)
BIOSIS; Silver Platter Information Inc.

Biotechnology Citation Index
Institute for Scientific Information (ISI)

Biotechnology Engineering Citation Index
Institute for Scientific Information (ISI)

BIRD (Database on the Child and His Environment)
Centre International de l'Enfance

BookFind-CD MEDICAL
Book Data

British Medical Journal CD-ROM
Maxwell Electronic Publishing

CABCD
Silver Platter Information Inc.

CANCER-CD
Silver Platter Information Inc.

CANCERLIT
Compact Cambridge

Cancerlit - Knowledge Finder
Aries Systems Corporation

Cardiology MEDLINE
Maxwell Electronic Publishing

CardLine
Aries Systems Corporation

CAT CD450 Medical Cataloging Collection
OCLC Online Computer Library Center Inc.

CD Plus/AIDSLINE (AIDS Information Online)
CD Plus Inc.

CD PLUS/HEALTH
CD Plus Inc.

CD PLUS/MEDfive
CD Plus Inc.

CD PLUS/MEDfour
CD Plus Inc.

CD PLUS/MEDLINE
CD Plus Inc.

CD PLUS/MEDtwo
CD Plus Inc.

CD PLUS/New England Journal of Medicine
CD Plus Inc.

CD-CATSS
Utlas International

CD-IRIS
Chibret International Documentation Centre

CD-MED - Anaesthesia
Questel; INSERM-IMA

CD-MED - Cardiovascular Diseases
Questel; INSERM-IMA

CD-MED - Gynecology
Questel; INSERM-IMA

CD-MED - Infectious Diseases
Questel; INSERM-IMA

Chest Radiology
Paediatric Chest Radiology (3-in-1 CD-ROM)

Combination Cancerlit/PDQ
Compact Cambridge

Compact Cambridge MEDLINE
Compact Cambridge

Compact Cambridge MEDLINE with Cumulative Index
Compact Cambridge

Compact Cambridge MEDLINE with Reference Update
Compact Cambridge

Composite Index for CRC Handbooks
EBSCO Publishing
Comprehensive Medline
EBSCO Publishing
Computerized Clinical Information System (CCIS)
Micromedex Inc.
Consult Scientific American Medicine
Scientific American Medicine
Core Journals MEDLINE
Aries Systems Corporation
CORE MEDLINE
EBSCO Publishing
Critical Care & Emergency MEDLINE
Maxwell Electronic Publishing
CSIC
Micronet S.A.; La Ley Division
Informatica
Derwent Drug File on CD-ROM
Derwent Publications Ltd.
Electronic Book - Medical Terminology
Nichigai Associates Inc.; Kinokuniya
Company Ltd.
Emergency Medicine MEDLINE
Maxwell Electronic Publishing
EMERGINDEX System
Micromedex Inc.
EMF DATABASE
Information Ventures Inc.
Excerpta Medica - Drugs and Pharmacology
Silver Platter Information Inc.; Elsevier
Science Publishers Inc.
Excerpta Medica CD - Anesthesiology
Silver Platter Information Inc.; Elsevier
Science Publishers Inc.
Excerpta Medica CD - Cardiology
Silver Platter Information Inc.; Elsevier
Science Publishers Inc.
Excerpta Medica CD - Gastroenterology
Silver Platter Information Inc.; Elsevier
Science Publishers Inc.

Excerpta Medica CD - Immunology & AIDS
Silver Platter Information Inc.; Elsevier
Science Publishers Inc.
Excerpta Medica CD - Neurosciences
Silver Platter Information Inc.; Elsevier
Science Publishers Inc.
Excerpta Medica CD - Obstetrics/ Gynecology
Silver Platter Information Inc.; Elsevier
Science Publishers Inc.
Excerpta Medica CD - Pathology
Silver Platter Information Inc.; Elsevier
Science Publishers Inc.
Excerpta Medica CD - Psychology
Silver Platter Information Inc.; Elsevier
Science Publishers Inc.
Excerpta Medica CD - Radiology & Nuclear Medicine
Silver Platter Information Inc.; Elsevier
Science Publishers Inc.
Family Practice MEDLINE
Maxwell Electronic Publishing
Gastroenterology & Hepatology MEDLINE
Maxwell Electronic Publishing
GenBank Nucleotide Sequence Database
IntelliGenetics Inc.
GeneWorks CD-ROM
IntelliGenetics Inc.
Health - Planning and Administration CD-ROM
Compact Cambridge
Health Devices Alerts - DIALOG OnDisc
DIALOG Information Services Inc.
Health Planning - Administration
EBSCO Publishing
Health Reference Center
Information Access Company
Healthcare Product Comparison System - DIALOG OnDisc
DIALOG Information Services Inc.

HealthPLAN-CD on Silver Platter
Silver Platter Information Inc.
Human Nutrition
Compact Cambridge
Infectious Diseases MEDLINE
Maxwell Electronic Publishing
Journal of the American Medical Association CD-ROM
Maxwell Electronic Publishing
LILACS/CD-ROM Latin American and Caribbean Health Sciences Literature
BIREME Latin American and Caribbean Center on Health Sciences Information
Martindale - The Extra Pharmacopoeia on the Computerised Clinical Information System
Micromedex Inc.
Medicats
Big Time
Medicine History
Fototeca Storica Nazionale Snc
Medicorom
Inter CD
MEDLINE - DIALOG OnDisc
DIALOG Information Services Inc.
MEDLINE Clinical Collection - DIALOG OnDisc
DIALOG Information Services Inc.
MEDLINE Express
Silver Platter Information Inc.
MEDLINE Knowledge Finder
Aries Systems Corporation
MEDLINE Professional
Silver Platter Information Inc.
MEDLINE Standard
Silver Platter Information Inc.
Molecular Structures in Biology
Oxford University Press
Morbidity & Mortality Weekly Report CD-ROM
Maxwell Electronic Publishing

New England Journal of Medicine
CMC - Creative Multimedia Corporation
OBGLine
Aries Systems Corporation
Obstetrics & Gynecology MEDLINE
Maxwell Electronic Publishing
OncoDisc
J.B. LippInc.ott
OrthoLine Database
Aries-Systems Corporation
Oxford Textbook of Medicine - Electronic Edition
Electronic Publishing
PASCAL CD-ROM
INIST Institut de l'Information Scientifique et Technique (INIST/CNRS)
PathLine Database
Aries Systems Corporation
PC/Gene Databanks
IntelliGenetics Inc.
Pediatrics in Review & Infectious Diseases Manual
American Academy of Pediatrics
Pediatrics in Review and Report of the Committee on Infectious Diseases
American Academy of Pediatrics
Pediatrics MEDLINE
Maxwell Electronic Publishing
Personal Medical Library CD-ROM
EBSCO Publishing
PharmaROM
OFAC
Physician's MEDLINE
Maxwell Electronic Publishing
Pill Book Version 3.0
Yakugyo Jiho Co Ltd.
PolTox Library (Pollution and Toxicology Database on CD-ROM) PolTox I
Compact Cambridge
POPLINE
Silver Platter Information Inc.

Quantarc Electronic Library
    Poulter Communications PLC
RadLine
    Aries Systems Corporation
Saishin Igaku Daijiten (New Medical
    Dictionary)
    Ishiyaku Publishers Inc.
Saishin Igaku Daijiten (New Medical
    Dictionary) (Data Discman)
    Ishiyaku Publishers Inc.
Science Citation Index
    Institute for Scientific Information (ISI)
Siemens X-Ray CD-ROM
    BERTELSMANN Electronic Printing
    Service GmbH
SIRS Science Text & Index CD-ROM
    SIRS Inc.
SPORT Discus
    Silver Platter Information Inc.
STAT!-Ref
    Teton Data Systems
Storia Della Miniatura Medioevale
    e Dei Codici Membranacei
    Fototeca Storica Nazionale Snc
SurgAnLine
    Aries Systems Corporation
Talking Dictionary of Medical Termi-
    nology (Anatomy & Physiology for
    Nurses)
    Victoria University of Technology
    (Footscray Institute of Technology)
Term-X
    Ouwehand Consultancy (Ye Olde Hand
    Consultancy)
The American Medical Directory,
    32nd Edition
    American Medical Association
The BEST Disc
    Longman Cartermill Ltd.
The Electronic MRI Manual
    Aries Systems Corporation

The Excerpta Medica Library Service
    1984-1987 and 1988-1989
    Silver Platter Information Inc.; Elsevier
    Science Publishers Inc.
The Family Doctor
    CMC - Creative Multimedia Corp.
The Lancet CD-ROM
    Maxwell Electronic Publishing
The Merck Veterinary Manual
    Merck Sharp & Dohme Research
    Laboratories
The New England Journal of Medicine
    CD-ROM
    Maxwell Electronic Publishing
The Pediatric Infectious Diseases
    Journal 1984-1990
    CMC - Creative Multimedia Corporation
The Physician's AIDSLINE
    Maxwell Electronic Publishing
THORAX on CD-ROM (Pediatric
    Pneumology)
    ICOME Ltd.; Institute for Medical
    Postgradual Studies
TOMES Plus System
    Micromedex Inc.
Toxic Release Inventory 1987
    US Government Printing Office (GPO)
TOXLINE on Silver Platter
    Silver Platter Information Inc.
TOXLINE Plus
    Silver Platter Information Inc.
Unabridged MEDLINE
    Aries Systems Corporation
VETCD
    Silver Platter Information Inc.
Viral Hepatitis Compact Library
    CD-ROM
    Maxwell Electronic Publishing

Additional Research and Statistics Titles

Academic Abstracts Full Text Elite
EBSCO Publishing
Academic Abstracts Full Text Select
EBSCO Publishing
Agricultural Census 1982
Space-Time Research Pty Ltd.
AIDS Compact Library CD-ROM
Maxwell Electronic Publishing
AIDSLINE
Silver Platter Information Inc.
Airborne Antarctic Ozone Experiment
NASA Ames Research Center
AQUALINE
Compact Cambridge
Aquatic Sciences and Fisheries Abstracts (ASFA)
Compact Cambridge
ARCHI-CD
AXIROM (Groupement Canope - Sédinov - UNSFA)
Arctic & Antarctic Regions (Cold Regions)
National Information Services Corporation (NISC)
ARIES
CD ROM de Mexico SA de C.V.
ATLA Religion Database on CD-ROM
American Theological Library Association (ATLA)
Bibliography of Mexican Research
Multiconsult SC
Biological Abstracts on Compact Disc (BA on CD)
BIOSIS; Silver Platter Information Inc.
Biological Abstracts/RRM (BA/RRM on CD)
BIOSIS; Silver Platter Information Inc.
Biotechnology Abstracts on CD-ROM
Silver Platter Information Inc.

Biotechnology Citation Index
Institute for Scientific Information (ISI)
BNI - British Newspaper Index on CD-ROM
Research Publications
Canada 1986 Census Profiles
Statistics Canada
Canadian Register of Research and Researchers in the Social Sciences
University of Western Ontario
CASPAR (Computer Aided Science Policy Analysis and Research)
Quantum Research Corporation
Catalogo Comune Delle Biblioteche
Universita Degli Studi di Milano - Dipartimento di Scienze dell' Information
CCINFOdisc - Series A2 - CHEMSource (Chemical Information)
Canadian Centre for Occupational Health and Safety (CCOHS)
CCINFOdisc - Series B2 - InterData (Occupational Health and Safety Databases Produced Outside Canada)
Canadian Centre for Occupational Health and Safety (CCOHS)
CD-AGSTATS
Space-Time Research Pty Ltd.
CD-Atlas de France (IBM)
ARGO Infographie S.A.; Chadwyck-Healey France; GIP Reclus
CD-Atlas de France (Macintosh)
ARGO Infographie S.A.; Chadwyck-Healey France; GIP Reclus
CD-GENE (Gene/Protein Sequence Database & Software)
Hitachi Software Engineering America Ltd.
CD-ROM I.N.S.
National Institute of Statistics - Belgium
CD-View Illustrators
CRC Research Institute Inc.

CD/Biotech
  PC-SIG Inc.

CDATA 86 - The 1981 and 1986 Australian Censuses
  Space-Time Research Pty Ltd.

CDCD (Climate Data Compact Disc)
  Space-Time Research Pty Ltd.

CEAREX Volume I
  National Snow and Ice Data Center

Census 86 - The 1986 New Zealand Census
  Space-Time Research Pty Ltd.

Cfarbase for Global Investing
  CIFAR - Center for International Financial Analysis & Research

Cfarbase for International Research
  CIFAR - Center for International Financial Analysis & Research

Choices
  British Market Research Bureau

CIMMYT'S Maize Germplasm Database
  CIMMYT; CGNET Services International

Colorado Revised Statutes on CD-ROM
  CD-ROM Resource Group Inc.

Combination Cancerlit/PDQ
  Compact Cambridge

COMLINE on Silver Platter
  Silver Platter Information Inc.

Compact Cambridge MEDLINE
  Compact Cambridge

Compact Cambridge MEDLINE with Reference Update
  Compact Cambridge

Compact D/Canada
  Disclosure Inc.

Compact International Agricultural Research Library CIARL Basic Retrospective Set 1962-1986 (CIARL-BRS)
  Consultative Group on International Agriculture Research (CGIAR)

Consu/Stats 1989
  Hopkins Technology

Consu/Stats I
  Hopkins Technology

Contributed Cataloging - Research & Academic MARC Records
  The Library Corporation

Countries of the World Encyclopedia
  Bureau Development Inc.

County Business Patterns 1985
  Space-Time Research Pty Ltd.

County Business Patterns 1986
  Space-Time Research Pty Ltd.

CRB InfoTech CD-ROM
  Knight-Ridder Financial Publishing Group

CRI Postman
  CSK Research Institute Corporation (CRI); Dai Nippon Printing Company Ltd.

CRIS/ICAR
  Silver Platter Information Inc.

CRISS
  CSK Research Institute Corporation (CRI)

Current Data Bases (Media & Marketing Research Data)
  Interactive Market Systems Inc. (IMS)

Current Research in Britain (CRIB)
  Longman Cartermill Ltd.

Current Studies Disc 1990
  Mediamark Research Inc.

DaTa - Deloitte & Touche Accounting & Auditing Knowledgebase Systems
  Deloitte & Touche

Digital Chart of the World (DCW)
  GEOVISION Inc.; Environmental Systems Research Institute (ESRI)

Digital Data Library
  Digital Library Inc.

DISCOTEXT 1
  Hachette

DMSP SSM/I Brightness Temperature and Ice Concentration Grids for the Polar Regions
  National Snow and Ice Data Center

DNASIS-DBREF 50
Hitachi Software Engineering Co Ltd.

Dun's BusinessLine
Dun's Marketing Services; Donnelley
Marketing Information Services (DMIS)

ECDIN
Commission of the European Communities Environmental Institute of the Joint
Research Centre

**EL CID Construction Information
Database**
Architech Publishing Ltd.

**ElectriGuide - EPRI Research
PowerDisc**
Electric Power Research Institute (EPRI)

EMF DATABASE
Information Ventures Inc.

English Vocabulary Learning Aid
CSK Research Institute Corporation
(CRI)

ERIC - DIALOG OnDisc
DIALOG Information Services Inc.

ERIC - EBSCO CD
EBSCO Publishing

ERS Electronic Data Products
Information Division, EMS, US Department of Agriculture

ESPACE-ACCESS
European Patent Office (EPO)

ESPACE-BULLETIN
European Patent Office (EPO)

ESPACE-EP
European Patent Office (EPO)

ESPACE-EP-B
European Patent Office (EPO)

ESPACE-FIRST
European Patent Office (EPO)

ESPACE-UK
European Patent Office (EPO)

ESPACE-WORLD
European Patent Office (EPO); World
Intellectual Property Organisation
(WIPO)

Europe in the Round
Vocational Technologies Ltd.

**Excerpta Medica CD - Immunology &
AIDS**
Silver Platter Information Inc.; Elsevier
Science Publishers Inc.

Farm Audience Readership Measurement Service
Interactive Market Systems Inc. (IMS)

Fedstat/Tiger - Digital Map Databases
US Statistics Inc.

**FERC Data on CD-ROM - Electric
Utilities**
Oil Pipeline Research Institute Inc.

**FERC Data on CD-ROM - Natural Gas
Pipelines**
Oil Pipeline Research Institute Inc.

**FERC Data on CD-ROM - Petroleum
Pipelines**
Oil Pipeline Research Institute Inc.

Fine Chemicals Database (Chemlink)
Chemron Inc.

Food/Analyst
Hopkins Technology

Food/Analyst Plus
Hopkins Technology

Foods Intelligence on Compact Disc
BIOSIS; Silver Platter Information Inc.

Gale GlobalAccess - Associations CD
Silver Platter Information Inc.

General Business File
Information Access Company

Geospace
ACT Multimedia

Grants Database - DIALOG OnDisc
DIALOG Information Services Inc.

**GRASS 4.0 (Geographic Resources
Analysis Support System)**
Young Minds Inc.

Haystack III
Information Handling Services Inc.

Helecon CD-ROM
Helsinki School of Economics and Business

Hospital Admission Records - Canada, Hospital Morbidity
Health & Welfare Canada

Hyper-ABLEDATA
Trace Research and Development Center

ICONDA
Silver Platter Information Inc.

IEA Coal Research CD-ROM
IEA Coal Research

Illustrator's Scrapbook
CSK Research Institute Corporation (CRI)

IMAGO - The Electronic Slide Table
CD Romics

INIS (International Nuclear Information System)
Silver Platter Information Inc.; International Atomic Energy Agency (IAEA)

Insight into American Life and Opinions
ORS Publishing

INSPEC - Physics Computing Ondisc
UMI (University Microfilms International)

International Pharmaceutical Abstracts
Compact Cambridge

International Pharmaceutical Abstracts (IPA)
Silver Platter Information Inc.

IntlEc CD-ROM - The Index to International Economics, Development, and Finance 1981-1990
Chadwyck-Healey Ltd.

Investext
Information Access Company

Investigating Chinese Poetry
CSK Research Institute Corporation (CRI)

IRESIE
Universidad de Colima

Jane's Strategic Weapon Systems
Jane's Information Group

Japanese History
CSK Research Institute Corporation (CRI)

Life Sciences Collection
Compact Cambridge

LISA Plus
Bowker-Saur Ltd.

Lotus One Source - CD/Investment - International Equities
Lotus Development Corporation

Lotus One Source - CD/Investment - US Equities
Lotus Development Corporation

Magazine Article Summaries (MAS) Full Text Elite
EBSCO Publishing

Magazine Article Summaries Full Text Select
EBSCO Publishing

MarketPlace Business
MarketPlace Information Corporation

Master Search Bible - Comparative Bible Research
Tri-Star Publishing

Metropolitan
London Research Centre; Réseau URBAMET

Microlog - Canadian Research Index
Micromedia Ltd.

Monterey Bay Regional Sampler
US Geological Survey (USGS)

Moody's Bank & Finance Manual & Disc
Moody's Investors Service

Moody's Transportation Manual & Disc
Moody's Investors Service

My Fair Lady/CAN
CSK Research Institute Corporation (CRI)

NADbank
Interactive Market Systems Inc. (IMS)

NATASHA - National Archive on Sexuality, Health, & Adolescence
Sociometrics Corporation

National CD-ROM Sampler - An Extension Reference Library
Interactive Design & Development

National Meteorological Center Grid Point Data Set, Version II
National Center for Atmospheric Research, Department of Atmospheric Sciences (University of Washington)

NERIS on CD-ROM
NERIS

New Car and Truck Buyer Media Report
Interactive Market Systems Inc. (IMS)

New England Journal of Medicine
CMC - Creative Multimedia Corporation

New England Law Library Consortium CD-ROM Union Catalog
New England Law Library Consortium (NELLCO)

NHK English Conversation
CRC Research Institute Inc.

NHK English Conversation (CD-I)
CRC Research Institute Inc.

NIJ Drugs and Crime CD-ROM Library
Abt Books Inc.

Nimbus-7 SMMR Brightness Temperature Grids for the Northern Hemisphere
NASA/Goddard Space Flight Center, Oceans and Ice Branch

North American Indian Anthropological Series
Quevillon Editions

NTIS
Silver Platter Information Inc.

NTIS - DIALOG OnDisc
DIALOG Information Services Inc.

NYNEX Fast Track Digital Directory
NYNEX Information Technologies Company

OG/PLUS
Research Publications

Pan European Study
Interactive Market Systems Inc. (IMS)

Patent History
Research Publications

PatentView
Research Publications

Pediatrics in Review & Infectious Diseases Manual
American Academy of Pediatrics

Pediatrics in Review and Report of the Committee on Infectious Diseases
American Academy of Pediatrics

Physician's MEDLINE
Maxwell Electronic Publishing

Pilot Gas Turbine Start-Up Trainer
Southwest Research Institute

PMB Print Measurement Bureau
Interactive Market Systems Inc. (IMS)

PolarPAC
Western Library Network (WLN)

PolTox Library (Pollution and Toxicology Database on CD-ROM) PolTox I
Compact Cambridge

Poltox Library (Pollution and Toxicology Database on CD-ROM) Poltox III
Compact Cambridge

Real Estate Information
COURTHOUSE Records Inc.

Religious and Theological Abstracts on CD-ROM
Innotech Inc.; Religious and Theological Abstracts Inc.

RIA OnPoint
Research Institute of America Inc.

Salescan
Dun & Bradstreet International

San Jose Mercury News - DIALOG OnDisc
DIALOG Information Services Inc.

Scantrack Market Planner
A.C. Nielsen

Scholarly Book Reviews on CD-ROM
University Publications of America

Science and Geography Education (SAGE)
CSIRO (Commonwealth Scientific and Industrial Research Organisation) Australia

SciTech Reference Plus
Bowker Electronic Publishing

SESAME
CIRAD

Supermap
Space-Time Research Pty Ltd.

Supermap 1980 Census - Unit Records Population and Households -Hungary
Space-Time Research Pty Ltd.

Supermap 1980 US Census County Level
Space-Time Research Pty Ltd.

Supermap 1980 US Census Tract Level
Space-Time Research Pty Ltd.

Supermap 2 - The 1991 New Zealand Census
Space-Time Research Pty Ltd.

Supermap Hong Kong
Space-Time Research Pty Ltd.

Survey of Adults and Markets of Affluence
Interactive Market Systems Inc. (IMS)

SWRA - Selected Water Resources Abstracts
Compact Cambridge

Teenage Market/Attitudinal Study
Interactive Market Systems Inc. (IMS)

Telecom Business Finder
Space-Time Research Pty Ltd.

The 1991 TIME Magazine Multimedia Compact Almanac
Compact Publishing Inc.; Time Magazine Development Group

The BEST Disc
Longman Cartermill Ltd.

The CIA World Factbook
Quanta Press Inc.

The Earth Disc
Longman Cartermill Ltd.

The Merck Veterinary Manual
Merck Sharp & Dohme Research Laboratories

The North American Facsimile (Fax) Book
Quanta Press Inc.

The OCLC Computer Library
Silver Platter Information Inc.

The Physician's AIDSLINE
Maxwell Electronic Publishing

The Plastics and Rubber Materials Disc
Pergamon Press plc

The Ready Course
Interactive Knowledge Inc.

The Retail Census of Australia - 1985/86 Release
Space-Time Research Pty Ltd.

TOXLINE on Silver Platter
Silver Platter Information Inc.

Trade Opportunities CD-ROM
Wayzata Technology Inc.

TSR - Company Information Files
Tokyo Shoko Research Ltd. (TSR)

TURBO OUTRUN
CSK Research Institute Corporation (CRI)

Ulrichs Plus
Bowker Electronic Publishing

UNESCO CD-ROM Prototype
UNESCO

Union List of Scientific Periodicals in Japanese Language
Gakujutsu Joho Centre; Dai Nippon Printing Company Ltd.

US Coastguard Personnel and Naval Engineering Manuals
US Coast Guard

**Viral Hepatitis Compact Library
CD-ROM**
Maxwell Electronic Publishing

**Visual Information System for MH-53J
Helicopter**
Southwest Research Institute

**Voyage to the Planets Volume 1:
Uranus, Jupiter, Saturn**
Astronomical Research

**Voyage to the Planets Volume 2:
Neptune**
Astronomical Research

Voyage to the Planets Volume 3: Mars
Astronomical Research

Voyage to the Planets Volume 4: Venus
Astronomical Research

**Voyage to the Stars Volume 1: Deep
Space Galaxies**
Astronomical Research

Water Resources Abstracts
Silver Platter Information Inc.

Water Resources Abstracts, Volume I
National Information Services
Corporation (NISC)

World Climate Disc
Chadwyck-Healey Ltd.

World WeatherDisc
WeatherDisc Associates Inc.

Where To Buy: Hardware and Software Vendors

Look around at the nearest shopping mall: most computer hardware and software shops now stock CD-ROM hardware and software. Their prices are reasonable, in most cases, with up to 25 percent off the suggested list prices. Egghead Software, Electronique Boutique, Circuit City, CompUSA, Best Buy, and others are beginning to cover the software end of the business for games, home-based reference, and a small sampling of business applications. Drive availability and selection is, at best, abysmal in most chains and mall stores, with only low-priced—and mostly low-quality—multimedia upgrade kits available.

For the majority of the industrial-strength business applications, particularly those that entail a subscription-based fee, you have to deal directly with the manufacturer or through specialized distributors. Discounts, if any, are slight.

Mail-Order Sources for Hardware and Software

By no means is the following list of **mail-order firms** for hardware and software exhaustive—we've narrowed the list to those with which we've had direct experience, or those we know have excellent reputations for good prices, support, and service. Those marked "Highly Recommended" are companies we've dealt with directly and found to be excellent sources for CD-ROM products.

TIP

Mall or Mail Order?

You don't have to settle for the drives offered by the chains—their selection is terrible, and the majority of the drives are disappointing. The reputable mail-order firms we list here carry a wide array of drives, SCSI cards, cables, and accessories—and their prices are as much as 30 percent off list. Most carry CD-ROM software as well, and even have bundling prices: when you order a drive, they offer special pricing on a wide selection of CDs.

HIGHLY RECOMMENDED
ComputAbility

HIGHLY RECOMMENDED
Computer Discount Warehouse

ComputAbility

PO Box 17882
Milwaukee, WI 53217
Phone: (800) 558-0003
Fax: (414) 357-7814
Visa and MasterCard accepted

ComputAbility was founded in 1982 and is on the cutting edge of multimedia with a wide product line spanning everything from CD-ROM game software to high-end video-editing and laser-disc players. Most of the products discussed in this book are available at ComputAbility—from SCSI cables to video compression boards—and their prices are extremely competitive. Some of the **CD-ROM** drives they carry include the following:

➤ NEC
➤ Toshiba
➤ Hitachi
➤ Texel

Sound cards from Turtle Beach, MediaVision, and Creative Labs are available separately or in the bundled multimedia upgrade kits we spoke of in Chapter 3, "How To Select CD-ROM Drives." ComputAbility is also a good source for speakers and SCSI host adapters. We've ordered Adaptec cards from ComputAbility on numerous occasions—they're always priced right and arrive within days. ComputAbility carries the full Altec Lansing series of ACS speaker systems, too.

Computer Discount Warehouse (CDW)

2840 Maria Drive
Northbrook, IL 60062
Phone: (800) 326-4239
Fax: (708) 291-1737
VISA, Discover, and MasterCard accepted

CDW has been in the mail-order business for over a decade. They have a few Midwest showrooms and discount stores, but their primary business is mail order. The company stocks a good selection of CD-ROM drives, including the following:

➤ NEC
➤ Toshiba
➤ Hitachi
➤ Texel

Prices are excellent—usually 25 percent or more below list, and delivery and support are good. CDW also carries sound cards, an extensive assortment of SCSI adapters, and some multimedia upgrade kits. Ask about CD-ROM software bundling when you order a drive—they regularly run specials for drive purchasers, offering an assortment of CD-ROM starter titles for a low price.

The motto at CDW is "ask for it." With over 15,000 items in stock, they usually have—or can get quickly—whatever item you're looking for.

Dustin

20969 Ventura Blvd.
Suite 13
Woodland Hills, CA 91364
Phone: (800) 274-6611
Fax: (818) 884-6611
VISA, Discover, and MasterCard
accepted

Dustin claims to be the world's largest seller of CD-ROM software and hardware on the planet. They may be right. They offer an extensive line of software titles and multimedia upgrade kits from Creative Labs and MediaVision. Although their drive selection is limited, their software title list is impressive. And they offer extensive discounts on titles when you purchase a drive or multimedia upgrade kit. For example, the regular price of ProPhone software is $219; when you order it as part of a bundle, the price is $79.

Elek-Tek

7350 North Linder Avenue
Skokie, IL 60077
Phone: (800) 395-1000
Fax: (708) 677-1081
Visa and MasterCard accepted

Elek-Tek started out in the calculator business—the high-end HP calculators, back before the PC market was even a reality. So they've been in the business since the beginning of the PC boom. They carry an extensive line of software titles, multimedia kits, and drives. Technical support and service is very good.

TigerSoftware

800 Douglas Entrance
Executive Tower, 7th Floor
Coral Gables, FL 33134
Phone: (800) 888-4437
Fax: (305) 529-2990
Visa, MasterCard, Discover, and
American Express accepted

TigerSoftware is more than just software. The company has a great reputation in the mail-order business and offers an extensive line of software and hardware products, including multimedia upgrade kits, CD-ROM drives, and speakers. The main CD-ROM drive product they sell is NEC, with some other brands as well. TigerSoftware makes extensive use of bundling—check for prices on a number of options or ask for their latest catalog.

Mail-Order Sources for CD-ROM Software Titles

Following are mail-order sources for CD-ROM titles. These firms specialize in CD-ROM software and offer a wide range of the latest titles at a substantial discount. They'll probably beat the prices of many chain and mall stores.

RECOMMENDED
Dustin

RECOMMENDED
Elek-Tek

Mr. CD-ROM

123 South Woodland Street
Winter Garden, FL 34787
Phone: (800) 444-6723
Fax: (407) 877-3834
Visa and MasterCard accepted

Plenty of titles, fast delivery, and great discounts are a few of Mr. CD-ROM's highlights.

Walnut Creek CD-ROM

1547 Palos Verdes Mall
Suite 260
Walnut Creek, CA 94596
Phone: (800) 786-9907
Fax: (510) 947-1644
Visa, MasterCard, and American
Express accepted

Walnut Creek specializes in compilations of public-domain software on CD-ROM as well as an extensive library of programming source code. In addition, the company carries a complete line of the most popular CD-ROM software titles available today.

SofTec Plus

1200 E. River Road
Suite M176
Tuscon, AZ 85775-182
Phone: (800) 779-1991
Visa and MasterCard accepted

All the major educational, reference, and entertainment CDs can be ordered from SofTec Plus, most with prices 30 to 50 percent off list price. The company advertises that they won't be undersold.

This company specializes in public-domain and programming software on CD-ROM, but they also carry a great assortment of home and general-reference CDs.

Appendix E

Additional Sources for Information

The CD-ROM industry is dynamic and fast growing. Periodicals are a good source of information concerning product announcements; electronic information services are *the* best source for contacting fellow CD-ROM users; and company bulletin-board services are a must for obtaining the latest software drivers and software program revisions. The more information you have at your disposal, the better your CD-ROM expertise.

Magazines, Journals, and Newsletters

To keep up to date with the latest in technology and application development, you should check in periodically with at least some of the following publications.

CD-ROM Professional

462 Danbury Road
Wilton, CT 06897-2126
Phone: (800) 248-8466
Annual subscription price: $44.95

CD-ROM Professional, published bimonthly, is slick, well-designed, and always on top of what's new in the industry. Articles are written by professionals in the business, so the content is always accurate and appropriate. Geared as much toward the CD-ROM publisher as the end-user, the magazine has a lot of ground to cover—and to its credit, it does it well.

HIGHLY RECOMMENDED
CD-ROM Professional

CD-ROM World

Meckler Corporation
11 Ferry Lane West
Westport, CT 06880
Phone: (203) 226-6967
Annual subscription price:
$39 (personal) $87 (institutional)

Published bimonthly, *CD-ROM World* covers CD-ROM news from all over the globe. It has reviews, news, and user articles highlighting the uses of CD-ROM in a variety of educational, manufacturing, and other professional work situations.

New Media

901 Mariner's Island Blvd.
Suite 365
San Mateo, CA 94404
Phone: (415) 573-5170
Fax: (415) 573-5131
Price: $3.95 per issue

The multimedia market—from Apple Macintosh to PC to CD-ROM and beyond—is growing rapidly. *New Media* has staked out this considerable turf as its base of coverage in articles ranging from multimedia authoring software to game and reference reviews. Although the magazine is oriented toward the consumer and entry-level developer, it is written for the average user and is a pleasure to read and always up to date.

Wired

544 Second Street
San Francisco, CA 94107-1427
Phone: (415)904-0660
Fax: (415) 904-0669
Annual subscription price: $20;
$36 for two years

Wired is a bimonthly explosion of post-information-age news, views, and techno-editorial that is a joy to read and look at. Visually and intellectually alive, the content may not be for all readers, but you owe yourself at least one look. Not technology specific, *Wired* is more a guide to what's fringe, off the edge, or looming on the electronic horizon.

Business and Legal CD-ROMs in Print

Meckler Corporation
11 Ferry Lane West
Westport, CT 06880
Phone: (203) 226-6967
Annual volume price: $55

The *Business and Legal CD-ROMs in Print* is an annual review and digest that targets this most vital area of CD-ROM publishing. Any legal or business research professional needs this volume to keep up to date.

**HIGHLY
RECOMMENDED**
Wired

RECOMMENDED
New media

RECOMMENDED
Business and Legal
CD-ROMs in Print

Information Searcher

14 Hadden Road
Scarsdale, NY 10583
Annual subscription price: $24

Targeted at teachers, researchers, and library professionals, this quarterly newsletter covers both the on-line and CD-ROM markets in reviews, strategies, and tips. *Information Searcher* includes curriculum guides, conference coverage, and a CD-ROM directory for schools.

Electronic Sources

Following is a listing of the most popular CD and BBS reference sources for CD-ROM users. Note that CompuServe has an expanded CD-ROM vendor and user forum. Also note that nontraditional methods for accessing information about CD-ROMs can be found in places such as the Internet and other professional organizations that host electronic forums on America OnLine, CompuServe, BIX, and Prodigy.

Meckler CD-ROMs in Print

Meckler Corporation
11 Ferry Lane West
Westport, CT 06880
Phone: (203) 226-6967
CD-ROM version: $95
Printed version: $95

Meckler CD-ROMs in Print is a great disc-of-discs. Virtually all CD-ROMs in print, in the US and throughout the world, are referenced on this disc. Multimedia, hardware manufacturers, and much more are indexed and searchable. The disc is an excellent value and has a printed counterpart.

Nautilus

7001 Discovery Boulevard
Dublin, OH 43017
Phone: (800) 637-3472
Fax: (614)-761-4110
Per issue price: $9.95 (plus $1.50 shipping and handling)
Annual subscription price: $137.00 (includes shipping and handling)

A unique, multimedia CD-ROM magazine on CD-ROM disc, Metatec's Nautilus is filled with multimedia presentations, sound samples, photography, industry interviews, full-motion video clips, and shareware in a variety of categories. Worth a look if you're new to CD-ROM, you can get a sample disc of a past issue for $4.95.

CD-ROM Forum

This CompuServe forum is devoted to CD-ROM enthusiasts—both corporate and home. The CD-ROM forum is a clearinghouse for news, tips, and CD-ROM-related shareware programs. Libraries and topics include PhotoCD, CD audio, and Nautilus (the CD-ROM magazine from Metatec). To access the forum, type the following at any CIS prompt:

GO CDROM

CD-ROM Vendor's Forum

Software and hardware manufacturers have sponsored the CD-ROM Vendor's forum on CompuServe. Among the vendors on-line in this forum are the following:

➤ Trantor
➤ Meridian Data
➤ Bowker Electronic Publishing
➤ Best Photo Labs
➤ One-Off CD Shops
➤ Nimbus Information Systems
➤ QuickScan
➤ Bureau of Electronic Publishing

Other vendors are expected to come on board in the coming months. The forum includes demos, driver updates, press releases, and other information in addition to access to company representatives. To access the forum, type the following at any CIS prompt:

GO CDVEN

Multimedia Forum

The Multimedia forum on CompuServe hosts vendors and users of all multimedia equipment and software: Macintosh, Amiga, PC, and many other platforms are represented. Vendor representatives are available to answer questions, and shareware and demos can be found as well. To access the forum, type the following at any CIS prompt:

GO MULTIMEDIA

BIX

Byte magazine's information service (BIX) has a CD-ROM forum for users, developers, and manufacturers. Library files include demos and shareware. Select CD.ROM from the forum menu for access to the forum.

Internet

The Internet—that wonderful jungle of tons of information on virtually every conceivable topic—has, as you might imagine, a CD-ROM information forum with archive files and information files. The Internet address for this forum is **cdrom.com**.

Optical Publishing Association

PO Box 21726
Columbus, OH 43221
Phone: (614) 442-8805
Fax: (614) 442-8815

The Optical Publishing Association is for CD-ROM software title developers and publishers. Following is the information from the association for potential members:

Investigate your new career:

Join the Optical Publishing Association today! OPA: Linking markets and technology for a new era of publishing .

Your new career in optical publishing:

Whether you know it now or not, your involvement in CD-ROM—and its myriad implications—is changing your job description and your career path. The OPA will help provide the basic background you need to apply this new media to your problem. From SGML to new distribution channels, from writing the business plan to data conversion, OPA gives you the data you need to be successful in your project and product development.

Can you keep up on your own?

The Optical Publishing Association is the only professional and trade association dedicated to keeping its members informed about all the factors that constitute the emerging optical and digital publishing industry.

CDROM and multimedia integrate elements of the three most influential businesses in the communication economy: publishing, computing, and entertainment. OPA's primary goal is to provide a forum where these disparate interests come together to form the heart of a dynamic new industry.

With news and developments coming from many directions, it is exceedingly difficult for any individual to follow all the events that will impact the ultimate success of your business. OPA keeps tabs on the industry and maintains a number of programs to keep its membership informed, involved, and ready to meet the challenges of new media.

Publishing: communicating complex ideas at a distance:

At its heart, the publishing enterprise is the business of recording ideas for access by many potential customers. Multimedia and database publishing on CD-ROM combines the power of computing with traditional publishing models and techniques from a variety of communications and entertainment activities to deliver a vast spectrum of information: from basic text to motion video to new categories that integrate data in fascinating new ways.

Corporate publishers:

OPA keeps you current on techniques and technology. Whether your job is capturing and delivering corporate documents to employees or technical documentation to customers; whether your application for new media is sales support, training, or other innovative uses, OPA can give you the background to build cost-effective alternatives to your existing programs—and can even show you how to make new revenues from your information inventories.

Commercial publishers:

OPA wants to help you create successful new products for both existing customers and new markets. Effective business planning, marketing, team-building, the changing distribution landscape, and other issues are as important as the technology and new delivery platforms. OPA programs are intended to help you evaluate new opportunities and provide solid background on the technical choices that can turn those opportunities to profits.

Programs:

➤ "Digital Publishing Business" is the membership newsletter that presents new publishing technology in the context of successful business enterprise. DPB integrates the news of the many diverse players in an evolving enterprise. "Linking markets and technology in a new era of publishing."

➤ OPA publishes and resells publications relevant to the broad spectrum of digital production and marketing. Members receive some free (like the semiannual industry Executive Summary Report) and discounts on others.

➤ OPA Executive Director Rich Bowers is a sysop on CompuServe's CDROM forum, providing up-to-the-minute expert answers to both developer and consumer questions. A number of OPA lists and publications are also available for downloading, some exclusively for OPA members.

➤ The Technical forum is OPA's interface to the standards development process. OPA has been directly responsible for two standards that relate directly to CD-ROM production and interface design.

➤ OPA will produce a number of seminars during the year, with focuses on business issues, product design, and technical development. Members get discounts on attendance.

➤ Special-interest groups will emerge from the interests of the membership, with focuses on both corporate and commercial publishing issues.

➤ OPA members will receive periodic special offers and discounts on relevant products and services.

Join OPA Today!

In a rapidly changing industry, you have to know not only the latest news, but also how that news will impact your plans or current projects. Join professionals who share similar challenges and support the OPA in its efforts to provide the information you need! As an individual or corporate sponsor, your dues return real value throughout the year.

OPA Member Benefits. OPA promotes and encourages the development of optical publishing; educates the public about the benefits and applications of optical publishing technology; and serves as a conduit for the exchange of information, opinions, and analysis within the optical publishing industry. To accomplish these goals, the OPA offers the following services to its members:

Professional members: Professional membership is open to any individual with interests in optical publishing technology, production, and/or market development.

➤ One year subscription to "Digital Publishing Business," the OPA's newsletter dedicated to the business of CD-ROM and new media publishing.

➤ A membership package including:
• A Nautilus intro CD-ROM
• A starter kit for CompuServe (to access the CD-ROM forum and other services)
• A $50 discount coupon for a disc from One-Off CD Shops Inc.
• Semiannual "Executive Summary" of the commercial and corporate CD-ROM publishing enterprise
• Participation in OPA special-interest groups
• A membership certificate
• Discounts for OPA and other related publications
• Discounts for OPA business and product development seminars
• Discounted ads in the DPB Classified Index
• Other discounts and special offers for OPA members to be offered from time to time

Corporate sponsors: Corporate sponsorship/membership is open to any organization actively involved, or planning to be actively involved, in publishing using optical media, distribution, or sales, and/or hardware or software technology development for CD-ROM/multimedia products.

➤ Call for benefits and opportunities

Planned OPA programs: OPA plans to offer the following activities, based on interest and volunteer participation:

➤ Seminar series
➤ Organization of local/regional chapters
➤ Market research programs for specific market segments and technologies
➤ Special newsletters for OPA SIGS

Save $40! Join OPA now and receive a free copy of The CD-ROM Publishing Enterprise Executive Summary Report: 1992 Mid-Year.

➤ What is the installed base of CD-ROM drives and how fast are they selling?

➤ What is the penetration of CD-ROM in corporate publishing?

➤ What are the CD-ROM platform alternatives and how do they impact the business?

➤ How can you project sales for 1993 and beyond?

➤ What products and issues impact your planning?

➤ How can you evaluate market studies and reports?

➤ What are the essential issues for publishers?

➤ How is the distribution landscape changing?

The answers to these questions and more appear in this first semiannual report compiled by the Optical Publishing Association. If your job, your company, or your project depend on solid information about publishing on new media, you need this report. This publication is priced at $40, but you get it *free* with your membership in OPA.

Membership dues schedules:

Professional	$85 per year ($125 outside N. America)
100+ employees	$1000 per year

Care and Feeding of CD-ROMs

CD-ROM discs are extremely durable. Properly cared for, they should last indefinitely. They are not indestructible, however. When audio CDs were introduced, for some reason a rumor began that there was nothing you could do to hurt them. It didn't take long for the truth—or lack of truth—in this statement to be shown. Take a few precautions and you won't need to worry about your discs. If they do get damaged, there may still be hope.

Handling CD-ROMs

If you read about how a CD-ROM drive works in Chapter 1, "What Is CD-ROM?," you know that the surface of a disc is essentially an optical surface. It must pass a finely focused beam of laser light—first to the metallic layer beneath the plastic (which contains the data) and then back to the receptors. Dirt, scratches, fingerprints, and other imperfections interfere with the retrieval of the stored data.

In the case of an audio CD, there is a great deal of leeway in surface imperfections. Audio is a predictable, analog signal. It is possible for a CD player to interpolate (that is, make an educated guess) about any missing data. It works like this: assuming the scratch or dirt doesn't obliterate too much data, the circuitry of the player simply looks at the values before and after the unreadable information and "guesses" that the missing value is between the two. Although the guessed value may not be the missing value, because the data represents sound, it takes quite a few of these guesses to make the sound detectably different.

Computer data, on the other hand, has no such predictable pattern. It is absolutely necessary that a 1 be retrieved as a 1 and a 0 as a 0. Because small scratches are a fact of life, the CD-ROM must incorporate a scheme that makes it somewhat forgiving of such small damage. This scheme is called ECC (Error Correction Code). With ECC, a disc can sustain some surface damage and still be usable.

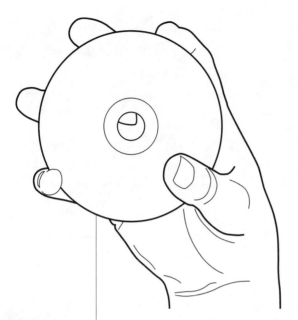

FIGURE F.1

Handle the disc by its edges to avoid putting fingerprints on its surface.

ECC works by recording data redundantly. That is, it uses a scheme that makes possible the reconstruction of any bits from the surrounding bits. While ECC does allow a CD-ROM to tolerate some degradation, your best bet is to handle your discs carefully enough to keep the surface in good condition.

➤ **Treat your discs as you do photographic negatives.** Hold discs only by the edges. Keep them free from dust. Store them in containers when not in use. The goal is the same in both cases: keep the surface free of scratches, fingerprints, and dirt.

➤ **If you must put a disc down, do it with the working surface up.** When you place a CD-ROM on your desk or other surface, make sure that you place it with the *unprinted surface up*. Doing so helps avoid getting dirt on the disc's surface or scratching it when trying to pick it back up.

➤ **If your drive uses caddies, buy enough for all your commonly used discs.** Caddies are relatively inexpensive—certainly cheaper than the CD-ROMs they protect. If all your commonly used discs are in caddies, you never actually have to handle the discs themselves.

Storing CD-ROMs

The CD is basically a plastic sandwich with an aluminum filling. It really does not require too much in the way of special storage. Common-sense precautions should suffice.

➤ **Try to keep your CD-ROMs at around room temperature.** Although CD-ROMs can tolerate a fairly wide temperature range without visible damage, extreme heat can be hazardous to their health. In addition to warping the discs by overheating, cyclic heating and cooling can damage the metallic layer inside the disc. A well-manufactured disc should last indefinitely, but, like any storage medium, radical changes in environment can damage it.

➤ **Keep your CD-ROMs in their packages when not in use.** If a CD-ROM is not in use (or in a caddy), store it in its package to help prevent dust or other contamination from getting on the disc. Dust itself does not damage the disc, but if enough accumulates, read errors can result. This means the disc must be cleaned, which is where the potential for damage lies. It is very easy to damage a disc while cleaning it. (The cleaning method itself may scratch the disc surface, or the dust may be abrasive enough that wiping it from the surface does damage). Keeping the disc in its package also limits the possibility of scratching the surface while handling it.

Cleaning CD-ROMs

If you follow the precautions on handling and storage, you should rarely need to clean your discs. When you do, however, a little care will make damage to them unlikely.

➤ **Use a very soft, lint-free cloth.** The plastic surface of the disc is soft. Paper towels, for example, scratch it. The cloth you choose should be of the type for cleaning lenses—you can find one at a photographic supply house. In fact, any lens-cleaning accessory is potentially useful for cleaning CD-ROMs.

➤ **Use radial strokes from the center to the outside edge to remove the dust.** Although the natural tendency is to wipe the CD in a **circular** fashion—this being the easiest—this method is the most likely to cause damage that the ECC can not overcome. Wipe from the inside out (see fig. F.2)

➤ **Use a mild glass cleaner to remove contamination that is more tenacious than dust.** Any mild commercial glass cleaner is appropriate for cleaning discs. Glass cleaner can remove accidental spills (like drinks, for example). Spray the area with the spot and let the cleaner sit for a while to allow the solvent to remove the spot without rubbing—which must be avoided. In extreme cases, careful washing in the sink with mild dish soap is also okay. Follow the same radial-cleaning method as for dust.

Using compressed gas—available in office-supply or photo stores—is good for preventative maintenance. You will find that if dust is allowed to accumulate, the spray alone cannot remove it. The dust adheres to the surface of the disc and requires mechanical action to remove.

Commercially available CD-cleaning systems are just fine for CD-ROMs. They are designed to provide the radial cleaning action and often come with some sort of liquid for use in conjunction with the machine.

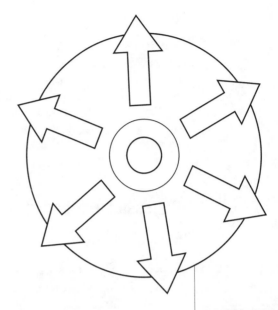

In Case of Damage...

Even if you've done everything right in handling, storing, and cleaning your discs, mistakes do happen. Fortunately, there are a few things you can do to restore a damaged disc to near-new condition.

CD Polish

There are various brands of polish intended for removing small scratches from CD-ROMs. You can find these products in audiophile stores or through magazines.

Metal Polish

Liquid metal polishes—like Brasso—are very similar in composition to the CD polish just mentioned. Use these polishes sparingly and with a very soft cloth to get rid of small surface defects.

FIGURE F.2

Cleaning strokes should be made from the center to the edge of the disc to limit scratch damage.

Why Not To Wipe in a Circular Motion

Because the information on the CD-ROM is recorded in a spiral, any scratch you may cause by wiping the disc in a circular fashion has a chance of obliterating a whole string of pits, making a large part of the data unreadable.

Keep Polishing Radially

When you rub the disc with toothpaste (or any other polish), remember to rub from the center of the disc to its edge rather than around the disc. The abrasives in polish are intended to repair existing damage, not cause additional damage. Although it may not make any difference if you polish around the disk, it's probably best to keep your cleaning strokes consistent.

Toothpaste

Yes, toothpaste—preferably one designed to give you "shiny white teeth"—can work wonders on more severe damage. Use your finger and gently **polish** out the defect with a small amount of the toothpaste using short reciprocating strokes. Carefully rinse the residue and then use a CD polish or metal polish to smooth the surface more if necessary.

Professional Plastic Polishes

In the most extreme cases, when the disc is irreplaceable and the damage is more than toothpaste and metal polish can repair, it may be possible to use methods normally reserved for working with lucite and other plastics after machining. These methods involve using successively finer grits of abrasive paper and ending with liquid-based polishes. This technique requires some skill and some practice. You can get the materials—and advice on use—from a local plastic-supply store. If you resort to this method, practice on some scrap plastic or a junk disc first; take your time when doing the job on the real disc.

Drive Maintenance

There isn't too much you have to do to maintain your CD-ROM drive. Its main enemy is the omnipresent dust in homes and offices. Dust can have detrimental effects on the mechanical components of the drive, but its most likely effect is to cover the laser's collimating lens. When this happens, it appears that all your discs are bad.

If you have a dirty lens, there are two courses of action available:

1. Disassemble the drive and dust the lens with a soft brush or pressurized air.

2. Buy a CD lens-cleaning disc from your local audio store.

Option 1 is probably beyond most of us. Very frequently, CD-ROM drives are sealed internally—an attempt to prevent the dust problem in the first place. This is a double edged sword: if the drive does get dirty, you can't easily open it for cleaning.

Option 2 is easy and should work. Lens-cleaning discs have a small, velour-like material attached to the disc; they instruct the drive to seek across the disc, wiping the lens as it seeks. Some discs just put the velour "brush" on the data track; when the drive attempts to initialize the disc, the lens is cleaned. Most drives then spit out the disc because it cannot be read.

Miscellaneous Hardware and Software Manufacturers

Hardware and software vendors—from speakers to multimedia boards—described or mentioned in this book are included in this appendix. Also included are vendors that we did not have the space and time to devote space to in the main text of this book but that are worth mentioning.

AimTech Corporation
20 Trafalgar Square
Nashua, NH 03063
Phone: (603) 883-0220
Fax: (603) 883-5582

Brightbill-Roberts & Company Ltd.
Suite 321 120 E. Washington Street
Syracuse, NY 13202
Phone: (315) 474-3400
Fax: (315) 472-1732

British Telecom Directory Products Unit
1st Floor, Columbia Center Market Street
Bracknell
Berkshire RG12 1JG
United Kingdom
Phone:(+44) 344-861961
Fax: (+44) 344-860872

C-Cube Microsystems
1778 McCarthy Blvd
Milpitas, CA 95035
Phone: (408) 944-6300
Fax: (408) 944-6314

Canadian Center for Occupational Health & Safety (CCOHS)
250 Main Street
East Hamilton, Ontario, Canada L8N 1H6
Phone: (416) 572-2981
Fax: (416) 572-4419

Canadian Telebook Agency
301 Donlands Avenue
Toronto, Ontario, Canada M4J 3R8
Phone: (416) 467-7887
Fax: (416) 467-7886

Capitol Disc Interactive
2121 Wisconsin Avenue NW
Washington, DC 20007
Phone: (202) 965-7800
Fax: (202) 625-0210

CBIS, Inc.
5875 Peachtree Industrial Blvd.
Building 100
Norcross, GA 30092
Phone: (404) 446-1332
Fax: (404) 446-9164

CD Romics
PO Box 221085
San Diego, CA 92122
Phone: (619) 546-8278

CD-ROM Galleries, Inc.
512 Gertrude Avenue
Aptos, CA 95003
Phone: (408) 685-2315
Fax: (408) 685-0340

CD-ROM Strategies
18 Chenile
Irvine CA 92714
Phone: (714) 733-3378
Fax: (714) 786-1401

CEDROM Technologies, Inc.
1290 Van Horne Avenue
Suite 209 Outremont
Quebec, Canada H2V 4S2
Phone: (514) 278-3373
Fax: (514) 270-4162

Centerpoint Communications Group
434 South First Street
San Jose, CA 95113
Phone: (408) 993-1040
Fax: (408) 993-1056

Claritas/NPDC, Inc.
201 N. Union Street
Alexandria, VA 22314-2645
Phone: (703) 683-8300

CMC - Creative Multimedia Corporation
514 NW 11 Avenue
Suite 203
Portland, OR 97209
Phone: (503) 241-4351
Fax: (503) 241-4370

Compact Publishing , Inc.
4958 Ashby Street NW
Washington DC 20007
Phone: (202) 244-4770
Fax: (202) 298-8487

Compton's NewMedia
345 Fourth Street
San Francisco, CA 94107
Phone: (415) 597-5555
Fax: (415) 546-1887

CoSA (Company of Science and Art)
14 Imperial Place
Suite 203
Providence, RI 02903
Phone: (401) 831-2672
Fax: (401) 274-7517

Crowninshield Software, Inc.
1050 Massachusetts Ave.
2nd Floor
Cambridge, MA 02138
Phone: (617) 661-4945
Fax: (617) 661-6254

Dai Nippon Printing Company Ltd.
1-1 Ichigaya-Kagacho 1-chome Shinjuku-ku
Tokyo, Japan 162-01
Phone:(+81) 3-266-2910
Fax: (+81) 3-266-4599

Dataflight Software, Inc.
10573 West Pico Boulevard
Suite 68
Los Angeles, CA 90064
Phone: (213) 398-2787
Fax: (213) 398-0194

Dataware Technologies, Inc.
222 Third Street
Suite 3300
Cambridge, MA 02142-1188
Phone: (617) 621-0820
Fax: (617) 621-0307

Diaquest, Inc.
1440 San Pablo Avenue
Berkeley, CA 94702
Phone: (510) 526-7167
Fax: (510) 526-7073

Digidesign, Inc.
1360 Willow Road
Suite 101
Menlo Park, CA 94025
Phone: (415) 688-0600
Fax: (415) 327-0777

Digital Audio Labs
14505 21st Avenue N.
Suite 202
Plymouth, MN 55447
Phone: (612) 473-7626
Fax: (612) 473-7915

Digital Video Arts Ltd.
Twining Center
715 Twining Road
Dresher, PA 19025
Phone: (215) 576-7920
Fax: (215) 576-7932

The DMR Group
57 River Street
Wellesley Hills, MA 02181
Phone: (617) 237-0087
Fax: (617) 237-3528

DNASTAR, Inc.
1228 South Park Street
Madison, WI 53715
Phone: (608) 258-7420
Fax: (608) 258-7439

EarthInfo, Inc.
5541 Central Avenue
Boulder, CO 80301
Phone: (303) 938-1788
Fax: (303) 938-8183

The EDGE Interactive Media, Inc.
150 S. El Molino Ave.
Suite 201
Pasadena, CA 91101
Phone: (818) 304-4771
Fax: (818) 796-0132

Electronic Arts, Inc.
1450 Fashion Island Blvd.
San Mateo, CA 94404-2064
Phone: (415) 571-7171
Fax: (415) 571-1893

Elmsoft, Inc.
7954 Helmart Drive
Laurel, MD 20723
Phone: (301) 470-3451

Folio Corporation
2155 North Freedom Boulevard
Suite 150
Provo, UT 84604
Phone: (801) 375-3700
Fax: (801) 374-5753

Gain Interactive
1807 Second Street
Suite 22
Santa Fe, NM 87501
Phone: (505) 982-3738
Fax: (505) 988-5951

Gaylord Information Systems
PO Box 4901
Syracuse, NY 13221
Phone: (315) 457-5070 or (800) 962-9580
Fax: (315) 457-8387 or (800) 272-3412

GEOVISION, Inc.
5680 Peachtree Parkway
Norcross, GA 30092
Phone: (404) 448-8224
Fax: (404) 447-4525

The H.W. Wilson Company
950 University Ave.
Bronx, NY 10452
Phone: (212) 588-8400
Fax: (212) 538-7507

Henco Software, Inc.
100 5th Avenue
Waltham, MA 02154
Phone: (617) 890-8670
Fax: (617) 890-7671

Hewlett-Packard Company
100 Mayfield Avenue
Mountain View, CA 94043
Phone: (415) 691-5587
Fax: (415) 691-5484

Highland Software
1001 Elwell Court
Palo Alto, CA 94303
Phone: (415) 493-8567
Fax: (415) 493-4506

Hitachi Software Engineering Co. Ltd.
6-81 Onoe-cho Naka-ku
Yokohama, Japan 231
Phone:(+81) 45-681-2111
Fax: (+81) 45-681-4914

I.S. Grupe, Inc.
948 Springer Drive
Lombard, IL 60148
Phone: (708) 627-0550
Fax: (708) 627-4086

ICOM Simulations, Inc.
648 South Wheeling Road
Wheeling, IL 60090
Phone: (708) 520-4440
Fax: (708) 459-3418

Image Concepts
33 Boston Post Road West
Marlboro, MA 01752
Phone: (508) 481-6882
Fax: (508) 481-4406

Imagetects
7200 Bollinger Road #802
San Jose, CA 95129
Phone: (408) 252-5487
Fax: (408) 252-7409

Infolink, Inc.
750 North 200 West
Suite 307
Provo, UT 84604
Phone: (801) 375-7507
Fax: (801) 375-7537

Information Access Company
362 Lakeside Drive
Foster City, CA 94404
Phone: (415) 378-5200 or (800) 227-8431
Fax: (415) 378-5420

Information Handling Services, Inc.
15 Inverness Way East
Englewood, CO 80150
Phone: (303) 790-0600
Fax: (303) 799-4085

Information Navigation, Inc.
4201 University Drive
Suite 102
Durham, NC 27707
Phone: (919) 493-4390
Fax: (919) 489-5239

Information Technologies Group, Inc.
7315 Wisconsin Avenue
Suite 1100 W
Bethesda, MD 20814
Phone: (301) 961-8580
Fax: (301) 961-8892

Inmagic, Inc.
2067 Massachusetts Avenue
Cambridge, MA 02140
Phone: (617) 661-8124
Fax: (617) 661-6901

Innotech, Inc.
110 Silver Star Blvd
Unit 107
Scarborough
Toronto, Ontario, Canada M1V 5A2
Phone: (416) 321-3838
Fax: (416) 321-0095

Intechnica International, Inc.
PO Box 30877
Midwest City, OK 73140
Phone: (405) 732-0138
Fax: (405) 732-4574

Interplay Productions
3710 S. n #100
Santa Ana, CA 92704
Phone: (714) 545-9001
Fax: (714) 549-5075

Iterated Systems, Inc.
5550-A Peachtree Parkway
Suite 545
Norcross, GA 30092
Phone: (404) 840-0310
Fax: (404) 840-0029

JAPAN Media
Tempelhofer Damm 4 1000
Berlin, Germany 42
Phone: (+49) 30-785-1713
Fax: (+49) 30-785-1993

Knowledge Access International
2685 Marine Way
Suite 1305
Mountain View, CA 94043
Phone: (415) 969-0606
Fax: (415) 964-2027

Knowledge Garden, Inc.
12-8 Technology Drive
Setauket, NY 11733
Phone: (516) 246-5400
Fax: (516) 246-5452

KnowledgeSet Corporation
888 Villa Street
Suite 410
Mountain View, CA 94041
Phone: (800) 456-0469
Fax: (415) 968-9962

KWA, Inc.
7125 West Jefferson Avenue
Suite 342
Lakewood, CO 80235
Phone: (303) 987-1729
Fax: (303) 987-2262

LaserLaw Corporation
1720 Loraine Street
Enumclaw, WA 98022
Phone: (206) 825-4093
Fax: (206) 825-9607

Library Systems & Services, Inc.
200 Orchard Ridge Drive
Gaithersburg, MD 20878
Phone: (301) 975-9800
Fax: (301) 975-9844

LinksWare Corporation
812 19th Street
Pacific Grove, CA 93950
Phone: (408) 372-4155
Fax: (408) 646-1045

Logical Data Expression
5537 33rd Street NW
Washington DC 20015
Phone: (202) 966-3393

Macromedia, Inc.
600 Townsend
San Francisco, CA 94103
Phone: (415) 442-0200
Fax: (415) 442-0190

Magnetic Press, Inc.
588 Broadway
New York, NY 10012
Phone: (212) 219-2831
Fax: (212) 334-4729

Mammoth Micro Productions
1700 Westlake Avenue North
Suite 702
Seattle, WA 98109
Phone: (206) 281-7500
Fax: (206) 281-7734

Management Information Technologies, Inc.
5 Vanderbilt Motor Parkway
Suite 403
Commack, NY 11725
Phone: (516) 265-3518
Fax: (516) 265-3643

Maxwell Data Management, Inc.
275 East Baker
Suite A
Costa Mesa, CA 92626
Phone: (714) 435-7700
Fax: (714) 751-1442

Maxwell Electronic Publishing
124 Mount Auburn Street
Cambridge, MA 02138
Phone: (617) 661-2955 or (800) 342-1338
Fax: (617) 868-7738

MECC
6160 Summit Dr. N.
Minneapolis, MN 55430-4003
Phone: (800) 685-6322
Fax: (612) 569-1551

Mentor Graphics Corporation
8005 SW Boeckman Road
Wilsonville, OR 97070-7777
Phone: (503) 685-7000
Fax: (503) 685-1202

Meridian Data, Inc.
5615 Scotts Valley Drive
Scotts Valley, CA 95066
Phone: (408) 438-3100
Fax: (408) 438-6816

Microboards
308 Broadway
PO Box 130
Carver, MN 55315
Phone: (612) 448-9800
Fax: (612) 448-9806

MicroRetrieval Corporation
One Kendall Square
Building 100
Cambridge, MA 02139
Phone: (617) 577-1574
Fax: (617) 577-9517

Midisoft Corporation
PO Box 1000
Bellevue, WA 98009
Phone: (206) 881-7176
Fax: (206) 883-1368

**Multinational Multimedia
Computing, Inc.**
800 Airport Boulevard
Suite 320
Burlingame, CA 94010
Phone: (415) 340-1700
Fax: (415) 347-6675

National Geophysical Data Center
Mail Code E/GC1
325 Broadway
Boulder, CO 80303
Phone: (303) 497-6826
Fax: (303) 497-6513

Nippon Courseware Co. Ltd.
4-16-6 Kuramae Taitoh-ku
Tokyo, Japan
Phone: (+81) 3-35687-9800
Fax: (+81) 3-35687-9822

**OCLC Online Computer Library Center,
Inc.**
6565 Frantz Rd
Dublin, OH 43017-3395
Phone: (614) 764-6000 or (800) 848-5878
Fax: (614) 764-6096

ON Technology, Inc.
155 Second Street
Cambridge, MA 02141
Phone: (617) 876-0900
Fax: (617) 876-0391

Online Computer Systems, Inc.
20251 Century Boulevard
Germantown, MD 20874
Phone: (301) 428-3700
Fax: (301) 428-2903

Open Text Corporation
180 King Street
Suite 550
South Waterloo, Ontario, Canada N2J 1P8
Phone: (519) 571-7111
Fax: (519) 571-9092

Optical Access International, Inc.
800 West Cummings Park
Suite 2050
Woburn, MA 01801
Phone: (617) 937-3910
Fax: (617) 937-3950

Optical Publishing, Inc.
Database Division
155 West Harvard Street
Ft. Collins, CO 80525
Phone: (303) 226-3466
Fax: (303) 226-3464

**OptImage Interactive Services
Company**
1501 50th Street
Suite 100
West Des Moines, IA 50265-5961
Phone: (515) 225-7000
Fax: (515) 225-0252

Optisys
8620 N. 22nd Avenue #109
Phoenix, AZ 85021
Phone: (602) 997-9699
Fax: (602) 944-4051

Optivision, Inc.
4009 Miranda Ave.
Palo Alto, CA 94304
Phone: (415) 855-0200
Fax: (415) 855-0222

OWL International, Inc.
2800 156th Ave. SE
Bellevue, WA 98007
Phone: (206) 747-3203
Fax: (206) 641-9367

Pacific CD Corporation
PO Box 31328
Honolulu, Hawaii 96820
Phone: (808) 949-4594
Fax: (808) 949-4594

Palisade Corporation
31 Decker Road
Newfield, NY 14867
Phone: (607) 277-8000
Fax: (607) 277-8001

**Pennsylvania Department of Education,
State Library**
333 Market Street
11th Floor
Harrisburg, PA 17126-0333
Phone: (717) 787-6704
Fax: (717) 783-5420

Personal Bibliographic Software, Inc.
525 Avis Drive
Suite 10
Ann Arbor, MI 48108
Phone: (313) 996-1580
Fax: (313) 996-4672

Personal Library Software, Inc.
2400 Research Boulevard
Suite 350
Rockville, MD 20850
Phone: (301) 990-1155
Fax: (301) 963-9738

Pinnacle Courseware, Inc.
4340 Stevens Creek Blvd.
Suite 202
San Jose, CA 95129
Phone: (408) 249-8383
Fax: (408) 249-8393

Pixel Productions
67 Mowat Avenue
Suite 547
Toronto, Ontario, Canada M6K 3E3
Phone: (416) 535-3058
Fax: (416) 535-2794

PRISM Interactive Corporation
751 Roosevelt Road
Building 7, Suite 200
Glen Ellyn, IL 60137
Phone: (708) 469-1215
Fax: (708) 469-1452

Quantum Access, Inc.
50 Briar Hollow West 515W
Houston, TX 77027
Phone: (713) 622-3211
Fax: (713) 622-6454

Research Information Systems, Inc.
Camino Corporate Center
2355 Camino Vida Roble
Carlsbad, CA 92009
Phone: (619) 438-5526
Fax: (619) 438-5573

Simmons Market Research Bureau
420 Lexington Avenue
New York, NY 10017
Phone: (212) 916-8900
Fax: (212) 916-8918

SoftWright
791 South Holly Street
Denver, CO
Phone: (303) 329-6388
Fax: (303) 329-0901

Sterling Resources, Inc.
10 Forest Avenue
Paramus, NJ 07652
Phone: (201) 368-8725
Fax: (201) 368-9024

Sun Moon Star Group
1941 Ringwood Ave.
San Jose, CA 95131
Phone: (408) 452-7811
Fax: (408) 452-1411

TerraLogics, Inc.
114 Daniel Webster Highway South
Suite 348
Nashua, NH 03060
Phone: (603) 889-1800
Fax: (603) 880-2022

TextWare Corporation
347 Main Street
PO Box 3267
Park City, UT 84060
Phone: (801) 645-9600
Fax: (801) 645-9610

Thunderstone/Expansion Programs International, Inc.
11115 Edgewater Drive
Cleveland, OH 44102
Phone: (216) 631-8544
Fax: (216) 281-0828

Tiger Media, Inc.
5801 E. Slauson Ave.
Suite 200
Los Angeles, CA 90040
Phone: (213) 721-8282
Fax: (213) 721-8336

Time Arts, Inc.
1425 Corporate Center Parkway
Santa Rosa, CA 95407
Phone: (707) 576-7722
Fax: (707) 576-7731

Titus Software Corporation
20432 Corisco Street
Chatsworth, CA 91311
Phone: (818) 709-3692
Fax: (818) 709-6537

TMM, Inc. (Total Multimedia)
299 West Hillcrest Drive
Suite 200
Thousand Oaks, CA 91360
Phone: (805) 371-0500
Fax: (805) 371-0505

TMS, Inc.
110 West 3rd Street
PO Box 1358
Stillwater, OK 74076
Phone: (405) 377-0880
Fax: (405) 372-9288

Trantor Systems Ltd.
5415 Randall Place
Fremont, CA 94538-3151
Phone: (510) 770-1400
Fax: (510) 770-9910

UniDisc
3941 Cherryvale Ave.
Suite 1
Soquel, CA 95073
Phone: (408) 464-0707
Fax: (408) 464-0187

United States Geological Survey National Geomagnetic
Information Center
USGS, Box 25046
MS 968 Denver Federal Center
Denver, CO 80225-0046
Phone: (303) 236-1365
Fax: (303) 236-1519

User Interface Technologies (U.I.T.) Corporation
PO Box 1698
Idyllwild, CA 92549
Phone: (714) 659-4580
Fax: (714) 659-4682

Virgin Games, Inc.
18061 Fitch Ave
Irvine, CA 92714
Phone: (714) 833-8710
Fax: (714) 833-8717

The Voyager Company
1351 Pacific Coast Highway
Santa Monica, CA 90401
Phone: (310) 451-1383
Fax: (310) 394-2156

VTLS, Inc.
1800 Kraft Drive
Blacksburg, VA 24060
Phone: (703) 231-3605
Fax: (703) 231-3648

Wayzata Technology, Inc.
PO Box 807
Grand Rapids, MN 55744
Phone: (218) 326-0597
Fax: (218) 326-0598

Young Minds, Inc.
1910 Orange Tree Lane
Suite 300
Redlands, CA 92374
Phone: (714) 335-1350
Fax: (714) 798-0488

Index

Symbols

A